Other Books by Otto Friedrich

GLENN GOULD

A LIFE AND VARIATIONS

GLENN

A LIFE AND

Random House New York

GOULD

VARIATIONS

OTTO FRIEDRICH

Library of Congress Cataloging-in-Publication Data
Friedrich, Otto.
Glenn Gould.
Includes index.
1. Gould, Glenn. 2. Pianists—Canada—Biography.   I. Title.
ML417.G68F7 1989   786.1′092′4 [B]   88-29676
ISBN 0-394-56299-2

Manufactured in the United States of America
24689753
First U.S. Edition

Book design by Bernard Klein

TO PRISCILLA

"The really important things in any biography are what someone thinks and feels and not what he has done. . . ."

—Glenn Gould

"Perhaps the author of the second book on Glenn Gould will attempt a 'conventional' biography. He will fail. Gould has protected his private life from public scrutiny, firmly but courteously, as no other celebrity among artists in our time has done. Moreover, unless I am much in error, his private life is in fact austere and unremarkable. A book on his life and time would be brief and boring. . . ."

—*Glenn Gould, Music and Mind,* by Geoffrey Payzant

" . . . Payzant, in fact, provides ample evidence for this contention with his own first chapter, a quick-and-dirty sketch of Gould's early years—which is indeed rather boring and by no means as brief as it should be."

—Gould's review of Payzant's book

Preface

I had just taken a leisurely sip of coffee and unfolded the Paris *Herald-Tribune* at a café in the Milan airport when I saw the front-page headline announcing that Glenn Gould was dead. It was like a physical blow. I remember saying aloud—with a sense of not only loss but anger at that loss—"Oh, God *damn* it!"

Gould had been a hero of mine for more than twenty-five years, ever since my friend Martin Mayer, then a music critic for *Esquire*, had manifested his enthusiasm for this young newcomer by giving me a copy of *The Goldberg Variations*. Like most people discovering that incredible performance, I was overwhelmed. I played the record over and over. I went and bought a copy of the music and practiced it for months, knowing perfectly well that I would never be able to play it, or anything else, the way Gould did. There was nothing left but to imitate Mayer and give away copies. Over the years, I have handed out perhaps twenty copies of *The Goldberg Variations*, thinking each time that there was no better present I could give to anyone.

When Gould died, I thought that would be the end of that particular obsession. I could still play the favorite records late at night, the Bach partitas or the Beethoven Second Concerto or the Wagner transcriptions, but there would no longer be the haunting sense of that mysterious presence somewhere up in Canada, that unseen force from which new ideas and new creations periodically emanated. That was all over.

About two years later, I got a telephone call from my daughter Molly, a literary agent in New York, who coolly asked whether I would be interested in writing a biography of Gould. Only then did I learn that when Gould died, he left the execution of his will to a Toronto lawyer named J. Stephen Posen, and that Posen was now looking for a biographer. Yes, I was definitely interested.

Posen's first problem had been to find out exactly what Gould's "estate" contained, apart from five pianos and a certain flow of record royalties. The explorers who went through Gould's Toronto apartment and his studio in a nearby hotel soon discovered that he rarely threw anything away and rarely paid much attention to where anything was. They came upon plastic garbage bags filled with unanswered mail, sheaves of manuscripts, heaps of unworn clothing. Ruth Pincoe, a professional bibliographer, took charge of cataloguing and dating, insofar as it was possible, the accumulation of letters, program notes, newspaper clippings, and all the rest of what eventually became "The Glenn Gould Collection" at the National Library of Canada in Ottawa. Perhaps the most remarkable of these papers was an assortment of lined note pads, scores of them. Gould never kept a real diary, but on these undated note pads, he scribbled whatever came to mind, ideas, letters, drafts of interviews, revisions of articles, stock-market holdings, medical symptoms, his own temperature, and the temperature of various cities in Canada as reported by his radio in the small hours of the morning.

Before opening Gould's papers to the public, Posen and the estate decided to commission some writer to go through all this material, to interview Gould's friends and relatives, and to write what might be described as the "official" or "authorized" biography. Posen assigned the task of finding this biographer to a Toronto agent, Lucinda Vardey, and she started on her assignment by writing to a lot of other literary agents to ask whether they had clients whom they would like to recommend as Gould's biographer. One of these inquiries almost inevitably ended on Molly's desk, and she responded with an impassioned letter declaring that she had been raised on the recordings of Glenn Gould. Ever since the appearance of *The Goldberg Variations,* when she was four, she had been hearing Bach partitas and Beethoven sonatas and whatever other new Gould recordings her father kept bringing home.

Molly's letter had a certain effect. Though a number of other names were recommended to the authorities in Toronto, Posen kept remembering Molly's heartfelt enthusiasm and wondering whether I might be the answer to his search. It was apparently not an easy decision to make. One problem, according to Posen himself, was that I was not a Canadian, and therefore there might be criticisms about his surrendering one of Canada's great cultural heroes to an outsider. Another problem was that I was not a professional musician or musicologist, and there might be criticisms about putting a great artist into the hands of a mere journalist. I could not deny the charges. I am an American and I have spent much of my life working for such periodicals as *Time, The Saturday Evening Post,* and the New York *Daily News.* On the other hand, I was ready to argue rather strenuously that art is international, that Gould was an international figure, that I had known and loved music all my life, and that journalism consists mainly of getting at the truth and reporting it in an interesting way.

After summoning me to a very pleasant interrogation over lunch at the Windsor Arms Hotel in Toronto, Posen and his associates decided to take their chances on me. In the contract that Posen drafted and I signed, we agreed on certain ground rules for this biography of Gould. Among other things, we agreed that I would "endeavour to be sensitive to, to look carefully into and to give close attention in the Biography to the impact of the country of Canada and way of life of Canada on Glenn Gould's development, life and work." I had no doubts or hesitations in signing such a pledge, for I do know that being a Canadian was important to Gould, and I also like Canada very much.

The Glenn Gould Estate gave me exclusive access to Gould's papers in the National Library, and so I spent the fall of 1986 in Ottawa, reading and listening and taking what finally amounted to about one thousand pages of typewritten notes. The Glenn Gould Estate also promised to help open whatever doors needed to be opened to whatever friends and relatives I wanted to interview. And all of this was done, and after more than eighty tape-recorded interviews, I amassed nearly two thousand pages of transcripts.

Despite the estate's official involvement, however, Posen's contract promised me that this would be my book, and that all the judgments in it would be my judgments. "Subject to the foregoing," as the document declares, "it is understood that the final decision on the content of the Biography will be yours. . . ." The contract called for my manuscript to be sent to Posen for his inspection, it gave him the right to point out anything he considered inaccurate or defamatory, and it required that I "act reasonably in considering any such notice." That is the extent of our agreement.

So this is my book, representing my views and my judgments, and if anyone is displeased by anything I have written, I alone am responsible. I hope, of course, that no such reactions will occur.

This book, finally, has required a good deal of help from a good many people, and now it is time to thank them. Thanks first to Steve Posen for his trust and confidence in me. Thanks to Herbert Russell Gould and Vera Gould for their help and cooperation; and to Ray Roberts, Gould's friend and assistant, for the hours he spent in answering my questions.

The process of interviewing has been a long and interesting one. For assistance of all kinds, large and small, I owe a debt of gratitude to (in alphabetical order): John Barnes, John Beckwith, Leonard Bernstein, Boris Brott, Martin Canin, Sam Carter, Schuyler Chapin, Robert Craft, David Diamond, Timothy Findley, Winston Fitzgerald, Elizabeth Fox, Malcolm Frager, Robert Fulford, Monica Gaylord, Nicholas Goldschmidt, Gary Graffman, Jessie Greig, Morris Gross, George Roy Hill, Dr. Fred Hochberg, Paul Hume, Don Hunstein, Deborah Ishlon, Andrew Kazdin, Nicholas Kilburn, Jon Klibonoff, Susan Koscis, Franz Kraemer, Polly Kraft, Jaime Laredo, William Littler, James Lotz, John McGreevy, Karen McLaughlin, Peter Mak, Sir Neville Marriner, Lois Marshall, Martin Mayer, Bruno Monsaingeon, Paul Myers, Nancy Newman, Richard Nielsen, Harvey Olnick, David Oppenheim, Dr. Peter Ostwald, Margaret Pacsu, Tim Page, Dr. Emil Pascarelli, Geoffrey Payzant, Judith Pearlman, R.A.J. Phillips, Ruth Pincoe, Mario Prizek, Alan Rich, John Peter Lee Roberts, Joseph Roddy, Roger Rosenblatt, Roxolana Roslak, Lillian Ross, Edward Rothstein, Alexander Schneider, Harold Schonberg, Richard Sennett, Robert Silverman, Robert Skelton, Janet Somerville, Dr. Irvin Stein, Frederic Steinway, Dr. Joseph Stephens, Annalyn Swan, Vincent Tovell, Lorne Tulk, Kurt Vonnegut, and Ronald Wilford.

A special word of thanks to Dr. Helmut Kallmann, head of the music department at the National Library of Canada, and to his staff, notably Stephen Willis, curator of the Gould collection, and Gilles St. Laurent, who runs the machines in the tape vault.

Thanks to Nancy Canning, who produced the bibliography and discography at the end of this book.

Thanks to Dorothy Marcinek, who transcribed many of the interview tapes and retyped the manuscript.

Thanks to Lucinda Vardey for originally discovering me. And, of course, to Molly.

Otto Friedrich

Locust Valley, New York
December 1, 1988

Contents

GLENN GOULD

A LIFE AND VARIATIONS

I

The Legacy

The television cameras came to watch the memorial service for Glenn Gould, to observe everything and to record everything that they observed. They silently inspected the stained-glass windows that color the Anglican Church of St. Paul in downtown Toronto. They silently surveyed the gathering of about three thousand friends and admirers, some of whom had known Gould well, some who had known him only in passing, and some who had known only his music, all crowded into that monumental church to pay homage. While the TV cameras watched, the microphones listened. They listened to Gould's admirers singing the "Old Hundredth," one of those stately hymns that he had loved ever since his childhood. "Oh, God, our help in ages past, our hope in years to come, our shelter from the stormy blast, and our eternal home."

The television cameras are always intruders, always asserting that all of life—even a memorial service for the dead—is mere raw material, fodder, film to be processed in the entertainment factory that serves us all. But the television cameras deserved their place as observers at the Gould service, for though the celebrated pianist had lived an unusually private and solitary life, though he had abandoned his extraordinary career as a concert performer, he had never abandoned what he once called "my love affair with the microphone." To him, the microphone and the camera brought a kind of artistic freedom that could be achieved in no other way. "I believe in 'the intrusion' of technology," he once wrote, "because, essentially, that intrusion imposes upon art a notion of morality which transcends the idea of art itself."

The television cameras know nothing of such things. They only watch and record. "Time present and time past/ Are both perhaps present in time future," as T. S. Eliot wrote at the start of *Burnt Norton*, "And time future contained in time past./ If all time is eternally present/ All time is unredeemable./ What might have been is an abstraction/ Remaining a perpetual possibility. . . ." Now, in October of 1982, now that Glenn Gould was dead, killed by a stroke just a few days after his fiftieth birthday, now the television cameras in the crowded Church of St. Paul watched Robert Aitkin play a Bach flute sonata and the Orford Quartet play the cavatina from Beethoven's Opus 130. They watched Maureen Forrester, in tears, sing "Have Mercy, Lord," from the *St. Matthew Passion*, that beautiful lament in which Gould had accompanied her at her first concert nearly thirty years earlier. They watched John Peter Lee Roberts, a Canadian Broadcasting Corporation executive who had been one of Gould's best friends, delivering his tribute. "When Glenn performed . . ." Roberts said, "he stood outside himself in an ecstasy which brought together music, mind and what I can only describe as a reaching toward God. The result was not so much an interpretation as a realization or re-creation of the music. . . . Glenn has gone now, but we must be grateful for his life and the rich legacy he has left us. . . ."

Then there sounded through the vaulted church a taped recording of the theme that symbolized that whole legacy, the stately saraband that Bach had used as the foundation of *The Goldberg Variations*. This had been Gould's choice for his spectacular debut on Columbia Records a quarter-century earlier, when he was a bold newcomer of twenty-three, and his reflective reinterpretation of that famous performance had just appeared on the market as the last of his fourscore recordings—and thus his testament.

And now, far more than when he was alive a decade ago, Gould has become the heroic icon to an increasingly widespread cult. This cult is based on the perfectly sound view that Gould was an extraordinary pianist, but it also extends considerably beyond that. It suggest that Gould's mastery of recording technology, his imaginative experiments in radio and television, and his extensive writings on all the communications media combine to make him a major contemporary thinker, an important theoretician of the postindustrial era. It also implies that in his much-publicized withdrawal from the competitive life, in his insistence on the value of solitude, Gould acquired a somehow superhuman persona, a spiritual power of the kind that would once have been attributed to martyred saints but now is more commonly ascribed to fallen movie stars—and that, accordingly, every relic of his private life deserves public enshrinement.

The rituals of ceremonial worship in our time are gigantically visual (even for classical pianists), and so when the New York Metropolitan Museum of Art invited Gould's admirers to come and hear him play a series of eight concerts in September of 1987, it invited them to watch him play on a screen about twenty feet high. The rituals are also intensely institutional. There is now a Glenn Gould Foundation and a Glenn Gould Prize, and the Canadian government extended the full weight of its beneficence in 1986 by sending a Glenn Gould exhibition to be seen by large crowds in Paris, Italy, and Eastern Europe. The institutional enthusiasm for organized discourse seems insatiable. The Canadian Society for Esthetics writes to invite one's participation in a "colloquium" on "the numerous facets of Gould's genius" at the University of Quebec in October of 1987. The Glenn Gould Society in the Netherlands, which publishes a glossy magazine about its hero, requests one's assistance in a Glenn Gould Symposium in Amsterdam in May of 1988. The National Library of Canada, in announcing a Gould exhibition to run throughout the summer of 1988, also announces a symposium on "Gould the Communicator."

In addition to all these official ceremonies, a number of admirers worship the icon in their oddly personal ways. The authorities guarding the relics receive frequent inquiries from supplicants who want to engage in various kinds of Gouldian research, Gould studies, Gould books, Gould catalogues. "There is a lady from Texas whose mother saw Gould in a dream," one of the pianist's friends writes from Toronto. "They were on a train, and he was telling the old Texas lady (who had never heard or seen Gould) that her daughter should work on a film project about his 'methods of creation. . . .'"

It may be useful to reassert the basic facts underlying the mythology. Gould was inexplicably gifted in childhood with a phenomenal natural talent for playing the piano. Blessed with understanding parents and a sympathetic teacher, he flowered, in his early twenties, into one of the world's very greatest pianists, one of the very greatest interpreters of both Bach and such modern masters as Schoenberg and Hindemith. Cursed, however, with a fear and even hatred of his natural environment, the concert hall, he managed to discover a way of escaping from the stage into the recording studio and continuing his career, behind clouds of self-created publicity, entirely in private. He made more than eighty records, which range across an enormous repertoire from Byrd and Gibbons through most of Bach, Mozart, and Beethoven and on into Wagner, Strauss, and Sibelius. These recordings, some of them glorious, all of them interesting, and now artfully preserved on compact disks, represent Gould's major contribution to art in our time.

There is something both exaggerated and poisonous, however, in our fascination with performing artists. As with our political leaders, we yearn both to idolize them and to possess them, and finally to degrade and destroy them. Gould's achievements would have been enough for most musicians to die rich and happy, but he was one of those restless souls who can see the falsities in the public admiration and who keep searching for new purposes in life. He worked hard at becoming a composer and even harder at creating compositions out of radio voices; he dreamed of writing both religious music and historical novels; he was beginning, in his last years, to create a new career as a conductor. And just as Gould rejected the richly rewarded role of virtuoso, the public that wanted to lionize him onstage eventually started to share his own idea that he was destined for greater things than performance, perhaps as a philosopher, perhaps as a saint.

But perhaps Gould finally saw through all such ambitions as well. There are many who thought he was crazy to give up a life that others keep struggling to achieve; there are some who believe that his undeniable eccentricity was simply his own way of dealing with life, and mastering it. The Canadian friend who wrote about the woman from Texas writes again to report that "a musician I know wrote a piece a while back called, 'Glenn Gould is alive and well in Orillia.' The basic premise is that he got bored, staged his own death, and is now sitting up in Orillia [the lakeside town where he spent his boyhood summers], watching all the fuss."

It is a pleasant thought, that Gould is alive and well in Orillia, but he is not. He is dead, dead, dead. And now it is time to start examining the legacy.

Bits and pieces of the Glenn Gould legacy survive in a large and silent room overlooking the lazy flow of the Ottawa River. On the fifth floor of the National Library of Canada, just a bit beyond the Supreme Court and the Justice Ministry and the splendidly Gothic revival Parliament—where a statue of a sword-wielding Sir Galahad commemorates the unsuccessful attempt by a young man named Henry Harper to rescue a girl named Bessie from the flooding river in 1901—there lie all of Gould's papers, boxes and boxes of letters ("Seventy-two meters of shelves," one librarian says proudly), radio scripts, canceled checks, Grammy nominations, newspaper clippings, medical prescriptions, and much more.

Some of the old passions still breathe. "You can't imagine the effect, the cheers, the happiness and the overwhelming joy . . . [you] produced upon me, my colleagues, and our students!" an admirer named Kitty Gvozdeva wrote from Leningrad. "We all welcome and greet you with the greatest love, admiration and affection we are capable of. . . ." Or from Budapest, in broken French: "Je suis Hongroise. J'aime beaucoup la musique. J'ai en entendu le votre concert en la radio. Je suis la votre appassioné ammiratrice. . . ." Or from somewhere in America, from an eighteen-year-old student: "Dear Glenn, You know, you make love to the piano keys, and it is the most beautiful thing I have ever seen." And from somewhere else in America: "Dear Mr. Gould: Please complete the following questionnaire and return to me at once, since my future depends entirely upon your answers: 1) Have you written any string quartets since your Opus 1? 2) Are you engaged? 3) Are you married? 4) If I come to Toronto, will you permit me to see you?"

He saved all these things. He saved a check stub for ten dollars, the first money he ever earned by playing the piano, when he won a Kiwanis prize back in the 1940's. He saved four battered leather wallets that the archivists have now labeled A through D, and a small earthenware mug that offers the familiar plea: "Please don't shoot the piano player. He's doing the best he can." And then there is a box containing several of those famous scarves and mufflers that he wore around his neck on the hottest days of summer. And a tan-covered book filled with blank pages and bearing the "humorous" title, *Essence of an Enigma.*

And half a dozen cardboard cartons full of Gould's own compositions, the surprisingly Brahmsian string quartet, the complex cadenzas to Beethoven's first piano concerto, even a mimeographed copy of a march entitled "Our Gifts," which states on the cover that it was composed by Glenn H. Gould in 1943, when he was a ten-year-old student at the Williamson Road Public School in Toronto. "We are the boys, we are the girls of all the Public Schools," he had written in a burst of wartime patriotism. "We have a Red Cross job to do, to furnish all the tools. . . ." And more than twenty cartons full of the music that he played, Bach, Beethoven, Mendelssohn, Hindemith, more Bach. There are several battered copies of the classic Ralph Kirkpatrick edition of *The Goldberg Variations,* one of them covered with Gould's private notations, like, at the bottom of *Variatio 3:* "N.B.—this is n.n. per se, but it needs a greater sense of cadence. . . ."

And here on these silent shelves in this silent room is a box containing a barometer and thirty-two black felt-tipped pens, the kind that Gould liked to use not only as a marker but as a baton, when he conducted his own recorded performances while listening to playbacks in the shrouded solitude of the studio control booth. And a box containing four pairs of sunglasses and another with three wristwatches, one stopped at quarter past one, one at quarter past five, and one at quarter past six. And a box containing nothing but "miscellaneous keys," dozens and dozens of them, on rings and chains and various bits of string, door keys, car keys, trunk keys, keys to God knows what forgotten cupboards or closets.

And cuff links, dozens of them too, squirreled away in three small containers, not chained sets of cuff links but the spiked kind that can be inserted hastily into the cuffs of white evening dress, pearl and mother-of-pearl, amethyst, gold, brass. He probably never wore a single one of them after that day in 1964 when, at the age of thirty-one, he walked off the concert stage forever. But he saved them. One unmatched cuff link has a rectangular plaque with a G clef inscribed on it; another bears the head of a goddess haloed by a ring of stars. Each single cuff link means that the other in the pair was lost somewhere in the scramble of the concert tour. And somewhere in the correspondence files, there is an unhappy letter from a young stage manager in Winnipeg, who wrote to remind Gould that he had loaned him a pair of his own cuff links, that "I was too excited by the whole thing to remember, and when I did you had gone." These cuff links had "only sentimental value to me," the manager wrote, but could Gould, wherever he now was, please send them back? "I do this so often that I can no longer remember which cuff links are mine . . ." Gould wrote back, barely acknowledging that the sentimental value was now a value forever lost. "The only thing I can suggest is that you go out and buy a pair like you had before and please send the bill to me. . . ."

And a jumble of books. The memoirs of Turgenev, Philippe Halsman's *Jump Book,* a deluxe edition of *Walden,* six plays of Strindberg, Waugh's *The Loved One,* a review copy of H. H. Stucken schmidt's biography of Schoenberg, Goncharov's *Oblomov.* An inscribed copy of Lillian Ross's *Picture;* an inscribed copy of Yehudi Menuhin's *The Music of Man.* A paperback edition of Robert Nozick's *Anarchy, State and Utopia,* marked only by Gould's interest in a passage about animals. "Because people eat animals, they raise more than otherwise would exist without this practice," Nozick had written. "To exist for a while is better than never to exist at all." With one of his black felt pens, Gould heavily underlined that last sentence.

And then there are several copies of Geoffrey Payzant's intellectual study, *Glenn Gould, Music and Mind,* and there is Tim Page's *Glenn Gould Reader,* which contains the review that Gould, who had read and approved Payzant's book before publication, wrote of it after publication. "Professor Payzant makes clear that he . . . has not attempted a biographical study," Gould observed, with the academic owlishness that he loved to affect, "that Gould's private life is, in fact, 'austere and unremarkable,' and that 'a book on his life and times would be brief and boring.'" Chinese boxes contain nests of smaller and still smaller boxes. How many men ever get a chance even to see their own biographies, much less to write reviews criticizing them? (And just as Gould had approved Payzant's book, Payzant had approved Gould's review of it.)

But Gould's dedication to technology provides even stranger

forms of Chinese boxes. Here, on a library shelf containing more than 150 of Gould's videotapes, cassettes that range from Bernstein performances of Beethoven symphonies to the insomniac Gould's tapings of *The Mary Tyler Moore Show,* here is a TV series called *Glenn Gould Plays Bach,* which begins with the camera staring at the score of Bach's *Art of the Fugue.* Then it stares at a portrait of Gould in profile, superimposed on the Bach fugue. Then the image of Gould in profile suddenly comes to life and begins playing the Bach score. Then the camera pulls back to show a TV screen, to demonstrate that what we had been watching was only an image of Gould playing Bach on that screen, and now the camera pulls back still farther to show us Gould's performance on the screen being watched by Gould in an easy chair, ready to discuss all these complexities with Bruno Monsaingeon, the French TV producer who arranged the whole affair.

Such are the marvels that technology can produce at the flick of a switch, but they have no substance, no reality, no life. Flick the switch again, and the music of Bach immediately stops, the image quickly shrinks to a shining dot at the center of the TV screen, and we are left sitting in the comfortable silence of the National Library of Canada. Silence—in the stillness of this shrine, one must keep reminding oneself that Gould's greatness derived from the sounds that he created, the patterns of sound, the music.

Gould's piano, his battered black Steinway grand, now stands in a lonely place of honor on the library's ground floor, in a kind of niche at the foot of a circling stairway. It is a ceremonial stairway for state occasions, all walled and floored in what appears to be white marble, and the ordinary visitors who use the nearby elevators rarely catch a glimpse of either the stairway or of Gould's piano. Actually, this is only one of five pianos that could be designated as "Glenn Gould's piano." Another Steinway that he kept in his apartment was sold to the governor-general's residence to be played on such ceremonial occasions as Canada Day. Another Gould piano was loaned to the Vancouver Museum, and still others are regularly sent out to various exhibitions of Gould memorabilia.

But this warm instrument under the stairway of the National Library was the one Gould loved best, and it bears its official Steinway name, "CD 318," stamped in gold letters deep in its covering top. It was built in 1945, and once Gould discovered it, he made it his own. He used it for most of his recordings, shipping it to and fro between Toronto and New York, until there inevitably came the day when careless movers dropped it from a considerable height and then shoved it into place and pretended that nothing had happened. "The plate is fractured in four critical places," Gould reported bitterly to Steinway in December of 1971 after examining the ruins of his piano. "The lid is split at the bass end and there also is considerable damage to it toward the treble end as well. The sounding board is split at the treble end. Key slip pins are bent out of line. . . ." Technicians labored for months over the carcass of 318, but it could never be restored to Gould's satisfaction. His last recording of *The Goldberg Variations* was made on a Yamaha.

Still, CD 318 is, more than any other instrument, except perhaps the tinkly old Chickering that he used throughout his boyhood, Glenn Gould's piano. So when the executor divided up the estate and consigned CD 318 to the National Library, he stipulated that it should not be treated simply as an object of veneration but worked on and played by other pianists. And so, in the fall of 1986, we gathered in the auditorium of the National Library to hear a young pianist named Angela Hewitt give CD 318 its first public workout.

She was very engaging, attractive, buoyant, confident. She had won the 1986 International Bach Piano Competition in Toronto, and now she had come to the shrine to perform for us. Gould's father, Russell Herbert Gould, was there to listen, an aged but still erect figure in evening dress, and so were Miss Hewitt's own parents. She looked charming, in a black velvet tuxedo and an absurd red bow tie, and she played beautifully—one of the French Suites and a Weber sonata—with just the right combination of precision and ardor. We were all filled with admiration, and with a sense of the occasion, and we all knew that her last encore would have to be, as it of course was, the theme of *The Goldberg Variations.*

There was a wine-tasting reception afterward, and then they took Gould's piano away, and soon it was once again standing in isolation at the foot of the stairway, with a great steel clamp holding the keyboard shut and silent.

But there are always the tapes, boxes and boxes of tapes, shelf upon shelf of tapes—miles of tape. We are now in the audio archive, on the third floor of the National Library, an archive walled by rows of cinder blocks all painted in baby blue. Somebody tried to use paint to bring light to this vault, but there is no real light except what comes from three or four unshaded bulbs hanging in the darkness and silence. Here is a shelf entirely devoted to rows of seven-inch tapes, each bearing a label that tells and does not tell what the box contains: Haydn piano sonata, Elizabethan keyboard music, Anhalt fantasia, Prokofiev piano music, Beethoven variations in C minor, Hindemith piano sonata No. 1, Schumann piano quartet. . . .

There is another Glenn Gould here too, the Gould who built a whole new career for himself, after his retirement from the concert stage, as an explorer at the outer limits of radio and television, an explorer who first interviewed and then cut and spliced and wove until he had achieved another kind of music that he liked to call "contrapuntal radio." Here the labels on the boxed reels of tape tell their story of work completed: "Quiet in the Land," Freissan interview; "Quiet in the Land," Horsch interview; "Quiet in the Land," Mrs. Toews interview; "Quiet in the Land," Hiebert interview. . . . "Quiet in the Land," which Gould worked on for several years, was a documentary about the Mennonites, who, as he quoted one of them saying, were "in this world but not of it." This was the conclusion of the series that Gould called his "solitude trilogy," all symbolically set in the Canadian North. The idea of North—that was his title for the first in the series—was very important to Gould. So was the idea of solitude.

When we enter the cinder-block vaults of the National Library of Canada, we come there not just to survey the rows on rows of more than fifteen hundred tapes but to hear, in the midst of the all-enveloping silence, the sound of one of the great artists of our time. On the machines that Gould loved, one can play not only such familiar wonders as Bach's partitas but also such unfamiliar wonders as the Gould version of Beethoven's *Hammerklavier Sonata*. And then there are half-remembered tapes of half-remembered Canadian television shows—Gould playing Scriabin preludes in front of a swirling cloud of Scriabinesque colors, Gould dressed up in a white suit to recite bits of William Walton's *Façade*. And in and out of the music, one keeps intermittently hearing that odd, nervous, clipped, self-conscious voice—returned, for a moment, from the dead—saying, "This is Glenn Gould—"

II

The Prodigy

Not long after Glenn Gould's extraordinary New York debut in 1955, when it first became internationally known that this young Canadian pianist could play like an angel, and looked rather like an angel too, Florence Gould received a letter from an old friend named Pearl. "How my heart leaped with joy knowing how delighted his dear little mother would be . . ." she wrote. "Knowing as I do what a good Christian girl you are I couldn't help but recall the words no good thing will He withhold from them that walk uprightly."

Pearl had not seen her friend since one summer day in the 1920's, when Florence was still Florence Greig and had come to visit her at her father's house in Moncton, New Brunswick. Pearl's aunt had been sick, and the girls' chattering disturbed her. "My father who loved music and thought so much of you told us to go outside and sing," Pearl wrote, "so we went out and sat on the back fence and sang. You told me some day you were going to marry and have a little boy and his name would be Glenn. I said I suppose he will be musical. You quickly said I'll see to that, with a twinkle in your eye. I shall never forget that day. You were never satisfied with just anything, you wanted only the best. . . ."

Florence Greig, who worked for many years as a teacher of singing, was proud to claim a dim connection to Edvard Grieg. Her only child, Glenn, occasionally joked about his own reluctance to record the famous Piano Concerto in A minor by the Norwegian composer, whom he liked to describe as one of his mother's cousins. Both Florence Greig and Edvard Grieg were actually descended from a fierce

Scottish tribe known as the MacGregors, who claimed a royal descent from Griogair, son of Alpin, King of the Scots in the eighth century. The family motto is "'S Rìoghal mo dhream" (Royal is my race). The MacGregors once owned much of Argyll and Perthshire, but they were such a warlike clan that they were entirely proscribed in the seventeenth century, in the reign of King James VI (James I of England). The use of the family name was decreed punishable by death, and so the MacGregors became Gregs and Gregsons and Greigs.

Family legend claimed that the MacGregors rose up to fight for Bonnie Prince Charlie at Culloden in 1746, and that one of the survivors fled to Norway and eventually became the great-grandfather of Edvard Grieg. There are always scholars who devote their efforts to investigating such legends—in this case, J. Russell Greig, author of *Grieg and His Scottish Ancestry,* 1952—and the investigation unfortunately demonstrated that Alexander Greig, who was only six when the Scots fought at Culloden, probably emigrated to Norway simply to seek his fortune. He made it as an exporter of Norwegian lobster and stockfish.

Most family histories are equally prosaic. Peter Greig, one of thirteen children of a Scottish farmer, emigrated to Canada in the mid-nineteenth century. He and his wife, Emma, had ten children, one of whom was Charles Holman Greig, who married Mary Catherine Flett, whose father, a carpenter from the Orkneys, died in a fall from the roof of the Bank of Montreal. One of their children, Florence, duly met and married Russell Herbert Gould, whose father's business card said: "Thomas G. Gould, Fur Salon, Designers and Manufacturers of Quality Fur Garments." Bert Gould inherited and managed his father's prosperous fur business, and passed on his middle name to the son whom his wife had long known she would name Glenn. She was forty-two (and had suffered through several miscarriages) when he was born. But even before he was born, according to her niece, Jessie Greig, "she did play music all the time she was carrying Glenn, with the hope that he was going to be a classical pianist."

Q: You think she had that in mind from the beginning?

A: I *know* she did.

And what can Bert Gould remember of his son's earliest days? Sitting with a cup of coffee in his sunny living room in Toronto, the old man smiles at the familiar question and offers a familiar answer. "When Glenn was just a few days old," he says, "he would reach up his arms like this. . . ." He raises his own aged arms toward the ceiling and wiggles his fingers to illustrate the idea of a week-old infant playing Bach. "Just a minute," he says, hurrying away to look for supporting evidence. "Here, this is something I did for that exhibition in France."

"As soon as he was old enough to be held on his grandmother's knee at the piano," the handsomely printed statement by Bert Gould declares, "he would never pound the key board as most children will with the whole hand, striking a number of keys at a time, instead he would always insist on pressing down a single key and holding it down until the resulting sound had completely died away. The fading vibration entirely fascinated him. . . ."

This is the stuff of legends, of course, a Christ child raising a hand to bless his worshipers, a boyish Napoleon brandishing a sword, a diminutive Mozart mesmerizing the courts of Europe by his agility at the harpsichord. But Glenn Gould really did have a talent that defied ordinary explanations. His father, who had played the violin in boyhood until he injured his hand, saw that easily. His mother soon realized that he had perfect pitch, and she began giving him piano lessons when he was three. He could read music before he could read words. She "used to play a game of note recognition with Glenn," according to Bert Gould's recollections. "He would go to a room at the far end of the house and his mother would strike a different chord on the piano in the living room. Invariably Glenn would call the correct answer."

The Goulds were obviously quite aware that their very left-handed child was unlike any others, and the child, though lucky in having such perceptive parents, was also quite aware of his own differentness, separateness, uniqueness. His father recalls that even as a baby, he wouldn't catch or play with a rubber ball. "And as he grew up," Bert Gould says, "if you threw a tennis ball—tried to get him to catch it—he'd turn his back and let it hit him, but he wouldn't catch it. Never would." Jessie Greig remembers when he came to her house for a visit at Easter time, when he was seven or eight, and he went outside to watch Jessie and her brothers playing marbles. "He watched for a long time, with his hands in his pockets," Miss Greig recalls, "and then he said, 'I'd like to play.' So we handed him some marbles, and he just put his hand down once to the cold earth, and he withdrew it *so* quickly—and he put his hands back in his pockets and said, 'I'm afraid I can't.' Even at that age, his hands must have been very, very sensitive, and he just said, 'I can't.' And he really wanted to. I can see him yet, kicking the earth with one toe, and wanting to join in and not being able to."

By then, the child seemed to have already decided on his future. "Oh, there was no doubt about that from the time he was three to five, anywhere in there," says Bert Gould. "In fact, at five years old, Glenn told me himself, 'I'm going to be a concert pianist.' He never changed his mind." But it was only a little later, when he was six, that the child was taken to his first concert, a recital by the legendary Josef Hofmann. "It was a staggering impression," Gould said later. "The only thing I can really remember is that, when I was being brought home in the car, I was in that wonderful state of half-awakeness in which you hear all sorts of incredible sounds going through your mind. They were all *orchestral* sounds, but *I* was playing them all, and suddenly I was Hofmann. I was enchanted."

There was something uncanny, unnatural, about Glenn Gould's gift. Most child prodigies work like galley slaves, many of them driven by their authoritarian parents or teachers, but Gould largely created himself. His indulgent mother was his only teacher until he was ten, by which time he had already mastered all of the first book of Bach's *Well-Tempered Clavier,* and then she turned him over to the almost equally indulgent Alberto Guerrero at the Toronto Conservatory. An émigré from Chile, Guerrero had conventionally definite views about how things should be played, but he easily recognized the uniqueness of the young Gould. "If Glenn feels he hasn't learned anything from me as a teacher, it's the greatest compliment anyone could give me," Guerrero's widow, Myrtle, once quoted him as saying. "The whole secret of teaching Glenn is to let him discover things for himself."

Gould not only taught himself, in the special music room that his father built so that the boy could play late at night, but he rarely worked very hard on anything that he wanted to learn. "I go days—not only days, but weeks—without touching the piano," he said to a slightly shocked interviewer in 1970. "I've never seen why it's necessary.... I play best after the two weeks or so that I've laid off." And he said it was that simple from the beginning. "I never bothered to practice very much—I now practice almost not at all—but even in those days I was far from being a slave of the instrument," he said in one of his long telephone talks with Jonathan Cott (*Conversations with Glenn Gould*). Gould professed to believe, in fact, that there was little to be taught or learned in the way of technique. "Given half an hour of your time and your spirit and a quiet room," he once said to a room full of educators, "I could teach any of you how to play the piano—everything there is to know about playing the piano can be taught in half an hour, I'm convinced of it."

Gould quickly added that he had never tried this experiment on any pupil, and there may have been a certain amount of hyperbole in his statement, perhaps a certain desire to *épater le pédagogue*. It seems more likely, however, that Gould's claim reflected a desire to generalize from his own experience, to deny the strangeness of his gift. After all, Bach himself had once said of his own skill as a keyboard virtuoso: "There is nothing to it. You have only to hit the right notes at the right time, and the instrument plays itself." But Bach also attributed his ability to hard work—"Whoever is equally industrious will succeed just as well"—whereas Gould seemed to feel very little need, at least on technical details, to work at all.

He could sight-read anything, and memorize at sight. John Roberts recalls Gould "flawlessly sight-reading" the Grieg concerto and then saying, "I just try not to look at the battlefield." Roberts also remembers an occasion when Gould challenged him to name any piece of music that Gould could not instantly play from memory. Roberts asked for specific sections of Strauss's *Burleske*, Prokofiev's Seventh Sonata, Beethoven's Opus 31, No. 3, "as well as other works, all of which he could do instantly."

These are all part of a fairly standard piano repertoire, of course, but Gould's head was full of orchestral and operatic works too. Roberts used to visit him at the summer home that Bert Gould had built on Lake Simcoe, about sixty miles north of Toronto, and there would be "sessions" at the piano that lasted until 3 A.M., sessions in which Gould seemed to transcribe the most complex orchestral scores as he went along. "I can remember him performing *Pelleas und Melisande* by Schoenberg with his eyes mostly closed . . ." Roberts recalled later. "Another example was the 'Four Last Songs' of Richard Strauss. He also had whole opera scores in the back of his head. Once he started Wagner's *Tristan und Isolde,* Glenn would be lost in another world, often oblivious to the presence of anyone else."

Judith Pearlman, the TV producer who made a television version of Gould's radio documentary, "The Idea of North," had a similar experience during her stay in Toronto. "After he had finished his recording session, I was in the control room, on the phone to New York, and he just sat down at the piano and started to play—all kinds of things. I knew he didn't like to have anybody listen to him, but after a while, I decided to come out of the control room. I *sneaked* out. I was terrified. Hearing him play live, which nobody ever heard—but he went right on playing. He said, 'Do you know this?' He was playing something from *Der Rosenkavalier.* And I said, 'Do you know *Die Frau ohne Schatten?'* And he just looked at me and then started playing the whole thing, from memory, and singing all the parts. I couldn't *move.* This is a big chunk of music, you know, and for him to have the whole thing in his head—"

Even that is not unique. Arthur Rubinstein once took the score of an unknown piano concerto aboard a plane to Spain and then performed it from memory, and without any rehearsal. Alicia de Larrocha has reported much the same thing. The pianist John Browning recalls that George Szell could sit down at a piano and play Beethoven string quartets from memory, or his own transcriptions of Strauss tone poems. "He could isolate on the piano, the viola part for a Schubert or Mozart quartet that he hadn't thought of in twenty years," Browning told David Dubal *(Reflections from the Keyboard).* These are no ordinary gifts, of course, but neither are they unimaginable. Gould's gift virtually was. He seems to have heard and perceived and taken in sound in a way that was quite different from the way these things are done by ordinary people. He himself became aware of this strange faculty when he was about thirteen, when he was working on a Mozart fugue in C minor (K. 394), and a surly household maid was determined to interrupt his work by turning on her vacuum cleaner.

"Well, the result was," as Gould recalled in an address to the graduating class at the Toronto Conservatory in 1964, "that in the louder passages, this luminously diatonic music ... became surrounded with a halo of vibrato, rather the effect that you might get if you sang in the bathtub with both ears full of water and shook your head from side to side all at once. And in the softer passages I couldn't hear any sound that I was making at all. I could feel, of course—I could sense the tactile relation with the keyboard ... and I could imagine what I was doing, but I couldn't actually hear it. But the strange thing was that all of it suddenly sounded better than it had without the vacuum cleaner, and those parts which I couldn't actually hear sounded best of all."

John Cage, during his period of absorption with aleatory music, or music of chance, was once reported to have listened with an expression of boredom to a recording of a familiar Brahms symphony—then to have smiled with pleasure when he heard the symphony suddenly interrupted by a doorbell. This was not because he welcomed the prospect of a visitor but because he welcomed the opportunity to hear for the first time the chance combination of a Brahms symphony and a ringing doorbell. Gould's perception of Mozart and the vacuum cleaner was not just an acceptance of an odd combination of sounds but an almost complete separation of his sense of music from his sense of hearing.

He liked to play two radios simultaneously, he once told Richard Kostelanetz, and "quite mysteriously, I discovered that I could better learn Schoenberg's difficult piano score, Opus 23, if I listened to them both at once, the FM to hear music and the AM to hear the news." Kostelanetz further recorded that Gould could read magazines while talking on the telephone and could "learn a Beethoven score while carrying on a conversation." Gould was not doing this to show off; he had simply discovered in himself a remarkable capacity to hear different things at once (notably the intertwining voices in Bach's fugues), and he found that this capacity somehow helped him to absorb music almost instantaneously. "If I am in a great hurry to acquire an imprint of some new score on my mind," he told the students at the Toronto Conservatory as an elaboration on his story of the vacuum cleaner, "I simulate the effect of the vacuum cleaner by placing some totally contrary noises as close to the instrument as I can. It doesn't matter what noise, really—TV westerns, Beatles records; anything loud will suffice—because what I managed to learn through the accidental coming together of Mozart and the vacuum cleaner was that the inner ear of the imagination is very much more powerful a stimulant than is any amount of outward observation."

Gould not only could hear and take in and memorize several things at once, but he heard with an incredible precision. Karen McLaughlin, who worked on the second recording of *The Goldberg Variations,* recalls that the sound engineers were amazed to find that Gould could differentiate between the playbacks from two different digital recording systems. "One was a Sony and one was a Mitsubishi, and the technical specifications were identical," she says, "and yet Glenn could unerringly tell them which was which. And that just amazed them. Nobody else could hear that kind of thing."

Despite a certain amount of theorizing and rationalizing, Gould seems to have been unable to understand the mysterious workings of his mysterious gift. "He was never terribly conscious of landing on right notes or worrying about that kind of thing," John Roberts remembers. "Once he began to think pianistically, it was destructive. I actually believe that at a certain moment, Glenn began to wonder, 'Well, how do I do this?' But he could never know how he did it. He just did it. And any kind of questioning, any conversation which veered toward how things are done really brought quite a reaction. He couldn't stand to talk about anything like that. That's why he disliked talking to other pianists. He had to try and protect himself from that."

Even for these disturbing aspects of his gift, though, Gould developed a theory, a metaphor, a source of authority. "Schoenberg once said," he observed, "that he would not willingly be asked by any of his composition students exactly why such-and-such a process served him well, because the question made him feel like that centipede who was asked in which order it moved its hundred legs, and afterwards he could move no legs at all—there's something impotent-making about that question. I'm rather afraid of it."

Perhaps the best analogy to Gould's strange gift lies in the ability to play chess blindfolded, even to play several such games simultaneously. This is not something that can be taught; it is simply there or not there. The prize example is Paul Morphy, of whom it has been said that having his mind must have been like having the boxing ability of Joe Louis when everyone else in the world was five feet high. Morphy took up chess at eight and could defeat anyone in his native New Orleans when he was ten. At nineteen, having won his law degree but being too young to practice, he went to New York to compete in the first American Chess Congress, which he won easily. Moving on to Europe, where he soon defeated the unofficial world champion, Adolf Anderssen, Morphy gave an exhibition in Paris by playing blindfolded against eight opponents at once, a world record at that time. The next day, he could still recite all the moves in all the games. He then planned to play blindfolded against twenty opponents, but friends dissuaded him on the ground that such an effort might cause a mental breakdown.

Thwarted in his ambition to overthrow his last rival, the British champion Howard Staunton, who evaded every challenge from the young American, Morphy sailed back to a hero's welcome in New York ("One smile, one glow of pride and pleasure, runs all over the land . . ." wrote James Russell Lowell). But after a competitive career that had lasted only about a year and a half, Morphy gave up chess, with a Gouldian abandon, and never again played a major match. Indeed, he seems to have acquired an intense distaste for the game. Even his friends could see that something had gone wrong. Morphy returned to his mother's home in New Orleans, dabbled at the law, engaged in a protracted litigation against a brother-in-law who he thought had defrauded him. He claimed that enemies were trying to poison his food. For two decades, he emerged from his mother's house at noon every day, walked alone through the streets, swinging his cane, often talking to himself. At night, he went to the opera. One summer morning in 1884, when Morphy was forty-seven, his mother found him dead of a stroke in his bathtub.

One cannot help wondering what chess meant to Morphy. (Ernest Jones once wrote an elaborate psychoanalytic study, *The Problem of Paul Morphy*, suggesting that "the unconscious motive activating the players is not the mere love of pugnacity characteristic of all competitive games but the grimmer one of father-murder.") How would his life have been different if chess had been more systematically organized in those days, and if it had been possible for him to become the world champion? Conversely, what would his life have been like if he had never seen a chessboard, if he had lived in a society where the game of chess was completely unknown? Would that extraordinary brain have turned to some other form of strategic planning—to the manipulation of the stock market, for example—or would it have remained forever passive, dormant? And what of Glenn Gould, if, say, his mother had never owned a piano? Might that piercing mind have devoted itself to chess (Bert Gould did teach his son to play)? Or to investment banking (Gould later did invest his earnings very profitably)? Or to who knows what?

From another perspective, of course, Gould was destined to spend much of his early life as just another little boy growing up in just another neighborhood. The Goulds lived in an intensely WASP area known as The Beaches, and it was just a short walk from their modest house at 32 Southwood Drive down to the amiable streetcar line on Queen Street and then to the even more amiable boardwalk along the shore of Lake Ontario. Even now, if one looks westward toward downtown Toronto, a spit of land blocks the entire city from sight. One is completely cut off, in a very pleasant enclave.

Outside that enclave lay a world strange and ominous. "The most vivid of my childhood memories in connection with Toronto have to do with churches," Gould recalled in his script for a television show, "Glenn Gould's Toronto." "They have to do with Sunday evening services, with evening light filtered through stained-glass windows, and with ministers who concluded their benedictions with the phrase, 'Lord, give us the peace that the earth cannot give.' Monday mornings, you see, meant that one had to go back to school and encounter all sorts of terrifying situations out *there*...."

Single children almost always encounter difficulties in their first collisions with other children, but Gould's collisions at the Williamson Road Public School, a three-story brick fortress about two blocks from his home, seem to have been particularly bruising. "I found going to school a most unhappy experience," he once told an interviewer, "and got along miserably with most of my teachers and all of my fellow students." The fellow students had similar memories. "He was somewhat isolated from the rest of us," Wayne Fulford, general manager of a bus equipment firm, told a reporter after Gould's death. "I mean, he wasn't somebody who pretended to be interested in hockey or baseball when he wasn't.... He didn't always mix in."

Gould was often bullied, sometimes came home crying. "I can remember him saying that the worst bully followed him nearly home and finally took a swing at Glenn," John Roberts recalls. "And Glenn just went for him. And hit him so hard that this kid wondered what had struck him. Then Glenn grabbed him by the lapels and shook him and said, 'If you ever come near me again, I will kill you.' And this kid was absolutely scared out of his mind, and the thing which also frightened Glenn was that he realized that it was true."

The Fulfords lived next door to the Goulds on Southwood Drive, and Wayne Fulford's older brother Robert, former editor of the Toronto magazine *Saturday Night,* has similar memories of the young pianist's loneliness. "I remember him as a child being much more puritanical than our district and our time in history would require," Fulford says. "He was a boy very much unlike other boys in that regard, as in a thousand others. Couldn't stand to hear boys blaspheme or use obscenities. And he would actually beg you not to. His mother had a kind of idea of what was a good child, and he bought it and internalized it. She was a bit of a dragon."

Q: But she wasn't harsh with him, was she?

A: Can't remember her being harsh with Glenn, but there's a way of nagging without being harsh that can be pretty controlling. I can remember her saying, "Glenn, you should do this, Glenn, you should do that." You don't need harshness if you're persistent. And she didn't like him to have opinions that were too confident.

Q: Too confident?

A: Too showing off. She was a real old-fashioned Canadian in that way. Don't come out of hiding too much, and never give an opinion that isn't well considered, and probably don't give it at all. I'd say she was a very narrow person in every way except musically, and maybe musically she was narrow too.

Elizabeth Fox, a CBC producer who became friends with Gould a few years later, has somewhat more amiable memories. "When you'd go to his home, it was just so warm and nice," she says. "I can remember eating well and being treated well, lots of lights on. I liked both his parents. I don't know what they were like with other people, but they were sure nice when I was there. But they constantly— they certainly deferred to him. I thought later of E. B. White's *Stuart Little,* about these people who have a mouse as a child. And he's dressed up as a human being, but he goes up and down the drains and all the rest. Well, when you were at the Goulds' house, you'd think, these people have produced something that is not of them. He's dressed *somewhat* like a human being, and he plays the piano, but it was—they were constantly in awe."

In this difficult period, Jessie Greig came into Gould's life as a kind of rescuer. He had always known her as a cousin living in nearby Uxbridge, but when he was thirteen and she was eighteen, the Goulds invited her to live with them while she attended teacher's college in Toronto. "We were very, very close, and our closeness came from my year there," she says. "He was sort of a capricious, very outgoing child, outgoing in the sense that he could join in any conversation, and did. He was interested in everything. And he had great confidence in everything. And his desire to learn everything was just boundless."

The Goulds clearly thought it would be a good idea for their rather lonely adolescent to acquire a big sister, and that is what Jessie soon became. She taught him, and took care of him, and fought with him, and loved him. "One night," she recalls with a laugh, "I had scrubbed the kitchen floor and waxed it and got the vegetables on. They were going out after dinner, so I said, 'I'll do the dishes,' and they said, 'Glenn will help you.' Well, after they'd left, he took and threw water on the freshly waxed floor, just to make me angry, and so I started to chase him. I grabbed a wax rag from under the sink, and I caught him on the stairs, and I waxed his face, you know, just like two kids would do. And he was very upset. He said he was going to die of germs.

"He said he was going to wring my neck—that was always his favorite expression—so I ran upstairs, and I got in the bathroom, and I locked the door. He went in my room, and he got my notebooks from school, and he kept ripping out a page and putting it under the bathroom every hour or so. I kept saying, 'Glenn, I'll fail.' And he'd say, 'That's all right. If I studied as much as you, I'd be through the university by now.' Then another page ripped, and under the door. Then we both heard the car come in, and we both flew to our respective rooms, and he slept all night in his clothes. And the next morning, his mother said, 'How did things go?' And Glenn said, 'Fine, just fine.'"

Apart from Jessie, Gould had few close friends. He easily persuaded himself, as he often told interviewers, that he liked animals better than people. One of the first long newspaper stories about him, in the Toronto *Star* of February 21, 1946, reported that the thirteen-year-old pianist kept goldfish named Bach, Beethoven, Chopin, and Haydn, as well as a budgerigar named Mozart. The bird, according to the *Star*, "perched on the score [and] attempted to accompany him." "He can't talk yet," Gould was quoted as saying, "but he knows his music." The Toronto *Telegram* took a similar approach a few years later and photographed Gould's shaggy dog next to him at the piano. "The English setter, Nick, sat motionless as Glenn played variations of La Ricordanza by Carl Czerny," the *Telegram* reported, in that infinitely patronizing tone that newspapers use toward both musicians and children, "and seemed to enjoy watching his master's fingers race over the keyboard."

Gould created his own journalistic account of these years by founding a newspaper that he named "THE DAILY WOOF—The Animals Paper, Etided [sic] by Glenn Gould." Only one neatly penciled issue survives. The two lead stories are headlined BACH DIES OF FUNGUS and MOTZY BELIEVED TO HAVE LICE. The latter goes on to report: "AAP Jan. 4 A matter still under examined [sic] is whether or not Motzy, the budgy has lice. His recent scratchings have given the impression that he had." At the bottom of the page, under the headline SQUIRREL ATTRACTS ATTENTION, and the logo "Special to the WOOF," the paper reported: "A black squirrel attracted much attention here yesterday P.M. when he dragged a large chunk of bread across the street spreading crumbs on the lawn. He is wanted for questioning by local authorities in other recent thefts."

Most children quickly learn that their parents claim a God-given right to kill any animals they choose. Gould never really learned that, or never accepted it. Gould's father, the furrier, was a devoted fisherman, as were many of the neighbors who lived near the Goulds' summer cottage on Lake Simcoe, and Gould was just six when one of these neighbors took him out on the lake for his first actual fishing expedition. "I was the first to catch a fish," Gould remembered years later, when he was a famous pianist being interviewed by the Toronto *Star*. "And when the little perch came up and started wiggling about I suddenly saw this thing entirely from the fish's point of view. And it was such a powerful experience, I sort of picked up my fish and said I was going to throw it back. At that moment—this has remained with me as a sort of block against people who exert influence over children—the father suddenly pushed me back into my seat, probably for the sensible reason that I was rocking the boat. Then he took the fish out of my reach, at which I went into a tantrum and started jumping up and down, stamping my feet and pulling my hair and stuff like that. And I kept at it until we got in to shore. . . ."

Gould's father, who did subsequently give up fishing at his son's urgings, remembers that there was once a skunk prowling for garbage outside the cottage, and the boy built a trap that would catch the animal without harming it. When the skunk was duly trapped, the father told the boy to go and deal with it, assuming that the confrontation would soon lead to the skunk being turned loose. "Within a few minutes, Glenn had him eating out of his hand," Bert Gould recalls. Skunks are handsome animals, but they can be fierce as well as smelly, and perhaps there was something about the wildness of the animal he had trapped that appealed to the boy. There remains in the archives of the National Library of Canada a fragment of a song that Gould wrote in honor of his new friend. "I am a skunk, a skunk am I," it goes, "skunking is all I know, I want no more, I am a skunk, a skunk I'll remain. . . ."

Near the end of his life, when he appeared in "Glenn Gould's Toronto," the pianist recalled that one of the unfinished works of his childhood was an opera that "was to deal with the ultimate catastrophe of nuclear destruction. In Act I the entire human population was to be wiped out and in Act II they were to be replaced by a superior breed of frogs." Gould claimed that he had actually composed "a few bars" of a chorus for frogs in the key of E major, "which I always felt to be a benign and sympathetic key," but he acknowledged that there would have been a "casting problem."

These few remnants of genocidal childhood fantasy finally served only as an introduction to an unusual scene in "Glenn Gould's Toronto," in which Gould, after recalling that he had once sung Mahler songs to some cattle grazing in a field, ventured out to the Toronto zoo in the silent emptiness of dawn and sang these same Mahler songs to a troop of captive elephants. The elephants listened in wonder for a few moments, then turned and flapped their giant ears and wandered away.

For the most part, Gould's summers on Lake Simcoe were idyllic. "Glenn was very proud of his first boat," according to Bert Gould, "which was a fifteen-foot cedar skiff which I had equipped with an electric motor and two twelve-volt storage batteries. This boat Glenn steered and controlled from a wheel at the bow. . . . Glenn was never happier than when on the water with his boat and his dog Nick in charge of the front deck. . . ." Bert also remembers one stormy day when he feared that his son might be lost, and so he set out in another boat to find him—and did find him, waving like a conductor at the waves that broke over the bow.

This amiable lakeside life led to an accident that was to become quite important in Gould's later years. His father built a long rail from the house to the beach, to help Glenn haul his boat up out of the water. When the boy was about ten, his father recalls, something went wrong. "Glenn and a number of others got on the boat and started it down the rail," he says, "and somehow Glenn slipped and fell off the back of it and hit his spine on the rocks."

Q: How high a fall was that?

A: Well, it's not a great fall, I suppose a couple of feet, but a vertical drop to the rocks.

Q: Did he complain of pain then?

A: Oh, yes.

Q: Did you take him to a doctor then?

A: Oh, yes, we took him to doctors for a long time afterwards. . . . We had him to every specialist we could think of. Started with the medical men and then osteopaths and chiropractors—the works.

Q: How long did that go on?

A: I'd say two or three years anyway.

Such back injuries are mysterious and powerful—this may well have been the "obscure hurt" that haunted Henry James all his life—for they periodically seem to be cured, for months on end, and then the pain suddenly returns and seizes the victim, as though he were being grasped by a giant claw. Beyond that, the injury affects the neck, the arms, the wrists, the hands.

Gould's health was to remain something of an enigma throughout most of his life, to himself as well as to his doctors, his friends, and his public. Bert Gould still says emphatically that he "was never really sick a day in his life," but from the earliest concerts on, Gould often complained of debilitating ailments, and often canceled performances because of them. He seems to have suffered from some kind of circulatory problem that made his hands feel cold, and so he began using mittens, hot water, various pills. He felt susceptible to drafts, which led to sore throats and chills. He lived in dread of germs, viruses, infections. It is quite possible that these difficulties were largely imaginary, or a response to the stresses of playing in public—and Gould freely admitted to hypochondria—but just as a hypnotized man's arm can turn red and blistered when he is told that he is being burned by a cigarette, so a hypochondriac's imagined pains really do hurt. Gould consulted many doctors throughout his life; few brought him any real relief.

Like any other schoolboy, though, the vulnerable young pianist set off every day to learn spelling and fractions and all those other disciplines that the adult world considered necessary. After Gould had served his apprenticeship at the Williamson Road Public School, he moved on to a nearby public high school named Malvern Collegiate, but he went there only in the mornings, so that his afternoons could be reserved for the piano. The teaching at Malvern was rigorous. What was the Concordat of 1801? What was the Directory? What was the effect of the American Civil War on the development of the Canadian West? "In Kipling's address on Values in Life, what type of man does the author hold up for our admiration? Why is he admirable? What *advice* and what *comfort* does he offer to youth when depressed by a sense of his own worthlessness?" What is the difference between the Shakespearean sonnet and the Petrarchan sonnet? "Qu'est-ce que vous prenez comme petit déjeuner?" "Je prends d'habitude du céreal chaud, de la pain et du café. . . ." The teacher duly noted Gould's mistake in the gender of the word for bread. "Qu'avez-vous l'intention de faire l'année prochaine?" "J'ai l'intention étudier la musique."

Most of Gould's schoolbooks show a dutiful dedication to his work, extended notes on *Pride and Prejudice* and the history of Canada, but there was also a deplorable tendency toward romantic rhetoric. "Far down, through the concrete channel, a myriad of flustered flotsam floundered against a flurry of the windsquall," one paper for his English class began. "From far up, I saw a vacillating abstract of surrealistic shape whose every minute movement only multiplied my misconceptions of their unity. For I, a stranger to their city, saw a mass—controlled, directed, pushed—as one. I felt the incessant onward motion of the crowd, but I, aloof then, failed to see that each small, separate movement was a symbol of their individuality. . . ." And so on. Gould's teachers did not encourage this sort of thing. "In this paragraph you are using words for their own sakes," one of them commented on one of his efforts. "The result is that your style is obscure and seems forced." Another judgment was even more blunt: "Vague answers will not suffice." And another still more so: "Just stuff and nonsense." The cruelest of these comments came from a teacher who quite accurately declared that much of Gould's paper on *Macbeth* was a "waste of words," and who then added: "You are absent too often and miss too much work. Your knowledge is not thorough, nor your application of it sufficiently exact. Your bad spelling also has contributed toward your failure as you see. . . ."

As with the school bully whom he threatened to kill, Gould stood ready to combat his teachers. In one of those standard assignments on "my plans for the school year," he defiantly wrote: "I am at something of a disadvantage in writing on this subject, for my adventures in the halls of learning are curtailed at the close of the fourth period each morning. The remainder of my day is spent in music, with the exclusion of an hour or so in the evening which I rather grudgingly bequeath to Macbeth, the Treaty of Ghent and the subjunctive mood. . . . My plans for this season include a number of solo recitals and appearances with the Hamilton and Toronto Symphony Orchestras. Although very little of this is relevant to the title, I think it will be sufficient to show why I have not a moment to spend on extra-curricular activities at school. My plans for the school year, therefore, are nonexistent." To this bitter observation, the teacher wrote in the margin, "That cannot be." At the end, this same teacher wrote, "Clever," and graded the paper B-minus.

If the piano added something of a burden during Gould's school years, it was also an escape. "I think I was truly determined upon a career in music at the age of nine or ten," he told an interviewer, Bernard Asbell, in 1962. "I was determined to wrap myself up in music because I found it was a damned good way of avoiding my schoolmates, with whom I did not get along." He did not see himself specifically as a concert pianist, however. "I saw myself as a sort of musical Renaissance Man, capable of doing many things. I obviously wanted to be a composer. I still do. Performing in the arena had no attraction for me. This was, at least in part, defensive. Even from what little I then knew of the politics of the business, it was apparent that a career as a solo pianist involved a competition which I felt much too grand ever to consider facing."

Gould's mother was the most encouraging of teachers, and it was probably important that she was not a professional piano teacher but rather a singing coach. "His mother did a very important thing," John Roberts observes. "She made him sing, all the time. As he played notes, as a small child, he had to sing them. I think that had something to do with his being able to hear in his mind as well as he could. And his mother used to listen to all his playing—he played rather than practiced—and if she thought something was not right, she would call out to him immediately. So as a small child, he never learned mistakes, because they were always perceived instantly. It wasn't until Glenn was ten that there was any need for him to go to another teacher. Glenn always said to me that he considered himself self-taught."

Raising a child endowed with such gifts is not easy. (What must Leopold Mozart have wondered in the darkness of some sleepless night?) The desire to protect and shelter and defend is repeatedly challenged by self-accusation, by the anxiety that one may not be doing enough to help the child become whatever it is destined to become. Mrs. Gould took her son to the Toronto Conservatory to be examined, like some medical wonder. "Dear Mr. Gould," said the letter to the seven-year-old boy from Fredk. C. Silvester, Examination Registrar, "We have pleasure in informing you that the mark you received in your recent examination for Grade IV piano was the highest in the Province of Ontario. This entitles you to the Conservatory's Silver Medal, which you will receive in the early part of October. . . ."

After a good deal of consultation, the Goulds decided to consign their prodigy to the care of Alberto Guerrero. It seems to have been a wise choice. By then already in his middle fifties, with a balding head and rimless spectacles, Guerrero had once founded and conducted the first symphony orchestra in Santiago, Chile. He gave premiere performances of Debussy and Ravel. In the 1920's, he migrated northward, and, according to an obituary notice in the Toronto *Star* in 1959, it was through his performances that "Toronto heard for the first time the major piano works of Hindemith, Schoenberg, Stravinsky, Milhaud, and others."

Guerrero also had some important idiosyncrasies that he taught to his pupils. "He sat lower in relation to the keyboard and played with flatter fingers than most players," according to another one of his students, John Beckwith, now a composer and professor at the University of Toronto. "His performances of light rapid passages had not only fluency and great speed but also exceptional clarity and separation of individual notes. . . . One practice-technique for finger separation consisted of playing the music for each hand separately, very slowly, but making the sound by tapping each finger with the non-playing hand. One learned from this how very precise and economical the muscle movements needed for fast playing really could be. It was indeed a 'pure finger-technique' in that virtually no hand-action was applied—the fingers did it all."

"Glenn was not taught in the usual way, 'Do this' or 'Do that,'" according to the recollections of Guerrero's widow, Myrtle. "Alberto exposed him to all kinds of music, and they would enjoy analyzing the music together. . . . The lessons were of great duration because Glenn insisted on getting every sound just right. He would linger over just one or two things until he had it. Alberto would say, 'Oh, it's all right, Glenn,' but Glenn would say, 'No, it's not!'" "My studies with Guerrero, in my later teens, were essentially exercises in argument," Gould recalled many years later. "They were attempts to crystallize my point of view versus his on some particular issue, whatever it was, and . . . I think that for me, anyway, it worked very well."

There still survive some amateur recordings of the two of them playing piano duets, the first movements of the great Mozart four-hand sonatas in C and F, the young Gould playing the upper part brightly and eagerly, like a yearling newly turned loose on a racetrack, and Guerrero providing a watchful accompaniment, knowing full well how this animal could run. They played croquet together too, the Guerreros and Glenn and his mother, for the Guerreros had a cottage not far from the Goulds' place on Lake Simcoe. Like any boy who announces a hatred of competition, Gould also hated losing, and croquet, like chess, brings out the worst instincts. "Glenn was a furious competitor," Mrs. Guerrero recalled, "and if he didn't win, it was a tragedy."

The Goulds did not want their son to be a public prodigy, committed to the public rituals of a Rubinstein or a Menuhin, but they inevitably began wondering whether it was fair to a child of such enormous talent to keep that talent hidden. The Goulds were devoted churchgoers, so it seemed natural to them to offer up their son's talents on the altar of the church's social evenings. One elderly lady who heard Gould perform at a meeting of the Women's Missionary Society at the Emmanuel Presbyterian Church in Toronto recalled to an interviewer just a few years ago that the boy wore a white satin suit with short pants. A surviving letter from the Reverend W. J. Johnston of the Eglinton United Church thanks the Goulds for bringing their eleven-year-old son to "our church social last evening" and for making him "entertain us so wonderfully at the piano. He certainly is a lad of parts."

Gould's first formal public appearance, in 1945, came not at the piano but at the organ. He had been studying both instruments at the Toronto Conservatory, and he liked to claim in later years that his labors at the organ had taught him the significance of a bass line, and of a detached touch, and, of course, of the genius of Bach. The organ also provided Gould with his first (and last) job. He was hired to accompany the services at an Anglican church, but he had a habit of losing his place when the congregation sang. There was an embarrassing mistake, a rustle of disapproval, and then an abrupt dismissal. In his solo premiere, though, one newspaper review praised "Glenn Gould, a nipper who looks about 11, may be older, but announced his encore in a voice which has not yet changed. . . ." Edward Wodson of the *Telegram*, on the other hand, was astute enough to see that although Gould was "just a child, really, a loose-jointed, gracious, smiling boy . . . he played the organ last evening as many a full-grown concert organist couldn't if he tried. A genius he is . . . and in every detail his playing had the fearless authority and finesse of a master." Gould first attracted serious attention as a pianist when he entered a Kiwanis festival in February of 1946 and emerged as one of the thirty-two winners out of nine thousand contestants. "Serious attention" is perhaps too strong a term for a competition on which the Toronto *Star* reported only that "Gould was a poetic wizard with a Bach prelude, but too sinuously intense for the Fugue." The newspaper's critic, Augustus Bridle, devoted far more attention to "Miriam Smith, age 6, [who] dangled her bootees far above the pedals to play a Bach Gavotte," which Bridle said she had turned into "a fairyland fandango." A somewhat less idiotic review in the *Telegram* reported that the thirteen-year-old Gould had played a Bach prelude and fugue "with remarkable feeling and finesse, these characteristics in a degree rather beyond his years." The critic went on to conclude that "his performance at the piano as a whole, however, was too consciously mannered." Gould preserved the stub of the ten-dollar check that he won for this performance, but it may be possible to glimpse in these accounts of the Kiwanis festival one of the origins of his lifelong dislike of both competition and newspaper critics. "The Scribbler," he wrote years later in an unpublished fantasy entitled *The Gouldberg Variations*, "[was] a noxious little wart from, of all venalities, the daily press— that loathsome compendium of assaults, insults, vagaries, untruths, half-truths, libels, vulgarities, pomposities and even dichotomies. . . . There was not an ounce of goodness in this wretched chap, not from the greasy morass that stood proxy for his hair to his syphilitic little toe."

It was only a matter of time, and not too much time, before Guerrero wrote to Gould in 1946 to report the Toronto Symphony Orchestra's invitation to a major piano debut. "You have been chosen to play in the opening concert of the Secondary School Series . . ." he wrote. "You would play the G Major Beethoven concerto. Sir Ernest [MacMillan] will conduct. There is a nominal fee of $75. . . . I have missed very much a game of croquet."

How casually it is said. You would play the G major Beethoven Concerto, a work that happens to be one of the masterpieces in the literature of the piano, and also a work to which thousands of amateurs have devoted many thousands of wasted hours. Gould was then thirteen, still writing school papers on Kipling and the history of Canada. Like every young pianist of that period he knew and played and loved Artur Schnabel's recording of the Beethoven Fourth with the Chicago Symphony Orchestra under Frederick Stock. "Almost every day," he later recalled, "some or all eight 78-rpm sides served as accompaniment for practice sessions in which I faithfully traced every inflective nuance of the Schnabelian rhetoric, surged dramatically ahead whenever he thought it wise . . . and glided to a graceful cadential halt every four minutes and twenty-five seconds or so while the automatic changer went to work on the turntable."

Gould claimed—his memory on these matters was, not infallible—that Guerrero forced him to surrender his beloved Schnabel recording and to bow down to the teacher's authority, and that the teacher professed himself satisfied only when Gould played the concerto at the more brisk tempo recorded by Rudolf Serkin. "On the day of my debut it rained," Gould later wrote, "and that evening— it was early May, the first week of daylight saving, and the sun set at eight—the low-pressure area moved eastward, the ceiling lifted, and the skyline of Toronto took on that misty, orange-shaded cyclorama effect that Walt Kelly would soon celebrate in the color installments of 'Pogo' at Okefenokee. . . . This was a time for personal statement—a moment to grasp and to make one's own." Gould walked onto the stage and began playing the Beethoven concerto exactly as he pleased. He remembered long afterward that "I left in high spirits, my teacher was shattered, and the press, on the whole, was quite kind." There was only one small annoyance in the Toronto *Globe and Mail,* which reported that this great concerto had been "left in the hands of a child," and the reviewer wondered, "Who does the kid think he is, Schnabel?"

Even at this age, the child was already becoming a hero. Fourteen years later, a housewife in New Westminster, who had been fifteen years old on the occasion of Gould's concert, wrote him to tell him not only that she had been there but that she had recorded the event in her diary. "Glenn is fourteen but he looks much younger," she had written. "I think he must have been scared because at the beginning . . . after he had played a few chords, and was sitting while the orchestra was playing, he was sort of fidgety—kept pushing his hair back and mopping his brow with a large white handerchief. He was round-shouldered and seemed to bend over the piano as he played; his playing, however, more than made up for his idiosyncrasies. He was marvelous! The audience nearly brought the house down. Finally he played an encore—a Chopin Valse. His fingers moved like lightning. . . . I wonder whether, 10 or 15 years from now, we'll be hearing from him on the concert stages of the world?"

That performance in May of 1946 actually involved only the first movement of the concerto, and it was not until the following January that Gould played the entire work with the Toronto Symphony under the baton of an Australian guest conductor, Bernard Heinze. Pearl McCarthy then wrote in the *Globe and Mail* that "the boy played it exquisitely," but she also sounded a theme that was to become an obsession among reviewers throughout Gould's concert career. "Unfortunately," she wrote, "the young artist showed some incipient mannerisms and limited his self-control to the period when he himself was playing. As he approaches adult status, he will undoubtedly learn to suppress this disturbing fidgeting. . . ."

Gould, as usual, had an explanation, and in this case it involved his English setter, Nick (officially Sir Nickolson of Garelocheed), who was in the process of shedding hair. "As I was getting into my best dark suit prior to the concert," Gould later recalled, "my father cautioned me to keep my distance from Nick, but that, of course, was easier said than done. Nick was an affectionate and concerned animal and not one to see a friend off on an important mission without offering his good wishes." Gould's trousers, in short, were covered with long white dog hairs, but it was only during a pause in the slow movement of the concerto that be became aware of the dog's contribution. One of the strangest things about public performance is that one is capable of losing all sense of where one is, and just as it becomes possible to play a difficult piano concerto without even noticing the hundreds of watching faces, so it is also possible to start wondering, in the middle of that concerto, whether one should try to remove some dog hairs from one's trousers.*

Gould came to the absurd decision that the third movement would give him an opportunity, for there is a long orchestral tutti after each

---

*Gould retained a lifelong practice of thinking about different things at once. When an admiring friend once said that his playing showed "incredible powers of concentration" on the work being performed, Gould retorted, "That's not true at all. I just played with the Chicago Symphony, and during the last movement of the concerto, all I was thinking was, Is the driver that I hired going to be backstage when I'm finished so I can make a quick getaway?"

statement of the rondo theme. The one problem, which had never occurred to him, was that each statement of the theme was identical but then led to a different interlude, and that a pianist engaged in picking dog hairs from his trousers might lose track of which tutti the orchestra was playing. And so it happened. "Major tuttis went by and the [hair-removal] operation was ninety percent complete," Gould recalled. "Only one question remained in my mind: how complete was the concerto? Was this the tutti which, upon my entrance, I lead toward the dominant? Was it the one which I echo in the minor key? Or was it the one which points the way to the cadenza? The problem didn't occur to me until the last few bars of whichever tutti it was. I tried desperately to remember what besides picking setter hairs I'd been doing for the last five minutes or so and placed an inspired bet on tutti no. 3. The cadenza lead-in was, indeed, upcoming, but I had learned the first valuble lesson of my association with the T.S.O.—either pay attention or keep short-haired dogs."

Gould enjoyed his early success. "Performing before an audience gave me a glorious sense of power at fifteen," he told one interviewer. He probably had very little idea what an arduous process the climb to worldwide fame would become. The first solo recital was a student concert in April of 1947, which Gould later described only as "a brace of fugues and some Haydn, some Beethoven, some Mendelssohn, some Liszt (which I haven't played since in public)." GOULD DISPLAYS GROWING ARTISTRY, said the *Globe and Mail*. Looking back at his young self, Gould later declared that he was "not nervous at all. It was all part of a game, really. . . . In those days, one was blissfully unaware of the responsibility. I just wish I could feel that way again. Now you accomplish the same thing by sedatives."

Gould's memories of those days are not completely reliable. He did play Liszt's *Au Bord d'une Source* at his first official recital under the management of an energetic young Toronto impresario named Walter Homburger in the Eaton's department store auditorium in October of 1947. He also offered a rather un-Gouldian assortment of works by Scarlatti, Couperin, Beethoven, Mendelssohn, and Chopin. (Yes, the Impromptu in F-sharp major, Opus 36, and the Waltz in A flat, Opus 42. And Robert Fulford, who lived next door, says that his strongest memories of summer evenings on the veranda were "the sound of him playing Chopin.") But while Gould's memories are selective, the Toronto music critics of the time are hardly more reliable. Bridle of the *Star,* for example, wrote of that October recital: "Spiderlike fingers, flexible rubberish wrists, pedals infallible, nose a foot above the keys, he was like an old man on a music spree. . . . In a Beethoven sonata, Opus 37 [he meant Opus 31], he outdid Rachmaninoff for intensively supple art. Vivid re-etching, such as Ludwig never dreamed into a sonata, was the essence of this youth-technique. . . ." And so on. But Bridle did add, after all that gushing, "This boy is on the road to pianistic fame."

Radio provided another road, an important road, to that fame. For those who have grown up with television, it is hard to understand how important radio was in the 1940's. It was everything that TV is today, plus whatever radio still is, plus a lot more. It was the one national and even international system of communication, of both messages and fantasy. It alone brought us the soothing voice of President Roosevelt at his fireside and the shrieking voice of Hitler on his rostrum—both of whom derived a lot of their political power from their mastery of radio—as well as the weekly chatter of Walter Winchell's news broadcasts to "Mr. and Mrs. America and all the ships and clippers at sea," and the weekly absurdities of Fred Allen interviewing Senator Claghorn or the boxes and baskets tumbling out of Fibber McGee's hall closet. TV destroyed all this phantasmagoria by its relentless insistence on what TV people call "the visuals," on showing us exactly what everything looks like, which is usually less than we had imagined. Imagine a TV adaptation of Orson Welles's *War of the Worlds* setting off a nationwide panic.

Radio also served to unite people. It created, among other things, a standardized national accent and also a national schedule. Sunday afternoon was the time for the New York Philharmonic—and thousands later remembered the news from Pearl Harbor as an interruption of Arthur Rubinstein's performance of the Brahms B flat Concerto—just as Sunday night was the time for Winchell (who sold Jergens lotion), Charlie McCarthy (who sold Chase and Sanborn coffee), and Jack Benny (who sold Jell-O). Nowhere was this more true than in the Canada of Gould's youth, a vast and relatively empty land that was still rather nervously examining the connective fibers of its own identity. "So I went back to my work in CBC and stayed with the organization throughout the war," says the radio broadcaster who serves as hero of Hugh MacLennan's novel, *The Watch That Ends the Night*. "Strange years which now have become a blur. While the war thundered on, Canada unnoticed grew into a nation at last. This cautious country which had always done more than she had promised, had always endured in silence while others reaped the glory—now she became alive and to us within her excitingly so. . . . And sometimes, thinking with shame of the Thirties when nothing in Canada had seemed interesting unless it resembled something in England or the States, I even persuaded myself that here I had found the thing larger than myself to which I could belong. . . ."

Unlike anything south of the border, the CBC is, of course, a government-funded national network, and the people in charge of it were fully aware of their role in this national awakening. The organization had been founded in 1936, according to a magazine article recently tacked to the door of the CBC radio archives in Toronto, for the official purpose of "fostering national spirit and interpreting national citizenship." Over those great spaces, it was the CBC radio that provided the neurons to connect Montreal and Toronto with Winnipeg, Moose Jaw, Yellowknife. And against the constant buzz of broadcasting from the United States, the CBC needed and searched out and supported Canadian journalists, Canadian talkers and tellers, and, of course, Canadian musicians. Gould, unlike some of his admirers, was never a Canadian nationalist. "Our country," he wrote to a young American pianist in the 1950's, "having passed out of the stage when the foreign-born were considered indispensible, is now in an equally revolting nationalist stage in which all outside attractions ought to be dispensed with." Still, the young Gould, that nipper, that lad of parts, seemed made to order for the Canadian radio network's needs.

And it for him. "One Sunday morning in December 1950," he wrote in an essay titled "Music and Technology," "I wandered into a living-room-sized radio station, placed my services at the disposal of a single microphone belonging to the Canadian Broadcasting Corporation, and proceeded to broadcast 'live' two sonatas: one by Mozart, one by Hindemith. It was my first network broadcast, but it was not my first contact with the microphone; for several years

I'd been indulging in experiments at home with primitive tape recorders—strapping the mikes to the sounding board of my piano, the better to emasculate Scarlatti sonatas, for example. . . . But the CBC occasion . . . was a memorable one: not simply because it enabled me to communicate without the immediate presence of a gallery of witnesses . . . but rather because later the same day I was presented with a soft-cut 'acetate,' a disc which dimly reproduced the felicities of the broadcast in question and which, even today, a quarter-century after the fact, I still take down from the shelf on occasion in order to celebrate that moment in my life when I first caught a vague impression of the direction it would take . . . when my love affair with the microphone began."

So he knew even then, at the age of eighteen, that technology could provide him with an alternative method of performing music, a method that could do away with all the staring faces, all the coughs and rustlings, all the anxieties. But he also knew perfectly well that he still had a great deal to learn. It is all too easy for an inexperienced youth to devote himself to the official classics, Bach and Beethoven, to become a specialist and even a partisan of what little he already knows. Gould was more ambitious. "My first experience of contemporary music was via Paul Hindemith and particularly *Matthias the Painter*," he later recalled. "I was 15 at the time, a complete reactionary. I hated all music after Wagner, and a good deal of Wagner, and suddenly I heard *Matthias the Painter*, in a recording with Hindemith conducting, and flipped completely. This suddenly was the recreation of a certain kind of Baroque temperament that appealed to me tremendously, and I, as a 15-year-old, came alive to contemporary music. . . ." And so he became alive to Schoenberg and Webern and Prokofiev, even to Krenek, Casella, and Anhalt.

Hindemith's Third Sonata became one of Gould's basic works when he started giving local concerts. He played it at the University of Toronto early in 1950, along with Bach's *Italian Concerto* and Beethoven's *Eroica Variations*, and the young reviewer for *Varsity* declared that "one can only shout superlatives." He played the same Hindemith sonata at the University of Western Ontario a few months later, together with the Bach Toccata in E minor, a Mozart fantasia and a Chopin étude. The London *Free Press* praised his "singing tone."

By now, Gould had to decide on his future course. He had already decided that Malvern was of no future use to him, and that the only question was how to devote his life to music. "I was rather young to have taken a step like that," he later recalled. "I did so, I think, very much over the objections of my family, who thought it was an outrageous token of presumption for any kid of 19 to decide that he had had enough book learning." At the same time, though, Gould also decided that he had had enough conservatory learning, and his parents opposed that decision too. "I can still see tears in Glenn's eyes," Jessie Greig remembers. "He never really cried, but there'd be tears—he'd get so angry about it, because he felt he had outgrown Guerrero."

No matter what anyone else thought, Gould simply broke off his studies with Guerrero and retired to the cottage on Lake Simcoe. "I didn't approve of my teacher," he later wrote to a friend. And to another: "I was equipped with everything except the kind of solidarity of the ego which is, in the last analysis, the one important part of an artist's equipment." He now spent endless hours playing Bach on the old Chickering, endless hours going for walks with his dog (Nick had developed a growth on his back, and so he had been superseded by a collie named Banquo), and then still more hours playing Bach on the Chickering. He may have been undergoing a kind of crisis over the question of what to do with his life, but his father remembers that time with equanimity. "He was just practicing," says Bert Gould, "and preparing himself."

No longer under the tutelage of Guerrero, Gould looked toward Homburger for guidance, and Homburger decided that it was time for the nineteen-year-old virtuoso to explore a bit of the world beyond Toronto. He sent Gould, under the watchful care of his mother, to play the Beethoven Fourth in Vancouver, where he received what the Vancouver *Daily Province* described as "a rousing five curtain calls." And to Calgary, where the *Herald* bravely called his playing of the Bach Fifth Partita, the *Eroica Variations,* and the Hindemith sonata "one of the finest performances ever heard on the Calgary stage." The local press was hungry for more details. The *Albertan* asked Mrs. Gould "if she had any advice to hand on to mothers of other musical children," and Mrs. Gould promptly replied "that mothers must sacrifice and give of their time, often to the curtailment of social activity. . . . 'When Glenn practiced at noon I was always there and when he came home after school to practice again I was always home,' she commented." And now that he had reached the age of nineteen, was he "interested in girls"? the *Albertan* inquired. "No, he hasn't time for them yet, his mother says, adding with a smile, 'And I'm glad he hasn't right now.'"

Gould returned to Toronto to play the Beethoven Second Concerto. ("The Glenn Gould touch was a caress—" the *Telegram* gushed, "forceful as compulsion of tyranny, but lovely as faith, hope and charity in perfect unison. . . .") And the Canadian premiere of Schoenberg's Suite for Piano, Opus 25. And Beethoven's Opus 101, and the Berg Sonata, and some short pieces by Orlando Gibbons for the Ladies' Morning Musical Club in Montreal. ("One of the great musical personalities of this generation," said the Montreal *Star*.) And Beethoven's Opus 109, at the Technical School Auditorium in Ottawa. ("Fascinating to watch the long, sensitive, animated hands of this slight, unassuming young man," said the Ottawa *Citizen* in one of the silliest of the many silly newspaper commentaries on the young Gould. "A Surrealist painter might feel tempted to paint these two hands, fantastically enlarged, as two huge living beings, with a small human body attached to them.")

That sonata had given Gould problems far beyond the Surrealist imaginings of the Ottawa critic, problems that only Gould could have created and only Gould could have solved. There is a difficult passage in the fifth variation of the last movement, an upward run in the right hand, which Gould described as "a positive horror." "You have to change from a pattern in sixths to a pattern in thirds, and you've got to do that in a split second," Gould later told Cott. "I had always heard this piece played by people who, when that moment arrived, looked like horses being led from burning barns— a look of horror would come upon them."

When Gould began a little practicing on Opus 109, just two or three weeks before his first public performance of it, he made the mistake of beginning with that difficult passage, "just to make sure there's no problem." As he tried it, "one thing after another began to go wrong," and within a few minutes he discovered that he had "developed a total block about this thing." That block paralyzed him until three days before the concert—"I couldn't get to that point without literally shying and stopping"—and so he decided to re-create the lesson of the maid with the vacuum cleaner and try what he called the Last Resort method. "That was to place beside the piano a couple of radios [and] turn them up full blast." This helped, but only partly. Keeping the radios on as loud as possible, Gould then concentrated all his attention on four unimportant accompanying notes in the left hand, and concentrated on playing them "as unmusically as possible." When he had mastered that, and finally turned off the radios, the block about the difficult right-hand run was gone.

And then Stratford. It had been founded as a Shakespeare festival, about seventy-five miles west of Toronto, but someone had inevitably had the idea of adding music, and so Stratford soon became the kind of festival where musicians could experiment, relax, enjoy themselves. Some veterans still recall the extraordinary 1954 production of Stravinsky's *A Soldier's Tale*, starring Marcel Marceau in his first North American appearance, and featuring Alexander Schneider as the wandering violinist. And that was how Schneider met Glenn Gould.

Sitting now by the picture window overlooking the shrill traffic on Manhattan's East Twentieth Street, he remembers the twenty-one-year-old pianist as "a very strange guy." Schneider was supposed to give a recital of Bach, Beethoven, and Brahms, and so he was introduced to the local prodigy. "And he came without any music," Schneider recalls. "He said, 'I play by heart.'" Schneider had never before encountered a pianist who knew the whole violin repertoire by heart. He himself prefers to play with the score in front of him, "so you can relax, you know, and make music." Gould was not like other musicians, as Schneider soon learned, and "he played *very* well."

So the word kept spreading. Another American musician, Harvey Olnick, who had come to teach at the University of Toronto, heard Gould play *The Goldberg Variations* at a small university recital. "I was bowled over, absolutely," he recalls. "I was absolutely thunderstruck. After the concert, he was just standing there, as you went out, and I said, 'I'd like to talk to you sometime. I don't understand this. Where did you come from? I know your teacher. He's a Romantic. Where did you learn to play Bach like this?'"

Olnick sent a pseudonymous review to the *Musical Courier*, the first report on Gould in an American periodical. "The public will soon be confronted with an artist in no way inferior to such artists as Landowska and Serkin," it said. That confrontation was soon scheduled when Walter Homburger booked his young client into the Phillips Collection in Washington and Manhattan's Town Hall early in 1955. Olnick went on beating the drums. "I called Winnie Leventritt in New York and I said, 'Winnie, go to this concert. This guy's a kook, but he's fantastic! Incredible!' And she had a party at her house, and so news got around."

With all the confidence of a youth of twenty-two, Gould ignored the traditional debut repertoire of a little Mozart, a little Chopin, and chose for his first American appearance in Washington only a few of his own favorites, a pavane by Orlando Gibbons and a Sweelinck fantasia, Bach's Fifth Partita, and five of the Three-Part Inventions, Beethoven's Opus 109 (difficult run and all), the thorny Berg Sonata, and the even more thorny Variations by Anton Webern. The most important witness to all this was Paul Hume, who wrote a remarkable review in the next day's Washington *Post*. "January 2 is early for predictions," Hume began, "but it is unlikely that the year 1955 will bring us a finer piano recital than that played yesterday afternoon in the Phillips Gallery. We shall be lucky if it brings us others of equal beauty and significance."

It is rare for a music critic to abandon all the usual cautions and hedgings and commit himself so boldly to a newcomer. The classic instance was Robert Schumann's marvelous salute to the appearance of Chopin's Opus 2 Variations on *Là Ci Darem la Mano:* "Hats off, gentlemen, a genius!" Gould was no Chopin, and Hume no Schumann, but there still is something moving in the critic's attempt to describe an extraordinary experience. "Gould is a pianist with rare gifts for the world," Hume concluded. "It must not long delay hearing and according him the honor and audience he deserves. We know of no pianist like him at any age."

"I had not listened for two minutes before I thought, I am listening to something more than extraordinary," Hume still recalls. Now retired, he is sitting in the boardroom of a Toronto bank, where the first Glenn Gould Prize of fifty thousand dollars has just been awarded to the Canadian composer R. Murray Schafer. "I thought,

I have never heard *this* kind of playing before," Hume says. "Gould made some of the *most* glorious music I have ever heard from any piano. The gift of prophecy is one that a critic must use with great care, but there was no question that he could have the greatest career in the world. I just sat there and thought, My God, how beautifully this piano is being played by this man."

The musical world is not very large, at its upper levels, and Hume's review very quickly became known in New York. The musical capital of the world was always ready to listen to a new challenger, to listen with skepticism and arrogance, but to listen. Like all young musicians, Gould had to pay his own expenses, had to pay $450 to rent Town Hall, and about $1,000 more for advertising, programs, and promotion. But New York was willing to pay attention. David Oppenheim, the director of Columbia Records' Masterworks division, was visiting Sasha Schneider's house on East Twentieth Street, and they listened to a recording by the great Romanian pianist Dinu Lipatti, who had died just five years earlier at the age of thirty-three. "I think I had maybe brought the Lipatti record to him," Oppenheim recalls. "And I said, 'Why can't we find another one like that?' And he said there was one, a person in Toronto named Glenn Gould, who was, alas, a little crazy but had a remarkable, hypnotic effect at the piano." Schneider remembers the discussion in much the same way. "So I said, 'Well, why don't you go and listen to—there is a boy coming from Canada. Go and take a contract with you right away, and sign him up, because if you liked Lipatti, you may like him.' So he went. . . ."

So he went. And others went too—not a great many, perhaps two hundred at most, but they were interested and important listeners. The young pianist Paul Badura-Skoda was there ("I marvel at his ability to give expression to three voices"). Eugene Istomin was there, with his colleague Gary Graffman. "It was a fantastic concert," Graffman still recalls. He is sitting now in his apartment near Carnegie Hall, which is filled with Chinese art, and he is sipping a mixture of tea and apple juice. "He had a hand in his pocket as he walked out. And as soon as he started to play, everybody—or at least *I*—sat on the edge of the chair, and I just listened to music and was absolutely floored. It was more than just hearing a very talented newcomer. It was a unique personality already."

And Winston Fitzgerald of the house of Steinway remembers the occasion just as vividly.

Q: What was the atmosphere at that debut?

A: Electric.

Gould's father, Bert, sat proudly in the audience on that memorable evening, but most of his Toronto friends were present only in the telegrams they showered upon him. ALL OUR VERY WARMEST WISHES FOR TREMENDOUS SUCCESS TONIGHT and KNOW YOUR CONCERT WILL BE WONDERFUL and ALL GOOD WISHES FOR A GREAT NY DEBUT AND BRILLIANT CAREER and ARISE AND SHINE FOR THY LIGHT HAS COME. And though it was not a big event by New York standards, the Toronto press covered it with characteristic enthusiasm. The *Star*'s Hugh Thomson described the young hero as "Toronto's 22-year-old pianist and composer, Glenn Gould, the youngest student to graduate from the Royal Conservatory." The *Telegram*'s George Kidd not only called him a "Toronto-born pianist" but felt compelled to appear blasé about the atmosphere of excitement. "For Canadians, it was no surprise that the 22-year-old pianist received such a response," he wrote. "His work has long been known from coast to coast. . . ."

Taking no chances before this important audience, Gould played the same pieces he had played so successfully in Washington. The *Telegram* correspondent noted that he wore a dark business suit instead of the customary white tie and tails. "His shyness was apparent as he stepped onto the large stage with its gleaming white walls and brown backdrop," Kidd wrote. "There was a hesitancy as he acknowledged the warm applause that swept up to him from the other side of the footlights. But once he began to play, the shyness departed. . . ."

The applause demanded an encore even at the intermission, and when the recital was all over, more than a hundred people crowded backstage to shake Gould's hand and congratulate the new star. The great rite of passage had been passed. Even the imperious New York *Times* was moderately impressed. "A debut recital of unusual promise," said the critic who signed himself "J.B." (John Briggs). "The challenging program Mr. Gould prepared was a test the young man met successfully, and in so doing left no doubt of his powers as a technician. The most rewarding aspect of Mr. Gould's playing, however, is that technique as such is in the background. The impression that is uppermost is not one of virtuosity but of expressiveness. One is able to hear the music." The *Herald-Tribune* was equally appreciative: "This young pianist is clearly a dedicated, sensitive poet of the keyboard; he has a wonderful control of finger articulation and tonal levels, while every fragile nuance . . . bespeaks the real artistic nature."

These were both rather short reviews, however, of the kind that get published every day. Both the *Times* and *Herald-Tribune* devoted more space and attention to a Carnegie Hall recital by a violinist named Julian Olevsky. Neither of them seemed to realize that a major event had just occurred. One man who did realize it, though, was David Oppenheim of Columbia Records, who decided that night that the great Lipatti was not without successors. A tall man, graying now, Oppenheim still remembers the very first notes of Gould's recital. "It started with something very slow—Sweelinck, I think it was," he says, "but it might have been someone else from that period—something that, in anyone else's hands, would have been just a crushing bore. And he did it in such a—he set such a religious atmosphere that it was just mesmerizing. And it didn't take more than five or six notes to establish that atmosphere, by some magic of precise rhythm and control of the inner voices. . . . And I was—thrilled. And looked around to see if there were any of my colleagues from other record companies there—didn't see them— and moved as quickly as I could to get to his manager the next day to propose a deal."

Nobody could remember a major recording contract ever having been offered after just one Town Hall recital. It was a contract that was to bring Gould worldwide fame, and to endure for more than twenty-seven years, until the day of his death.

III

The Goldberg Variations (I)

When Gould met with an executive of Columbia Records to decide what he should play for his first recording, he startled the executive by announcing that he would like to begin with Bach's *Goldberg Variations*. The executive, whom Gould did not identify in his subsequent account of this meeting, objected. Surely, he said, Gould would not want to stake his fledgling career on something so obscure, so difficult, so complex. ("It may be doubted," Sir Donald Francis Tovey had written, "whether any great classic is really so little known. . . .") The executive also felt obliged to observe that the redoubtable Wanda Landowska had already recorded *The Goldberg Variations* on her redoubtable harpsichord, and that most connoisseurs associated the work with her. "Don't you think the Two-Part Inventions would make a better debut choice?" he asked.

"I'd rather record *The Goldberg Variations*," Gould persisted, politely deaf to all objections.

"You really would, eh?" the executive said. "Well, why not? Let's take a chance."

It is, as Gould was to teach us, a magnificent, magical work. *Aria mit verschiedenen Veraenderungen*, Bach had modestly called it, an aria with different variations. As with many masterpieces, it is now encrusted by legends, which are not necessarily false. Legend reports that Bach journeyed from Leipzig to Dresden in 1741 and there visited one of his young pupils, Johann Gottlieb Goldberg, who was employed as a harpsichordist by Count Hermann Karl von Keyserling, the Russian ambassador to the court of Saxony. Count Keyserling suffered from neuralgia, which kept him awake at night.

Legend says that he asked Goldberg's teacher to write him something that would help him pass through these dark hours.

We do not know why this mundane request inspired Bach to write one of the masterpieces of Western music. Probably he himself did not know. He took as his theme a little saraband that he had already jotted down some fifteen years earlier in the *Notenbuch* that he provided for his twenty-year-old second wife, Anna Magdalena. Then, in contrast to most other variations by most other composers, he never again used his theme as the material to be varied. Instead, he relied only on the bass line, that stately progression downward from G to D, tonic to dominant, as the foundation for the thirty variations that were to become a kind of cathedral of sound, and of the Baroque imagination.

Perhaps the most extraordinary aspect of this cathedral is that every third variation, every third vault and groin in the construction, was a canon, a perfect replication of itself, at intervals that extended from a canon at the unison to a canon at the second and on to a canon at the octave, and then, as a kind of proof of Bach's unmatchable virtuosity, a canon at the ninth. But these are all technicalities. In between such casual demonstrations of virtuosity, Bach wrote a gorgeous collection of songs, dances, declamations, meditations, all based on that rudimentary progression downward from G to D. And yet it was emblematic of Bach's genius that the canons are among the most beautiful of all the variations. Count Keyserling was pleased. He sent Bach a golden goblet containing 100 louis d'or, apparently the biggest payment that Bach ever received for any single composition in his life. And according to legend, the count loved to listen to Bach's creation in the dark of a sleepless night. "Dear Goldberg," he would say, "please come and play me my variations."

It is difficult now to determine just how the young Gould acquired his passion for *The Goldberg Variations*. They really were very rarely played in those days, and they did have a reputation for being austere and academic, like some combination of Palestrina and Schoenberg. Guerrero occasionally performed them, so he may well have recommended them to his pupil, but Gould often roamed through volumes of Bach on his own, so he may have discovered them by himself, may have instinctively seen in that elaborate structure something that appealed to his sense of pattern and control.

He first performed them outside Toronto, two months after his New York debut, at an assembly of the Morning Musical Club at the Technical High School in Ottawa. The only record we have of this occasion is in the commentary of local critics like Lauretta Thistle of the Ottawa *Citizen*. "In the vast fairy cavern of The Goldberg Variations Mr. Gould is completely at home," she wrote, "and he makes an admirable host, communicating his own enjoyment in the treasures."

To make his first recording of *The Goldberg Variations*, Gould arrived that June of 1955 at the Columbia studio in an abandoned Presbyterian church at 207 East Thirtieth Street in New York, bringing with him a large supply of personal idiosyncrasies. He brought his own personal chair, which his father had built for him, which enabled him to sit just fourteen inches off the floor, so that he could keep his wrists at or below the level of the keyboard. ("I tried to find something fairly light in a folding chair," according to Bert Gould, "and then I had to saw about four inches off each leg, and I made a brass bracket to go around each leg and screw into it, and then welded the half of a turnbuckle to the brass bracket so that each leg could be adjusted individually.") He brought a bulky collection of sweaters and scarves in even the warmest weather, and he brought a large assortment of pills. When he played, he often gestured like a conductor with one hand while he attacked the keyboard with the other. And he sang, groaned, sighed. Gould had fairly good reasons for his odd behavior—it was easier to bring along his own low chair than to hunt for one in each new city, for example, and the scarves and pills all reflected a justifiable anxiety about his uncertain health—but many observers regarded all this as pure eccentricity, either a manic desire for self-indulgence or a manic yearning for publicity. Or perhaps those were both the same thing. In either case, Columbia was eager to publicize its boy wonder, to publicize him not only as a splendid pianist but as a bizarre personality.

"Columbia Masterworks' recording director and his engineering colleagues are sympathetic veterans who accept as perfectly natural all artists' studio rituals, foibles or fancies," said a Columbia press release about the recording of *The Goldberg Variations*. "But even these hardy souls were surprised by the arrival of young Canadian pianist Glenn Gould and his 'recording equipment.' ... It was a balmy June day, but Gould arrived in coat, beret, muffler and gloves. 'Equipment' consisted of the customary music portfolio, also a batch of towels, two large bottles of spring water, five small bottles of pills (all different colors and prescriptions) and his own special piano chair. Towels, it developed, were needed in plenty because Glenn soaks his arms and hands up to the elbows in hot water for twenty minutes before sitting down at the keyboard.... Bottled spring water was a necessity because Glenn can't abide New York tap water. Pills were for any number of reasons—headaches, relieving tension, maintaining circulation. The air-conditioning engineer worked as hard as the man at the recording studio control panel. Glenn is very sensitive to the slightest changes in temperature, so there was constant adjustment of the vast studio air conditioning system...."

Columbia not only sent out this kind of publicity but invited musical journalists to come and see for themselves, and the journalists, sensing a good story, were glad to cooperate. "Debbie Ishlon at Columbia called me and said, 'There's something *happening* at the studio on Thirtieth Street,'" says Martin Mayer, who was then writing a monthly music column for *Esquire*. "She said, 'We're doing these recording sessions, *The Goldberg Variations*, and we've got this nut, and everybody's talking about how absolutely marvelous he is, you never heard anything like this.' So I went down there, to Thirtieth Street. Gould was listening to tapes when I came, and he didn't like some of what he heard. The producer would say, 'That's good,' and he would say, 'We'll see.'

"There was a little room off in a corner of this church—which was what this studio had been, you know—and there was a hot plate, and there was a kettle on the hot plate that was simmering, and there was a ewer on the table, a pitcher and a basin, and Gould came and put his hands in the basin and he poured in *scalding* water, and he said, 'This relaxes me.' Then he went out, and his hands were relaxed, and *red* they were. And the first thing I noticed was the way he played—like this—with his wrists below the level of the keyboard, which I'd never seen before. I watched and listened for about an hour and a half.

"Debbie had arranged for us to have lunch, and the first question I asked him was, 'Isn't it terribly hard to play the piano that way, not being able to put any of your upper body into getting a forceful action?' And he said, 'Oh, yes, you have to develop a lot of muscles behind your back, but that's the way my teacher taught me, and I can't change now.' And I said, 'I should think that would distort the way all the muscles in your arms and shoulders work.' And he said, 'My teacher's the biggest hunchback in Canada.'

"We went back to Gould's hotel in the Fifties, on Central Park—was that the St. Moritz? It might have been the St. Moritz. Anyway, he went to the bathroom and opened an attaché case, which opened up into a triple layer of medications. He reached in and took a bottle and took two pills. He said, 'These are my blood circulation pills. If I don't take them, I don't circulate.' I said, 'Well, by all means take them.' I really thought he was unique, a very, very great artist."

Gould was, of course, a willing participant in all this publicity. "My policy," as Joseph Roddy quoted him in a *New Yorker* profile, "has long been to cut the cloth to fit the corner newsstand." And so the press kept being invited to ogle his "eccentricities." "Gould puts on an astonishing and vivid show for those who attend recording sessions . . ." Herbert Kupferberg wrote in the *New York Herald-Tribune*. To the familiar tales of scarves and hats, he added that Gould "spurns the sandwiches sent in to the recording crew, subsisting instead on arrowroot biscuits washed down with his special spring water or skimmed milk." Jay Harrison went to cover the spectacle for *The Reporter* and noted that "a small Oriental rug had been placed beneath the pedals, for Mr. Gould finds himself unhappy when his feet rest on bare wood; and directly to his right, though the day was mild, an electric heater had been set up to keep him ultra-warm. . . . Gould finally began to play. He got through his opening phrase and then, without warning, flung his arms up. 'I can't,' he said plaintively. 'I can't. There is a draft. I feel it. A strong draft.' At this, a flock of workmen poured into the hall to track down the mysterious wind. . . ."

This kind of behavior naturally inspired the press to extravagant commentary. One Toronto columnist observed that Gould's melodramatic swaying over the keyboard resembled a combination "of the last act of *Macbeth* with an imitation of a proposal of marriage by a man who had just swallowed a fly." The press was also pleased to find that Gould could provide snappy answers to its questions.

When Ronald Collister of the Toronto *Telegram* asked him why he liked to take his shoes off during recording sessions, Gould replied, "I am naturally a foot-loose type." In repartee like that, Gould was starting to sound like another new keyboard phenomenon named Liberace.

But he did keep trying to explain himself. He knew that his hands were capable of a kind of magic that he could not fully understand, and so he naturally felt an extraordinary need to protect them. He tried to avoid shaking hands because some men like to apply crushing grips. He wore several pairs of gloves, he told Collister, because "My hands react badly to air-conditioning and dampness." "The melted paraffin wax he rubs on his hands 'makes me feel that I have new hands,'" Collister's story went on. "And the circulation pills he takes keeps his arms and hands supple. They are not studied eccentricities, he explains. 'I don't think about them. If I did, I would become so self-conscious I would have to give up this business.'"

As for Gould's use of pills, it is worth recalling that this was the era of Miltown, a time when the newly discovered tranquilizers and energizers seemed to provide everyone with a harmless method of dealing with the stresses of life. Gould joked about this in a letter to a young pianist in Washington, on which he inscribed the heading, GOULD'S CLINIC FOR PSYCHOPSEUMATIC [sic] THERAPY. "Due to my experience with internal medicine practice I am unusually alert to the problems of neurotic artists . . ." Dr. Gould wrote in his recommendation of various pills. "The yellow sleeping pills are called Nembutal. The white sedatives are called Luminal. I believe that both will have to be obtained through your doctor. Luminal is perfectly harmless and can be taken generally three times a day;—one after the noon meal and two at bedtime. I strongly advise however that you do not make a habit of Bevutal. It should definitely be reserved for the nights before special occasions and to break chronic sleeplessness. . . ."

The press kept wanting to know more. PIANIST USES 'STOP,' 'GO' PILLS, said a headline that December in Victoria, where Gould went to play the *Emperor Concerto*. "The tensions of traveling and playing concerts make a pianist's life an artificial existence, says Glenn Gould of Toronto . . ." the newspaper reported. "To keep up the pace, Mr. Gould has a bag-full of pills to stop perspiration before a concert, to increase circulation temporarily, stimulants 'to keep going' and sedatives fast and slow."

All this publicity, this kind of publicity, helped to make Gould, still in his early twenties, an international star. "Men we'd like you to meet," sighed a headline in *Glamour* in April of 1956, "A frail, loose-jointed Canadian with a bumper crop of light-brown hair, he bolsters legend with idiosyncracies: carts around pills, bottled spring water, a special chair; his views on diet (A friend: 'What did you eat that disagreed with you, Glenn? Food?')." *Vogue* the following month sounded even more feverish: "Glenn Gould . . . has caused this year a glow of jubilant bonfires among American critics. . . . Tense, emaciated, with blueberry-blue eyes, Gould approaches his piano as he might an unbroken horse, bringing forth a tone both strong and lyrical. . . ."

The important thing, though, was that Gould's version of *The Goldberg Variations* was a great performance and a great recording, one of the greatest ever made. We who had not been present at Town Hall, the thousands of us, now had our first chance to discover Glenn Gould. Here we learned for the first time that Bach's variations (and, by implication, all of Bach) were not some cerebral construction to be respected from a respectful distance but rather a creation of passionate intensity and immense beauty. Here we learned too that Gould could play the piano like nobody else in the world. He had all the essential talents, a singing tone, a very precise articulation, a skillfully controlled dynamic range, but he also had two gifts that were rare if not unique. One was the ability to give this benign music an incredibly propulsive rhythmic drive. Being able to play with such precision even at high speed, he could make Bach's creation leap and plunge and fly; he filled it with a nervous energy that filled it with life. Gould's other extraordinary gift was the ability to make all three voices in three-part counterpoint remain completely independent even as he wove them inextricably together. The canons of *The Goldberg Variations* acquired an implicitly religious quality—as they must once have had in the mind of Bach—of being simultaneously one in three and three in one.

It took Gould just a week to make this extraordinary recording, and the last thing he taped was the opening theme itself. "I found that it took me twenty takes," he recalled later, "in order to locate a character for it which would be sufficiently neutral as not to prejudge the depth of involvement that comes later in the work. It was a question of utilizing the first twenty takes to erase all superfluous expression from my reading of it, and there is nothing more difficult to do. The natural instinct of the performer is to add, not to subtract." When the last notes of the "Aria da Capo" had finally died away, Gould shook hands with all the technicians and smiled and departed, with all his pills and his special chair in hand, and returned to Canada, to the summer cottage on Lake Simcoe.

The reviewers were reasonably appreciative, though none of them had the judgment or courage to commit themselves in the way Paul Hume had done when he wrote: "We know of no pianist like him at any age." Harold Schonberg of the New York *Times,* who was to become a kind of mossy boulder in Gould's path, began a record roundup in the Sunday edition by saluting Vlado Perlemuter's performance of the complete piano music of Ravel, and only after praising Robert and Gaby Casadesus's version of the Mozart four-hand sonatas did he get around to noting that there was "rather unusual playing" in a young Canadian's account of *The Goldberg Variations.* "Gould has skill and imagination, and the music appears to mean something to him," Schonberg acknowledged. "He also has a sharp, clear technique that enables him to toss off the contrapuntal intricacies of the writing with no apparent effort. Best of all, his work has intensity. . . . Obviously, a young man with a future."

The other reviews were rather similar, full of praise but mainly offering encouragement for the future rather than recognition of a great achievement. "This 23-year-old Canadian pianist has more promise than any young North American keyboard artist to appear since the war," said *Newsweek.* "His Bach is sensitive and superb, and with his musicianship and technique further revelations are to be expected. . . ." And Irving Kolodin in *The Saturday Review:* "Gould not only has all the finger discipline that can be taught, but also a kind of darting finesse that cannot. . . . He has made a mark for himself with this clean-lined, soberly expressive effort that will take considerable doing to excel."

And perhaps he never did. That extraordinary album of thirty variations, with that cover containing thirty snapshots of the shirt-

sleeved young Gould playing, singing, explaining, listening, argu-
ing—that record changed many people's lives, changed their ideas
and feelings about Bach, about music, about themselves. It became a
kind of talisman, something that had been mysteriously seen out at
the edge of the universe and then brought back to us. It was a commercial phenomenon too, of course. The best-selling classical
record in the year of its appearance, 1956, it never went out of print
during the following quarter of a century, and the only man who
would try to drive it out of print was Gould himself, when he rerecorded it shortly before his death. Even then, there are those of us
who still prefer the original version, who prefer to the acutely self-
conscious Gould of fifty the brashly confident Gould of twenty-two,
the brilliant young virtuoso who felt, believed, knew that he could
do anything.

In practical terms, though, what the huge success of *The Goldberg
Variations* meant was that the young pianist who had delighted a few
hundred people at his concerts in New York or Washington or
Toronto now confronted the demands of the whole world. What
did that success mean to you? Gould was asked by one interviewer.
"Well, it meant a great deal to me," Gould confessed. "But it also
launched me into the most difficult year I have ever faced."

IV

The Virtuoso on Tour

In the popular imagination, a concert pianist lives a rich and glamorous life. He strides onstage, under the spotlights, with the mysterious authority of a Lohengrin. Outfitted in the most elegant white tie and tails, he sits down at the piano, silences the expectant audience, and begins, with complete ease, to play. Almost by magic, from memory, the Chopin preludes flow forth, or the *Appassionata*. The audience explodes into applause, the men admiring, the women adoring. The pianist bows graciously and disappears into the night.

The reality is quite different. There is, of course, great music, and sometimes great emotion on both sides of the footlights, but there are also leaden pianos, coughing audiences, witless newspaper reviews, delayed flights, lonely hotel rooms, bad food, and constant anxiety. "We're just slave labor," John Browning once said to Elyse Mach *(Great Pianists Speak for Themselves)*. "We go to a hall and practice; then we rest, eat, and dress for the concert. We play the concert, go to an after-theater party, retire for a few hours' sleep, then catch a morning plane to the next stop. It becomes very routine. . . . On the other hand, no performing artist is ever in complete control over a situation, either. I think stage fright plays some part in the final product. Every performance has some of that. It begins to build in the morning and reaches a climax by mid-afternoon. That's when it's worst. I don't have bad nerves, but I often wake up with a tight knot in the stomach which gets tighter as the day progresses. . . ."

Many other pianists report similar difficulties. "It can get to you, year in and year out," Leon Fleisher told David Dubal. "It's terribly stressful to go from one imperfect situation to another, lousy piano, noisy audiences, drafts—you name it." And Philippe Entremont: "People think the life of a touring musician is glamorous. They don't realize the enormous amount of work involved, the incredible toll on the nerves. . . ." And Paul Badura-Skoda: "There are times when you feel that the public is just waiting for your slightest mistake. Concert halls are not always benevolent places." And Ruth Laredo: "I remember listening to Gina Bachauer on the radio . . . describing the life of a woman on the road, and what it's like after the concert, going back to your hotel room, and being alone so much of the time. It can be a very . . . difficult life." Fleisher recalled that when he was six or seven, his mother took him to hear Rachmaninoff and then rushed him backstage to shake the great man's hand. "Suddenly, in between encores, he came over to me," Fleisher said, "he peered down at me and asked, 'Are you a pianist?' And I looked up at this Empire State Building of a figure, and nodded my head. He then shook his head and said, 'Bad business.'"

Many artists nonetheless love to perform. The excitement overwhelms all difficulties. Arthur Rubinstein was perhaps the best example, and so when Gould undertook an interview with him, the two soon found themselves totally at odds. Rubinstein, like Madame Sosostris, had a bad cold, but he had nonetheless given his annual recital in Toronto, and when Gould came to meet him backstage, Rubinstein said, "You would have canceled the concert, wouldn't you?"

Gould equivocated. "I'm not sure, actually," he said. "I suppose that I. . . ."

"Of course you would have . . ." Rubinstein said. "I see it in your eyes."

Rubinstein then began interviewing his interviewer. "Was there never a moment when you felt that very special emanation from an audience?" he added.

"There really wasn't . . ." said Gould, who by then had not appeared in a concert hall for seven years.

"But you never felt that you had the soul of those people?" Rubinstein persisted.

"I didn't really want their souls, you know," Gould said. "Well, that's a silly thing to say. Of course, I wanted to have some influence, I suppose, to shape their lives in some way . . . but I didn't want any power over them, and I certainly wasn't stimulated by their presence as such. . . ."

"There we are absolute opposites, you know," Rubinstein said. "We are absolute opposites! . . . If you would have followed the pianistic career for many years as I have—over sixty-five years, you know—you would have experienced this constant, constant, constant contact with the crowd that you have to, in a way, persuade, or dominate, or get hold of. . . ."

Gould never wanted that. He never had the slightest intention of giving concerts for sixty-five years or of dominating crowds. He saw public performance only as a phase to be passed through, a phase that would bring him the money and celebrity to do other things. "For practical reasons, if nothing else, I suppose I will always remain to some extent a performer," he told an interviewer from the Toronto *Globe and Mail* in 1956, his first year on the concert tour. "One can too easily become enamored of the glamor, which I think is non-existent. My interests lie more in the literature of music, in composition, in conducting. . . . "

Gould's next big expedition after the New York debut was to Detroit in March of 1956, his first American appearance with orchestra, and that involved a fairly typical series of mishaps. Originally, he was supposed to play the Beethoven Fourth Concerto with the Detroit Symphony Orchestra across the river in Windsor, Ontario, but when a French pianist named Eliane Richepin cabled that she was unable to make a scheduled appearance in Detroit, Gould was asked to fill in. He arrived at the Masonic Temple auditorium to try out the piano but found that it was being tuned for a recital by Arthur Rubinstein. "Mild-mannered and agreeable," according to a report in the Detroit *News*, "Gould agreed to go away until the tuner had finished, and to end his own practicing in time for the stage to be set for Rubinstein."

Gould's concert was a public triumph, but the reviewers' criticisms of his physical mannerisms at the keyboard came close to being personal attacks. "Seldom has a more exquisite performance been heard . . . or a worse one witnessed," wrote J. Dorsey Callaghan in the Detroit *Free Press*. "Gould's storm-tossed mane of hair, his invertebrate posture at the keyboard and his habit of collapse at the end of each solo line were sheer show business. His interpretation and performance of the music . . . sheer genius." Harvey Taylor of the Detroit *Times* was even more patronizing. "The Beethoven fourth piano concerto . . . emerged with stunning beauty," he wrote. "He has obviously conquered the piano and now, to flower fully as a performing musician, he has only to conquer himself. In his current phase of development it is his tragedy that his behavior at the piano produced laughter in his audience. . . . Why do pianists feel that they can indulge in these fantastic emotional ecstasies?"

The Windsor *Daily Star* took a patriotic approach. "Canada triumphed last evening," its account began. The *Star* went on to describe Gould as "Canada's finest concert pianist and Canada's greatest contributor to the perfect interpretation and development of piano literature," and it reported that "our young Canadian artist captivated an audience which virtually filled the 5,000-seat auditorium. His ovation was tremendous. He took eight curtain calls. There were bravos, whistles, cheers." When Gould arrived in Windsor to play there three days later, however, the pressures upon him had apparently become nearly unbearable. In the dressing room before the concert, he suffered what the *Detroit News* called a seizure of "nervous tension" and announced that he could not play. "After extended discussion with symphony officials and insistence that he was too ill to play, Gould consented to 'try' and went to the piano," the newspaper reported. As for the actual performance of the Beethoven Fourth, the *News* said that "the extraordinary contortions and twitchings were missing," but it added that the "quiet and sedate" Gould gave "a performance that was almost colorless and marked by little of the brilliance for which Gould has been uproariously acclaimed. . . . He was far less of a pianist than he had been the preceding Thursday night."

Looking back on these difficult early years on the concert stage, Gould said that he had originally been quite unconscious of the physical mannerisms that many critics regarded as an attempt to attract publicity. (In surviving tapes of Gould's concerts, the most disturbing distraction is actually the ceaseless coughing from the audience.) "I had not regarded any of the things attendant upon my playing—my eccentricities, if you like—as being of any particular note at all," the pianist told Bernard Asbell. "No one made any fuss about them. Then suddenly a number of well-meaning . . . people in the arts . . . said, 'My dear young man, you must pull yourself together and stop this nonsense. . . .' The fact that I tend to sing a great deal while I'm playing, that I tend to conduct myself with one hand—all that sort of thing. . . . I had never given any thought to the importance, at least to some people, of visual image. When I suddenly was made aware of this in about 1956, I became extremely self-conscious about everything I did. The whole secret of what I had been doing was to concentrate exclusively on realizing a conception of the music, regardless of how it was physically achieved. This new self-consciousness was very difficult."

Musical commitments are generally made a year or more in advance, and Gould was now committed to endless touring. A solo recital in Toronto's Massey Hall. Bach's Fifth Partita, and the Beethoven Opus 109, and the Hindemith Third Sonata. "Mr. Gould employed a new gimmick," the *Telegram* reported. "During the entire work, his left leg was carelessly draped over his right knee."

The Beethoven Third Concerto in Pittsburgh. "He played brilliantly," said the *Press,* but "why must he crouch like a panther over the keys? Why should he pounce upon the notes like a leopard leaps upon its prey for the kill?" And the *Sun-Telegraph:* "He seems to forget that he is on a concert platform, that sort of exhibitionism having gone out more than 40 years ago. The discovery of new drugs and vitamins can cure such contortions, much as the witches exorcised them centuries ago." In Montreal, he played the Bach Concerto in D minor and the Strauss *Burleske.* "Canadians are unused to the possibility of a native excelling in the arts," said the *Star.* And a recital at Ohio Wesleyan. "There was hardly a listener who was not overwhelmed," said the Delaware *Gazette.*

That was a test run for his first reappearance at a recital in New York, where he played all of Bach's fifteen Three-Part Inventions, four pieces from *The Art of the Fugue,* and the third sonatas of both Hindemith and Krenek. "Astounding," said the *Herald-Tribune.* Then to Dallas for what the *Morning News* called an "interesting and provocative" performance of Beethoven's *Emperor Concerto.* Then a recital in Spokane, which included Beethoven's Opus 110, Mendelssohn's *Variations sérieuses,* and two Brahms intermezzi.

"Gould has marvelous talent and a masterful technique," said the *Daily Chronicle,* adding, as usual, that his "unusual mannerisms had most of the large audience buzzing by intermission time."

The journalistic obsession with Gould's "mannerisms" led to problems of a kind that no other pianist had to face. George Szell, the brilliant but irascible conductor of the Cleveland Orchestra, apparently took offense at Gould's hiring a carpenter to build blocks under his piano during a rehearsal of a concerto they were to play together. This incident took place during a break in the rehearsal, and Szell never said anything at the time, but a subsequent *Time* cover story on the conductor reported that Gould's fussiness had wasted so much of the orchestra's rehearsal time that Szell had angrily told him, "Perhaps if I were to slice one-sixteenth of an inch off your derrière, Mr. Gould, we could begin." Szell had never said any such thing, Gould told Jonathan Cott, so when Gould later met the man who had written the *Time* story, he asked him the source of this anecdote and learned that Szell had told it himself. The press not only prints authoritative lies but feeds on them. When Szell died in 1970, Gould was dismayed to see the same anecdote reappearing not only in the *Time* obituary, but also in slightly different form in *Newsweek,* and then in *Esquire.* There the quotation was substantially altered into what Gould recalled as "'I vill personally stick . . .'—I can't remember the exact words but it really doesn't matter—'stick one of zose legs up your rear end.'"* Gould finally wrote, and *Esquire* printed, his categorical denial of the scene. It included Gould's vow that if Szell had ever made such a remark, the Cleveland Orchestra "would have been obliged to find themselves a new guest in a hurry."

Fairly often, Gould rebelled at the whole system and canceled his concerts, sometimes because he felt bad, sometimes because he said he felt bad. "He became a notorious canceler," says Morris Gross, who was then Gould's attorney, "and I would get calls from all over the place. He would arrive in some major center in the United States and find himself unwilling—or he would say unable—to play. I

---

*These are Gould's versions, but such stories change in the retelling. As a matter of record, the *Esquire* version said: "Accounts vary as to whether [Szell said that Gould] should take the handle that adjusted the height and 'screw it up your ass' or whether he merely suggested that if the bench were too high Gould should simply 'squeeze down on your asshole.'"

would have to try to—provide a scenario which was acceptable to the impresario who was going to be losing a lot of money each time. And Glenn would promise to return, and sometimes he wouldn't even play the return concert. But sometimes, it was his offbeat appearance that would get him in trouble. I remember once he was doing a concert in Sarasota, Florida, and I got a phone call from him, and he said, 'I was sitting out on this park bench, and I guess they're trying to preserve their image of being a very warm area in the middle of winter. I was sitting there in my usual—doing nothing unusual—and they've run me in. The police.'"

Q: He was wearing all his coats and mittens, damaging the image of the city?

A: Exactly. I said, "What were you wearing?" That's exactly what happened.

And then came the news that the Soviet Union had invited Gould to play in Moscow and Leningrad in the spring of 1957. Russia in those days was still a land of fear and mystery. Scarcely four years had passed since the death of the terrible Stalin and the beginning of what Ilya Ehrenburg christened "the thaw." Westerners had barely heard of names like Gilels and Richter, and Russians had just experienced their first encounter with an American troupe that had come to perform *Porgy and Bess*. "When the cannons are silent, the muses are heard," as Truman Capote entitled his marvelous account of that Gershwin expedition. Gould, by now twenty-four, was the first classical musician from North America to be invited behind what was persistently called the Iron Curtain. He was delighted. Taking along his manager, Homburger, he flew to Moscow and established himself in the Canadian embassy. Officials there persuaded him that his Communist audiences would be offended if he clung to his habit of performing in a dark business suit, and so he reluctantly agreed to white tie and tails.

MOSCOW HAILS GOULD, cried the headline in the Toronto *Star*. At a time when the heavily censored Western press coverage of Moscow was minimal, the *Star* had shrewdly signed up Homburger as a special correspondent, and Homburger now reported on Gould's concert with breathless enthusiasm. "The famed Bolshoi Hall of the Tchaikowsky Conservatory of Music in Moscow was filled to capacity last night as Toronto's Glenn Gould became the first Canadian musician ... to perform here," said the story under Homburger's by-line, which actually sounds rather like the work of a rewrite man on the *Star*'s cable desk. Gould had chosen several of his favorites, four selections from Bach's *Art of the Fugue*, the Sixth Partita in E minor, Beethoven's Opus 109, and the Berg Sonata. "By intermission, bravos could be heard all over the hall," Homburger reported. "As Gould took his second bow a huge basket of blue chrysanthemums was carried up the aisle toward the stage. ... During intermission the director of the Moscow Philharmonic came to pay his compliments and said, 'Bach must be your great passion; we have never heard fugues like this.'

"At the end of the recital, bravos and applause again echoed through the hall," Homburger went on. "Soon the applause turned into a rhythmic clapping, the greatest compliment an artist can be paid in this country. And then the encores began: First a fantasia by Sweelinck, then two of the Goldberg Variations by Bach. Still the audience clamored for more and Gould added another set of three variations. ... Even after the house lights had been put on the audience did not wish to leave and Gould had to take innumerable bows. By the time he came back to the dressing room many musicians were crowded into the dressing room to congratulate him. Still the audience persisted in their applause, so in the middle of receiving congratulations Gould was rushed out on the stage once more and as a final encore he played another five of the Goldberg Variations. ..."

Even the most triumphant concerts remain fairly standard public rituals (performed in white tie and tails), but in this era of the thaw, the people who most passionately hungered to hear the young visitor from the West were the students at the Moscow Conservatory. Gould willingly agreed to go and play for them, on condition that he be allowed to choose whatever he pleased, with no program announced in advance. He then decided to play only modern music, meaning only music of the twentieth century.

"When I first announced what I was going to do, i.e. that I was going to play the sort of music that has not been officially recognized in the U.S.S.R. since the artistic crises in the mid thirties, there was a rather alarming and temporarily uncontrollable murmuring from the audience," Gould later reported in a letter to Yousuf Karsh, the photographer. "I am quite sure that many of the students were uncertain whether it was better for them to remain or walk out. As it turned out, I managed to keep things under control by frowning ferociously now and then and the only people who did walk out were a couple of elderly professors who probably felt that I was attempting to pervert the taste of the young. However, as I continued playing music of Schoenberg ... Webern and Krenek, there were repeated suggestions from the student body, mostly in the form of discreet whispers from the committee on the stage but occasionally the odd fortissimo suggestion from the audience, that they would prefer to spend their time with Bach and Beethoven. . . ."

Gould had a grand time in Russia. "It was a sensation equivalent to that of perhaps being the first musician to land on Mars or Venus . . ." he wrote to Karsh. "It was a great day for me!" It was also a great day for the inhabitants of Mars. The pianist Bella Davidovich recalled that her husband was in the hospital and heard Gould's first Moscow concert on the radio, and he told her, "When you get to Leningrad, Glenn Gould will be there. Please stay one more day, you must not miss him, you cannot imagine the concert he gave." Mrs. Davidovich did stay on and did go to hear Gould, though she had great difficulty in getting a ticket. "After he played in Moscow," she recalled, "everybody was calling Leningrad, saying, 'Run to the concert—go to hear Gould.' The tickets were gone in a minute. We had never heard such playing."

Everywhere Gould appeared, he was greeted by cheering crowds. Women handed him bouquets of lily of the valley. In Leningrad, extra seats were installed onstage, an unusual concession to popular demand, and extra police had to be assigned to the crowds that milled around the lobby. For his last orchestral concert, when he played the Bach D minor Concerto and the Beethoven Second, the management had not only sold all 1,300 seats but also 1,100 standing-room tickets, which meant that the crowds jammed into every bit of floor space, and still more waited outside in vain hopes of getting in.

"It was a sight I shall not soon forget," Homburger cabled back to the Toronto *Star*. "Even those orchestra members who were not required during the concertos stood backstage to listen and gave Gould an ovation as he came offstage. The crowd once again was most demonstrative with immense bunches of flowers being tossed onstage and the hall resounding to the continuous roar of applause and bravos.

"Gould had originally decided not to play any encores after the concertos," Homburger went on. "However, the following message was delivered to him during intermission: 'Dear Sir, We implore you to play some Bach without the orchestra. Many of us had no opportunity of attending your concert on the 16th and had been waiting in the street for a long time and all in vain. [Signed] Your Russian admirers.' Of course, Gould did not want to disappoint anyone and so began another marathon of encores.

"At one point, Mr. Slovak, the conductor of the concert, said to me, 'I think I might as well go home. Gould can finish the concert. I don't think the public wants to hear the last orchestral piece.' I finally convinced the stage manager to move the piano to the side of the stage and Gould and I went back to the dressing room. It must have been all of five minutes when the stage manager returned and informed us that the audience was still applauding. So Gould took a final bow in his overcoat, cap and gloves."

Neither in Toronto nor in New York had Gould experienced anything quite like this, this outpouring of adulation and admiration, even love. "It was overwhelming and just a bit frightening," he later said. Canadians like to complain that their artists are not taken seriously until they achieve success in New York, but as Van Cliburn was to discover a year later, neither Canadians nor Americans stage the rituals of artistic triumph with the éclat of the Russians. Gould's family was well pleased too. "I am very proud of you and the work you are doing," his father said in an oddly formal cable to Moscow. "Every thinking Canadian has reason to thank you. Your music may have a very real part in establishing a better feeling between east and west. We do hope and pray that it will." The Canadian press took it all as a national event. "Mr. Gould represents Canada abroad with distinction," said the Toronto *Telegram*, "and in doing so he broadcasts the message that Canadians are interested in a world climate where music and its artistic allies can flourish uninterruptedly. Canada is proud of Glenn Gould. . . ."

The Russians were more warmly represented by Kitty Gvozdeva, a middle-aged teacher and translator in Leningrad. "I wish you, Glenn, darling, golden boy, all the love, and luck and happiness of this best of all possible worlds!" she wrote in one of the first of her many effusions. Gould was touched, and wrote back, and their affectionate correspondence lasted the rest of his life. Despite Kitty Gvozdeva's warmest pleadings for another visit, Gould never returned to the Soviet Union, but he always retained an affection for all those Russians who had showered him with lily of the valley, and they for him.

Gould was by now committed to the international concert track, and the track led next to Berlin, to a performance of the Beethoven Third Concerto with Herbert von Karajan and the Berlin Philharmonic. Gary Graffman recalls meeting Gould several times in Berlin because the two pianists were both practicing in the Steinway building.

Q: But he often said that he practically never practiced at all.

A: He was practicing a lot.

Q: He was practicing a lot?

A: He was practicing a lot.

Graffman also recalls that Gould "had a thing about adjusting to time changes and adjusting to food and adjusting to water," and when they went out to dinner together Gould wanted only a well-done steak. "I remember ordering escargots," Graffman says, "and when they came, I said to him, obviously not seriously, I said, 'I hope this doesn't disgust you.' And he said, 'Oh, that's perfectly all right. I just won't look while you're eating.' He was serious."

Gould's Berlin debut was a triumph. "A young man in a strange sort of a trance . . ." wrote the doyen of German critics, H. H. Stuckenschmidt. "His technical ability borders on the fabulous; such a combination of fluency in both hands, of dynamic versatility, and of range in coloring represents a degree of mastery which in my experience has not appeared since the time of Busoni. A marvel, an experience, an incomparable delight. . . ." Then southward-bound to Vienna, and Gould, having caught another cold, decided to take the train. "My cold is still lousy . . ." he wrote to his father. "Sympathy but no flowers please. . . . Actually I spent a pretty miserable day with sinus pain—much like the time I came home from Texas and was deaf. . . . Aeroplanes can wreak havoc with a cold. Anyhow I stayed in Frankfurt (which is a very beautiful city from what little I saw of it)—then took the train last night to Wien."

Gould loved the Germanic landscape ("Beautiful forests and any number of quaint little towns dominated by Baroque churches," he wrote to his father), and it inevitably reminded him of a Germanic past to which he felt mysteriously attached. "I stayed up till 11:30 specially to sing *Die Meistersinger* as we went through Nürnberg," he wrote. Then came a painful dawn. "This morning at 6:30 the porter came around to give me back my passport when we had crossed into Austria and as I was opening the door of my compartment he suddenly pushed it shut again on my left thumbnail. Said thumbnail is now turning slightly blue and making it a bit difficult to write...."

Gould found the legendary Vienna of Mozart and Haydn a little disappointing ("Too much rococo architecture for my rather severe tastes"), but his concert there was another triumph. "Encores upon encores," Homburger reported, "cheers upon cheers, house lights on, stage lights out, more applause, and a final bow in overcoat, hat, and gloves." From all this, Gould might have expected a triumphant welcome back to Toronto, something between a press conference and a ticker-tape parade, but he characteristically slipped home almost in secret. He didn't even give advance notice to his parents, with whom he still lived. "It was deliberate," he subsequently told an inquiring reporter from the Toronto *Telegram*. "I didn't want any fanfare. I was in New York, and it was hot, so I decided to come home.... I feel that I did the best playing of my career over there. Now that I'm home I just want to get away from everything for a while."

For a star pianist, though, there is no such thing as getting away from everything for a while. Gould returned to Toronto in June of 1957, and the *Telegram* reported that same week that he would hit the trail again in August, and the trail would take him that season to Montreal, Hollywood, Washington, Syracuse, Rochester, Pittsburgh, Cincinnati, St. Louis, New York, Oberlin, Miami, Philadelphia, New Orleans, Kingston, Buffalo, Winnipeg, Saskatoon, Seattle, Tacoma, Boston, Lexington, Ottawa....

Gould's contract with Columbia called for him to make three records in two years, and his next choice was no less daring than his insistence on *The Goldberg Variations*. It was also a major miscalculation. He came to New York in February of 1956 and proceeded to record the last three sonatas of Beethoven, Opus 109 in E major, Opus 110 in A flat, and Opus 111 in C minor, all works of extreme subtlety and beauty and complexity. It was then considered rather bold for anyone to play any one of the three sonatas as the climax of a recital, and there were some critics who thought it presumptuous for any pianist to attempt a public performance of these masterpieces before having attained a considerable maturity.

Gould had played the Opus 109 often, the others rarely, and his conceptions of all three included some ideas that were extremely unorthodox. Much of his Opus 109 was splendid, but when he ventured into the beautiful variations in the final movement, he began violating what Beethoven had written, not just misinterpreting but violating. At the start of the fourth variation, specifically, Beethoven had carefully noted that it should be played "Un poco meno andante ciò è un poco più adagio come il tema," and he added, since he was then in a patriotic phase, a German equivalent, "Etwas langsamer als das Thema." Somewhat slower than the theme, which is andante. Since this beautiful piece comes between the vivace third variation and the stern counterpoint of the allegro fifth variation, it is obvious that Beethoven wanted to emphasize the contrast in the marvelous serenity of this variation. Ignoring the composer's written wishes, Gould played it at high speed, made it glib, superficial, flashy.

His hurried version of Opus 111 was still worse. This is one of Beethoven's very greatest works, one of those grand statements of heroic purpose, like the Fifth Symphony and the *Emperor Concerto*, and Gould only later acknowledged that he disliked this most popular aspect of Beethoven. ("The supreme historical example of a composer on an ego trip," he said, " a composer absolutely confident that whatever he did was justified simply because he did it.") Whenever Gould performed a piece that he disliked but didn't want to admit disliking, he tended, for mysterious reasons of his own, to speed up the tempo. (Some months later, when a critic in Cincinnati ventured to ask him why he had raced through the Opus 111, Gould first "put his hands in his pockets and said he felt it that way," then "explained further [that] the piece was weak in spots; it needed greater speed. . . .") Conversely, Gould said many years later, when discussing his rerecording of *The Goldberg Variations*, that the music he loved best was music that he wanted to hear played slowly. He attributed this feeling to his recollections of the old Presbyterian hymns of his boyhood.

Now he played the heroic first movement of Opus 111 at a frantic speed that deprived it of all its grandeur, made it sound like a stunt. Perhaps only Gould could play it that fast; only Gould would want to. He had said more than once that there was no reason to record a classic work unless one had a new interpretation to offer. "If there's any excuse at all for making a record, it's to do it differently," he declared in a recorded interview entitled "Glenn Gould: Concert Dropout," "to approach the work from a totally recreative point of view, that one is going to perform this particular work as it has never been heard before. And if one can't quite do that, I would say, abandon it, forget about it, move on to something else. . . ." These Gouldian theories were essentially misconceived, however. While an interpreter should have considerable latitude, there is really no reason for any pianist to ignore Beethoven's clearly stated wishes simply for the sake of expressing his own wishes, or simply for the sake of being different. There are limits, in other words, on the interpreter's freedom; the theme of *The Goldberg Variations* must not be played presto, not even by Glenn Gould. Heard today, more than thirty years after he made the recording, Gould's rushed and crashing performance of the Opus 111 remains a botch. It is a botch, one should add, that could only have been perpetrated by someone who was twenty-three years old, and a genius, but it is still a botch.

Partly because the Beethoven sonatas are so well known, in contrast to *The Goldberg Variations*, the critics were quick to pounce. "Unfortunately, his new Beethoven recording is more notable for eccentricity than for musical substance . . ." said one of the first newspaper reviews, in the Baltimore *Morning Sun*. "The whole impression, despite technical accomplishment, is one of childishness." *Time* accused Gould of merely "skimming the surface." "At every point one hears his mind operating attentively and independently," B. H. Haggin wrote in *The New Republic*, "and since the mind is not only powerful but willful and even eccentric, its operation is interesting but the result is largely unacceptable." And Harold Schonberg of the New York *Times* was as lordly as ever: "Not only are the performances immature; they are actually inexplicable.

The scramble through the finale of Op. 109 and the last variation of Op. 111 are something that the young Canadian pianist will look back on as an aberration in about ten years."

Gould was not someone who enjoyed admitting mistakes. In a letter to John Roberts, he sounded quite defiant: "I can only say that those alterations of dynamic or tempo indications with which I took license were the result, not of whims, but of rather careful scrutiny of the scores. . . . Since so many listeners and critics (trustworthy ones too) have taken exception to my conception of late Beethoven I cannot claim that it is the most convincing recording that I have made. However, I do feel that, if only as a personal manifesto, it is the most convinced." In a later letter to John Conly at *High Fidelity*, Gould said that his conception of late Beethoven "does come from an abiding personal conviction," and that he hoped to record more of it, even "if, as I expect, it will be similarly condemned." Gould never fulfilled that plan. Though he performed both the Opus 101 and the *Hammerklavier*, Opus 106, he never made a commercial recording of either one, nor indeed of any sonata after the *Appassionata*. And with the coming of stereo, Gould never rerecorded Beethoven's last three masterpieces; the original mono versions were quietly allowed to go out of print.

Nearly a year after this miscarriage, Gould made his New York orchestral debut in January of 1957 with Leonard Bernstein and the Philharmonic, and they reached the happy choice of Beethoven's Second Concerto. It was and perhaps still is the least known and least appreciated of Beethoven's five concerti, but Gould loved it, played it brilliantly, and made it virtually his own. His performance also illustrated some of the lesser known of his own qualities: charm, gaiety, effervescence. Even the dour Harold Schonberg was impressed, somewhat. "Mr. Gould strolled on stage," he wrote, with the customary atmospherics, "sat at the piano, crossed his legs during the opening tutti, gazed calmly upon audience and orchestra, and then untangled his legs and got to work. He presented a sharp, clear-cut reading that had decided personality." Leonard Bernstein was characteristically more effusive about Gould's performance. "He is the greatest thing that has happened to music in years . . ." he said.

Bernstein, like so many people, had first encountered Gould

through his recording of *The Goldberg Variations*. It had appeared when Bernstein's wife, Felicia, was pregnant with their first son; while she had to wait out the last month during a New York heat wave, that record "became 'our song.'" Bernstein's most vivid personal memory of the young Gould came slightly later, when they were preparing to record the Beethoven C minor Concerto, and Bernstein invited the pianist to dinner at his place in the Osborne apartment house, just across from Carnegie Hall. "He was all bundled up," Bernstein recalls, sipping on his Scotch and soda and taking another cigarette from his silver cigarette box, "and he had an astrakhan hat over some other kind of cap, doubly hatted, doubly mittened, and endlessly muffled and mufflered. And Felicia said, 'Aren't you going to take your hat off?' He said, 'No, no, that's all right, I'll keep it on.' A few minutes later, she asked me, in an aside, over drinks, whether this was a religious matter with him, and I said, 'As far as I know, it isn't!' So she brought it up again to him and said, 'Really, I think you ought to take your hat off, if you don't have any reason for having it on, because it's very warm.'

"And you know, he did. And when he had taken his hat off, Felicia said, 'But this is impossible!' I mean, he had—this was a mat of hair, soaking wet, and just unnourished, and no air. It was hair that hadn't breathed in God knows how long. And while I was fixing drinks or something, she lured him into the bathroom, sat him down at a stool, and cut his hair. And washed it, and combed it. And he came out looking like some kind of archangel, radiant, with this beautiful hair, which one had never seen the color of, quite blond, and shining, haloed-ish. It was really a very beautiful thing to see, what she did, his acceptance, equally beautiful, and the result, which was thrillingly beautiful."

When Gould and Bernstein appeared at the Columbia recording studio on Thirtieth Street, though, there were other dramas of a kind that everyone who worked with Gould was beginning to recognize. For their first collaboration, on the Beethoven Second, Gould arrived with the usual collection of scarves and pills and briefly took up his position at the piano. "With the opening tutti under way," Jay Harrison wrote in *The Reporter*, "Mr. Gould, having nothing to do during the first portion of the concerto, slid out from behind the piano and loped casually about the hall. He shook his head, waved his arms, beat time, and acted generally in a manner that any conductor less accustomed to the ways of genius might have found trying in the extreme. Bernstein, who was himself a prodigy once, took no notice. . . ." When they were finally ready for Gould to start taping, he couldn't be found. A Columbia salesman reported that he was in the men's room soaking his hands in scalding water.

"I love him, you know I love him," said Howard Scott, the recording director for Columbia, banging his head in exasperation. "But why does he have to soak his hands now. Why?"

"Don't rattle him," said the salesman. "He'll sell like crazy—thousands of albums, thousands. He's great and Columbia's got him."

The recording session, when it finally got under way, went well. Gould, for all his oddities, was a consummate professional. But also a perfectionist. Bernstein, very pleased with the performance, declared that "if we can't get great Beethoven out of what we've already done, we never will," but Gould dismayed everyone by saying, "I noticed some trills I'd like to redo."

"Trills," Scott muttered. "We just recorded fifteen of the best trills on records and he wants to redo them. Glenn, take it from me, we'll put together a record from out of all this that you'll be proud of, Lennie will love, and the critics will adore. I know."

He was right. Gould was proud of it, and Bernstein loved it. "I am as proud as you are . . ." he wrote to Gould, "and I hope the critics get the point & perceive for once in their lives what is really going on." The only taint was a bit of gossip, repeatedly told, most fully reported by Abram Chasins in *Speaking of Pianists,* and strenuously denied by Gould. The story was that in the exhilaration of their first public performance of the concerto, Bernstein had urged that they record it together "while it was hot," and that Gould declined, and that Bernstein bewilderedly asked why, and that Gould coolly said, "Because Bernstein isn't ready." B. H. Haggin maliciously repeated the tale, which Bernstein now says he never heard, and went on to comment on the recording: "The orchestra's tense, hard-driven, harsh-sounding playing make it evident that Bernstein still wasn't ready, but Gould makes Bernstein's unreadiness glaring with each piano phrase that he articulates and shapes so perfectly and with such repose and executes with such precision and such beauty of sound." Schonberg of the *Times* was for once more gracious: "The results are beautiful ... Mr. Gould can play with considerable dash, and he does when necessary; but the overall impression is one of well-balanced plasticity, of piano merging with orchestra and veering out again, of fine ensemble and musical finesse."

Only after that triumph, at the end of 1957, did Columbia release the third of Gould's great early recordings, the Fifth and Sixth of the Bach partitas, which he had actually taped somewhat earlier. As with the Beethoven sonatas, this combined a piece that Gould had performed a lot, the Fifth Partita in G major, with one that he had hardly played at all, the Sixth Partita in E minor. And as with *The Goldberg Variations* and the Beethoven Second Concerto, Gould was now taking hold of a relatively neglected part of the piano repertoire, demonstrating that both of these partitas were masterpieces, and making them unmistakably and forever his own. Thousands of people who had never before heard a Bach partita would hear them forever after as Gould alone had articulated and dramatized them.

The only one who disapproved of this superb recording was, strangely enough, Gould himself. He even made his dissatisfaction part of his subsequent indictment of the whole process of concert performances. "I had just returned from my first European tour ..." he told an interviewer, Elyse Mach, "and during that tour ... the Fifth Partita, which is a great favorite of mine, was an integral part of almost every program.... During those concert experiences I had to project that particular piece to a very large audience in most cases and, as a consequence, I had added hairpins—crescendi and diminuendi, and similar un-Bachian affectations—where they didn't need to be. I had exaggerated cadences in order to emphasize the separation of sentences or paragraphs, and so on. In other words, I was making an unnecessarily rhetorical statement about the music, simply as a consequence of having attempted to project it in very spacious acoustic environments.... So the result is that the record made in the summer of '57 is a very glib, facile effort, because a series of little party tricks which just don't need to be there had been added to the piece. Now the interesting thing is that, at the same time, I also recorded the Sixth Partita, which I had played very rarely in public ... and that's a good recording. No party tricks."

They are both far more than good recordings; they are both great recordings. The strange thing is that Gould, who couldn't see how he had gone terribly wrong on the late Beethoven sonatas, also could see only flaws and failures in his marvelous recording of the Fifth Partita. For once, the critics were more perceptive than he. "One is electrified . . . by the very first phrase of Bach's Partita No. 5 . . ." Haggin wrote in *The New Republic*, "by the power, the authority, the sustained tension that compel one's continued fascinated intellectual attention. . . . Both his intellectual power and his technical mastery are evident. . . . I can't recall another pianist achieving anything like this playing of counterpoint."

"Gould is back on the high road to enduring accomplishment . . ." Irving Kolodin wrote in *The Saturday Review*. "It is an enlivening experience to hear the music take shape under his hands, disciplined yet flexible, thoughtful but animated, properly restrained and still possessed of a dynamic rise and fall. . . . An interpreter who can conceive of a printed page with this much sophistication need only be true to his own best impulses. . . ."

Back on tour in August of 1957, Gould appeared to Canadians as a national hero. When he joined the Montreal String Quartet in playing the Brahms Quintet in F minor, Eric McLean of the *Star* reported not only that the performance was "electrifying" but that scalpers had been hawking tickets for as much as thirty dollars apiece, "something unheard of in the local history of chamber music."

South of the border, things were somewhat more difficult, for while the press fanned Gould's celebrity, it also seemed totally obsessed with what it kept calling his "mannerisms" or "eccentricities." Even Paul Hume, who had written that prescient review in the *Washington Post* three years earlier, now turned on Gould. After the usual complaints about the pianist's low chair and his little rug, after grumbling that Gould crossed his legs and massaged his wrists while the orchestra was playing, Hume went on to say that "for him these habits may now be necessities. But nothing like them has ever been needful to many pianists who have played this music more powerfully, more beautifully, and more poetically than Glenn Gould." On the other hand, celebrity begat celebrity. Gould's performance of *The Goldberg Variations* (and the Schoenberg Suite, Opus 25) attracted to Carnegie Hall an audience that included Arthur Rubinstein, Leonard Bernstein, Dimitri Mitropoulos, and Elisabeth Schwarzkopf, and it began winning more serious respect from Schonberg of the *Times*. "Always there was variety, a fine musical intelligence, an extraordinary ability to separate voices and a pair of hands that were unerring," Schonberg wrote. "For this kind of Bach playing one is content to put up with all the personal idiosyncrasies that Mr. Gould can conceive; though, in truth, it is difficult to see how he can conceive any more."

Most of the piano tour, though, involved provincial critics and provincial audiences in provincial cities. "The fabulous young Canadian pianist with the currently soaring reputation played his debut recital in the Miami area Friday night," the Miami *Herald* said of the man who had already dazzled New York, Washington, Berlin, and Moscow. Then came a recital in Philadelphia, and an orchestral concert in New Orleans, and then a performance of the Beethoven Third Concerto in Buffalo inspired the sage of the Buffalo *Evening News* to declare that Gould "has nothing like the technique of a young Horowitz [and] the Third Concerto in the hands of the incomparable Backhaus is undoubtedly closer to the wisdom involved in the Beethoven poetry."

Still, the New York press could be equally problematic. When Gould played the Schoenberg concerto and the Bach D minor with Dimitri Mitropoulos and the New York Philharmonic in March of 1958, Paul Henry Lang of the *Herald-Tribune* became positively indignant. "I found the performance nothing less than shocking," he wrote. "The same Glenn Gould who played the Schoenberg concerto with fine musicianship pounded and punched his way through this intimate chamber piece. His tone was harsh, at times downright brutal. . . . The whole thing was a caricature of a baroque concerto." Winthrop Sargeant of *The New Yorker*, by contrast, found the same performance "a masterpiece of coherence, control and fine musical taste." It was left to Hugh Thomson of the Toronto *Star* to report that Gould was "so carried away" in his performance of the Bach concerto that "he cut his thumb on the keys in the excitement of the finale. Then, when he began to play this Schoenberg concerto, blood kept spreading over the keys. This was probably all to the good, because if there ever was a work that needed some blood, it's Schoenberg's piano concerto."

Gould again appeared to be nearing a breaking point, both physically and psychologically, though he seems not to have realized what was happening. The first major symptom was an unusual sort of indifference to the quality of his own public performances. In Boston that same March, he came out after intermission and announced that he would play the Mozart Sonata in C major (K. 330) instead of Beethoven's Opus 110 because he hadn't practiced the Beethoven. "With innocent good humor," the Boston *Globe* reported, "he added that he hadn't practiced the Mozart either." And in Montreal, when he once again played *The Goldberg Variations,* Eric McLean shrewdly observed not only that "the finger work in the fast movements was not as clean as usual" but that Gould seemed to be getting bored. "It was as though excessive familiarity had caused Gould to lose interest in the primary melody of the movement," McLean wrote, "and had transferred all his attention to the tenor part. This is cavilling, of course. By general standards it was unusually brilliant and musical playing. It was only by the Gould standard that it fell short of perfection."

To Gould, of course, the Gould standard was the only standard, and he now felt a strong conflict between the drumming sense of duty and commitment and the desire to escape from that same drumming sense. In the summer of 1958, he had promised to return to Europe, to perform the Bach D minor at the Salzburg Festival with Mitropoulos and the Concertgebouw Orchestra, and then on to Brussels for Canada Day at the World's Fair, on to Berlin and Stockholm and Wiesbaden, Florence, Tel Aviv. . . . Looking back on that frantic period in his life, Gould daydreamed about the attractions of being some kind of a prisoner locked in a cell.

"I've never understood the preoccupation with freedom as it's reckoned in the Western world . . ." Gould wrote in a rather peculiar work, "Glenn Gould Interviews Glenn Gould about Glenn Gould." "To be incarcerated would be the perfect test of one's inner mobility and of the strength which would enable one to opt creatively out of the human situation." Gould found another way to opt creatively out of the human situation: he got sick, a severe attack of tracheitis that he blamed on the air conditioning in the Salzburg

Festspielhaus. Testifying on his own behalf, Gould described this illness as a reprieve. "My tracheitis was of such severity," he said, "that I was able to cancel a month of concerts, withdraw into the Alps, and lead the most idyllic and isolated existence."

Gould actually canceled only one recital in Salzburg, and two weeks later he got himself to Brussels to play the Bach D minor with Boyd Neel at the World's Fair. *Le Soir* aped the American newspaper coverage of Gould by complaining of his "orang-outang style," and the Toronto press aped its own coverage by reporting the Brussels attack as though it were significant news. Gould drove himself on. "I was terribly depressed," he later told Bernard Asbell. "I was going to be there [in Europe] for three months, terribly out of touch with all the life that I knew, and everything seemed ridiculous and I wished I were home. Before the first concert . . . in Berlin, I was walking to the rehearsal and suddenly said to myself, 'Well, who the hell said it was supposed to be fun anyway?' I must say this pulled me through several weeks. I settled on it as a motto."

Gould needed that motto during his actual concert with Karajan and the Berlin Philharmonic. Once again, the Bach D minor. It should perhaps be explained that this concerto begins with both piano and orchestra playing the sturdy main theme in unison, but that Bach himself later used the theme canonically, that is, restating it two beats after the original statement so that the theme accompanies itself. Now, on the stage of the Hochschule für Musik, after a speech by Mayor Willy Brandt, after the world premiere of an overture by Wolfgang Fortner, Gould and Karajan joined in what Gould later called "one of the most embarrassing beginnings this concerto has ever had."

What was embarrassing was that Gould misunderstood Karajan's cues. "I looked up at K," Gould later wrote in one of his many unfinished manuscripts, "saw, or thought I saw, his preparatory upbeat, and three-quarters of a second later, as his arms emphatically described the bottom of their trajectory, I made my entrance—alone—For K., up is down and vice versa—in the matter of prep. beats. The orch entered as I answered at the second beat—Happily canonic voice-leading met all academic requirements—I took ¾ of a second off to compensate and rejoined them in the middle of the bar. Apart from that, the afternoon was quite uneventful. We exchanged a final glance of mutual support, indicating to each other that a state of mutual preparedness was at hand. He then, as is his wont, closed his eyes for the duration. . . ."

And so, on to Stockholm. There is probably no way to capture all the turmoil and anxiety of this concert tour, or any concert tour, but among Gould's miscellaneous papers there is a memorandum, apparently written many years later,* which gives some sense of the young man on the run. It bears the title "A Season on the Road," and it is nothing but a series of notes, scraps. "Preambule," it begins, "summer of 58 Salzburg—Mitrop [Dimitri Mitropoulos]—Concertgebouw. . . . Premonitions of disaster. El Al Flt (J-Pl-R-Z) Berlin (the sweat in the night) Hochschule Karajan. . . . the continuing unwellness; contrast Berlin reaction to Spr 1957 (first exp. etc.). The chiropractor; Stockholm George-Walter (?) Jochum's lebensraum lecture from Nietzsche; 'the flu;' Bechstein-Steinway; the dinner party; Nordic hedonism; the letter 'flying under the flag;' 'Gt.' Dictator Chaplin . . . Wiesbaden, Sawallisch; cut finger, the drive down the Rhine; Koln, the paternoster; cancellation No. 1; the endless bath; chess . . . the flight to Hamburg—fever and pain; the chiropractor (Palmer method); 102 in the eve.; sweat in the morning; to Vierjahreszeiten—the Inner Harbor. Dr. Storgaharm: 'Remember Chopin.'"

Gould probably knew in Stockholm that he was getting seriously ill. "I have fallen victim to another flu à la Salzburg (current temperature 101 degrees)," he wrote to Homburger on October 2. "Sunday's concert may have to be canceled." But he pressed on to Wiesbaden and Cologne and then collapsed completely at the Hotel Vier Jahreszeiten in Hamburg. "I have chronic bronchitis in the right lung," he wrote to Homburger on October 18. "This we found out by X-rays yesterday. Since I don't know too much about this I am not sure that the practitioner who is seeing me is the best person for the job. . . . [He] is very much a Nature Boy type—milk and honey, cold cloths on the right side—all that sort of thing—I

---

*This probably was a set of notes for Gould's unwritten autobiography. Robert Silverman, editor of *The Piano Quarterly*, repeatedly pressed him to write his memoirs, and when they met in 1981, Silverman recalls, "He said, 'I'm going to write my biography in sections. I'm going to write about every year of my career when I was touring. . . . I'm going to work backwards and forwards, and I'm going to re-create a diary of my life.'"

am sure this kind of doctoring would suit you perfectly but it doesn't seem to be getting me any improvement. . . . I have a high fever every evening (last night up to 100.8). . . . If I see no hope of speedy recovery, I am going to cancel the works and head for Die Zauberberg." And then on October 24: "The doctor concluded his diagnosis yesterday and I have been put to bed for ten days on a no-protein diet. The idea seems to be to give the kidneys a rest as much as possible. X-rays showed there was nothing wrong with them whatever organically but that they had some way been affected by this virus. Quite frankly, I don't think I can stand ten days with nothing substantial to eat. . . ."

Gould's many friends and admirers were eager to offer advice. "We are all very sad about your illness," wrote a Berlin harpsichordist named Sylvia Kind, who recommended massages. "When the circulation is intensive, the poison goes out from the body," she wrote. "The masseur who saved my health (a half-Indian) . . . will come to your hotel. I rang him up and told him about you. . . ." Gould's grandmother wrote him about "that lame back" and said: "Next time, try my remedy, a *thin* coating of mustardine or musterole spread on a cloth and worn over the achy spot. It eases all my aches. . . ." From New York, the Columbia Records publicist Debbie Ishlon cabled: HAVE YOU TRIED YOGI EXERCISES?

The most concerned of these well-wishers was the impresario Wolfgang Kollitsch, who had organized Gould's concerts in Germany. "During the first days of the treatments he drove us crazy by phone begging us to come back to Berlin where he was sure there were better doctors," Gould wrote to Homburger. "Finally he called again on Monday night and announced, and I quote, 'I feel that in this hour of decision it is my duty to stand by your side.' No protests were any use and at 8:00 the next morning he arrived in Hamburg. He accompanied us to the hospital and when the doctor told him I really had been sick he was quite thunderstruck. (I found out afterwards that he had begged the doctor to change his mind while I was off having an X-ray or something.) Anyway when the doctor stood firm Kollitsch acquiesced entirely. . . . He stayed in Hamburg till evening and after dinner . . . I saw a new side of Kollitsch—the hard-headed businessman in the guise of the Viennese gallant—He spoke of his loss of the amount he had spent to book the tour, of the commissions he had lost. . . ." On his sickbed, Gould agreed to a settlement in which Kollitsch kept all the money he already owed Gould, a matter of perhaps one thousand dollars, a settlement that Homburger described as "most generous—but definitely uncalled for."

Despite all these harassments, though, Gould loved playing the role of convalescent at the Vier Jahreszeiten in Hamburg. It is one of the great hotels of Europe, with marvelous chandeliers, and huge claw-footed bathtubs, and a superb view out over Hamburg's inner harbor. To live there in such splendor, with that wonderful sense of irresponsibility that comes with illness, could only have struck Gould as a blessing. "The best month of my life," he once described it to Cott, "—in many ways the most important precisely because it was the most solitary. . . . Knowing nobody in Hamburg turned out to be the greatest blessing in the world. I guess this was my Hans Castorp period; it was really marvelous. There is a sense of exaltation . . . it's the only word that really applies to that particular kind of aloneness." Nor was Gould fazed by the mysteriousness of his illness. A couple of years later, on hearing that Leonard Bernstein was suffering from "an exotic ailment," Gould wrote him a jocular (and prophetic) inquiry: "Do you have a title for it yet? If you are stuck in that department I have several titles for diseases which I am expecting to have in later life and have not yet had occasion to make use of. I always find that a good disease title will impress your average concert manager no end. . . ."

The only thing that could have made Gould's incarceration even better was a sense of the admiration of the outside world. And this too came to him in the new recording of his glittering performance of Beethoven's First Concerto, which included his own rather densely contrapuntal cadenzas. "I have been exulting for two days now in our Beethoven #1, which was sent me," he wrote to Vladimir Golschmann, who had provided the orchestral accompaniment. "I hope you have heard it and are as proud of it as I am. There is a real joie de vivre about it from beginning to end." And then there occurred a charming scene, when Gould was playing his new record of the Beethoven concerto in his hotel sickroom, and a chambermaid stopped to listen. "The maid," he wrote, "is standing entranced in the doorway with a mop in her hands, transfixed by the cadenza to movement #1 which is on the phonograph—it's just ended and she's just bowed and gone on to the next room."

After a month in the Hamburg hotel, Gould was ready to resume his tour in Italy, but he wanted to abandon the idea of going to Israel. Homburger was aghast. "Your suggestion of getting out of the Israeli tour, but continuing in Europe, is based on dreams rather than reality," he wrote. "It just can't be done. They would know about your playing and it would antagonize them to such a degree that it might even have reverberations over here."

It was in Italy, actually, that Gould encountered some novel difficulties. The Accademia Santa Cecilia in Rome didn't want him to play a Bach concerto and proposed instead that he perform Liszt, Chopin, or Mendelssohn. "While I should like to do everything possible to accommodate the Accademia," Gould rather stiffly responded, "I regret that it will not be possible for me to program any of the concerti which they suggested. My repertoire is built almost exclusively around preromantic music. . . ." They eventually compromised on the Beethoven Second.

But then, when Gould played a recital in Florence, he underwent for the first time the very unpleasant experience of being booed. "I had just concluded a performance of the Schoenberg suite, Op. 25," he later wrote, "which, although it was at the time thirty-five years old, had not yet been admitted to the vocabulary of the Florentines. I arose from the instrument to be greeted by a most disagreeable chant from the upper balcony, which was at once contradicted by feverish encouragements from the lower levels. Although I was new to this experience, I instinctively realized that no harm could come to me so long as I permitted the spectators to vent their fury upon each other. Therefore, I cunningly milked the applause for six curtain calls. . . ."

When Gould finally got to Israel, they loved him, as only the Israelis (or the Russians) could love a young Canadian who had come to play them *The Goldberg Variations*. Gould was heavily booked for other things too—the Beethoven Second Concerto three times in four days in Tel Aviv, then the Bach F minor and the Mozart C minor the following day, and then the Beethoven Second in Jerusalem the day after that, and so on, eleven concerts in eighteen days. Every performance was sold out, and the critics struggled to find their way into the transcendental. "Only words from the theological terminology would express this unique manifestation of the spirit from a higher sphere," wrote the reviewer for *Haaretz*. "This is indeed religious music; those are religious sounds.... Gould's playing comes nearest to the conception of prayer.... No praise, however high, could do it justice."

Israel was still a fledgling nation, still only ten years old, still surrounded and beleaguered, and that perilous condition colored the Israelis' perception of Gould, and his of them. "He made front-page news in the local papers," Homburger reported back to the Toronto *Star*, "when it was discovered that, unannounced and unescorted, he had visited a communal settlement within one mile of the Jordanian border. Glenn was exploring the countryside in his rented car. He picked up a hitch-hiker, who turned out to be an immigrant from India, returning to his communal settlement.... Gould was invited in and offered tea. When he requested milk, his host, without batting an eye, rolled up his sleeves, set off for the barn and called over his shoulder: 'Just a moment, I'll get it.'"

This frontier quality in Israel also affected Gould's customary idiosyncrasies. When he was supposed to play the Beethoven Second in Jerusalem on a cold December day, he found the hall impossible. "I don't think I'll play in Jerusalem tonight," he said. "I've just been with my manager to see the hall and it's too cold. There's no heating in it at all." He was told, of course, that the concert had been sold out, and that thousands of ticket-holders were coming to sit in the frosty hall to hear him. "Well, look, I'm susceptible to colds," Gould said. "I see no point in being heroic about it. If I get sick, I won't be able to go through with the rest of my concerts here."

They put eight heaters on the stage in the hope of providing a Gouldian environment, but nobody knew what the visitor would do. When he had not arrived at the scheduled time, a member of the orchestra walked to the front of the stage and announced to the shivering audience that Gould was "suffering from a cold." At that very moment, according to an Israeli reporter, "In loped Mr. Gould, wrapped in a long overcoat and a muffler. He slouched into his unique position at the piano and proceeded to turn in an unforgettable rendition of Beethoven's Second Piano Concerto."

That Beethoven concerto gave Gould difficulties that his Israeli audiences never imagined, or rather it was the "absolutely rotten" piano that the Israelis provided that gave him those difficulties. "I'd gone through a miserable rehearsal," Gould later told Jonathan Cott, "at which I really played like a pig because this piano had finally gotten to me. I was playing on *its* terms ... and I was really very concerned because I simply couldn't play a C-major scale properly."

Gould was then staying at a resort about fifteen miles outside Tel Aviv, and he decided to get into his Hertz car and seek a solution out in the wilderness. "I went out to a sand dune," he said, "and decided that the only thing that could possibly save this concert was to recreate the most admirable tactile circumstances I knew of." In other words, he decided to rehearse the Beethoven concerto by *imagining* himself playing it on his favorite piano, the turn-of-the-century Chickering that stood on short, stubby legs in his parents' cottage on Lake Simcoe.

"When you were sitting in the car in the desert," Cott asked, "were you performing the piece in the air, on the dashboard, or ..."

"Neither, neither," Gould said. "The secret is that you must never move your fingers. If you do, you will automatically reflect the most recent tactile configurations that you've been exposed to."

So Gould sat in his rented car, looking out at the Mediterranean Sea, and imagined the living room in the cottage on Lake Simcoe, imagined each piece of furniture, imagined the old Chickering piano, imagined himself playing through the Beethoven concerto from beginning to end. "I ... got the entire thing in my head and tried desperately to live with that tactile image throughout the balance of the day," he said. "I got to the auditorium in the evening, played the concert, and it was without question the first time that I'd been in a really exalted mood throughout the entire stay there— I was *absolutely* free of commitment to that unwieldy beast. Now, the result, at least during the piano's first entrance, really scared me. There was a minimal amount of sound—it felt as though I were playing with the soft pedal down. . . . I was shocked, a little frightened, but I suddenly realized: Well, of course, it's doing that because I'm engaged with another tactile image, and eventually I made some adjustment, allowed for some give-and-take in relation to the instrument at hand. And what came out was really rather extraordinary— or at least I thought so."

Others thought so too, among them Max Brod, Franz Kafka's friend and literary executor, who came wandering backstage with a woman whom Gould took to be his secretary. Aping her German accent, Gould remembered her saying that they had heard several of his performances but that this concert "vas somehow, in some vay, somesing vas different, you vere not qvite one of us, you vere—your being vas *removed.*" Gould bowed deeply and said thank you, "realizing of course that she had in fact put her finger on something that was too spooky to talk about." Kafka's friend's friend—and Gould was a great admirer of Kafka—rather spoiled this moment of insight by saying that Gould's performance of the Beethoven concerto was "unquestionably ze finest Mozart I haf ever heard."

When Gould returned to Toronto in December, the *Telegram* quoted him as saying that his touring had been "a little hectic," that he had lost twelve pounds, "but I still reach 160," and that he hadn't even had time to get his hair cut. "This is the remains of a production number a Berlin barber gave me, slightly overgrown," he said. He added that he planned to cut down the number of his performances in the coming year to perhaps no more than twenty-five in North America and ten in Europe, but now his schedule called him, and, on Christmas Day, he set out to play the Bach F minor and the Mozart C minor in Detroit. "Unfortunately Gould affects strange mannerisms to his own detriment," the Detroit *Free Press* said in that familiar litany. "The tittering audience is too busy wondering what he'll do next to appreciate his skilled playing. . . ."

In January of 1959, Pierre Berton of the Toronto *Star* caught Gould back at the family cottage on Lake Simcoe and persuaded him to talk about some of his childhood fears. "When he was a boy of eight, a schoolmate standing near him was physically ill," Berton wrote. "All eyes turned on the wretched child and from that instant on Gould was haunted by the spectre of himself being ill in public. That afternoon he returned to school with two soda mints in his pocket, a small tousled boy on guard against the moment when he might lose face. The soda mints were soon supplemented by aspirins and then by more pills. In school, Gould literally counted each second until lunch hour (10,800 seconds at 9 a.m., a comforting four-figure 9,900 at 9:15), and prayed that nothing might happen to humiliate him. Nothing ever did. He has never been ill in public. . . ."

But every time he walked onto the concert stage, before a hushed and expectant audience, Gould saw himself walking into a gladiatorial arena, where the audience sat ready to give the thumbs-down signal for his death. Even the piano that he had learned to master then seemed a wild beast. "It is very easy to let the piano become your enemy when you have lived with it and worked with it—especially when the majority of the pianos are ones you don't like," Gould said to Berton. "The piano symbolizes the terror of the performance and the only thing you can do is hypnotize yourself so the actual ordeal is less great."

Up until now, in his late twenties, Gould still lived at home with his parents. Or rather, he lived in a ragged series of hotel rooms in Chicago and San Francisco and London and Dallas, and then returned to seek haven in his parents' home in Toronto. Now he began thinking that it was time to live on his own, but even though he almost inevitably had become somewhat estranged from his father, he found the break difficult. "At one stage, he had a room in the Windsor Arms Hotel in Toronto," John Roberts recalls, "and he had another room in which he had a piano, at a certain point, when he was trying to find a way of living away from home. And then he took an apartment. And then he decided he didn't like it so he never moved in."

Then came what Gould himself called "a longing for grandeur," and so, "more or less on a whim," he rented a riverside estate called Doncherry, fifteen miles outside Toronto. Writing to a friend in Germany, he reported that Doncherry had twenty-six rooms, "if one counts the seven bathrooms, the breakfast room, the scullery." It also had a swimming pool and a tennis court, for a man who neither swam nor played tennis. And a view. "The view from down below looking up, and especially at night with flood lights, was like looking at Salzburg castle from your own strawberry patch," Gould wrote. "Oh, yes, there was one of those too." His manager, Homburger, apparently expressed misgivings about this château, which Gould took to mean that he "was terrified that I was giving up the piano." Homburger's secretary, Gould went on, "was convinced that I was having an affair with the upstairs maid (who hadn't yet been engaged, to do housework, that is) and my mother, I'm sure, was convinced that I was secretly married. . . ."

Gould invited Winston Fitzgerald of Steinway & Sons to come and admire his new palace. "He said, 'I'm going to take you for a ride,'" Fitzgerald recalls. "We drove out to this neocolonial house, and I thought he was going to introduce me to some friends of his. When we got to the door, he reached in his pocket and took out a key and opened the house, and it was empty. So he was showing me around the house and asking me how I liked it. We went upstairs and—there were two wings to the house, and he was telling me where he was going to have his studio, where his piano would be, and his new recording studio. It was all going to be in one wing of this house, and then we went to this other wing, and I said, 'What are you going to do here?' He said, 'Oh, this is going to be—my manager's going to live here.' And I said, 'You mean to tell me Walter Homburger's going to come out here and live?' He said, 'No, I mean my personal manager.' And I said, 'Who's that? I didn't know you had one.' And he looked me square in the face and said, 'You.' That was the way Glenn did things. Well, of course, I almost went through the floor. But I ultimately did not go to manage him, for many reasons, not the least of which was that he had a habit of calling me at two or three o'clock in the morning, and this happened several times a week for years. I did not tell him that I was afraid of being a prisoner of his whims. I said I had a lifelong obligation to Steinway's, and I just couldn't leave, and he accepted that."

Even in less baronial circumstances, the process of establishing a home is more complicated than somebody who has always lived with his parents might realize. John Roberts, who had helped Gould in his house-hunting, now watched him confront the problems of furnishing his château. "And of course, poor Glenn, whenever he went into a department store, he was instantly recognized, and people rushed up and asked for his autograph, which he got very tired of. And so I began to organize things—we bought a stove, and a fridge, and I can't remember what, just reams and reams of things. And then he rang me up and said he'd changed his mind. And I said, 'Well, what did it?' And then there was great laughter, and he said to me, 'Well, it's when the brooms crossed the threshold that I realized that domesticity had hit me, and I realized that this is not for me at all.' So eventually he settled on this six-room penthouse on St. Clair Avenue. But to get used to it, he didn't actually live there at first. He would go and sleep there, but he also had the Windsor Arms situation, and he phased himself in. . . ."

Not too long after the move to St. Clair, Gould learned that another tie to his youth had been cut. Banquo, the last of his pet dogs, was hit by a car. "I was taking Banquo out for his walk at night," Bert Gould recalls, "and he heard another dog yelping, as though he'd been hit or something, and Banquo just left me on the sidewalk and dashed across the street. He ran right in front of a car and was killed on the spot. I went back home, got the wheelbarrow, and took him back to the house, but he was gone. I called Glenn and told him, and he was terribly upset. . . ."

Q: And he never wanted another dog?

A: Well, I won't say he didn't want another one, but he wasn't at home for me to get him another one. I had an oil painting of Banquo done especially to give to Glenn. It's down in the basement.

And at the end of 1959, Gould suddenly found himself unable to give any more piano concerts. The implications of that discovery must have been devastating, but what had actually happened was almost ludicrous. After playing Beethoven's Fourth Concerto in Oklahoma City that December, Gould went to New York for some discussions at the house of Steinway, whose pianos he always used, and there he had an ill-fated encounter with the chief Steinway technician, William Hupfer. Though Gould's subsequent lawsuit treated Hupfer like some sort of a ruffian, he was scarcely that. Schuyler Chapin, who had by now succeeded Oppenheim as head of Columbia Masterworks, described him as "a quiet, thoroughly professional man" and "the only one allowed to tune and regulate Horowitz's piano." Exactly what Hupfer did to Gould we do not know for sure (a recent inquiry at Steinway prompted a suave young man in a pinstriped suit to say regretfully that Hupfer "passed away about five years ago"), but the affidavit that Gould filed in federal court charged that Hupfer had engaged in "unduly strong handshakes and other demonstrative physical acts." Ignoring widespread reports that Gould was a man of "extreme and unusual sensitivity to physical contact," the complaint said, Hupfer approached him from behind and "recklessly or negligently let both forearms down with considerable force on the plaintiff's neck and left shoulder, driving the plaintiff's left elbow against the arm of the chair in which he was sitting."

Winston Fitzgerald, the Steinway official in charge of artists and repertory, and the man at whose desk the incident took place, dismisses Gould's whole account as fanciful. According to Fitzgerald, Gould and Hupfer had increasingly sharp professional disagreements, which they both repressed. "They had distinctly different ideas about the voicing of pianos," Fitzgerald says, "and Glenn wanted all sorts of things done to pianos that Mr. Hupfer would not do, did not consider good piano practice, and so this friction developed."

On the day of their encounter at Fitzgerald's desk, Fitzgerald recalls nothing "reckless or negligent." "Mr. Hupfer just laid his hand gently on Glenn's shoulder, and Glenn suddenly went into a state of gloom," Fitzgerald says. "And when Mr. Hupfer left, I said, 'Glenn, what's wrong?' And he said, 'He *hurt* me.' Well, I saw this, and I mean, he just put his—he *couldn't* have hurt him."

Q: But something happened. Gould *was* injured.

A: So he *said*.

Q: You think he didn't have injuries? He had to cancel a whole lot of concerts.

A: Well, I don't know. Certainly they didn't ensue from that incident. He may indeed have had some problems, but I can assure you that it was not from this incident with Mr. Hupfer. Hupfer was barely there two seconds. He just walked by and sort of lightly patted Glenn on the shoulder, and immediately there was this cloud of gloom hanging over him, and he said, "He *hurt* me."

Fitzgerald expressed some of his skepticism in a letter to Gould at the time, and Gould replied rather sharply that he "was a little surprised at the tone of your letter in so far as you seem to express some bafflement about the nature of my malaise." The only reason that several newspapers had been told that he had suffered from a "fall," he said, "was to avoid a fuller explanation which would perhaps cause some embarrassment to Steinway & Sons."

The only other surviving witness to the encounter, Frederick (Fritz) Steinway, corroborates Fitzgerald's account. "Fitzgerald said no, and I believe it," Steinway says.

Q: Then why did Gould claim to be so seriously injured?

A: Because he was a hypochondriac, as you well know.

Q: Why did he cancel a lot of concerts on account of this?

A: Artists are very apt to do that sort of thing for all kinds of reasons, some of which make sense and some of which do not.

When Gould eventually sued Steinway for $300,000 in damages, the press treated the whole affair as a light comedy. Gould really did feel, however, that he had suffered a serious injury to that fragile mechanism with which pianists perform their art. "The initial injury was to the left shoulder and when X-rayed the shoulder blade was shown to have been pushed down about one-half inch," Gould wrote to a friend a month after the incident. "That problem has basically been cleared up now but has caused a secondary reaction much more troubling. The nerve which controls the fourth and fifth fingers of my left hand has been compressed and inflamed or whatever, with the result that any movement involving a division of the left hand, as in a sudden leap to the left side of the keyboard, is, if not actually impossible, accomplished only by a considerable effort of will. . . . I have been having two treatments per day on different aspects of it—one medical and one chiropractic—and while no one seems to feel that it is likely to become permanent, I must say I am becoming rather dissatisfied with the relative lack of improvement."

Gould blamed his condition on "what may gallantly be called an 'accident' . . . entirely due to the idiocy of one of Chez Steinway's senior employees." He said this nemesis "may have forced me to become a full time composer," but he remained reluctant to announce any details in public. He simply canceled all concerts for the next three months ("I am back to cancelling concerts for a living," he wrote to Bob Barclay, the music publisher who had recently produced the score of his string quartet), and when he reappeared to perform the Beethoven Fourth in Baltimore, he said to the *Morning Sun* only that he had been "seeking relief from the effects of a strained shoulder." To a friend in Berlin, he attributed his recovery to cortisone. "It has really worked a miracle with the arm," he wrote. "I still am not able to give recitals because I don't feel that I can play for a whole evening without great fatigue, but I did play my first concerto appearance in three months last week. It was with the Baltimore Symphony and it was a great success despite the fact that my arm was quite sore and tired by the time I was finished. Nonetheless, to have got through it was something of an achievement and I am feeling much more optimistic about the full recovery of my arm."

Cortisone is an unreliable friend, however. "The arm is very, very much better," Gould wrote to Schuyler Chapin at Columbia in March. "The cortisone is having a truly miraculous effect, except that it makes me wretchedly nauseous but I have developed a system of taking it one day, being sick the second day, eating the third day, taking cortisone the fourth etc." And then it didn't work. "The temporary improvement during March, which enabled me to play some concerts, turned out to have been due to the taking of cortisone," Gould wrote to Robert Craft that May, "but it was a temporary improvement only and the trouble came back in full force."

Yet there remained a certain element of mystery as to what was really wrong with Gould, if anything. Dr. Joseph Stephens, a friend who both played the harpsichord and taught psychiatry at Johns Hopkins, speaks somewhat derisively of Gould's "imaginary illnesses."

Q: Were they really imaginary?

A: Oh, well, he became so obsessed by this shoulder thing that I had him seen at Hopkins by a very fancy neurologist, and he insisted that I sit with him while he was being examined, and the neurologist said to me, "Not a thing wrong with him."

Eugene Ormandy, the conductor of the Philadelphia Orchestra, warmly recommended in May an orthopedist named Irvin Stein, and so Gould went to Philadelphia to see him. "It was in relation to a difficulty with his neck and arm, which he had developed, according to him, subsequent to an extremely hearty push and slap on the top of his shoulder," Dr. Stein recalls from his retirement in Florida. "And it was associated with an immediate pain on the left side of his neck that went into his arm and affected his playing."

Q: Did you have any reason to doubt his story about how the injury was caused?

A: Well, I don't know. This is what he described to me.

Dr. Stein declared that the only solution was to encase Gould's whole arm and shoulder in a plaster cast, a cast that held the arm upward and outward. There is a photograph in the Ottawa Library that shows Gould in this portable prison, naked to the waist, the precious arm outstretched and immobilized, like the branch of an espaliered apple tree. He is somewhat unshaven in this photograph, and he looks terrified, like a trapped animal. To some extent he was.

Dr. Stein remembers those months with tranquility. "He tolerated very well having the shoulder in a plaster," he says, "so that we could bring his shoulder up toward his neck and reduce the stretch on the nerves in the brachial plexus, which is the thing that goes from the spine into the upper extremities. And he did very well after a few weeks of that, and then some gradual exercises. It apparently cleared up." In Gould's letters of that year, however, there is a good deal of agitation and anxiety. "I finally had to cancel the balance of the season and try to get this thing put in shape once and for all . . ." he wrote to a friend in early May. "What a season this has been!" And to another friend at the end of May: "I have just returned from Philadelphia and regret to say that . . . the treatment there was by no means wholly successful. . . . There has been, however, some improvement in the arm, I believe, and I am beginning to wear a metal cervical collar." And in early June: "When the arm was completely at rest in the cast, there was indeed a great deal of relief but, unfortunately, when it was taken out and once again required full support from the shoulder, the problem returned. . . . The problem is essentially one of endurance. Due to the stretching of the muscle complex of the shoulder, the arm fatigues terribly quickly."

By July, he felt well enough to go to New York for a recording session. "My arm, I think, was in the best shape it has been since last winter," he wrote Homburger. "I have been wearing the collar at all times when practising and having a great deal of physiotherapy, and I was quite sure that I could get through the recording with no difficulty. . . . The Monday session went very well indeed. I did Opus 31, No. 2 [Beethoven's Sonata No. 17 in D minor, the so-called *Tempest Sonata*] . . . and I think it will be a superb recording but by Tuesday with the exposure to air-conditioning (possibly), and without as much physiotherapy as I had been used to, the arm had tightened up again in exactly the same way and finally on

Wednesday we abandoned the recording of the Eroica variations [by Beethoven, Opus 35], cancelled Thursday's session and will take up again the end of August. This is, needless to say, very disappointing because I had certainly expected better results by this time. The symptoms are exactly the same as before—same knot, same aches, same fatigue. Next week Stratford begins and I am determined to try to get through it . . . but at this point I frankly don't see how."

He got through it by willpower, and because Stratford represented an odd kind of liberation. The authorities of the annual Shakespeare Festival had had the inspired idea in 1956 of making Gould a codirector of the new musical programs (along with the violinist Oscar Shumsky and the cellist Leonard Rose), and so he acquired the authority to organize unusual programs, all Mendelssohn, for example, or all Hindemith. But even before that, he enjoyed the idea of taking part in a festival. Instead of endlessly repeating his concert repertoire, endlessly playing Beethoven's Opus 109 and the Berg Sonata, he could try out all kinds of things. At this 1960 festival, for instance, he joined with Oscar Shumsky in playing Beethoven's Violin Sonata in C minor, and then with Shumsky and Leonard Rose in Beethoven's *Ghost Trio*. With the festival orchestra, he played not only Bach's D minor Concerto but also the Fifth Brandenburg Concerto, conducting both from the keyboard of a specially doctored piano that he called a "harpsipiano." GLENN GOULD AT STRATFORD 'BETTER THAN EVER,' said a headline in the Toronto *Star*. "It is perhaps conceivable that somewhere in the world one might hear greater performances of chamber music than those presented at the Festival Theatre here this afternoon," John Kraglund wrote in the Toronto *Globe and Mail*. "I have neither heard them nor heard of them, so I can only sympathize with the more than 1,000 persons who made fruitless efforts to secure tickets to a concert that had been sold to its capacity of nearly 2,300 seats several weeks ago."

And so Gould was back on the road. Mozart's C minor Concerto in Vancouver, and the same in New Haven, and the Strauss *Burleske* in Detroit, and the following night the Beethoven Second, and then the *Emperor* in Buffalo. "Having once experienced the threat and fear of not being able to play," he wrote to a friend, "has, understandably, made me perhaps for the first time really anxious to do so and I feel that some of the best performances I have given have been in these last few months." But there was still that inescapable sense of routine. "In South Bend, Indiana, if I remember correctly," says John Roberts, "he was climbing the stage to perform at a concert, and he said, 'Glenn Gould, what in God's name are you doing? Another platform, another place.'"

And there were the same old aggravations. Not only his shaky health ("I still have good days and bad days," he wrote to a friend in Berlin in September), not only the sometimes idiotic newspaper reviews ("I have never heard a concert with monotony carried to such extremes," said the Akron *Beacon Journal*), but sometimes moments of pure terror. One night, flying into Toronto, the plane coming in ahead of Gould's plane crash-landed, and Gould's flight had to be diverted to Ottawa. "Another time," according to Bert Gould, "they had the trays on their laps, and all the trays flew up and hit the ceiling, and stuff came down. It scared him, you know, and two or three times something like that gets you."

Then there were still the importunings of his admirers. A woman in Bethesda, Maryland, wrote to complain that she and a friend had driven all the way to Philadelphia to hear Gould play. "It wasn't until we were seated in the hall that we discovered a substitution had been made two days before," she wrote. "What induced our feeling of real shock, however, was the fact of having seen you just a few hours earlier at the Drake Hotel—you were checking out as we were checking in.... Please understand I have no wish to intrude. It's simply that the incident has left an uneasiness that refuses to subside...." Gould felt obliged to explain to her that he had been visiting his Philadelphia doctor. "That, then, was the reason for my presence at the Drake Hotel on November 3 and the reason that you observed me checking out of the hotel that afternoon."

The following month, December of 1960, Gould finally filed his damage suit against Steinway in federal court in New York. He said that Hupfer's overly "demonstrative" salutation had cost him $3,600 in medical bills and $21,400 in lost earnings, and he asked $300,000 in compensation. Steinway hemmed and hawed for about nine months and then settled. "They wanted him in their stable," says Fitzgerald. "He was a star." "To all to whom these Presents shall come or may concern, greetings," the settlement proclaimed. "Know ye, that Glenn Gould, over the age of 21 years . . . for and in consideration of the sum of nine thousand three hundred seventy-two and 35/100 ($9,372.35) lawful money of the United States of America, to him in hand paid by Steinway & Sons and William Hupfer, the receipt whereof is hereby acknowledged, have remised, released and forever discharged and by these Presents do for his heirs and executors and administrators remise, release and forever discharge the said Steinway & Sons and William Hupfer . . . from all, and all manner of action and actions, cause and causes of actions, suits, debts, dues, sums of money, accounts, reckonings, bonds, bills, specialties, covenants, contracts, controversies, arguments, agreements, promises, variances, trespasses, damages, judgments, extents, executions, claims, and demands, whatsoever in law or in equity, which . . ." And so on.

But the injury was not so completely healed. There was by now almost no part of Gould's soul and spirit—and perhaps this is just as true for all of us—that did not show signs of scar tissue. He was supposed to go to Philadelphia late in 1961 to play the *Emperor* with Ormandy and the Philadelphia Orchestra, but shortly after the Steinway settlement, he suddenly decided that he couldn't bear the idea of playing in Philadelphia. "Dear E," he wrote to Ormandy, "I imagine you have received some strange requests from time to time, but I daresay that few will be as startling as the one I am now going to make. I have been trying to summon courage to call you . . . but I feel that what I have to ask you is so unusual that only by writing can I give it some kind of form. I have developed (if that's the word) over the past months what I can only describe to you as a great apprehension in regard to giving concerts in Philadelphia. Never before in my life have I experienced anything at all similar to it, for I have come to feel something approaching terror at the thought of playing in Philadelphia. I'm afraid that the association of Philadelphia in my imagination has become inextricably confused with my weeks there and with the fact that during those weeks I was immobilized, at least pianistically. . . ."

Gould was writing on the stationery of the Edgewater Hotel on Lake Mendota in Madison, Wisconsin, and he had great difficulty in saying what he wanted to say. "Dear E," he began again. "I hope when you read this that you will forgive me for having written instead of called. To be honest, I have tried to find the courage to telephone you for some days but I felt that it would be most difficult to give an intelligent presentation which I must describe to you. I have developed over the past few months what I can only describe as a very great apprehension about giving concerts in Phil. Never in—similar to it [sic] for I have come to feel something approaching terror.... What has happened is that in my imagination the assoc. of Phil has become hopelessly confused with the memories of the weeks I spent there in a cast last year.... The more I try to argue with myself against the illogic of this assoc. the worse it becomes. I had a dream for instance just a few nights ago in which I seemed to be walking just offstage in the Academy [the Philadelphia Academy of Music] and as I moved toward the stage I fell over a rope of some kind and the dream ended as I apparently broke my arm. Believe me, Eugene, I know how foolish this all is, and I would feel greatly embarrassed to detail such unreasoned fears to anyone but you...."

But then he also had to write to the woman who had organized this concert, Emma Feldman, director of the Philadelphia All Star Forum Series, Inc. "Dear Emma," he began, on the stationery of the Greater Radisson Hotel in Minneapolis, "I imagine this letter will come as something of a shock to you and I can only assure you that it is no easy letter for me to write.... I have tried desperately but unsuccessfully to rid myself of a totally foolish and illogical phobia about giving concerts in Philadelphia.... As I am sure you will guess it is inextricably confused with the unpleasant memories of those very difficult weeks which I spent in a cast in Philadelphia last year, and in some mysterious way I have come to feel a great inhibition, even horror, of playing there. However idiotic this sounds to you I hope you will realize that in writing this I am in fact understating the case rather than exaggerating it....

"As I said to Eugene there are only two courses open to me," he went on. "One, the sensible, maybe even restorative one, I suppose would be—" At that point, Gould reached the end of the second page of this letter. He then began the third page by writing, "Onl," and then stopped. He began again by writing on a new sheet of the stationery of the Greater Radisson Hotel, "Only two courses open to me," and then he stopped again. There were finally six different versions of this critical third page (and he saved all the drafts), and he finally said, "When one has dwelt upon this sort of phobia so intensely the very concentration on its circumstances is likely to produce an atmosphere of unusual tension and I should be most reluctant to give a concert on an important series like yours under such circumstances. . . . I am sure you know that I will make every possible effort to reimburse you for any loss on this engagement. . . ."

The Philadelphians did their best to help. Emma Feldman denied that she was "shocked" by Gould's cancellation of the concert and said only that she was "both sad and upset about your—shall we say attitude about Philadelphia. . . . You should have a very warm feeling about Philadelphia, since I believe we did get you practically cured here." Eugene Ormandy was more understanding, in a rather strange way. When Gould had canceled his performance of the *Emperor*, Ormandy had recruited Van Cliburn to replace him, and now he wrote to Gould: "Perhaps it will give you a chuckle when I tell you that every time I talked to Van, for some psychological reason, I called him Glenn. The third time it happened, he said he didn't mind at all because he loved Glenn and he considered it an honor and a pleasure to be called by that name. So in the subconscious, you are really still with us. . . ."

It was not true. In the subconscious, Gould was already seeking his freedom from "the terror of the performance." At the end of *Lohengrin,* when Elsa breaks her pledge and asks the mysterious knight who he is, she then can only watch helplessly as he renounces her and sails away.

V

The Abdication

From the very beginning of his concert career, Gould talked freely about abandoning it. "I went on record once saying to a reporter from the Toronto Telegram that I would retire at 23," he wrote to Karsh. "Unfortunately I said it when I was 22, and he reminded me of it when I was 24." Not long after his New York debut, Gould told an interviewer in Winnipeg: "I'm more convinced than ever that I'd rather be a composer. I don't particularly care to play before the public. I love playing for myself." And back in Toronto early in 1956: "I am not very fond of the concert business. I am not endeared to the footlights at all. And it is a devastating road if you can't endure traveling."

By 1959, when he was not yet twenty-seven, Gould was talking quite openly about a complete withdrawal. "He is making plans to retire," Jay Harrison wrote in the New York *Herald-Tribune*. "Or so he says, with something less than the ultimate in conviction. As he put it last week: 'I certainly don't intend to work beyond my thirty-fifth year—not if I can help it. I really would like the last half of my life to myself. Then I could do what I can only do part-time now—compose.'" And a month later, to Dennis Braithwaite of the Toronto *Star:* "I hope that I will be able to retire by the time I am 35. If I can't I shall be very disappointed in myself and go out selling insurance or something else. But I want to be in a position to give up playing the piano, at least publicly, altogether."

Though he joked about selling insurance "or something else," the prospect of abandoning a very lucrative career (his fee had climbed to $3,500 per concert, and he earned more than $100,000 per year)

was a little frightening. How would he make a living? Would anyone buy the recordings of an unseen artist? Would a fickle public
turn away and reject him just as he had rejected it? Retirement at
such an age was virtually unprecedented. Franz Liszt had more or
less abandoned the concert stage at thirty-six, but only to become
court conductor and composer at Weimar. Still, the idea of retirement kept ripening in Gould's head. In April of 1962, when he was
just a few months short of his thirtieth birthday, he made what
seems to have been his first definite (though private) announcement
in a letter to Humphrey Burton at the BBC in London: "I am not,
at the moment, planning any tour in Europe for next season, or
indeed at the moment for any season. This is due to the fact that, as
of two months ago, I decided that when next season is over, I shall
give no more public concerts. Mind you, this is a plan I have been
announcing every year since I was 18, and there is a part of my
public here that does not take these pronouncements too seriously,
but this time I think I really mean it."

Gould made no official announcement. The plan just sort of solid-
ified, like ice congealing in a river. Sometimes he spoke of it as lim-
iting himself to a minimal number of concerts, sometimes as a total
withdrawal but only for a short period of time, a year or two. He
couldn't be sure. Early in 1963, he wrote to a fan who had asked
him to play in Prince Edward Island: "I have remained quite firm up
to now about my semiretirement plans. As a matter of fact, next year
I am doing only a very few engagements in the major American cities—just by way of reminding myself how to do a concert, and
really intending to spend a year thinking and composing." To an
interviewer in Portland, Oregon, he was still more specific. "His
own plans call for retirement from the concert stage next year," she
wrote, "save for a token 15 appearances, in order to devote more
time to television and composing. 'After all, one must quit by 30,'
he mused." And then, to a friend in New York: "I have, as you
know, attempted to maintain a semiretired state so far as concert-
giving is concerned, and . . . I have accepted only a minimum number of concerts next year . . . and I really feel that I must stick to
this resolve. In Canada, for instance, I do no public concerts now
except Stratford. The reason for all of this is that I felt it was essential, sooner or later, to find out what sort of a composer I could
become and to also have as much time for writing as possible."

Part of Gould's dislike of the concert tour was his dislike of travel, or rather his dislike of travel under pressure. He dreaded airplanes (that whole generation of touring pianists was acutely aware that one of its most brilliant members, William Kapell, had been killed in a plane crash at thirty-one), and after 1962, he simply refused to fly. But travel also meant missed connections, unheated trains, flat tires, second-rate hotels, and second-rate food. "Usually, whenever musicians get together and talk about our traveling," says Jaime Laredo, a cheerful soul who recorded the Bach violin sonatas with Gould, "we always somehow manage to talk about this great restaurant in this city, or that wonderful hotel or that wonderful hall. But with Glenn, every city that you mentioned was some terrible experience. 'That's where I came down with the worst cold in my life,' or 'That's where the hotel bed was so soft that I couldn't sleep.' And it made me feel bad because I realized how much he had suffered, what an incredible ordeal it had been for him."

Gould's determination to abandon the concert stage appeared to many such observers at the time as a bizarre renunciation of everything to which young musicians should and did aspire. What was it, if not the chance to perform great music before applauding audiences, that drove Gould's contemporaries to spend long hours in arduous and disciplined practicing? And they were indeed a talented group—Gary Graffman, Leon Fleisher, Van Cliburn, Eugene Istomin, Julius Katchen, Jacob Lateiner, Seymour Lipkin, Lorin Hollander—all young and energetic and ambitious and eager to compete for the rewards of success. Yet the mere recitation of such names today suggests a whole generation devastated by the demands of the competition that Gould rejected. Graffman and Fleisher were both stricken by crippling hand injuries, and though they still perform the limited repertoire for left hand, both of these highly gifted artists now devote most of their time to teaching. ("Yes, I think perhaps we were driven more than the previous generation," says Graffman. "I wonder whether recordings had something to do with it. Audiences now expect a note-perfect performance.") Cliburn, who once received a ticker-tape parade down Broadway after his spectacular triumph in Moscow, has remained mysteriously absent from the stage for most of the last ten years. Katchen is dead. And the others? Their careers tend to corroborate Gould's judgment and to imply that his act of apparent abnegation was actually an act of affirmation, of prudence, of survival.

Apart from all questions of personal convenience, Gould had acquired a real loathing for the gladiatorial aspects of the concert hall. The audience's eager participation in all "those awful and degrading and humanly damaging uncertainties," Gould felt, made a piano recital one of "the last blood sports." "Some people feel," an interviewer argued in 1962, "that one of the joys of listening to music arises from the 'one-chance' risk of performance—that no one, neither player nor listener, knows quite how it will come out."

"To me this is heartless and ruthless and senseless," Gould said in a great rush of feeling. "It is exactly what prompts savages like Latin Americans to go to bullfights. When I hear it I want to retire. The spectator in the arena who regards musical performance as some kind of athletic event is happily removed from the risk, but he takes some kind of glee in what goes on there. This is entirely separate from what is really going on: an effort by the performer to form a powerful identification with the music. A performance is not a contest but a love affair. . . ."

And then there always came that dismal ritual of the newspaper critics publishing their commentaries on the love affair. In retrospect, these critics' obsession with Gould's platform behavior seems to fluctuate between the rude and the silly. "He was a joy to hear," Howard Taubman wrote in the New York *Times*, for example. "But his mannerisms at the piano were not a joy to see. If Mr. Gould cannot help himself, one can only sympathize. If, during rests, he must fling himself back like an exhausted gladiator, if he must cock his head to one side like an absorbed parrot, if he must fuss with his handkerchief and look as if he will miss the start of the cadenza, why then he must. He had better realize, however, that he is not only doing himself a disservice but also distracting attention from the music. On all sides, one could see listeners smirking and giggling at Mr. Gould's extra-musical behavior instead of paying heed to Mr. Gould's celestial song. . . ." But imagine if Mr. Taubman were expected to dress up in white tie and tails to write *his* celestial song, if he were permitted no mistakes and no rewritten sentences in the creation of his review, and if some other critic, assigned to the maintenance of Grub Street's highest standards, then published a commentary not only on Taubman's views and Taubman's prose but also on his haircut, his costume, and any gestures he might happen to make while at work.

Like most artists, Gould professed indifference to these tiresome observations on his performances; like most artists, he was fibbing. Beyond the pretense of indifference to public attacks on one's personal behavior, there are only three alternatives: to suffer in silence, to talk back, or to revel in the role that has been assigned. Gould intermittently tried all four courses, notably the last.

In London in 1959, for example, he appeared at a press conference tousled and unshaven, and wearing a knee-length jacket, heavy overcoat, and two pairs of gloves. "What makes you think I'm eccentric?" he inquired of the reporters who had assembled to record his eccentricities. One reporter pointed out to Gould that his right shoelace was untied, apparently hoping that Gould would live up to his reputation by trying to tie it with his gloved hands. "The pianist shrugged it off," according to the Associated Press report published back in Toronto, "put down his drink (a glass of pineapple juice), and kept his gloved hands—insured with Lloyd's for $100,000—in his pants pockets." The swaddled Gould did in fact have a fever from flu and subsequently had to cancel one of his London concerts, but if the London press wanted to patronize this visitor from the colonies, the Canadian press was prepared as always to defend him as a national treasure. "So they've been having a gay time in Britain, tagging our Glenn Gould with the label eccentric . . ." said an editorial in the Toronto *Star*. "Canadians should always remember why he's really unusual: Because he's a great pianist, a genius. . . . Mr. Gould admits being 'a hypochondriac, in a small way.' Maybe. Without any doubt, however, he is an artist and Canadian in a big way."

Perhaps the most controversial of the public criticisms involved one of the most unusual of Gould's concert imbroglios, his very public disagreement with Leonard Bernstein in 1962 about how to play the Brahms Concerto in D minor. Gould strongly disliked all the competitive and heroic aspects of the Romantic piano concerto, and he never performed any of those beloved war-horses by Chopin, Liszt, Schumann, Tchaikowsky, or his distant cousin Grieg. But he loved Brahms, and he knew that Brahms had originally conceived his first concerto as a kind of symphony for piano and orchestra, and he himself had been "gradually evolving" a new view of this music. "I have begun to find, I think, a way of playing the middle and late 19th century repertoire," he wrote to a friend, "in which the predominant characteristic will be the presence of organic unity and not the continual . . . coalition of inequalities which, it seems to me, underlies most interpretations of 19th century music. If this sounds fancy and a bit arbitrary, it is not really. All that I am doing is deliberately reducing the masculine and feminine contrast of theme-areas in favour of revealing the correspondence of structure material between thematic blocks. . . ."

The most dramatic aspect of Gould's interpretation of the Brahms D minor was his insistence that it be played very, very slowly. Brahms's only indication of the tempo he wanted was *maestoso*, which could mean almost anything, but Gould's interpretation of "majestic" was worthy of the marble statue of the Commendatore in *Don Giovanni*. "Glenn had called me a week or two earlier from Toronto," Bernstein recalls, lighting another cigarette, "and said, 'Oh, Lenny, get ready for this! Have I got news for you about Brahms! Wait till you hear the D minor Concerto. I've discovered it. I know how it has to go, finally.' And I said, 'I'll bet slow,' knowing about his Mozart sonatas. And he said, 'Forget everything you ever heard about the D minor. This will shock you.' And I said, 'Well, I'm ready for anything. You can't shock me. *You* can't shock me.' He said, 'Believe me, this will throw you.'

"So he came to the house, and we played on the two little pianos that I had back-to-back. And I was really amazed at how slow it was.* And he played the first movement, almost all of it, in six [beats per measure], so that the second movement, the adagio which is also in six-four time, sounded like a continuation of the first movement. That was one of his big points, you see, that the quarter-note remains consistent throughout and holds this whole huge thing together. And I said, 'Of course, you're exaggerating. You're not

*"Gould was wrong, and I can prove it," says the pianist Malcolm Frager. "Because if you've ever been to Vienna—the manuscript of the first movement has a metronome marking, which is not in any printed score, but it's in Brahms' handwriting. It's 56 to the dotted half, and it's quite fast—*Pom*—pom—pom—pom—pom so playing it twice that slow is *not* what Brahms had in mind. It's provable."

going to really do it this way. You're just showing me what you've found, with these mathematical relationships between one movement and another.' And he said, 'No, this is the way we'll play it.' And I said, 'All right.'"

Bernstein believed that the Philharmonic could not play the concerto at Gould's tempo without a special rehearsal, and at that rehearsal, he tried to give the players some extra encouragement. "I told the orchestra to be ready for this," Bernstein says, "and that we must take it very seriously because this guy is such a genius. And even if he's *wrong*, it's going to be gorgeous, and we must go along with him. He's adventurous, I'm adventurous, and let's do it."

Bernstein apparently felt that his audiences needed similar reassurances, and since he had begun a tradition of giving informal talks during his Thursday night concerts, which were treated partly as dress rehearsals, Bernstein decided to talk about "this extraordinary performance." He insists that he told Gould exactly what he was going to say, and that Gould agreed completely. By now, after all these years, Bernstein remembers Gould as the most enthusiastic of collaborators. *"Together,"* he says, "we wrote on the back of an envelope some notes for what I was going to say, and he was simply delighted. Because he was made of that kind of sportsman's stuff, he was taking a chance on everything."

The event really does not sound quite the way Bernstein remembers it. Listening to a tape of this bizarre occasion a quarter of a century later, one feels a sense of shock at the announcer suddenly declaring, "I think Mr. Bernstein will have something to say to the audience," and then Bernstein starting to propose, in that mellifluous voice, what he called "this small disclaimer." He praised Gould as "a thinking performer," and said that his version of the Brahms concerto had "moments . . . that emerge with astonishing freshness and conviction." But he also declared that this would be "a rather—shall we say—unorthodox performance . . . a performance distinctly different from any I've ever heard, or even dreamt of, for that matter." Two artists are entitled to a difference of opinion, of course. Yet Bernstein not only made a public spectacle of the difference but publicly wondered why he took part in a performance of which he disapproved. Partly because Gould was "so valid and serious an artist," he said, and partly because "there is in music what

Dimitri Mitropoulos used to call 'the sportive element,' that factor of curiosity, adventure, experiment, and I can assure you that it *has* been an adventure this week collaborating with Mr. Gould."

That was perhaps the worst of it, that Bernstein played to his audience and played it for laughs. There were chuckles when he started by saying, "Don't be frightened—Mr. Gould is here." There was laughter when he asked about this controversial conception of Brahms, "What am I doing conducting it?" There was loud and prolonged laughter when he said that he had only once before in his life "had to submit to a soloist's wholly new and incompatible concept, and that was the last time I accompanied Mr. Gould."

What could Gould—touchy, nervous, mercurial Glenn Gould— have thought about all these witticisms as he waited in the wings of Carnegie Hall and listened to the audience laugh? He later said, surprisingly enough, or perhaps not so surprisingly, that he didn't at all resent being the butt of Bernstein's humor. "Despite all the wild accusations that have been flying about, the speech was completely charming," he wrote to a friend. "Indeed, done with great generosity, and far from having precipitated a feud (as the newspapers suggest) we have never been better friends." Bernstein too took pains later to proclaim that he had not tried to degrade or embarrass Gould. After Gould's death, he kept saying that Gould had approved of his talk, that he had meant no harm. "It was a marvelous evening," he says. "And it was something very fresh. He really did find wonderful things in that concerto, and I *adored* him for it. But that *goddamned story* that I can never seem to get rid of. I tell you, that story drives me crazy. It makes me—uh—inarticulate to talk about it."

Everyone who was at the concert remembers it differently, each perhaps according to his own prejudices, but we have the surviving testimony of the tape recorder. On first hearing the incredibly slow opening to this concerto, one is almost inevitably overwhelmed by the lumbering and ungainly tempo. It seems almost absurd, and it certainly fails to achieve Gould's concept of a symphony. Yet as the movement proceeds, one begins to appreciate other aspects of Gould's performance. The slow tempo enables him to bring to this music a clarity that is rarely heard in more conventional versions, and he plays the lyrical passages with an unsentimental sweetness that is extremely beautiful. Finally even the heroic sections, which seem so awkward at first, acquire a stately majesty of their own.*

The audience's applause at the end was enthusiastic—an ovation—but the tradition-minded critics were predictably merciless. Irving Kolodin wrote in *The Saturday Review* that Gould's performance was "slow to the point of sluggishness," and Winthrop Sargeant of *The New Yorker* was even more harsh. "The pace, indeed, was such that all the work's stirring momentum was lost, and a kind of agony set in, similar to the feeling of impatience one experiences while riding in a delayed commuter train and counting off the interminable stops that separate one from one's goal." Paul Henry Lang wrote in the New York *Herald-Tribune* that he must "strenuously protest" because Bernstein had "violated elementary obligations of professional conduct" and because his disavowal of Gould was "an irresponsible act of high-handedness." But Lang's view of Gould was even more critical. "Mr. Gould is indeed a fine artist, unfortunately at present suffering from music hallucinations that make him unfit for public appearances. . . ."

Harold Schonberg, probably the most powerful critic in New York, was inspired to a ponderous attempt at humor. "Such goings-on at the New York Philharmonic concert yesterday afternoon!" his review in the *Times* began. "I tell you, Ossip, like you never saw. But maybe different from when we studied the Brahms D Minor Concerto at the Hohenzellern [sic] Academy." This Ossip, whom Schonberg kept addressing throughout the review in the tones of a Borscht Belt comic, was apprently meant to invoke Ossip Gabrilowitsch, a famous virtuoso who had often played the Brahms, but since Gabrilowitsch died in 1936, when Schonberg was twenty-one, it remained unclear what the fancied relationship between them was supposed to be, or what role Schonberg imagined himself to be playing, or what any of this *commedia dell'arte* had to do with Gould's

---

*The controversy over this performance never seems to die. Alan Rich, who never even heard the concert, wrote in *Keynote* in 1985 to take issue with Bernstein's public statement that the Gould version had required "well over an hour." With stopwatch in hand, Rich reported that Gould had taken only fifty-three minutes and fifty-one seconds, which was twenty-three seconds less than a recent recording by Krystian Zimmerman, for which Bernstein had felt no need to make a speech. Bernstein's angry defense against this clockwork is that Gould had played considerably faster at his second performance on Friday afternoon, the one that was taped and broadcast.

performance of the Brahms concerto. But Schonberg pressed relentlessly on. "So then the Gould boy comes on, and you know what,
Ossip? ... The Gould boy played the Brahms D Minor Concerto
slower than the way we used to practice it. (And between you, me,
and the corner lamppost, Ossip, maybe the reason he plays it so slow
is maybe his technique is not so good.)"

"Isn't that awful?" Bernstein observes when the twenty-five-year-
old review is quoted to him.

"Yes."

"How dare he? Really! That goes too far."

Schonberg's celebrated review was so malevolent—"that disgust-
ing and supercilious review," as Schuyler Chapin refers to it—that
one cannot help wondering about the origins of the critic's hostility.
Schonberg himself says that the only time he ever met Gould was at
a lunch organized by a Columbia publicist. "Debbie Ishlon thought
that life in the Western Hemisphere would not be complete until
Gould and I were brought together," the critic recalls. "We looked
at each other, and I won't say it was hate at first sight, but we certainly operated on different frames of reference. Now, I'm primarily
a nineteenth-century man, and you know what he thought of the
nineteenth century. So there were some stabs at conversation, and
his lip curled, especially when I—he was talking about concertos to
record, and I mumbled something about the Hummel A minor,
which I think is a masterpiece that leads straight to Chopin. He
broke into laughter. And the lunch went downhill from there. And
that was it."*

Q: And why Ossip?

A: What happened—I came back to the office, and I had plenty
of time, instead of my normal forty minutes, and I wrote a normal
review, and then I looked at it and said, "Oh, for God's sake," and
I threw the thing out and went for the Ossip review. That was all.

Q: But why Ossip?

A: I don't know, I thought the name was funny.

For Leonard Bernstein to take a serious artistic disagreement and
make a joking public disclaimer was bad enough, but for the senior

---

*In private, Gould liked to refer to Schonberg as Homer Sibelius, and he once wrote to
Diana Menuhin: "It is my unshakable conviction that anything Homer Sibelius can know
about on Monday, I can know about on Sunday."

music critic of the most important newspaper in the United States to review this performance with an elephantine version of Yiddish humor, and to say in the course of all this humor that one of the world's great keyboard technicians played the Brahms concerto so slowly because he didn't have the technical ability to play it properly—well, is it really so surprising that retirement from the concert stage came to seem more and more attractive? "He was *very*, very upset by that Harold Schonberg comment that suggested that maybe he couldn't play the Brahms, which was completely absurd," says Dr. Stephens, the Johns Hopkins psychiatrist. "It was so stupid, it really was a terrible thing to write, but he was very hurt by that, I mean more hurt than angered." This is not to suggest that Gould retired because he couldn't stand newspaper criticisms, only that the critics' inanities were yet another element among the many that made his life on the concert tour acutely unpleasant. "At live concerts I feel demeaned, like a vaudevillian," he said.

And the harassment went on and on. In Chicago later that month, the critic for the *American*, a Hearst paper that liked to print headlines in red ink, said of Gould's concert: "His appearance is careless and somehow disheveled. His clothes don't fit, his hair needs cutting and grooming, he appears to have his trouser pockets stuffed with grapefruits, and he walks like an impersonation of Henry Fonda impersonating the young Abe Lincoln. By being himself a parody, he is beyond parody. . . ." Donal Henahan of the *News* was a little better but not much: "Music's most successful hipster, Glenn Gould, finally slouched onto the Orchestra Hall stage after three cancellations. . . . Seating himself at the Ouija board on a sawed-off rickety relic of a chair that was held together with wires, the disheveled recitalist sang and stomped and conducted. . . ."

It was perhaps appropriate that Chicago was the site, two years later, of Gould's next-to-last public recital, on March 29, 1964, and that Henahan was one of those who reviewed the performance. It was Easter Sunday, and it snowed, and Henahan began by saying, "To point out at this late date that Glenn Gould plays extraordinary Bach is like saying that it sometimes snows on Easter Sunday, but in both cases the obvious still comes as a shock when it happens. For it is an elemental excitement that Gould's Bach exudes. . . . In the Bach of no other pianist today will you find the pulse of the

composer beating so powerfully. . . ." Gould played the Fourth Partita, and four fugues from *The Art of the Fugue* (and Beethoven's
Opus 110, and the Krenek Third Sonata). "For the record," Henahan concluded, "yes, the man did have the piano up on blocks; he
did sit on his wobbly chair; he did have a glass of water at the ready
(not used this time); he did sing intermittently; he did conduct with
whatever hand was not busy at the moment, and he did sit side-sad-
dle most of the time, knee almost to the floor. So all right if it makes
him happy."

There was only one last commitment, in Los Angeles, a fortnight
later, April 10, 1964. Gould played the same Bach he had played in
Chicago, but he substituted, as he often did, Hindemith's Third
Sonata for the Krenek and Beethoven's Opus 109 for Opus 110.
The *Herald-Examiner* found his Beethoven "the ultimate of poetry
and eloquence," but in the larger and more important *Times,* Dion
Winans wrote of the same piece that it was "a misfortune throughout . . . headlong . . . sentimental . . . hardly Beethoven to
remember."

None of them realized—possibly Gould did not realize it himself—that when he bowed and smiled and walked off the stage of
the Wilshire Ebell Theater in Los Angeles that April evening, he
was departing from the concert stage forever, at the age of thirty-
one. The waves of applause that bade him farewell would never be
heard again.

VI

The New Life

The first thing that Gould did after his retirement was to do nothing, or nothing professional. He spent a lot of time at the cottage on Lake Simcoe, still rather wintry in those lengthening days of early April. He had not yet figured out exactly how he wanted to spend the rest of his life. He wanted to write, to make radio and television shows, to lecture—to teach, in effect—but the details were vague. He had no master plan ready to be carried out. He wasn't even completely certain that he would never give another public concert.

"He did a lot of thinking," Jessie Greig recalls. "His mind was made up that there would be no more travel, that he would stay right here. He never said it in as many words, but it was quite evident in conversations that he had made up his mind that he was going to leave the stage and just be himself, you know. He felt that onstage he wasn't himself. He was someone else. I think that he was really deep in thought about it, but he knew where he was going. He was studying all the time. I went to the cottage once, and I can remember seeing the pile of books that he had to read. It was just an enormous amount."

Q: What were they? Can you remember some of the titles?

A: I really can't remember. I just remember the enormous pile of books. I think it covered everything.

When Gould felt a need for personal contact, he turned to the telephone. Unlike ordinary social intercourse, the telephone brought him immediately into contact with friends in New York or London or Berlin. The cost of long-distance calls was no obstacle— he willingly paid monthly bills of hundreds and hundreds of dollars—and so he developed a habit of spending long evening hours on the telephone, not just talking but reading aloud, singing, playing games.

And although Gould liked to wear old clothes and let his hair grow, his life in retirement was by no means ascetic. A listing of his possessions for an insurance company included not only two pianos and a Zao Wou-Ki painting that he valued at $4,500 but also "one four-seater Chesterfield . . . one small mahogany chest of drawers, two fruitwood tables, two lamp tables, one walnut and one mahogany, two lamp tables with marble base, one table lamp with gold leaf design," and so on. Also one Siemens diathermy unit and one ultrasonic therapy unit. He valued the whole array at $19,800, which, for a bachelor in 1962, was a not inconsiderable sum.

Gould emerged from his privacy that June to give a graduation address at the University of Toronto, and to receive an honorary degree as doctor of law. He did the same, in red robes, at the conservatory that November. "I am compelled to realize," he said to the graduates, perhaps referring to his own uncertainties, "that the separateness of our experience limits the usefulness of any practical advice that I could offer you. Indeed, if I could find one phrase that would sum up my wishes for you on this occasion, I think it would be devoted to convincing you of the futility of living too much by the advice of others." A reporter from the Toronto *Star* interviewed him after his address and quoted him as saying "that he's definitely giving up concert work 'after I finish the few obligations I still have left over. Nobody will believe me when I say it, but it's true.'"

His TV recital for the CBC that June may have been one of those "few obligations." He played once again some of his most familiar pieces, the Sweelinck fantasy, some of *The Goldberg Variations*, Beethoven's Opus 109, and the Berg Sonata. A reviewer in the *Globe and Mail* complained once again of his "mannerisms." It was clearly time for things to change. And yet because Gould had never officially announced his permanent retirement, only a reduction in commitments or a temporary "sabbatical," nobody took his absence too seriously. His manager, Walter Homburger, wrote to an official at Schirmer's in the fall of 1964 that Gould would perform the Schoenberg Concerto in Cincinnati the following January. Indeed, even a year later, Homburger was announcing that Gould would play the Schoenberg with the Baltimore Symphony in April of 1966. By this time, Gould was formally rejecting all such invitations. "I am afraid that I am not able to accept any engagements for next season," he wrote to Cincinnati. And to Newfoundland: "I am not able to accept any engagements for this coming season." And to Cleveland: "I am not by any means reneging on my promise to you that if I decide once again to give some concerts the Cleveland Symphony will certainly be among them, should you so desire, but my sabbatical is proving so productive in so many ways that I have not for the moment at least much intention of altering course."

The course was still not completely clear, though. Gould had already begun, for example, a sporadic and rather ill-conceived career as a lecturer (why should a man who does not want to play the piano in public want to read a lecture in public?). In February, a few months before his retirement, he had appeared at Hunter College in New York to talk about piano music, and particularly about Beethoven's Opus 109. It was not a very happy occasion. Gould began by leaning against his piano, announcing what he wanted to talk about in the first of two lectures and adding, "You may not see me next time." Raymond Ericson of the *Times* reported that Gould then "moved to the lectern and to the reading of his script. There he stayed, with occasional trips to the piano to illustrate a point, at which he might stay on the piano bench and continue reading. It was obvious that some listeners would have preferred to hear Mr. Gould make music and not talk. After he had played just a few measures early in the evening, he was greeted with prolonged applause. To this he merely shook his head, indicating that he was intent on giving his lecture.... Several persons walked out because they apparently had expected more music." Eric Salzman of the *Herald-Tribune* wrote even more sharply of the disparities between Gould and his listeners. "The large audience at Hunter College, which had obviously come to hear him play, were restless and bored ..." he reported. "Gould was talking about the whole subtle relationship of tonal and harmonic thinking to musical structure and expression in an age of rationality and revolution; it was brilliant, stimulating, informative and nearly totally lost on the audience.... One had the uneasy feeling that maybe five people in the audience were interested, alert and able to follow."

Gould tried this lecture again at the Gardner Museum in Boston two days later, and then began working on something quite different. When an admirer at the University of Cincinnati invited him to lecture there, he lectured on the works of Schoenberg. There are no surviving reports of bored listeners, and Gould must have been pleased when the University of Cincinnati published his lecture in book form in November of 1964, Gould's first, last, and only book. "Gould's view of Arnold Schoenberg is that he is much less revolutionist than inspired seer," said Arthur Darack, who had also written a foreword to the book, in the Cincinnati *Enquirer*, "a composer who pointed the way out of the dilemma of all artists who find themselves in a cul de sac imposed by the sterility of their times."

Gould liked writing, liked both the analytical and the hortatory aspects of the craft, and he liked the fact that a writer generally works alone, keeping his own pace, free to revise his creations again and again. Indeed, Gould periodically told interviewers that if he had not been a pianist, he would have been a writer, as though it were a simple matter of free choice. He had, in fact, been writing about his own performances from the beginning, and he would go on providing liner notes for his recordings until the end. The only Grammy he ever won during his entire life was for these liner notes. And in the rather specialized world of musical journals, Gould found the doors wide open to such periodicals as *High Fidelity* or *Musical America*. Robert Silverman, who paid him no money but published seventeen of Gould's articles in *The Piano Quarterly*, recalls the terms he offered: "I said to him at the beginning, 'You can write about anything you want. It doesn't have to be about music—anything you want to write, I'll publish. Carte blanche. No editing and there's no limit to the length.'

"The telephone calls were almost always in the same pattern," Silverman goes on. "He would call, and he would start off by saying, 'I've written the following, and I'd like to know if you like it.' And then he'd start, and he'd read the whole thing. He'd always tell me it was a draft, but I could not detect if there was anything different when I got the typed-up manuscript."

Q: And you had to accept it on the phone?

A: It didn't matter what he wrote—I was going to publish it. I took everything as a gift.

Yet the gap between Gould's piano-playing and his writing about that playing is a large one. It is the gap between an enormously gifted musician and an intelligent but rather inhibited literary amateur. Compare, for example, the enthusiastic brilliance of his performance of *The Goldberg Variations* with the affected pedantry of his commentary: "One hears so frequently of the bewilderment which the formal outline of this piece engenders among the uninitiated who become entangled in the luxuriant vegetation of the aria's family tree that it might be expedient to examine more closely the generative root in order to determine, with all delicacy, of course, its aptitude for parental responsibility."

That demonstrates not only Gould's weakness for pedantry but also those same faults that his schoolteachers had complained about, a prose style that attempted witty elegance but actually sounded mannered and artificial. Only occasionally does one catch glimpses of a slightly manic clown kept prisoner inside Gould's head. This alter ego made one of his first appearances in an article about the CBC written late in 1964 for *Musical America*. It appeared under the pseudonym of Herbert von Hochmeister (Gould's clowning was often ethnic, often Germanic), "the fine-arts critic of *The Great Slave Smelt*, perhaps the most respected journal north of latitude 70°." (Gould's clowning, somewhat mysteriously, often involved the Arctic.) "From beneath the High Victorian turrets of a folksy house in downtown Toronto, known affectionately—and nationally—as the Kremlin, a shrewd covey of white-collar conciliators devote themselves with dedicated anonymity to governing our cultural life. . . ." Perhaps inevitably, Gould's humor was not appreciated everywhere. He never forgave John Kraglund of the *Globe and Mail* for having once written that it was "as light and frothy as a tub of wet cement."

More interesting than this essay itself is Gould's subsequent analysis of his shift in identity. "I . . . was incapable of writing in a sustained humorous style until I developed an ability to portray myself pseudonymously . . ." he told Jonathan Cott about the creation of Herbert von Hochmeister of the Northwest Territories. "The reason for that metaphor was that Herbert could thereby survey the culture of North America from his exalted remove, and pontificate accordingly. The character was also vaguely based on Karajan. Von

Hochmeister was a retired conductor and was always spouting off about Germanic culture and things of that nature. At least that's how I got into the character. . . . Once I did that, I found it no problem at all to say what I wanted to say in a humorous style. Until then, there was a degree of inhibition that prevented me from doing so. But then the floodgates were open, and subsequently I developed a character for every season."

It all sounds very lighthearted, but these were rather uncertain times. "The last year has been quite awful for me," Gould confessed early in 1965 to Kitty Gvozdeva, who had the merit of living in faraway Leningrad. "I've written a great deal for one thing—many lectures and magazine articles of one kind or another, and my first book—a small one and on Schoenberg, so you won't approve! And it's given me the urge to publish more. The last year has also crystallized my feelings about travelling and concert giving. . . . I simply can't conceive of going back to that awful, transient life." And change seemed to bring a remarkable improvement in his somewhat fragile health. "Since I stopped giving concerts, I've scarcely had so much as a sniffle," he told one interviewer, Richard Kostelanetz. "Most of my earlier illnesses were psychosomatic—a sheer protest against my regimen."

At about this same time, Gould wrote to a friend in Berlin that he had just finished a ninety-minute radio documentary "about the recording industry and its effect upon the lives of modern man. It is a rather fascinating program, I think. [It was made] with interview material taken from conversations with a number of friends as well as a good deal of my own narration." A year later, Gould reorganized these views into an article featured in the fifteenth-anniversary issue of *High Fidelity* magazine. Entitled "The Prospects of Recording," it was one of the most interesting and important pieces he ever wrote.

Gould began this long essay, as he began many of his early writings, with a defense of his retirement from the stage. More specifically, he repeated an earlier prediction "that the public concert as we know it today would no longer exist a century hence, that its functions would have been entirely taken over by electronic media." This, he said, appeared to him "almost as self-evident truth," but it had been widely disputed, and so he wanted to elaborate on it. He recalled how brief the supposedly eternal tradition of the concert hall actually was, no more than about a hundred years, and he ridiculed almost every aspect of that tradition. Why, indeed, should it be necessary, with or without tuxedo, to trek through the snow at some fixed time to some cavernous hall to hear the same old repertoire played to an accompaniment of rustling and coughing? (Gould himself almost never went to concerts.) The only thing that kept the concert tradition alive, he argued, was the oligarchy of the music business, plus what Gould called "an endearing, if sometimes frustrating, human characteristic—a reluctance to accept the consequences of a new technology."

Recording in itself was hardly a very new technology. Thomas Alva Edison built and named his first phonograph in 1877, primarily as a dictating device, and so the machine preserved the voice of Gladstone and the piano-playing of Brahms. What was remarkable in the technology of recording was that it kept changing, radically, repeatedly devouring all its children. In 1888 came the shellac disk to replace Edison's waxed cylinder. Enter Caruso, Joachim, Grieg. In 1925 came the first electric records, which rotated at a standard 78 r.p.m. In 1948, Columbia introduced the LP, which turned at 33⅓ r.p.m., contained a whole Mozart symphony on one side instead of eight, and could not be broken. All 78 r.p.m. records had to be thrown away. At the same time, acetate and shellac began to be replaced in the 1940's by magnetic tape, which could be spliced to get rid of all mistakes.

In 1958 came another revolution, stereophonic sound from different speakers, which made all previous monaural recordings obsolete. In 1965, just as Gould was writing about the resistance to new technology, the tape cassette began to threaten the record itself. Now you could hear Beethoven not only in your own home but in your car, and, eventually, even while jogging through the park. In 1979, during Gould's last years, Decca introduced digital tapes, much clearer than anything before, and in 1983, after Gould's death, Sony and Philips brought forth the even clearer compact disk, yet another revolution, yet another devaluation of all previous recordings.

One of the most controversial aspects of this evolving technology was that splicing led to charges of trickery and even fraud. The classic case occurred when Elisabeth Schwarzkopf was hired to sing a high C that was secretly spliced into a Kirsten Flagstad recording of *Tristan*. But Gould was heartily in favor of what he called "creative cheating." In his article "Music and Technology," when Gould recalled how he had recorded a 1950 CBC performance of Mozart and Hindemith on a second-rate studio piano, he reveled in the accidental discovery "that if I gave [the acetate] a bass cut at a hundred cycles or thereabouts and a treble boost at approximately five thousand, the murky, unwieldy, bass-oriented studio piano could be magically transformed." Splicing and editing tapes, like altering pitch, enabled Gould to achieve combinations that he had hardly imagined while actually playing a piece. The goal of a recording, he believed, should be not historical authenticity but the highest possible quality.

Critics of such "creative cheating"—and there were and still are many—insist that there is a kind of mystical unity and power in an uninterrupted performance, particularly a live performance, that there is an arching melodic line that cannot be mechanically imitated. Gould had an answer to that too, which he entitled "The Grass Is Always Greener in the Outtakes: An Experiment in Listening." He began with a quotation from the enemy, specifically André Watts: "I can't help wishing that all recordings were live performances. . . . If this is totally unfeasible, then at least I'd like to know that there was no splicing within movements. . . . The whole intimidating idea of having all those guys around while you have to stop and ask for a retake . . . can be pretty terrible, especially if you have to start again and again. It can get you very uptight." Gould's answer was to explore the basic question: Can anybody really tell the difference?

With a weightiness worthy of Herbert von Hochmeister, Gould created a test panel from among his friends and acquaintances: six professional musicians, six audio experts, six "laymen." Half were men, half women. To all of these, he presented a tape of eight performances ranging from Byrd and Bach to Scriabin and Schoenberg, from a Gould solo to a George Szell performance of part of Beethoven's Fifth. Each panelist was asked to play the half-hour tape three times and then tell how many splices could be detected (they ranged from zero to thirty-four per piece). "That took a prodigious number of hours and hours and hours," says Steve Posen, Gould's attorney, who was one of the panelists, "first to prepare the material and then to sit with people as they went through it—hours and hours to come up with this information. He was infinitely patient when he got onto something." Gould was happy to report that nobody came even close to counting the splices correctly, and in elaborate breakdowns of the results, he was also happy to report that the professional musicians fared worst, and the "laymen" best. The two highest scores went to a male physician and a female librarian.

While Gould was trying so hard to demonstrate that the studio recording was artistically superior to the live concert, the great piano event of 1965, the year after Gould's retirement, was the return of Vladimir Horowitz to Carnegie Hall after an absence of twelve years. Columbia released a two-record album of "an historic return," and that inspired a wave of new recorded concerts, in which the coughs and clinkers were all treated as part of the atmospherics. This was, of course, a recording trend diametrically opposed to Gould's beliefs. His shift from the concert hall to the recording studio was not just a matter of personal convenience but of artistic conviction (if, indeed, the two can be separated). In contrast to all those who took pride in the possibilities of re-creating a live recital, Gould objected to what he called "the non-taketwoness" of the concert stage. A recording, he insisted, should be completely different from a recital, not simply reproducing a live performance but perfecting it, exploiting all the technical possibilities that could not even be attempted in the concert hall.

Gould was not, of course, entirely alone in these beliefs. As early as the 1930's, the English impresario and recording executive Walter Legge had committed himself to the basic proposition: "I wanted better results than are normally possible in public performance: I was determined to put onto disc the best that artists could do under the best possible conditions." Legge was not a believer in splicing, which was then just beginning to become possible; "the best possible conditions" meant to him primarily a studio where the artists could record take after take in the search for perfection. Far more Gouldian was John Culshaw (1924–1980), who produced for Decca between 1958 and 1964 the first complete recording of Wagner's *Ring* (conducted by Sir Georg Solti). Culshaw passionately believed that the coming of stereo made it possible to record operas that would sound quite different from theatrical performances. "It can bring opera to life in the home in a way that was quite unimaginable twenty years ago," he wrote in *Ring Resounding*. "The effect is nothing like that of the opera house, for several reasons. The listener at home is not a member of a community, and whether he admits it or not his reactions in private are not the same as his reactions in public. . . . The sound of a good stereo recording . . . will tend to engulf the listener, and may draw him psychologically closer to the characters of the opera than when he is in the theater. The sense of being inside the drama is heightened by the absence of a visual element. . . . Instead of watching someone else's production, he is unconsciously creating his own."

Andrew Porter, reviewing Culshaw's version of *Das Rheingold*, captured the idea perfectly. "Listening to these records is not like going to the opera house without looking at the stage," he wrote in *The Gramophone*. "In some mysterious way they seem to catch you up in the work . . . more intimately than that." Opera conductors and singers do not greatly appreciate having their physical appearance be made secondary to the positioning of microphones, but Culshaw affected to scorn all such objections. "As a rule," he wrote, "artists today understand that the actual techniques of recording are best left to those who understand them."

Gould, of course, was one of those who understood them completely, and his mastery of recording technology gave him something that was psychologically very important to him: total control over his own musical performances. But to return to "The Prospects of Recording," Gould wanted to demonstrate not that miking and splicing could provide technical benefits to him but that recording had changed the whole nature of music. Purely in terms of the music played, the enormous broadening of the available repertoire— specifically the popularity of early music—occurred entirely after World War II and as a direct result of the LP record. Composers like Vivaldi and Telemann, not to mention Josquin or Machaut, rather suddenly became once again part of the culture.

No less significant was the change in the way music was performed, and thus heard and understood. Because the musicians no longer had to fill large spaces with sound, the whole process of making music began to put more emphasis on clarity of tone, and particularly clarity of polyphony. Chamber music flourished. Old instruments came back to life. Though Gould resisted that last tendency, insisting that Bach could be played on any instrument, that it was part of Bach's genius to ignore the special characteristics of various instruments, he nonetheless insisted on playing pianos that were dry and clear and light-toned. So the sound of a Horowitz playing a Rachmaninoff concerto by now sounds to the contemporary listener almost as deliciously old-fashioned as Stokowski's lush sonorities in Bach.

"One of the first musicians to grasp the significance of recording to the composing process," Gould said, "was Arnold Schoenberg, who ... remarked: 'In radio broadcasting, a small number of sonic entities suffice for the expression of all artistic thoughts; the gramophone and the various mechanical instruments are evolving such clear sonorities that one will be able to write much less heavily instrumented pieces for them.' Intentionally or not, the development of Schoenberg's own style demonstrates his understanding of the medium and its implications. . . ." This evolution became all the more clear when Schoenberg's works were performed by musicians who really understood and appreciated them, specifically not just Gould but also Robert Craft, with whom Gould had recorded the Schoenberg Piano Concerto back in 1961.

"For Craft, the stopwatch and the tape splice are tools of his trade," Gould said, "as well as objects of that inspiration for which an earlier generation of stick wielders found an outlet in the opera cape and temper tantrums." Gould compared Craft's recording of Schoenberg's *Pelleas und Melisande* with the "glowingly romantic" account of the same score by an older German conductor, Winfried Zillig. "Craft applies a sculptor's chisel to these vast orchestral complexes of the youthful Schoenberg," Gould wrote admiringly, "and gives them a determined series of plateaus on which to operate—a very baroque thing to do. He seems to feel that his audience—sitting at home, close up to the speaker—is prepared to allow him to dissect this music and to present it to them from a strongly biased conceptual viewpoint, which the private and concentrated circumstances of their listening make feasible. . . . We must be prepared to accept the fact that, for better or for worse, recording will forever alter our notions about what is appropriate to the performance of music."

One of the strangest aspects of technology is not only that it creates new processes but that it cancels—or makes possible the cancellation—of widely accepted older processes. The computer revolution supersedes the industrial revolution, making obsolete all that centralization and standardization that led to the assembly line; the computer can just as easily make a suit or an automobile to "customized" individual measurements as to uniform measurements, and so farewell to Blake's dark Satanic mills. Gould's theories of technology similarly implied a reversal of a musical tradition that dated all the way back to the Renaissance. It was then, according to Gould's historical vision, that Western music took a radically wrong turn, toward specialization. All the milestones that are usually treated in musical-history classes as cultural triumphs—the arrival of the professional composer like Haydn or Mozart, the professional orchestra like that of the Esterhazys, the professional piano virtuoso, the professional conductor whose musical performance consists of waving a baton—all these impressed Gould as steps downhill toward the large and competitive musical marketplace of today. Impresarios send vainglorious virtuosos out on tour, star conductors jet from one guest appearance to another, composers remain largely ignored, and the audience consists of thousands of automatons assembled in uncomfortable culture palaces.

What had been lost in the Renaissance—which also created, along with a lot of great art, the capitalist system that thereafter bought and sold art—was the tradition of artistic community. Just as the great Gothic cathedrals had been largely built by anonymous designers and volunteer labor, music in the precapitalist age was an art in which composers, performers, and listeners were all more or less the same. Whether it was a case of a market crowd listening to a street band or a king singing his own songs—is it conceivable to imagine any president of the United States performing in public, like King Frederick II of Prussia, a flute concerto of his own composition?—music had once been a shared and communal activity, not a spectacle provided by a hired specialist.

Gould's visions of this pre-eighteenth-century Utopia may have been quite unrealistic, but the interesting thing is that Gould believed it could all be re-created by the wonders of recording technology. Some of this was already happening. New composers like

Boulez and Stockhausen had long since introduced taped sounds into the concert hall, and now they were playing their own compositions on synthesizers. Gould was particularly impressed by a fad recording of 1968, *Switched-on Bach,* in which a gifted amateur musician named Walter Carlos bleeped and pinged his way through various Bach selections on a Moog synthesizer. Gould called it "the record of the year (no, let's go all the way—the decade!)." He went further and organized a CBC radio show in which he combined selections from *Switched-on Bach* and interviews with Carlos and a Canadian visionary, Jean Le Moyne. Carlos, in a high-pitched voice that heralded his coming transformation into Wendy Carlos, rattled on about the technical details of his synthesizer: "The keyboards don't generate sounds—they're nothing but voltage sources. . . . So that C might be three volts, and the C above that might be four volts and D is four volts plus one twelfth of four volts. . . ." Le Moyne went on to hymn the glories of technology. "Machines in themselves are good," he declared, and even "the much-maligned mills of the Victorian era . . . have clothed more men . . . than all the charity of all the kings and all the lords and all the saints of humanity." Indeed, Le Moyne seemed to believe that machines had replaced saints as mediators between God and man. "What the machine teaches us," he said, "is a kind of . . . commentary on that passage of Saint Paul to the Philippians when he said about Christ that he did not hold himself jealous of the rank that equaled him to God, but he went down and became man and became obedient. . . . And in that way, I think there is a kind of Christification going on in the machine world, in technology. . . ."

Gould himself was hardly less visionary. The culmination of this technological revolution in music, he believed, would be the liberation of the listener, or rather the transformation of the listener from a passive into an active participant. "Dial twiddling is in its limited way an interpretive act," he wrote in "The Prospects of Recording." "Forty years ago the listener had the option of flicking a switch marked 'on' and 'off' and, with an up-to-date machine, perhaps modulating the volume just a bit. Today, the variety of controls made available to him requires analytical judgment. And these controls are but primitive, regulatory devices compared to those participational possibilities which the listener will enjoy once current laboratory techniques have been appropriated by home playback devices."

The highest delight, in Gould's view, would come when this "new kind of listener" could reedit all the tapes in his vast collection. "Let us say, for example, that you enjoy Bruno Walter's performance of the exposition and recapitulation from the first movement of Beethoven's Fifth Symphony but incline toward Klemperer's handling of the development section, which employs a notably divergent tempo. . . . With the pitch-speed correlation held in abeyance, you could snip out these measures from the Klemperer edition and splice them into the Walter performance without having the splice procedure either an alteration of tempo or a fluctuation of pitch. . . ."

It is probably inevitable that any vision of paradise shows primarily what the visionary wishes for himself; he tacitly assumes that everyone else would like the same. Brünhilde promises to the warrior Siegmund a Valhalla where "dead heroes in a splendid body will embrace you kindly and welcome you solemnly." T. S. Eliot, on the other hand, predicts that the hippopotamus will eventually take his place among the saints, "performing on a harp of gold," washed as white as snow and "by all the martyred virgins kist." So Gould dreamed of a day when the music lover might return home from a hard day at the office and proceed forthwith to his Gouldian studio to spend his evening splicing tapes. "The listener," said Gould, "can ultimately become his own composer."

Gould was spinning out this fantasy during a BBC television interview with Humphrey Burton in 1966 when Burton interrupted with a fundamental objection. He said he had no desire whatever to hear a self-created pastiche of Walter and Klemperer, he wanted to hear Klemperer's Beethoven exactly as Klemperer chose to play it. But when it was possible to buy and edit ten different versions of a Beethoven sonata, Gould insisted, Burton *should* want to. To another interviewer, Richard Kostelanetz, Gould imagined all ten versions emerging from one of his own recording sessions. "I'd love to issue a kit of variant performances and let the listener assemble his own performance," he said. And so Gould went right on preaching and proselytizing for the technological paradise that lay just beyond the horizon.

Not long after the Burton encounter, Gould was conducting a radio interview with Leopold Stokowski, whom he revered partly because of his pioneering broadcasts and recordings of the 1930's, when he misguidedly referred to the fashionable theories of Marshall McLuhan. What did Stokowski think, Gould inquired, about Professor McLuhan's view that we were nearing a time when there would be no need for any professional performers, only the creators, the consumers, and the computers? This was seven years after *The Gutenberg Galaxy* and five years after *Understanding Media*, and various experts had exhausted themselves in debating the significance of "hot" and "cold" media in "the universal village." It is hard to believe that Stokowski wasn't fully aware of this, but he answered Gould's question by calmly saying, "Who is Professor McLuhan?"

When Gould informed him, Stokowski dismissed the theorist with a lordly declaration that "he has a right to his opinion." Later on, though, when he grandly acknowledged uncertainty on some point, he added another jab. "I don't know," he said, "but I doubt if Professor—what is his name? McLuhan?—knows either."

It is easy enough now to observe that Gould's prophecies about the end of the concert have not come true—any more than the appearance of the new listener in his secluded electronic studio—and the conservatories still turn out virtuosos ready to don their tuxedoes and fly to Omaha for yet another *Emperor Concerto*. Remember, though, that Gould's prophecies applied not to the present but to the coming century. And although a Brendel or Barenboim can still fill Carnegie Hall with the familiar fans listening to the familiar pieces—"We have been, let us say, to hear the latest Pole/," as Eliot wearily wrote, "Transmit the Preludes. . . ."—we also hear cries of alarm about the declining interest in such things. "Pianists . . . are thus even more susceptible than others to certain market considerations . . ." said one such threnody in the New York *Times* late in 1987. "Pressures from managers and presenters, especially outside of New York, dictate that standard fare is essential to attract what seems to be an ever-dwindling audience for piano recitals. . . ."

While the subsidized conservatories still feed the subsidized concert machine—and what could be more unreal than the process of young black singers being elaborately trained to sing German or Italian in an art form to which virtually no major new works have been added in nearly half a century?—much of Gould's philosophy is now taken for granted in the admittedly simpler recording of popular music. It goes without saying that the best and most successful pop singers write their own material, sing their own creations, and it took the Beatles very little time to evolve from pink-cheeked guitar strummers into the technicians who created the synthetic sounds of *Sergeant Pepper's Lonely Hearts Club Band* inside their electronic laboratory. Evan Eisenberg, who has explored what he calls the phonography of both classical and popular music, has even written in *The Recording Angel* that Gould "as a classical pianist . . . could not construct records as ambitiously as people like . . . Phil Spector and Frank Zappa could." On the basic point, though, Eisenberg suggests a very Gouldian conclusion: "History may conclude that Gould was the one sane musician of the century; and his colleagues who work the continents like traveling salesmen, unpacking their hearts from Altoona to Vancouver, may seem as pathetic to our grandchildren as the bowing and scraping geniuses of the eighteenth century seem to us."

Such judgments may seem to imply that Gould believed not only in art for art's sake but in the coronation of art's sake over everything else, that Gould believed art to represent the highest good, the godhead of its own religion. In fact, he believed quite the opposite. He might well have read with sympathy Plato's arguments on why Homer should be censored for the sake of public virtue in the Utopian Republic, or how the sensuous sound of flutes should be forbidden, except to shepherds, or how even subversive harmonies should be outlawed. "Which are the harmonies expressive of sorrow . . . ?" Socrates asks. "The harmonies which you mean are the mixed or tenor Lydian, and the full-toned or bass Lydian, and such like," says Glaucon. "These, then, I said, must be banished. . . ."

Gould might well have listened just as sympathetically to the outcries of Pozdnuishef, the tormented hero of Tolstoy's *The Kreutzer Sonata*, who was driven to frenzies of jealousy by hearing his wife perform Beethoven's violin sonata with another man. "That sonata is a terrible thing," he says. "And especially that movement. And music in general is a terrible thing. . . . They say music has the effect of elevating the soul—rubbish! falsehood! . . . Its effect is neither to elevate nor to degrade, but to excite. . . . It transports me into another state ... under the influence of music it seems to me that I feel what I do not really feel, that I understand what I do not really understand, that I can do what I can't do. ..."

Perhaps Gould might have sympathized even with the angry reflections of Lenin on Beethoven. "I don't know of anything greater than the Appassionata," as Tom Stoppard quotes Lenin in his recounting of the famous scene in *Travesties*. "Amazing, super-human music. It always makes me feel, perhaps naïvely, it makes me feel proud of the miracles that human beings can perform. But I can't listen to music often. It affects my nerves, makes me want to say nice stupid things and pat the heads of those people who while living in this vile hell can create such beauty. Nowadays ... we've got to *hit* heads, hit them without mercy. ..."

In all these quotations, music appears not as purely something of beauty—of a beauty that serves as an end in itself—but rather as something essentially false, something that falsifies the truth as it seduces the true believer. The church had good reasons for forbidding any counterpoint or other artistic complications in the musical settings of its liturgy. Gould's private cosmology remains uncertain, for he had long since left behind the devout Presbyterianism of his parents, but he continued searching after some kind of spiritual truth. He read a great deal of theology, Kierkegaard and Tillich, late at night. He explored the outer edges of spiritualism, astrology, mind reading, prophecies. One aspect of his childhood Presbyterianism that remained extremely strong was his yearning for virtue, to do good, to be good. He repeatedly referred to himself by the title of George Santayana's sole novel, *The Last Puritan*. His ethical system remained as undefined and unformulated as his cosmology, but it seems to have been based on a rigidly controlled code of behavior, a code that prescribed isolation from others. To thine own self be true.

All of Western society has been organized on a completely different basis, however, on the basis of relationships with other people, at best love and communion, but in everyday life competition and commerce. In one of his most forthright and striking statements, Gould once declared in an interview: "I happen to believe that competition rather than money is the root of all evil." He had undeniably known and thrived on competition since his childhood, from the days when he won the Kiwanis piano competition for ten dollars, when he won the highest marks ever scored in earning his diploma at the conservatory, when he concentrated fiercely on defeating his elders and betters on the croquet field, but as he looked back across that world from which he had done his best to retire, the competitive instinct struck him as destructive, sterile, evil. And since he was an artist, he expressed that moral judgment in terms of art, and vice versa. "To rephrase the fashionable cliche," he wrote in "Glenn Gould Interviews Glenn Gould about Glenn Gould," "I do try as best I can to make only moral judgments and not esthetic ones. . . ."

That dictum sent Gould spiraling off (he was interviewing himself, after all) into an increasingly bizarre series of declarations of belief. Starting with the statement that all houses should be painted battleship gray, because "it's my favorite color," he proclaimed that anyone who wanted to paint his house red should be prevented from doing so, not only for aesthetic reasons but because such a change "would . . . foreshadow an outbreak of manic activity," and ultimately, "a climate of competition and, as a corollary, of violence." Interrogator Gould protested that this represented "a type of censorship that contradicts the whole post-Renaissance tradition of Western thought." Gould easily retorted that "it's the post-Renaissance tradition that has brought the western world to the brink of destruction." Or as he put it in a much later interview with Tim Page, "I would like to see a world where nobody cared what anybody else was doing."

The ultimate goal of art, Gould believed, was "the gradual, lifelong construction of a state of wonder and serenity." More immediately, its purpose was "essentially therapeutic and remedial." As for all its competitive forms, its concerts, shows, exhibitions, prizes, applauding audiences, all of that, those were simply flowerings from the root of all evil. "I feel that art should be given a chance to phase itself out," Gould finally said to himself in his self-interview. "I think that we must accept the fact that art is not inevitably benign, that it is potentially destructive. We should analyze the areas where it tends to do least harm, use them as a guideline, and build into art a component that will enable it to preside over its own obsolescence. . . ."

Earlier in this interview, Gould had seemed to startle his interviewer by proclaiming that one of his ambitions in life was "to try my hand at being a prisoner ... on the understanding, of course, that I would be entirely innocent of all charges brought against me. ..." Now it only remained for the interviewer to suggest that Gould should return to the drafty Salzburg Festspielhaus and give another concert there, so that he could once again catch a virus that would bring him the martyrdom he so clearly sought. "There could be no more meaningful manner in which to scourge the flesh," said Interviewer Gould, "and certainly no more meaningful metaphoric mise en scene against which to offset your own hermetic life-style, through which to define your quest for martyrdom autobiographically, as I'm sure you will try to do, eventually."

"But ... I have no such quest in mind," Gould protested.

"Then and only then," said the interviewer, "will you achieve the martyr's end you so obviously desire. ..."

VII

The Classical Records

It was not at all certain that an unseen pianist could earn a living from nothing but recordings. Virtually nobody had ever done it before. But Gould was determined to make the attempt, and Columbia, though it regretted the loss of concert publicity, was ready to back him up. "We used to talk about it a lot, about his hatred of the stage," says Schuyler Chapin, the head of Columbia's classical music department. "Because he wanted reassurance that his retirement from the stage was not retirement from the piano. And his records had sold pretty well. There was no question about the fact that the company was anxious to keep him."

Q: But he did take a big drop in pay, didn't he, when he first retired?

A: Yes. But he had saved his money, made a good start.

Gould also enjoyed proving the skeptics wrong. Walter Homburger had strongly advised him not to leave the stage, says John Beckwith. "Homburger said, 'That's a very risky thing to do, the public forgets about you, and you can't pick it up again—be careful.' And the next five or six years, Glenn would phone him every year and say, 'Walter, I just got my check from Columbia. Guess.' And Walter would guess, and it was always ten thousand dollars higher than Walter guessed."

Since Columbia gave Gould a very free hand in choosing what he wanted to record, he happily chose large quantities of Schoenberg. In 1964 alone, the year of his retirement from the stage, he recorded the *Phantasy* for violin and piano (with Israel Baker), the Suite for Piano, Opus 25, and two groups of songs, Opus 2 and 3 (sung by

Ellen Faull, soprano; Helen Vanni, mezzo-soprano; Donald Gramm, bass-baritone). The following year, he added four sets of piano pieces, Opus 11, 19, 23, and 33, *The Book of the Hanging Gardens* (Helen Vanni), and the *Ode to Napoleon Bonaparte*, (with John Horton as speaker and the Juilliard Quartet). Under the benign reign of Goddard Lieberson, who was then president of Columbia Records, the company felt a now-forgotten obligation to record major contemporary composers even if their works did not bring large profits. Lieberson committed Columbia to Stravinsky's authoritative performances of everything he wrote, so he felt no qualms about encouraging Gould in his passion for Schoenberg.

Most of Gould's labors during the later 1960's, however, were devoted to the fundamentals of the classical repertoire. He had already recorded the Beethoven First Concerto with Golschmann, and the next three with Bernstein; his performance of the *Emperor* with Stokowski would complete that cycle in 1966. Having miscalculated in his distorted early reading of the last three Beethoven sonatas, he now turned back and began a fairly systematic recording of the more congenial early sonatas, the three of Opus 10 in 1964, the two of Opus 14 and the *Pathétique* in 1966. And the following year, he began the ambitious and somewhat ambiguous project of recording all the Mozart sonatas.

The bedrock of Gould's career, though, was his unique mastery of Bach. He played Bach unlike anyone else, and he probably understood Bach better than anyone else. After the spectacular recording of *The Goldberg Variations*, his hardly less spectacular performance of the fifth and sixth partitas implied that he would record them all, which he completed in 1963. His admirable readings of the concerti in D minor (with Bernstein in 1957) and F minor (with Golschmann in 1958) implied that he would record all the concerti too, which he finished in 1969. Not all of these implications were inevitably fulfilled. He had often performed excerpts from *The Art of the Fugue* in his concerts, and he began recording this work on the organ in 1969, but although his splendid album of the first nine fugues cried out to be completed, Gould inexplicably left the project unfinished.

The main implication, though, was that Gould was planning to become the first pianist ever to record the complete keyboard works of Bach, and that inevitably brought him face to face with what Robert Schumann had called "this work of works," *The Well-Tempered Clavier*. Gould seems to have been a little hesitant, possibly even a little overawed. He had learned all the twenty-four preludes and fugues of Book I under the aegis of his mother before he was ten years old, and Alberto Guerrero must have devoted many of their hours together to the wonders and mysteries of Book II. Yet Gould almost never played any of these marvelous pieces on the concert stage. And it is remarkable that although he loved to indulge himself in both pedantries and parodies in the liner notes to his recordings, he left the liner notes for Bach's masterpiece to someone else.

To write about *The Well-Tempered Clavier* is indeed difficult. "The fact that the work today has become common property may console us for the other fact that an analysis of it is almost as impossible as it is to depict a wood by enumerating the trees and describing their appearance," Albert Schweitzer wrote back in 1905 in his rather quirky biography of Bach. Unlike Gould, though, Schweitzer had no qualms about undertaking the impossible. "We can only repeat again and again—take them and play them and penetrate into this world for yourself," he wrote. "Aesthetic elucidation of any kind must necessarily be superficial here. What so fascinates us in the work is not the form or the build of the piece, but the world-view that is mirrored in it. It is not so much that we enjoy the *Well-Tempered Clavichord* [sic] as that we are edified by it. Joy, sorrow, tears, lamentation, laughter—to all these it gives voice, but in such a way that we are transported from the world of unrest to a world of peace, and see reality in a new way, as if we were sitting by a mountain lake and contemplating hills and woods and clouds in the tranquil and fathomless water." Perhaps this is just the transcendental style of the period—Thomas Mann wrote similarly about Wagner—but there seems to be something in Bach that inspires the Germanic soul to ululate. "I said to myself," Goethe wrote after hearing some of Bach's organ works, "it is as if the eternal harmony were conversing within itself, as it may have done in the bosom of God just before the Creation of the world. . . ."

Gould was not like that. He did write a preface for a new Peters edition of *The Well-Tempered Clavier*, but it was, as might be expected, restrained, respectful, even reticent. He wrote mainly about the fugues, often citing examples not from *The Well-Tempered*

Clavier but from *The Art of the Fugue*. And he was technical to the point of scholasticism: "The very first fugue of volume one, for example, tolerates only the most modest of modulations and in its stretto-ridden way resourcefully characterizes the fugue subject itself—a bland diatonic model of academic primness. Other fugues, like that in E Major from Book II, exhibit the same sort of modulatory disinclination and here so tenacious is Bach's loyalty to his six-note theme, and so diffident the modulatory program through which he reveals it to us, one has the impression that the intense and fervently anti-chromatic ghost of Heinrich Schütz rides again. . . ." Or consider this: "He sets forth his material in many different harmonic guises and spot-lights some structural phenomena latent within it at each of the major modulatory turning-points. Thus, when he dissolves into the mediant and establishes his theme for the first time in a major key (D flat) a canonic duet ensues between the theme itself, now ensconced in the soprano part and, one beat delayed and two octaves plus one note lowered, an imitation in the bass. For this episode the chromatic counter-theme temporarily vacates the scene and in its stead, subsidiary voices append their own quasi-canonic comments. . . ." And so on.

Gould's recordings of *The Well-Tempered Clavier*, begun shortly before his retirement, are similarly idiosyncratic. Some of the preludes and fugues are quite miraculous—those in both C-sharp major and C-sharp minor, for example, sound tense and energetic and full of feeling. Some others are interesting but distinctly peculiar. Gould believed, for example, that the lyricism of the famous C major Prelude was "just prosaically prefatory," and that he could enliven the piece by playing the flowing figure in the right hand partly staccato. He seems to have thought too that he could improve the Prelude in F-sharp major by playing it at half speed, and the Fugue in A flat by playing it at double speed. Bach allowed him much more latitude than other composers, of course, for he rarely specified how fast he wanted his music played, or how loud or soft, or even on what instrument. Then there were other pieces that Gould simply played rather dutifully, as though they had to be included just to make the work complete. Let it be remembered, though, that Gould being peculiar or even just dutiful generally meant piano-playing at a level that virtually nobody else could approach.

Some critics rebelled at the eccentricities in this new version of *The Well-Tempered Clavier.* "A resounding 'nuts!' to Gould," said an unsigned review of the first album in the Washington *Post.* "He has tampered with the tone of the piano, and with Bach's phrasing, producing a caricature in many cases, and rarely offering insights of value. The tone is unpleasant, the performances a constant irritation." B. H. Haggin of *The New Republic* sounded almost equally fretful. "Admirer though I am of Gould's playing," he wrote, "I find that the carefully thought-out peculiarities of touch and phrasing in some of the performances . . . make it impossible for me to go along with them as convincing and acceptable statements of the pieces."

Most critics were far more approving. "Few pianists match Gould in the discipline, sharp focus and scrupulous artistry he brings to Bach," said the Minneapolis *Tribune.* "Played in compelling style, with a rhythmic flexibility that maintains the tension in each complex work," said the Philadelphia *Inquirer.* "One can hardly wait for the rest of the series," said the Detroit *Free Press.* And in *The Saturday Review,* Irving Kolodin offered his magisterial endorsement: "This introduction is as stimulating to the attention as it is unconventional to the ear. One thing is certain: at his most forthright and unsentimental, Gould is nevertheless deeply involved with the music's meaning as he conceives it; passionately pursuing the ebb and flow of thought wherever it may lead. . . ."

In contrast to the concert hall, where only one star performer is out onstage alone under the spotlights, the recording studio is a somewhat more collaborative scene. The pressure is still there. "Gould is tense and anxious at recording sessions—sometimes desperately so, and much more than he was when he played concerts," according to Geoffrey Payzant. But the pianist shares the arena with engineers and technicians. The chief of these, throughout most of Gould's long recording career, was Andrew Kazdin, a heavyset and thickly bearded man who had the unusual credentials of both a music degree from the New England Conservatory and an engineering degree from the Massachusetts Institute of Technology. He was two years younger than Gould, but he also had a remarkable authority and a mastery of detail, and in the year of Gould's retirement from the stage, Columbia hired Kazdin, not yet thirty, to help produce records.

By some accounts, Kazdin could be a stern taskmaster. Helen Epstein's *Music Talks,* for example, contained a scene in which the highly gifted Ruth Laredo spent four and a half hours making forty takes and inserts for Rachmaninoff's thirty-minute *Variations on a Theme by Chopin.* "I'm not sure we're covered on the first bar of the seventh variation," Kazdin said at one point. "I'm certain," Mrs. Laredo answered wearily. "I'm not. Maybe we should hear it," Kazdin repeated. "Look—I'm sure I didn't play any wrong notes," Mrs. Laredo protested. "I'm not talking about wrong notes," Kazdin insisted, "I'm talking about notes that didn't speak. Can we do it again?"

It is hard to imagine Gould accepting that much direction, and Kazdin makes no attempt to imagine it. "Two different cases," he says. "As record producers you have to be in a kind of communion and fit yourself to the artist you're going to work with in the way that will allow that artist to function—you know, the freest, the most comfortably—in what the artist has to do, which is to record an interpretation that is faithful to the artist's conception."

At the same time, though, Kazdin feels that "it's always the responsibility of the producer to try to at least point out technical flaws, and hopefully get them fixed. There have been rare instances where an artist will refuse to fix it. I haven't been so afflicted, but I've seen it in recording sessions. . . . When it came to wrong notes, nobody needed to tell Gould, because the way we recorded was such that he had a chance to listen to everything right on the spot. . . . Occasionally, I do remember— He almost always played from memory, and occasionally he memorized something wrong. Sometimes it was very insignificant, a question of whether there was supposed to be a little *Pause* or not. When I saw that happen, I would always— I figured it was my responsibility at least to mention it once."

Q: You were following with the score then?

A: Oh, *yes.* Oh, *yes.* That question means that as soon as I finish this sentence, I'm going to have to tell you a whole lot of stuff. So if I saw that he was doing something that *may* have been an oversight, you just stated, you know, "Are you aware that my score"— you put it as tactfully as possible—"my score has a *Pause* in bar 42?" And then you could have two kinds of answers: "Yes, I know, but it doesn't make any sense to me, so I'm going—" Fine. Or, "It *does?*" And then that kind of answer yields part A and part B. "My gosh, so it does. Doesn't make sense, so I won't do it." Or, "Oh, my gosh, I never saw that. Sure, I'll start doing it." So you feel the responsibility of at least mentioning it. But from an interpretive point of view, it was your life's blood not to mention anything.

Q: You never would say, "I don't think that's right"?

A: No. That's the way to make that your last session. You could feel it through the soles of your feet—that you just didn't tell him how to play the piece. . . . That's suicide.

Fundamental, says Kazdin, is the score itself. Not only the pianist but also the producer must have studied it, analyzed it, annotated it. It carries notes not just on how a piece should be played but where technical mistakes have occurred, where engineering changes have been made, where future splices should come. "The score becomes the bible of that particular record," Kazdin says. "It becomes, like *the* one document."

After the recording sessions comes the elaborate process of editing, splicing, and mixing. Some musicians leave that part mostly or entirely to the producer. Gould did it all himself. "Gould was the only one who could choose his own takes," Kazdin says. "We supplied him with copies of everything that had taken place, but he was the only one who was able to—because only in his head could reside— You see, the splicing with Gould wasn't just to eliminate wrong notes or fix fluffs of any sort. It also very often was the way that the profile of the piece was established. I mean, the interpretation of the piece emerged sometimes only in the juxtaposition of various takes. This was only in his head. Nobody could second-guess that. So what would happen is, we'd supply him with copies of everything that took place in the recording session, which he would hopefully file away (or sometimes lose). Because the record wasn't always issued with any kind of close proximity to the recording sessions themselves—it could be a matter of years. And he preferred to let years pass. In other words, if the choice was, edit it now and then put it away and wait, or put it away now and then edit it when CBS says they want to release it, he preferred the latter. He felt it gave him perspective, you know. He was too close to it sometimes. Later, he could see more what he wanted to do with a piece, or what he had in fact done with the piece at the recording sessions. So when it came time, he would exhume those tapes, listen to them, put whatever hours into them—and this is rather rare among artists. Few of them go to the trouble he went to."

Gould himself once offered a striking example of how he edited his tapes, not to correct mistakes but to create a completely new version of what he had recorded. The piece in question was the monumental Fugue in A minor from Book I of *The Well-Tempered Clavier*. It was "a contrapuntal obstacle course . . ." Gould recalled in "The Prospects of Recording," "even more difficult to realize on the piano than are most of Bach's fugues, because it consists of four intense voices that determinedly occupy a register in the center octaves of the keyboard—the area of the instrument in which truly independent voice leading is most difficult to establish." Gould recorded eight different versions of this fugue at one session in 1965, then decided that takes 6 and 8 (both made without any breaks or splices) were the best, and about equally good. Then he decided to wait for several weeks before trying to decide between them. When he came to make that decision, he discovered a surprising new element. "It became apparent that both had a defect of which we had been quite unaware in the studio: both were monotonous."

Both versions of this fugue had been played at the same speed (which, let it be noted, was considerably too fast) but in very different styles. "Take 6," Gould wrote, "had treated it in a solemn, legato, rather pompous fashion, while in take 8 the fugue subject was shaped in a prevailingly staccato manner which led to a general impression of skittishness." Without saying who actually made the final decision—one can guess—Gould reported that "it was agreed that neither the Teutonic severity of take 6 nor the unwarranted jubilation of take 8 could be permitted to represent our best thoughts on this fugue," and that "someone noted" that both versions were the same speed, and so "it was decided" to combine them.

The final version begins with the Teutonic severity of take 6, but at the end of the exposition, "the more effervescent character of take 8 was a welcome relief in the episodic modulation with which the center portion of the fugue is concerned." Gould then cut back to the solemnities of take 6 for the recapitulation and conclusion. And he was very proud of all this, not only what had been done but the way it had been done. "What had been achieved," he wrote, "was a performance of this particular fugue far superior to anything that we could at the time have done in the studio. . . . By taking advantage of the post-taping afterthought . . . one can very often transcend the limitations that performance imposes upon the imagination."

This decision sounds as though it had been made rather easily in some conference, dominated by Gould, but much of Kazdin's work with his star performer was more complicated than that. "With him being a resident of Toronto and me being a resident of New York," Kazdin recalls, "we operated on the telephone. I would have my score, he would have his score, and he could read me what he wanted. Splice—"

Q: Like "splice at bar 42"?

A: Sometimes more than that. Something on the fourth 16th of bar 32, on the E flat, we change from take 3 to insert 4 in take 2. And I would duplicate in my score what he had painstakingly worked out in his score. Then I would do the work, and then I would play it to him. I worked out a way of playing him the tapes on the telephone. I made a direct connection on my end, which bypassed the weakest link, which is the microphone. The earphone actually isn't too bad. Certainly there were niceties about the sound that could not be detected this way, but who cared—he *knew* what the tapes sounded like, so we'd go on making improvements, and then he'd approve it, and that would be that.

For all his pride and willfulness and eccentricity, Gould was remarkably adept at chamber music, which requires exactly the opposite characteristics: restraint, diplomacy, modesty, a sense of communion. Gould delighted in accompanying singers in the rather difficult songs of Schoenberg, and he made beautiful recordings of chamber works as diverse as the three Bach sonatas for viola da gamba and harpsichord (with Leonard Rose) and the Brahms Quintet in F minor (with the Montreal String Quartet).

Jaime Laredo had never even met Gould when somebody at Columbia suggested in the mid-1970's that they join forces to record the six Bach violin sonatas. "I was very apprehensive when I went to Toronto," Laredo says of what had become Gould's newest recording operation, "because, you know, one heard all sorts of stories about Glenn Gould, and I had no idea what to expect. And from the very beginning, I was amazed at how well everything went—how nice he was, how amenable he was. It was not the kind of situation where, you know, 'This is my show and we play things my way.' Not at all. It was very much give-and-take. Not one argument or impasse or anything. It was all really enjoyable. The only thing I didn't find enjoyable was working in the middle of the night."

Q: It started at 4 P.M. or something?

A: Oh, how I wish it had started at 4 P.M.! In those days, you know, he used to make all his records in the auditorium at Eaton's department store, so we had to wait for the store to close, which was 9 o'clock. We never really started the first tape until around 11 P.M., and we worked until 4 or 5 in the morning. And I wasn't *used* to that. I had to switch gears every time I went to Toronto and sort of, you know, night is day and day is night.

"We had done a little bit of rehearsing over the phone," Laredo goes on, "and he would actually sing through an entire movement, because he wanted to talk about, you know, are you happy with this tempo, or how does this seem? Knowing Glenn's mind, how brilliant he was, I thought there would be a lot of analysis at the recording session, but we just started playing. And we played over and over again. The way of rehearsing was not taking things apart or analyzing, but we'd play a movement, and we'd play it again, and then we'd play it a third time or a fourth time. If either of us thought, Well, that really wasn't very good, then we didn't even bother listening to the tape. When we did a take that both of us thought, Hey, that was pretty good, then we'd go and we'd listen to that take. Then we'd come back out and do another one.

"I had always thought of Glenn as this intellectual, thinking musician, but until I actually heard him in the studio, I never really appreciated what a fabulous, great pianist he was. You know, when we were—two or three or four in the morning, and we were waiting for Andy to change tapes or whatever—and Glenn would start playing the piano and rambling on. I remember one night he started playing me some Liszt transcriptions, and I tell you, it was absolutely— I mean, I was just—I was sitting there with my mouth open. I'd never heard piano-playing like that. I mean, I'd never heard anybody with a technique like that. The control that he had of the piano, and the sounds were so beautiful. It was absolutely astounding. Absolutely astounding.

"Then we'd go back to Bach. There were some movements of certain sonatas that he felt very strongly about, and he said, 'Oh, it really just must be this way.' But many others he was very willing to, you know—'Oh, you really want to do it a little faster? Or a little slower? Fine.' Whatever. And there were a lot of things that we played quite differently. By differently, I mean that whereas my playing in certain movements tended to be a little bit warmer, a little more romantic, his tended to be a little bit more detached, a little bit more aloof. It was not that we were at odds in any way—it just, you know, the combination really worked. And there was not one unpleasant moment."

The music critics only gradually became aware of Gould's disappearance. In the New York *Times* of December 5, 1965, more than a year after Gould's retirement, under a headline that said, "The Vanishing Glenn Gould," Howard Klein reported, mistakenly, that "there have been no announcements . . . but the 33-year-old Canadian pianist has let it be known that he will appear in public now just often enough to keep in minimal touch with his public." Klein went on to praise the new recording that completed Book I of *The Well-Tempered Clavier,* but still with the familiar references to the famous eccentricities. "As usual he can be heard singing lustily away in the background," Klein wrote. "His engineers must have some time keeping his vocal counterpoint to the minimum they achieve. . . . But give him a really complex fugue, such as the C sharp minor, No. 4, and he is in his element, separating lines with his well-regulated control and putting them back together with master's concentration. And his virtuoso sprint with the B flat (No. 21) is all dash and pianistic bravura. . . ."

The new reviews of Gould's recordings generally demonstrated a somewhat changed attitude on the part of the music critics. Gradually, they began to show an increasing respect and restraint. There are several possible explanations for this. It may have been simply that the critics no longer could see Gould, weaving to and fro on his pygmy piano stool, and so they no longer felt the need to report on his physical behavior. Perhaps they sensed that he would never again appear among them, and that their caustic commentaries might have had something to do with his disappearance. Or perhaps it was simply that many record reviewers remain on a somewhat lower level than concert reviewers, and so they feel less need to assert their own personalities. All of these possibilities, of course, confirmed Gould's own view that the public piano recital was "the last blood sport," and that the mysteries of art could best be fulfilled in the privacy of the recording studio.

Klein returned to Gould's recordings the following year with a glowing account of his Schoenberg. "Gould achieves in his Schoenberg recordings what may be his best recordings to date . . ." he wrote. "Gould plays Schoenberg with love, not just affinity. . . . There is a profound technical, intellectual, and emotional identification with the music." The year after that, Klein somewhat more restrainedly praised Gould's Beethoven, in this case the *Pathétique* and the two sonatas of Opus 14. "Gould, as everyone knows, is an iconoclast," he wrote, "with an enormous talent for music as well as iconoclasm. The direction the talent takes is sometimes questionable. . . . But the talent is still there, as can be heard on this new disk. The Pathetique . . . is given a stormy, quasi-operatic performance that, despite departures from Beethoven's own markings, creates a spontaneous and dramatic effect. . . ."

The ambiguity in some of Gould's Beethoven recordings reflected his views on the composer himself. "I have very ambivalent feelings about Beethoven," he told one interviewer. Though he did not like all of Bach—he made several derogatory remarks about the improvisations in the Chromatic Fantasy and the fugues in the early toccatas, for example—he almost always spoke of the composer with admiration and affection. But there was something about the theatrical, self-important side of Beethoven that irritated him. He liked the bright and cheerful compositions of Beethoven's youth very much—and even the *Moonlight Sonata*—but as Beethoven grew more complex and more grandiose, Gould liked only the enigmatic and eccentric transitional works like the *Les Adieux Sonata* and the F minor Quartet, the Eighth Symphony rather than the Seventh or Ninth. Of the mighty *Hammerklavier Sonata*, by contrast, he wrote that "it is . . . the longest, most inconsiderate, and probably least rewarding piece that Beethoven wrote for the piano."

Gould nourished a special dislike for one of Beethoven's greatest and most popular masterpieces, the *Appassionata*. He criticized it, quite possibly because of its popularity, on rather obscure technical grounds: "The relation of first and second themes, both of them spawned by an arpeggiated triad figure, is somehow out of focus. . . . The development segment is similarly disorganized. . . ." As though aware that such objections would win little support, Gould then attacked the piece on personal and emotional grounds: "At this period of his life Beethoven was not only preoccupied with motivic frugality; he was also preoccupied with being Beethoven. And there is about the 'Appassionata' an egoistic pomposity, a defiant 'let's just see if I can't get away with using that once more' attitude, that on my own private Beethoven poll places this sonata somewhere between the *King Stephen* Overture and the *Wellington's Victory* Symphony."

This diatribe appeared, oddly enough, in Gould's liner notes to his own recording of the despised sonata. And as though to demonstrate what a bad piece it was—and to carry out his theory that there was no point in playing a familiar piece unless it could be played differently—Gould proceeded to play the *Appassionata* rather badly. He adopted a funereal tempo, so that the grand first movement sounded halting and hesitant, broken into fragments, and completely lacking the one thing that the *Appassionata* must have, namely passion.

Yet in the same year in which he recorded this burlesque of the standard Beethoven, 1967, Gould perversely brought forth from relative obscurity one of his oddest triumphs, the Liszt transcription of the Fifth Symphony. In theory, every criticism that Gould had made of the *Appassionata* applied just as well to the Fifth Symphony—was ever a work more imbued with "egoistic pomposity"?—and the clangor of that famous opening theme became all the more clangorous by being transferred from the orchestral strings to the piano. And all this from Liszt, a composer whom Gould never otherwise recorded and never mentioned without a sneer. Yet because Gould now took both Beethoven and Liszt at their own self-valuations, because he played this almost-laughable combination with the utmost seriousness, he brought it off with complete success. It is one of his most admirable recordings.

And because he recognized this success, and recognized the elements of tacit parody in it, he shrewdly avoided in his liner notes the temptation to defend his work. Instead, he wrote a series of parody reviews attacking his own performance. "No keyboard version of this work has previously been available in our shops," Sir Humphrey Price-Davies is quoted from *The Phonograph*, "and I fancy that the current issue will find little favour in this country. The entire undertaking smacks of that incorrigible American pre-occupation with exuberant gesture. . . ." And in the *Münch'ner Musikologische Gesellschaft*, Prof. Dr. Karlheinz Heinkel begins by quoting from another Gouldian creation, Karlheinz Klopweisser: "Is it not notable that in his poetic-cycle 'Resonance-on-Rhine' *(Resonanz-am-Rhein)* Klopweisser's second stanza concludes the thought: 'With this oft-strident note let man now pause. . . .'"

This is Gouldian wit of a kind that only Gould could love, and yet the best joke is that Gould's silly ethnic parodies served to blur the real joke, which was simply that the celebrated classicist was presenting, completely deadpan, a brilliant performance of Liszt's transcription of that most venerable of romantic clichés, Beethoven's Fifth Symphony.

After Beethoven, Gould's judgments on composers changed from unusual to bizarre. He denounced Chopin, Schumann, and Liszt, and more mildly dismissed Schubert. Indeed, of all the early Romantics, the only one he admired was Mendelssohn. He derided Verdi and all the Italian operatic masters. Among the early twentieth-century composers, he despised both Debussy and Ravel, and among contemporaries, he disliked Stravinsky, Bartok, Poulenc. On the other hand, he praised and recorded Oscar Morawetz, Jacques Hétu, and István Anhalt, Canadians all. Of all composers of all times, he insisted his favorite was Orlando Gibbons.

The strangest of all these judgments was Gould's lifelong dislike and disapproval of Mozart. He enjoyed telling interviewers that Mozart was "a bad composer," and that he had "died too late rather than too early." His reasoning for that uncharacteristically heartless declaration was that Mozart's best works were those of his early twenties, that what Gould "hated" were the later masterpieces like the G minor symphony and *The Magic Flute*, and that if Mozart had lived to threescore years and ten, he "would have turned into a sort of cross between Weber and Spohr." When challenged on such denunciations, Gould would offer a series of unconvincing rationalizations to the effect that Mozart's music was "hedonistic" (one of Gould's pet pejoratives), or that Mozart had failed to conform to Gould's dictum that all piano music should be contrapuntal. Yet it is not too difficult to see in all these accusations an echo of a childish desire to shock the grownups, and perhaps a touch of envy toward music's most celebrated child prodigy.

"Were you always out of symphony with Mozart, even in your student days?" asked Bruno Monsaingeon, a cherubic French violinist who had become interested in televised musical interviews and would become a major collaborator in Gould's later video work. Their "interviews," after some preliminary discussions, were generally written out in advance by Gould, questions as well as answers.

"As far back as I can remember . . ." Gould replied.

"But, as a student, you must have had to learn to play these works. . . . And you always disliked them?"

"What I felt at the time, I think, was dismay. I simply couldn't understand how my teachers, and other presumably sane adults of my acquaintance, could count these pieces among the great musical treasures of Western man."

In 1961, Gould recorded one of Mozart's greatest concerti, the 24th in C minor, K. 491, with the CBC Symphony Orchestra under Walter Susskind, "as sort of an experiment." Or, as he told another interviewer, Jonathan Cott, "because it's the only one that I sort of halfway like." It was a strong and stirring performance, and we can easily ignore Gould's compulsion to "improve" the score with various minor revisions, extra chords, trills, and arpeggiations. But after he had recorded this masterpiece, Gould also felt compelled to use it as the centerpiece of the TV show that he titled "How Mozart Became a Bad Composer."

This began with one of Gould's attempts to appear worldly and *au courant*. He flippantly described Mozart as someone "who could knock out a divertimento the way an accounts [sic] executive dispatches an inter-office memo. But in a way, that's his problem. Too many of his works sound like inter-office memos. . . . Like an executive holding forth upon the ramifications of a subject no one in the front office is much concerned with anyway. 'Yeah, well, Harry, as I see it, J.B. has got this thing about replacing the water cooler. . . .'" And so on.

From this nadir, Gould went on to make a number of interesting, if misguided, points. Starting with his view that Mozart's brilliant use of eighteenth-century conventions represented "an appalling collection of clichés," Gould went on to inquire how this had happened, how "those prodigious gifts which made Mozart as a young man the toast of Europe [had been] reduced in the end to skillful self-parody," how everything had finally succumbed to "that jaded, world-weary approach which beset Mozart in his later years." Gould's conclusion was that Mozart's "decline can be blamed on what should have been his greatest natural asset—a fantastic facility for improvisation." Public improvisation was a required skill among the musicians of Mozart's time (as among jazz musicians of our own time), but Gould naturally found this abhorrent. Improvisation, he wrote, is "pretty well limited to the sort of music-making that results from split-second reaction, and it must rely heavily on devices that have already secured a place in the mainstream of musical activity." In other words, clichés.

This view of Mozart led Gould on into an odd inquiry as to "whether the composer is, in fact, really necessary." We had already entered, after all, the age of aleatory art, in which John Cage wrote down whatever notes he received from the *I Ching*, and Jackson Pollock sprayed paint in all directions, and the devotees of "mixed media" danced under various combinations of flashing lights. The reigning theory was that the audience's reaction to a work of art was part of the art itself. Gould, who liked to imagine a future age when listeners would splice together different versions of some symphony to suit their own tastes, approved of any efforts "to draw the audience into the making of a work of art," but as an artist who privately enjoyed his own remarkable gifts as an improviser, Gould saw hidden dangers that others might never have noticed. "Not least among those dangers may be the hedonistic pursuit of improvisation as a way of life," he wrote. "And that's why I think we can learn from Mozart, why his reliance in his late works on a facility for improvisation provides a real object lesson for the Twentieth Century."

One of the listeners to this broadcast in 1968 was an Amherst professor who reported Gould's views to B. H. Haggin, the pedantic but respected music critic for *The New Republic* ("H. B. Haggle" was to become Gould's private name for him). Haggin, in turn, reported the Amherst professor's account back to Gould: " 'He'd play something marvelous from K. 491 and say "Nothing here. Arid. Mechanical clichés like inter-office memos." ' " Haggin sent Gould an article he had written about Mozart in the *Sewanee Review* and solemnly asked him "if you would be kind enough to mark on it any passages I refer to that you consider to be mechanical clichés like inter-office memos. . . . And while you are at it, would you add bar references to the passages in K. 491 that you so characterized in your television talk?"

Haggin had admired some of Gould's early recordings of Bach, but he believed strongly that a pianist had a duty to follow whatever instructions a composer had left for the performance of his music. Now, while he challenged Gould to document his personal attacks on Mozart, he also wanted to know why Gould so frequently ignored Mozart's instructions in his new recording of the first five Mozart sonatas. "I was of course surprised by your treatment of the opening statement of the first movement of K. 282," Haggin wrote with the most courtly pretense that he and Gould were talking the same language. "I looked at my *Urtext* edition, and found that the specified tempo was Adagio, and that the markings indicated that the statement was to be played legato. I would appreciate your telling me your reasons for making the tempo Andantino—not to say Allegretto—and playing the statement with a light non-legato touch, so that instead of the serious and even poignant *espressivo* that Mozart seems to have intended, the effect is *scherzando*. And concerning the passages after the opening statement, in K. 282's first movement, I have the same question as I asked about the Adagio of K. 280: what are your reasons for giving the left hand's mere accompaniment figuration without melodic significance emphasis equal to, and even greater than, that of the melody? These are serious questions, to which I hope you will give me serious answers."

Gould did answer seriously and even a bit defensively. He suggested that the broadcast had "suffered to a degree from that lack of distance and perspective which can help a program realize its own structural rhythm." But he added that "much (most?) of what I said

I meant, and I was careful I think to confine the less appreciative remarks to Mozart's concerto writing and to be (relatively) enthusiastic about the sonata output." As for his habit of playing Mozart accompaniments in a contrapuntal relationship to the melodies ("adding vitamins to the music," Gould once called this), he stood his ground: "The whole idea of a melodic attribute as distinguished from the component parts of a harmonic environment has always seemed to me anti-structural and even, dare I say it, undemocratic. . . . The more singable, likeable and memorable the tune one encounters the less likely it is that that particular melodic strain will require any special emphasis. . . ." But on the more important question of why Gould felt himself free to change or ignore what Mozart had actually written, the pianist offered no answer.

Nearly ten years later, Gould wrote somewhat differently about this "rather rocky relationship" with Haggin. There had been problems as early as 1965, when *High Fidelity* wanted to accompany Gould's article on "The Prospects of Recording" with some brief comments from other authorities. One of those authorities had been Haggin, who then charged that his comment had been taken out of context and distorted. Both Gould and the editors of *High Fidelity* apologized profusely. On the subject of Mozart, though, Gould now reported to a friend that Haggin "wrote essay-length letters, complete with manuscript enclosures, showing how things *should* be phrased, dynamically graded, etc. I seem to recall also that he expressed his deep concern about my fondness for inner-voice manipulation and my indifference, as he saw it, toward melodic invention. These later letters, of course, went unanswered. . . ."

It remains something of a mystery why Gould should have undertaken to record the complete sonatas of a composer he disliked, disapproved of, and, as a necessary consequence, didn't understand. He did like the early sonatas, the most inconsequential ones. "These are glorious pieces," he wrote, "lean, fastidious, and possessed of that infallible tonal homing instinct with which the young Mozart was so generously endowed." He even wrote to Haggin, after the first volume was issued, that "the sonata project in general has been a joyous task." And he did have a grand time with those early sonatas. He played them all briskly—a bit too briskly—but with enthusiasm and affection.

As Mozart matured and his sonatas became more complex, how-ever, Gould seemed more and more determined, as with the later Beethoven sonatas, to deconstruct them. Some, like the A minor (K. 310) and the C major (K. 330), he played at blazing speed, which tended to reduce them to empty glitter. And the tone here was everything that Mozart should not be: cold, hard, distant, unfeeling. Gould's attitude seemed to be not just indifference or even dislike but actual contempt.* "The later sonatas I do *not* like," Gould later said to an interviewer, Tim Page. "I find them intolerable, loaded with quasitheatrical conceit, and I can certainly say that I went about recording a piece like the Sonata in B-flat major, K. 570, with no conviction whatsoever. The honest thing to do would have been to skip those works entirely, but the cycle had to be completed."

Some of these sonatas, Gould simply rewrote. The celebrated A major (K. 331), for example, begins with a theme and variations, *andante grazioso*. Gould played it about as slowly as is humanly pos-sible ("so maddeningly slowly that I had to get everyone's hackles aroused," as he told one interviewer, Humphrey Burton), because he had adopted a theory that, regardless of what Mozart wrote, each variation should be faster than the preceding one. So when he came to the penultimate fifth variation, which Mozart, with his own sense of contrasts, marked *adagio*, Gould undertook what he called "a really perverse thing" and played it *allegro*.

"Well, the idea behind that performance," Gould said in his inter-view with Monsaingeon, "was that, since the first movement is a nocturne-cum-minuet rather than a slow movement, and since the package is rounded off by that curious bit of seragliolike exotica [he meant the famous concluding *Rondo alla turca*], one is dealing with an unusual structure, and virtually all of the sonata-allegro conven-tions can be set aside. . . . I admit that my realization of the first movement is somewhat idiosyncratic."

Monsaingeon: It certainly is. . . . Did you assume that the melody was so well known that it did not need to be heard again?

Gould: Something like that, yes. I wanted—if I can invoke the name of Webern once more—to subject it to a Webern-like scru-

---

*On a much smaller scale, Gould had similar problems with Scarlatti, whom he also didn't understand or like or play well.

tiny in which its basic elements would be isolated from each other and the continuity of the theme deliberately undermined. The idea was that each successive variation would contribute to the restoration of that continuity and, in the absorption of that task, would be less visible as an ornamental, decorative element.

And as for the extremely slow pace of the concluding rondo, Gould added, "it seemed important to establish a solid, maybe even stolid, tempo, partly because, to my knowledge, anyway, nobody had played it like that before. . . ."

In his conversations with Jonathan Cott, Gould was more accusatory, and even more paradoxical. "I had more fun with those things," he said of the Mozart sonatas, "than anything I've ever done, practically, mainly because I really don't like Mozart as a composer." Gould did not seem to realize that his dislike was perfectly evident in the recordings, and that this dislike would prevent a listener from enjoying the performance. What pleasure can there be, after all, in seeing or hearing someone express his dislike for a great artist?

There is yet another mystery here: Did Gould play Mozart so glibly and harshly because he disliked it, or did he dislike it because he mistakenly thought that what he heard in his inner ear was what Mozart had intended? Did he hear the Platonic ideal of a Mozart sonata only in the unfeeling tones that he himself brought to Mozart's heartfelt music? Gould avoided such questions. He preferred to veer off into a simplistic differentiation between early and late Mozart, and he reasserted his notion that Mozart's growth and maturity was one long decline. "I love the early sonatas—I love the early Mozart, period," he said to Cott. "I'm very fond of that period when he was either emulating Haydn or Carl Philipp Emanuel Bach but had not yet found himself. The moment he did find himself, as conventional wisdom would have it, at the age of eighteen or nineteen or twenty, I stop being so interested in him, because what he discovered was primarily a theatrical gift which he applied ever after not only to his operas but to his instrumental works as well; and given the rather giddy hedonism of eighteenth-century theater, that sort of thing doesn't interest me at all."

From there on, Gould simply became abusive. Declaring his preference for the sonatas of Haydn (of which, necessarily, he made a far better recording toward the end of his life), he said, "One never gets the feeling that any two are cut from the same cookie stamp. I do get that feeling in Mozart, I'm afraid. I get the feeling that once he hit his stride, they're *all* cut from the same cookie stamp." And of Mozart's development sections: "Mozart never really did learn to write a development section, because, of course, you don't have to write a development section unless you've got something to develop." And finally, of the whole recording project: "I had fun with it precisely because you can play the damn things in the most deliciously straightforward manner, never yielding at a cadence . . . just going straight through to the end. . . . Now, the horror and the outcry that resulted from my Mozart recordings—I think it was the critic Martin Mayer who said about Volume 2: 'Finally, this is madness!' or something to that effect—is to me terribly funny, because all the critics are really responding to is a denial of a certain set of expectations that have been built into their hearing processes."

To claim amusement at being criticized is a fairly standard defense, but the "fun" was rather joyless. "Laughter is supposed to keep a man young," as Ring Lardner wrote in *Symptoms of Being 35,* "but if its forced laughter it works the opp." And Mayer was by no means alone in his condemnation of Gould's Mozart recordings. "Entering the Mozart lists once more, Glenn Gould delivers Volume Two of the Piano Sonatas . . ." Donal Henahan wrote in the New York *Times* in July of 1969, "with performances of expectably brilliant pianism. Brilliant, and yet disconcerting. Gould seems to see these sonatas . . . as technical challenges, which they seldom are in normal performance. And since the Canadian can perhaps play more notes in less time than anyone alive, the results here can be distressing. . . . Even when one grows more or less used to runaway tempos and loses himself in admiration at Gould's fantastic ability to hold a pulse rock-firm while bringing out every detail of embroidery, the voice of Mozart is hard to hear. . . . Gould misses the aristocratic note that Mozart's sonatas strike. . . ."

Worse reviews were to come. We are still among the early sonatas, which Gould said he loved, and if his glittering performances do not really demonstrate love, they do demonstrate interest and respect, which is more than these boyish works usually receive. And sometimes Gould did reach a level far beyond that. His version of the Sonata in D major (K. 311), for example, is completely admirable, beautiful, and full of verve. Henahan at the *Times* remained quite respectful through the third Mozart album in 1972. "Gould is at his mercurial best in these four Mozart sonatas . . ." he wrote, "flinging himself into the pieces with evident (sometimes audible) glee. It is impossible not to be infected by his joy in playing this music, even if one's own idea of Mozart is less headlong and clipped in phrase."

In the following year, 1973, the *Times'* coverage of the Gould/Mozart recordings fell into the hands of Peter G. Davis, who was considerably less sympathetic to Volume IV than Henahan had been to its predecessors. Davis was also reviewing Gould recordings of Beethoven and Hindemith, but he wrote that "the loudest anathemas will undoubtedly be reserved for the Mozart record, the fourth in an ongoing project. . . . One critic even went so far as to brand the previous disk in this series as 'the most loathsome record ever made.' The performances of Sonatas K. 331, K. 533, K. 545 and the D Minor Fantasy here will not make this sensitive soul any happier. They don't make me very happy either. It is very difficult to see what Gould is out to prove, unless the rumor that he actually hates this music is true. Tempos are painfully slow, the clipped, détaché articulation violates phrase structure (and many of Mozart's specific markings). . . . It all conjures up an image of a tremendously precocious but very nasty little boy trying to put one over on his piano teacher."

Nobody was more surprised by Gould's decision to record the complete Mozart sonatas than Andy Kazdin, his producer at Columbia. But Kazdin did not question the plan. "You know the joke—" Kazdin says. "'Where does your pet gorilla sleep?' 'Anywhere he wants.' It was, like, 'What's he going to record next?' 'Whatever he feels like.' Columbia was very enlightened that way. Basically, whatever he would do, they would accept. I mean, they knew they had something rather unique, and they would just sort of let him go."

Columbia indulged Gould even to the extent of moving the whole recording process from New York to Toronto. Ever since Gould had retired from the concert tours in 1964, he had chafed at the need to travel to taping sessions in New York about twenty times every year. He had not flown since 1962, and the train service all across the United States was becoming increasingly erratic, and the drive between Toronto and New York took at least ten boring hours each way. Then there was the nuisance and expense of shipping his piano to and fro, and of clearing it through customs each time.

Gould liked the acoustics in Toronto's Eaton Auditorium at least as well as those in any hall in New York, and so he began urging Columbia to let him make his recordings there. He was even willing to buy all his own equipment. "We came up with the plan that he would buy anything I told him to buy, which would be of a quality equivalent to what he could have used in New York," Kazdin says. "He would then charge back to CBS exactly the same hourly rates that our own engineering department charged the Masterworks department." Gould was boyishly proud of his new machinery. "It includes," he wrote to Ronald Wilford, who had become his manager after his retirement from the stage, "a Studer 8-track, 2 Ampex AG 440s, U87 microphones, matched sets of KLH speakers in my office and at Eaton auditorium, an extremely efficient cue-speaker system whereby the 'green room' is connected to the stage and insert takes are provided with the proper feeds from backstage. . . ." And so, from 1971 on, instead of Gould trekking to New York twice a month, Andy Kazdin made the trek to Toronto. "I was never crazy about flying either," says Kazdin.

As Gould acquired more and more control over his recordings, he seemed to work more and more slowly, more and more determined to achieve his own version of perfection, no matter what the cost. "I am by no means a fast worker in the studio," he wrote to Wilford in 1973. "A good session will consist of 2½ to 3 minutes per recording hour and, consequently, assuming the average record to include 50 minutes of recorded material, the best figure I can arrive at would be approximately 18 recording hours per album. . . ." (Gould's later radio work became comparably elaborate. William Littler of the *Star* noted that Gould had boasted of making 131 edits in a speech of 2 minutes and 43 seconds in his show on Richard Strauss, "about one edit per second. And you wonder why his documentaries take hundreds of hours to produce.")

And as Gould became more and more a media producer, he found more and more uses for a burly assistant named Ray Roberts. "It happened by a fluke," Roberts recalls over a pot of tea at the Windsor Arms Hotel in Toronto. "Glenn was recording in the old Eaton's Auditorium, and he had a whole lot of technical problems. An old friend of mine, Lorne Tulk, was doing the setups for him, and he asked me to just assist him on one particular occasion, and Glenn and I started talking, just in a casual way, and it became a regular occasion. This was in about 1970, when I was a salesman for Coca-Cola.

"Glenn had continual problems with his cars, and I started giving him advice on how to keep them running. I'm not a musician in any way, but I could make sure that things happened. We got equipment, we got transport, all of that, okay? I was a glorified gofer. But he also used me as a sounding board, to bounce ideas off. What do you think of X? Okay? He was very good to me, financially and in a lot of other ways. So that was fine."

Moving the recording sessions to Toronto brought an unusual dividend: Kazdin was now able to do the engineering work himself. As long as Gould recorded in New York, union regulations governed the editing process. "The physical act of splicing together tapes had to be done by a union engineer," Kazdin says. "There were some engineers who could read music, most often could not, and they had to work under the direction of the producer." Kazdin understandably felt that he could do all this work better himself. "When one does it oneself, there's a certain efficiency," he says. "It can be done faster than having to communicate to someone who, even if he's perfect, *some* part of the time there'll be a communications failure, and he won't understand, and you'll have to go back and do something again." But the union rules were the rules, and the rules forbade producers to work on tapes. "It was unheard of to even think about it," Kazdin says. "I couldn't even touch the tapes."

The union's jurisdiction did not extend to Toronto, however, and on anything recorded there, Kazdin became free to edit as he pleased, or as Gould pleased. "Then it occurred to me that there was absolutely no way they could tell whether I did it in Toronto or in my basement at home," he says, " and so in fact I did it there." And so it came to pass that the fourth volume of the Mozart sonatas included a credit for engineering by Kent Warden. "Warden I see as an anagram for Andrew," says Kazdin, "and Kent is a contraction of my middle name and my last name. I still am amused talking about this. My real masterpiece was the name for the editor, which was a complete anagram for all three of my names, which was Frank Dean Dennowitz."

Q: What is your middle name?

A: Fenton. So if you take Andrew Fenton Kazdin, you can unscramble that and come out with Frank Dean Dennowitz. Glenn, of course, knew all of this.

And how could Gould object to Kazdin's perhaps unintentional parody of Gould's schizophrenic love of alternate identities? How could the creator of Frank Dean Dennowitz receive anything but a wave of recognition from the creator of Herbert von Hochmeister (and, in future years, Teddy Slotz of New York, Sir Nigel Twitt-Thornwaite of London, and all the others)?

Kazdin, who is proud of his abilities, also gets satisfaction from the fact that he produced more than forty recordings by the headstrong Glenn Gould. "I've tried to figure out how it is that we made it work for fifteen years," he says, "and it must have been the fact that I was—to the extent that any human being can—just completely sublimating any form of ego. Just not intruding myself. Just knowing that my contribution to his record was going to be on the technical side, and that was fine. And if he was happy, then I was happy, and we were turning out very good records. I don't think two people can work together for that long without, you know, somewhere along the line, we must have bumped up against each other. I mean, there must have been some friction over maybe something foolish, you know, but it had nothing to do with the records. I mean, the facts speak for themselves."

Are we perhaps once again bumping up against something? Bumping up against memories of a Gould who was more than just eccentric? Kazdin is not surprised or thrown off balance by the suggestion. "Well, that's a good question because you're even asking it," he says. "You've already made an assumption in the asking of it. You want to know if his eccentricities went beyond— If you want to know how much your children have grown, you won't know as well as Uncle Fred, who sees them every three months. When you were thrown together with Glenn with such frequency, as I was in those years, as each new little thing came up, it was seemingly insignificant compared to what we had before. Nothing ever seemed to be terribly significant or important, and then, like the emperor's new clothes, some guy would walk in, and I'd be talking in a rather casual way, and I'd mention this or that, and he'd say, 'You mean he does that? And he does that? He sounds crazy!' And I'd say, 'No, no, no, no, no. He's just—' And then you'd start to think. You'd start to add up those things which snuck up on you, little by little, and you'd get into his way of working and thinking and being. So it's not a matter of whether I thought any of the things exceeded eccentricity, it's whether— Sometimes, I was unable to notice even the eccentricities, which got sort of caught up in the momentum of whatever the project was. The project would be his life, and you'd get caught up with him, and everything was supremely rationalized. He could rationalize anything, anything, better than anyone I've ever met in my life."

Q: That's also sometimes a mark of crazy people. Their most extreme crazinesses always make perfect sense to them. I'm not saying he was crazy, I'm just asking you about him.

A: You'll find people who are positive he was crazy, but I don't feel that I'm qualified, from a medical, psychological standpoint, to say when one crosses the line. I don't know. Eccentric was no question. Whatever that means. I mean that he had modes of behavior that seemed to defy logic but seemed to work for him, and he was happy, so you'd stand back and give him a little extra room. But while all that was going on, there was a supremely rational—I'm not talking about the artistic side, and I'm not talking about rationalizing—I'm saying there was a very rational person in there, who was very intelligent on many subjects besides music—could respond to logic, which many artists can't—and it was hard to believe that that person could be crossing the line. But he might have been. I didn't know then, and I don't know now. I'm sure there were many strange things that paraded under the banner of eccentricity. And, you know, you just let them go. I mean, in its own joky way, what I said to you how many minutes ago—"Where does your pet gorilla sleep?" "Anywhere he wants." He was a very valuable property to the record company, but he was—he was certainly unique in many ways.

About twenty years after Bach published the complete and self-contained twenty-four preludes and fugues of *The Well-Tempered Clavier,* he mysteriously started all over again and wrote in the same sequence of major and minor semitones the even more complex and elaborate and beautiful preludes and fugues that constitute what we now know as Book II of the same *Well-Tempered Clavier*. "I have just this week finished Volume I of the W.T.C., thank goodness," Gould wrote to an admirer in August of 1965, "and now I have little choice but to proceed onward into Book II."

Once again, some of his performances were miraculous, some peculiar, some dutiful. But no critic's commentary could provide so interesting a view of what was going on in Gould's mind as did Gould's own analysis, on a subsequent television show with Bruno Monsaingeon, of one fugue he particularly loved. Gould characteristically began by playing a rather hackneyed early fugue and denouncing what he described as the standard view that "because Bach turned out to be, arguably, the greatest craftsman of all time, he started out that way and produced masterpieces in his playpen, and *he did not*." That declaration led Gould, the great believer in rigorous counterpoint, into a rather emotional testimonial: "What he had, right from the earliest days, was the ability to write music of *incredible* intensity and pathos. The kind of recitatives that you get in the toccatas, even the earliest ones, could virtually have gone into the *Matthew Passion*—I mean, they're *extraordinary* things. But he did *not* have the ability to integrate that intensity with a real fugal craft until he was, I think, close to forty."

Monsaingeon's main function was to serve as straight man in these prewritten conversations. "Well, is there an example of integration that you could give us now?" he inquired.

"How about the—um—" Gould paused as though thinking about various alternatives, "the E major fugue from the second volume of *The Well-Tempered Clavier*?"

Despite Gould's theatrics, this is a splendid fugue, a brief and rather underestimated fugue, and Gould had thought deeply about it, and loved it passionately, and that all becomes clear in his presentation. These complementary elements are impossible to reproduce away from the television set, because Gould keeeps playing while he talks, and so his extremely technical analysis makes sense because he keeps illustrating what he is intently describing. And he keeps singing too, not in the strangulated tones of a concert virtuoso trying to suppress his instincts but in the full-throated enthusiasm of someone trying to express more contrapuntal voices than any piano can.

So imagine that you can see him playing and singing his way through the exposition of this stately and rather liturgical four-part fugue—he is wearing horn-rimmed glasses and one of his dark blue Viyella shirts, unbuttoned at the cuffs—and then listen to him start talking as he plays. "You know, it isn't exactly the world's most original thought," he says, "but what a choral piece this would have made! It's conceived vocally."

"Yes, yes," says the dutiful Monsaingeon.

"And maybe because he wasn't trying to cater to an instrument in any way," says Gould, still playing the exposition, "there's the sense that there isn't a wasted note, there isn't an artificial or superficial note. Everything is material to the material, everything absolutely grows out of the original subject, out of the original six notes which started it all [he plays that]. Even the first countertheme does [plays and sings that], because that countertheme is just the transposition of the subject [sings and plays it] to [sings and plays that] with a little bit of ornamentation."

Now things get more complicated. The first episode after the exposition is a stretto, that is, the theme is stated in one voice, and then, before that statement is finished, another voice echoes it, so that it moves in counterpoint to itself. This is, Gould says, "one of the first of those wonderfully compact, convoluted—in the best sense of the word—stretto overlaps. [He plays and sings it without comment for a while.] Only in this one, the countertheme gets its own stretto as well."

"The two ideas seem to develop in tandem," Monsaingeon offers.

"Exactly," Gould says. "And in tandem or otherwise, they move—well, one can't say they modulate together [continues playing], but they sort of bump into [laughs] the submediant key, C-sharp minor, thusly. And when he gets there, he does something rather cute. He takes the original subject and the original answer, starting on the original notes which they had started on, E and B respectively, and—transforms them, reharmonizes them, and finds a way of giving them a sort of tonal visa to pass through C-sharp minor. . . ."

It is possible that other pianists perform this brief fugue over an equally dense subtext of analysis, but it is hard to believe that many of them ever see so much in it as Gould saw, and amiably explained while he played. "Then they leave the orbit of C-sharp minor, if they were ever in fact in it," he observes, "and move, to the same extent that they were in C sharp, toward F-sharp minor. In which key, he does something very nice." Nice but very complex. Gould stops playing for a moment as he starts explaining. "He takes the theme, deprives it of the one expressive interval it had, the minor third [he plays that], and fills it in, as one would sing it in a scale [sings and plays], then makes the alto comment on that, also sort of filling in the pattern [plays and sings]. Except that in the alto, he starts to play around with the modes and goes up one way [plays a rising scale] and comes back down another. *Then* he adds a new countertheme in the bass [plays and sings], also based on the original idea, also expanding it to the interval of a fifth, and then puts *that* into a canon, in the tenor, just in case anybody'd missed the point. [He plays and sings that.] Then we leave F-sharp minor [still playing] by the same submediant C-sharp minor exit.

"Then you get another one of those glorious stretto occasions, as in the second sentence of the piece. And then, he does something very, very interesting—forgive me—after that stretto, for the first time, he introduces six diatonic notes in a row. Which doesn't seem like doing anything very special, but up till then, every motive that he's used has either been delineated by a fourth [he demonstrates] or by a fifth, as in the case of the countersubject [demonstrates]. He suddenly adds six notes successively [playing the fugue again now], then, in canon, seven [playing and singing], as though he were celebrating the ending that *seems* to be close by."

Monsaingeon has been allowing all this to run on far beyond the comprehension of anyone but a graduate student in harmonic analysis because he realizes that Gould is vividly demonstrating how his own mind works. This is where Gould lives, the interior citadel from which he observes a world unlike anything that anyone else sees or knows.

The "seeming" approach to the end of the fugue was, of course, only a seeming approach. There is still a coda to be explored and analyzed, and Gould continues full of enthusiasm. "So we have first the six-note thing, the seven-note extension, the eight-note extension," he says, "and—it's rudimentary material, but it makes for one of the most gloriously fulfilled codas he ever wrote, I think."

Monsaingeon is ready with his cue: "What about playing the whole fugue now?" Gould politely agrees that it is time to shift from analysis to performance. "One masterpiece coming up," he says. Then he begins to play.

VIII

The Composer

Gould had often declared that the main purpose in his retirement from the concert stage was to gain time to compose music of his own. "I saw myself as a sort of musical Renaissance Man, capable of doing many things," he told one interviewer. "I obviously wanted to be a composer. I still do." One can hear in such a declaration a certain hunger for a fame that would last. In no other art is there such a split between the immediate celebrity of the performer and the rewards that posterity grants to a great composer. Can we imagine a system in which a writer could become famous only by offering public readings of other men's works? Or a painter by staging slide shows? And what musicians do we remember from the past, some blazing piano virtuoso like Thalberg or Tausig (or Gould) or some relatively obscure creator like Franz Schubert? Yet it is Horowitz and not Elliott Carter who inspires people to stand in line all night outside Carnegie Hall.

To the young Gould, the idea of actually being a composer, of doing what Bach and Beethoven had done, was probably at least as important as the desire to compose something. "It's not that he wanted to become a composer—he wanted to become immortal," says Harvey Olnick. "Composition was a way of becoming more immortal." In "Glenn Gould's Toronto," the pianist very candidly recalled his youthful yearning to have his creations make an impression on the world. Before actually writing any music, he said, he would create elaborate title pages, which "were rather interesting because along with the name of the author in very large print there was also a totally fictitious publishing firm (always a different one) which was usually located in El Alamein or Murmansk or someplace I considered equally exotic."

Aside from a number of songs, which his mother had encouraged him to write ever since his childhood, Gould's boyhood compositions were mostly conservatory assignments. "The manuscript remnants of junior masterpieces occupy many drawers in my home," he later wrote. "They are tokens of that swift moving parade of enthusiasms which constitute the student life and they exhibit an attempt at every style from Palestrina (which was done to please my teachers) to Webern (which was done to annoy them). There were a great many quite professionally polished fughettas among them (I was good at fughettas, it was sort of like solving a jigsaw puzzle . . .)."

The first composition that actually got finished and performed was a suite of incidental music that the Malvern Dramatic Society asked Gould to write for a school production of Shakespeare's *Twelfth Night*. He was still only sixteen, but he had already performed Beethoven's Fourth Concerto, and he lived at such a level of publicity that the Toronto *Telegram* reported in February of 1949 that his music for *Twelfth Night* was "almost completed but not written down." This was not really incidental music in the traditional sense of accompaniment to a play but rather a piano suite that Gould played during intermission at the performance later that month. It contained four parts entitled "Regal Atmosphere," "Elizabethan Gaiety," "Whimsical Nonsense," and "Nocturne." Everybody was appropriately impressed.

As Gould's concert career became more and more complex, he often spoke of composing pieces that may have existed largely as sketches, or largely in his own imagination, a string trio that broke off after four pages, a clarinet sonata that no one ever seems to have heard. Early in 1950, he said he had written a piano sonata in the style of Schoenberg. The sonata was never finished, but there still survives a penciled manuscript entitled "5 Short Piano Pieces" and dated "1951–2." The piano pieces are each only about twenty bars long and resolutely written in the twelve-tone method, the resolute work of a resolute student.

At about this same time, Gould suddenly moved to a somewhat higher level by composing an atonal sonata for bassoon and piano.

Why the bassoon, that ungainly instrument that is so often used for comic or weird effects (e.g., the opening of Stravinsky's *Rite of Spring*)? One theory is that Gould's admiration for Alban Berg had led him to explore the possibilities inherent in Berg's Four Pieces for clarinet and piano; another is that his admiration for Hindemith led him to Hindemith's somewhat didactic but interesting series of sonatas for the flute, the horn, the oboe, the clarinet, and even the bassoon. Or perhaps it was simply that one of Gould's friends at the conservatory was a bassoonist.

Nicholas Kilburn is still a bassoonist. A taut, muscular man with a fierce white moustache, he makes his living with the Toronto Symphony Orchestra. He was once a pianist, but after he met and heard the young Gould—they were both then twelve—he decided to take up some other instrument. The bassoon seemed a good, remote choice, and so he eventually found himself giving a joint recital with the famous Glenn Gould. Now they were both nineteen. "The concert was very funny," Kilburn recalls, over a Greek salad in a restaurant across the street from the Toronto Symphony's rehearsal. "We walked out on the stage, and I looked at the audience, and I thought, What in heaven's name is going on? This room, the concert hall at the Royal Conservatory, was jammed to the rafters. But it wasn't jammed with my peers; it was jammed with all the intelligentsia, the musical intelligentsia of Toronto. Anybody who was anybody was there at that concert. I was staggered. . . .

"We did the Hindemith sonata, and the other one was Glenn's. How well it went, I don't recall. I do recall this—that the bow tie I was wearing was a clip-on. I'd never worn a bow tie in my life, and every time I took a breath, the clip-on bow tie would unclip, so I kept attempting to do the thing up. And finally, in a dudgeon, I just took it off and put it on the music stand. But it fell on the floor, and it looked to everyone as though I had just thrown it down.

"But the silliest thing of all was— You know, moisture collects in the crook of the bassoon, and the usual practice is that you remove the reed, and you blow into the crook to get the water past the S, or you take it off and you shake it. Well, I was so damn nervous that I took the crook with the reed in it, and I shook it. And the reed flew off, and flew back into the pipes of the organ at the back of the stage. Glenn was playing, and I hadn't another reed that

I could play. I had to retrieve that one. So I stood up, and Glenn looked up at me, wondering what in heaven's name I was doing. And as I went by him, I said, 'Vamp till ready.' That's a jazzer's term that says, 'Just keep going with that refrain until I get myself reorganized here, and we'll carry on.' Glenn didn't know what the hell I was talking about. I went back and picked up the reed, dusted it off, put it back on the bassoon, and we carried on with the performance. The poor chap didn't— Here was his great Toronto debut as a composer, and he's got some clown on the bassoon who's never played in public before."

Q: What did you finally think of the sonata? Is it a good piece?

A: Well, I've never played it again.

Q: Did you want to?

A: Not particularly. . . . I think Glenn was seeking something that he didn't quite achieve. Whatever it was. In fact, he was never happy with that bassoon sonata. Of course, he was very rarely happy with anything he wrote. After we'd finished performing the work, he insisted that it never be performed again. And any copies that I had, he wanted back. And the signature copy that I had, he destroyed.*

And then, almost out of nowhere, came a remarkable string quartet in F minor.† The most remarkable thing about it is that it is very beautiful. The disciple of Schoenbergian atonalism had suddenly regressed to an earlier Viennese tradition, that of Richard Strauss, Mahler, and particularly Bruckner, whose gorgeous Quintet in F major Gould had recently discovered.

Over a sustained pedal point on a low F, Gould made the second violin declaim a majestic four-note theme on which he constructed his entire quartet. (Perhaps unconsciously, Gould wrote a theme very similar to that of Beethoven's *Grosse Fuge* and also to the opening cello line in the A minor Quartet, Opus 132.) "This figure," Gould later wrote, "undergoes every adventure and enticement that

---

*Informed that a copy of the score and a recording still exist in the Gould archives, Kilburn said, "Well, that's his father's doing . . . part of this *history* that Bert was in the process of achieving."

†F minor was the key that expressed his own personality, according to one of the many such games that Gould liked to play. Asked by an interviewer to explain this statement, Gould said that F minor was "halfway between complex and stable, between upright and lascivious, between gray and highly tinted. . . . There is a certain obliqueness."

my technique would allow. All of the main sections of the work present themes which owe their derivation to this motive, however whimsically and fancifully its contours are altered in the progress of the work. . . . I was really attempting a giant romantic canvas to be composed of many minute pointillistic strokes."

Gould was almost too eager to be considered scandalous, scandalously melodious. He liked to compare his anachronistic quartet to the pictures of Hans van Meergeren, that unfortunate Dutch painter who achieved fame only in creating fraudulent pictures that he succeeded in selling as works by Vermeer. "How, in the midst of enthusiasm for the avant-garde movements of the day, could one find a work which would have been perfectly presentable at a turn-of-the-century academy . . . ?" Gould wrote in his liner notes to the Columbia recording of his quartet. "Well, the answer is really quite simple. Unlike many students, my enthusiasms were seldom balanced by antagonisms. My great admiration for the music of Schoenberg, for instance, was not enhanced by any counter-irritation for the Viennese romanticism of a generation before Schoenberg." Or, as he summed it up in an early draft of this essay, "I am constitutionally unfit to be a true rebel."

Gould claimed that his artful excursion into the 1890's soon became entirely spontaneous. "If this sort of theorizing suggests the same grim resolve with which every composer sets about an exercise in style," he wrote, "I must state that whatever may have been my academic motive initially, within a very few measures I was completely in the throes of this new experience. . . . I felt myself to be saying something original and my artistic conscience was clear. Whatever I had set out to prove pedagogically, it was soon evident that I was not shaping the Quartet—it was shaping me."

Well, perhaps, but the image of a creator in the throes of creation is not quite accurate. Donizetti wrote his marvelous *Don Pasquale* in eleven days, and when somebody mentioned that it had taken Rossini two weeks to finish *The Barber of Seville,* he said, "Rossini was always a slow worker." Gould spent two years laboring over his one-movement, half-hour-long quartet, and though he liked to consider himself a master craftsman, he had to keep telephoning friends to ask for guidance on the technical intricacies of bowing and double-stopping. Joseph Roddy remembers Gould even taking the manuscript to New York with him. "He was looking for some bowing advice," Roddy says, "and one night up in the Drake Hotel, I think it was, Sasha Schneider came up, and Debbie Ishlon of Columbia was there, and I was there, and there was the editing of the quartet to get the bowings right." Roddy tries mimicking their talk: "'I don't feel a down bow there— No, I don't— Are you sure?'"

"He used to call me sometimes at one o'clock in the morning because he had written three more bars to the quartet and he wanted to play the whole thing," Harvey Olnick recalls. "He wanted admiration the whole time, and indeed I thought it was miraculous. But as a piano piece, not as a quartet. Because he didn't really learn that you have to move registers around in order to make things interesting. And the composition was an act of will, of deciding beforehand that he wanted to do this."

So the work progressed. And there is probably no better way to describe it than to let Gould describe it, as he did in the long draft for his record-liner notes. "The development section in the classical symphonic structure is traditionally that place where the composer exerts all of his technical resources to elaborate and expand individually all the various themes and motives with which he has been working. It's obvious, I think, that this approach, this dissection of component parts, would be superfluous in my work since that is exactly what I have been doing from the beginning. Therefore, I allowed the development section to take an independent form—that of a fugue—indeed a very strict fugue. . . . The remainder of the development section of the Quartet is taken up with a series of chorales, three of them actually, whose function is to effect the return to the home key of F minor and hence the beginning of the recapitulation. . . ."

The supreme problem of any composer, of course, is to get his compositions performed. If Gould had written a piano sonata, he could have played it from Vancouver to Moscow, but since he had written a string quartet, he had to undertake the unfamiliar role of impresario for his own work. "Imagine then if you will the astonishment with which this work was met when I first played it on the piano for anyone that I could drag in to listen," he later wrote. "I well remember the first few piano read-throughs with some friends or other hapless callers in which the general tone of appreciation was something like, 'Ah, quit kidding.' 'Where did you dig this up?'"

That was in early 1955, when Gould was still just a Toronto prodigy, but 1955 was also the year in which Gould conquered Washington and New York, and so his quartet rather suddenly changed from the experiment of a provincial youth into the creation of an international celebrity. The following year, on May 26, it received its world premiere in Montreal by the Montreal Quartet (Hyman Bress, Mildred Goodman, Otto and Walter Joachim). Their performance prompted Marcel Valois of *La Presse* to high praise: "Serious, of high inspiration, pensive rather than lively, bathed in a discreet and slightly saddened coloring, the work . . . is of extraordinary interest."

When Gould became a codirector of the Stratford Festival, he brought along his quartet and put it in the middle of an unusual concert that also featured him playing the Berg Sonata and conducting from the keyboard Schoenberg's *Ode to Napoleon Bonaparte*. "Even though the [quartet] has a frankly acknowledged indebtedness to Bruckner and Richard Strauss, it was a moving and impressive work," Ross Parmenter wrote in the New York *Times*. Another listener, Walter Kaufman, the conductor of the Winnipeg Orchestra, wrote his praises directly to Gould: "Three days ago I heard your String Quartet . . . a most remarkable work. . . . You have much to say, and although you may say it differently in the years to come, whatever you say in your Quartet is good, solid, and honest music."

Gould found a small New York publisher, Barger and Barclay, who brought out the quartet in 1956, and then he began the long process of sending out copies and spreading the word. He hopefully sent it, for example, to Lukas Foss, then at Tanglewood. "It is a work that I am proud of but not altogether happy with," he wrote. "It was my first attempt at writing for strings and my old organist's habit of seeing the cello line as a pedal-board induced me to keep it for long stretches on the C string, among many other faults." And to Vladimir Golschmann. "I read the score," the conductor wrote back, "and feel delighted to realize that a very great pianist can be more than a very great pianist." Gould was "so happy" that Golschmann had "found some interest in my String Quartet." The next time they met, he wrote, "I would love to play it for you, either via the transcription which was made of it by the Montreal String Quartet or my much more exciting and much more inaccurate piano reduction."

And to David Diamond, to whom Gould somewhat mysteriously said that he was now struggling with a sonata for clarinet and piano, "which I am desperately trying to prevent from becoming a quintet." Diamond was rather chillingly professional: "I would like to discuss with you the voice-leading, notation for strings, and in general what I find is a very restricted range coverage of the instruments," but he did add: "I want to know more of your music." They next met, Diamond recalls, after a Carnegie Hall performance of Diamond's Sixth Symphony by Charles Munch and the Boston Symphony, a performance in which "Mr. Munch lost his place, and it was sort of a mess." Diamond, Munch, Gould, and others gathered in Leonard Bernstein's apartment across the street. Diamond remembers talking with Gould about his efforts to escape from atonalism. "I said, 'Although your texture is quite simple, and you use it very, very well, did you consciously work through the entire quartet in serial technique?' He said, 'Yes, I did. I even have twelve-tone serial charts.' Overall, I found his quartet a little on the dry side, and yet quite expressive, and for some strange reason I felt there was a kind of Wagnerian *melos* in it, especially in the slow sections."

All this lobbying finally helped persuade Columbia to bring out a recording, early in 1960, by the Symphonia Quartet (Kurt Loebl, Elmer Seltzer, Tom Brennand, and Thomas Liberti, all members of the Cleveland Orchestra), which had given the work its American premiere in Cleveland the previous year. ("While addressing women's associations is not one of my favorite pastimes," Gould wrote to Louis Lane, the associate conductor of the Cleveland Orchestra, "I am more than happy to barter a lecture on Schoenberg for a performance of the quartet.") This recording, of course, brought Gould's composition an international audience. The *Christian Science Monitor* found the quartet "an intensely beautiful work," and *The Saturday Review* was equally impressed: "Gould's materials have a shape and character of their own, beautifully suited, incidentally, to the medium in which he is working. . . . The impulse to 'sing' is also strong in him, and it comes as a sample of refreshing aesthetic candor to find a composer who dares to write what he feels."

Not everyone was so enthusiastic, of course. Eric McLean of the

Montreal *Star* raised some serious objections: "It is touched with genius like everything Mr. Gould sets out to do. . . . But its faults are great ones too. The string writing is almost completely out of character, with the instruments crowded into a narrow tessitura. Whenever he ventures into such things as double-stopping, tremolos at the bridge, or even pizzicato, the effect is rather self-conscious. . . . I still believe that the best way to hear this work is to have the composer play it on the piano, singing whatever his fingers cannot encompass, and cursing the page-turner." Despite such criticisms, though, Gould's quartet lingers in the memory of anyone who hears it. Writing in *Commentary* at the time of Gould's death a quarter of a century later, Samuel Lipman judged his Opus 1 "an enormously talented reworking of early Schoenberg, deeply moving, for all its derivativeness, and never less than brilliantly accomplished as a composition."

Gould was pleased and proud with the success of his first major composition. "Despite its atmosphere of faded elegance and rather bittersweet fin-de-siecle idiom, [it] has received on the whole marvelous critical notices," he wrote to a friend in Berlin. "There have been a few 'fashionable' reviews which have pointed out that it is rather inappropriate to revive the spirit of Richard Strauss in the age of Karlheinz Stockhausen (or is it really his age?), but the 'progressive' voices have, fortunately, been in the minority and have helped stir up reasonably healthy controversy."

More important, Gould saw this first substantial creation as the first milestone on the road to a career as a composer. "This Quartet represents a part of my musical development which I cannot but regard with some sentiment," he wrote in his characteristically formal liner notes for the Columbia recording. "It is certainly not unusual to find an Op. 1 in which a young composer inadvertently presents a subjective synthesis of all that has most deeply affected his adolescence. . . . Sometimes these prodigal summations are the harbingers of the true creative life. Sometimes the brilliance with which they reflect the past manages to excel all that their composer will do thereafter. In any event . . . it's Op. 2 that counts."

Although Gould did write other music, there was never to be any Opus 2. "I specialize in unfinished works," he confessed at one

point. Except for his densely contrapuntal 1954 cadenzas to Beethoven's first piano concerto, which Gould himself described as
"vastly inappropriate cadenzas . . . in the general harmonic idiom of
Max Reger," his only other published composition was a mildly
amusing little neo-Baroque exercise entitled "So You Want to
Write a Fugue?"

For just a trifle, this proved a remarkably popular work. Originally written as a five-minute finale for a television show called
"The Anatomy of Fugue," which Gould did for the CBC in 1963,
it was recorded for Columbia the following year by an ensemble
consisting of Elizabeth Benson-Guy, soprano; Anita Darian, mezzo-
soprano; Charles Bressler, tenor; Donald Gramm, baritone, and the
Juilliard Quartet, all conducted by Vladimir Golschmann. *HiFi/
Stereo Review* published a substantial article by Gould about this
work in April of 1964 and bound into that issue a thin plastic copy
of the recording. G. Schirmer published the score that same year,
with a pink cover ornamented by two angels. And Columbia finally
reissued the recording in 1980 as part of its *Glenn Gould Silver Jubilee Album.*

Gould's own description of this ponderous little fugue shows
how seriously he took his own attempts at humor, particularly on
the rather arcane (for television audiences) subject of counterpoint.
"The basso begins by suggesting that a certain degree of courage is
involved: 'You've got the nerve to write a fugue, so go ahead.' The
tenor is concerned with the utility of the finished product: 'So go
ahead and write a fugue that we can sing.' The contralto . . . advo-
cates an audaciously antiacademic method: 'Pay no mind to what
we've told you, give no heed to what we've told you and the theory
that you've read.' . . . As a gesture of tribute . . . the string quartet
now renders a quodlibet of four of Bach's more celebrated themes
(you'll note, among them, the second Brandenburg Concerto).
Then, appropriately, the quartet turns to the contralto for a brief
lecture on the perils of exhibitionism: 'But never be clever for the
sake of being clever.' This, with its attendant warning—'For a
canon in inversion is a dangerous diversion and a bit of augmenta-
tion is a serious temptation'—creates an entirely new thematic substance. Hereupon the string quartet renders a grandiose if minor-
inflected quotation from *Die Meistersinger*—the archtypical example

of musical cleverness—after which all concerned engage in joyous recapitulation. . . ."

This "joyous recapitulation" ends on a note of whistling-in-the-dark determination: "We're going to write a fugue. . . . We're going to write a good one now." That determination, of course, is exactly what was lacking in Gould's attempts to become a composer. "So go ahead," as the singers urged in the beginning, was an order that Gould could carry out only in terms of parody and pastiche. Near the end, he ventured warily into a mention of his own difficulties. "When you've finished writing it," the soprano promises, "I think you'll find great joy in it." The baritone can only answer: "Hope so. Well, nothing ventured, nothing gained, they say, but it really is rather hard to start."

Trio: Well?

Baritone: Let us try. Right now.

Trio: Now. We're going to write a fugue. . . .

And so on. Gould was a perfectionist, and perhaps he knew too much great music too well to accept the dispiriting contrast between his own efforts and those of the masters. He could obviously see the differences quite clearly, and he could not see much hope for narrowing them. For all his cleverness and skill, he knew that the innate gifts of a Beethoven or even a Scriabin—that compulsive creativity that Schoenberg once compared to an apple tree's need to flower and produce apples—was not in him. "I found that other men's music kept coming out," he admitted to William Littler of the Toronto *Star*. And so he fell back on the evasions of wit and humor. The sad question about the musical clowning in "So You Want to Write a Fugue?" is whether Gould knew how cruelly he was mocking his own failures.

As he got older, Gould kept returning to this kind of burlesque but for smaller and smaller audiences. Among his papers there remains an elaborately copied "Lieberson Madrigal," written for a testimonial dinner for Goddard Lieberson, who reigned as the king of Columbia Records for a quarter of a century. This starts with a four-part chorale of celebration: "Goddard, we wish you a happy anniversary, this is indeed a time for true rejoicing." But conflicting voices soon start bringing in office politics and inside jokes about "doting A & R . . . publicity that's seldom up to par, Creative Services that don't create, and sales force that gave poor John (and Frank) the gate. . . ." This inevitably leads into a fugue, to a text of "Lennie Bernstein wants to do Boulez, no Stockhausen . . ." over a sustained bass on a rival text: "No, no, Lennie, no you can't, why must you be so damn avant, damn avant, damn avant garde?"

In later years, Gould continued writing such things only for his friends. In one folder of his compositions, for example, there are ten pages of ink sketches leading up to "Monica—Her Madrigal" (presumably Monica Gaylord, a talented young black pianist from New York). The four-part lyrics are on Gould's standard level of comic verse: "Monica Anne, we've tried our best to guide you/ And though you've gone your own way, we've defied you./ Through every season, you've called it treason, yet we've still sought to reason with you./ We've clearly failed, for you have paled,/ You have now turned blue. . . ."

Gould's unfinished works were often ambitious (that may indeed be why they remained unfinished), from the boyhood chorus of postnuclear frogs to a cantata on Stalingrad that he took up in his thirties. "Future plans?" Gould was quoted as saying to an interviewer from the *CBC Times* in May of 1964, just after his retirement from the stage. "I'm recording like mad and working frantically on *A Letter from Stalingrad,* which I'm writing for soprano Lois Marshall. It's a very personal piece for me. The text is a letter from a German officer killed at Stalingrad, an extraordinarily moving thing, in which he instructs his wife in how she must conduct herself in the catastrophe of their world. He exhibits the remarkable schizophrenia of the German military character, coupling sentimental nostalgia with arrogant autocracy. My music is loose variations on a theme of Richard Strauss' *Metamorphosen.** I've also written the first draft of a short, quasi-autobiographical opera. . . ."

But what ever happened to "A Letter from Stalingrad"? One can try asking Lois Marshall on the telephone.

A: I really don't know. It's something I know nothing about.

Q: You never sang it?

A: No indeed. I never saw it, nor ever heard of it. It may be a myth. . . .

---

*Oddly enough, Gould also talked of writing a TV opera on Franz Kafka's *Metamorphosis.*

The "quasi-autobiographical opera" is about a Straussian composer who wants, like the composer of Gould's quartet, to write old-fashioned music. This brings him a certain success. "Think of all the performances of your works,/" runs one fragment of the prospective libretto, "Your symphony given by Bernstein,/ Your piano sonata played by Cliburn. . . ." But now the composer insists on writing an antiquarian opera, including a fugue, and his daughter anticipates nothing but trouble from fashionable critics. These early drafts can be dated to the early 1960's, since they were scribbled on the stationary of TWA and Continental Airlines, but other folders contain very different drafts.

In one of these, the composer's identity becomes quite clear, since it is entitled "Dr. Strauss Writes an Opera" (presumably based on Strauss's *Capriccio,* for the stage is set in Garmisch in 1940). It begins—cliché of clichés—with the telephone ringing and the aged composer crossing the stage to take a call from his English publisher: "Yes, yes, it is—uh—very good—yes, that is right, put him on, please—Herr Hawkes, *grüss Gott, wie geht's,* Herr Hawkes. . . ." In another version, the situation becomes more abstract, and Gould describes his cast of characters only as "the composer, the composer's daughter, her husband, a 12-tone composer. . . ." The plot remains roughly the same: "Comp. about 60 lives with daughter and her husband, who is reluctantly supporting him, and who is ambitious for . . . recognition of his talent. . . . He, however, lives a stormy interior life which is almost untouched by the daughter's plans for him. . . ." In one of Gould's fragmentary lyrics, the daughter denounces the composer with considerable bitterness: "Old man, you're failing,/ Old man, you're dying,/ Old man, your world will simply fade away. . . ." If Gould ever wrote any music for this "quasi-autobiographical opera," there is no evidence of it.

Perhaps the most extraordinary of Gould's unfinished compositions—unstarted compositions—was one that he planned for the end of his life. "Glenn said that at fifty he would retire and write," Jessie Greig recalls her cousin echoing the predictions of his youth. "And one of the things that he told me he was going to do was, he was going to write—he was fascinated by the book of Revelation in the Bible, and he was going to write something akin to Handel's *Messiah.*"

... And I stood upon the sand of the sea, and saw a beast rise up out of the sea, having seven heads and ten horns, and upon his horns ten crowns, and upon his heads the name of blasphemy ...

"We talked about it a couple of years, about the book of Revelation, about what it meant," says Miss Greig. "He had his own interpretations."

Q: What was his religion, exactly?

A: He believed in God, he believed in a hereafter. And you know that after his mother died [in 1975], I think that it was a more important part of his life, and he talked about it more often. He wanted to discuss certain things with me about the hereafter. His dreams were often about that.

Q: What dreams?

A: After his mother died, he dreamed about her a great deal, and he would tell me in great detail about this dream, about where she was living, and how she knew what we were doing, and so, you know, he really had a belief in the hereafter.

... And he showed me a pure river of water of life, clear as crystal, proceeding out of the throne of God and of the Lamb. ... And on either side of the river, was there the tree of life, which bare twelve manner of fruits ... and the leaves of the tree were for the healing of the nations. ...

We can never know why so little of the music that Gould thought of writing, and talked of writing, ever got written. "Between the idea/ and the reality/," as Eliot wrote, "Between the motion/ And the act/ Falls the Shadow. . . ." Part of Gould's failure as a composer perhaps did come from the distractions of other activities, of radio and writing and all the disturbances of daily life. "I have the feeling that he was the kind of person who was constantly engaged in research," Diamond says, "constantly writing these lectures or these liner notes, and you know how time-consuming these things are. And that was a kind of avoidance of getting to composition. When you have that kind of musical intelligence, composing is not hard. What *is* hard is just getting to that paper and sitting down with the ink or the pencils and *composing*."

Part of Gould's failure undoubtedly came from the curse of perfectionism, part perhaps from a deeply felt lack of first-rate creative talent—creative genius—part simply from a reluctance to explore the limits of his own imperfections. "He *hated* it that everything came out sounding like everybody else," says Leonard Bernstein, who has known his own conflicts between performing and composing, between one's own work and the influence of masters. "He said, 'I can't bear it.' I said, 'Well, a lot of Beethoven comes out sounding like Haydn, a lot of Schubert comes out sounding like Mozart—what're you going to do?' A lot of Mahler comes out sounding like everybody who ever wrote music before Mahler. But there's a personal voice there, in Schubert and in Beethoven and Mahler. It's a deep inner sound that a composer makes, which comes from the depths of him. Stravinsky stole from Tchaikowsky and Beethoven and Bach and Rimsky-Korsakov and Ravel and—*but* there's that *Igor* screaming through it all, an amazingly individual voice. And Glenn said, 'Well, I guess that's what I don't have.' And he couldn't stand it. He said, 'It's all either Schoenberg or Brahms, what I write.' He showed me some sketch of something he had worked on, as if to prove how *bad* he was as a composer. He said, 'Look at this—' I wish he had gone on, because I think he would have arrived—he would have written some fascinating music. That I'm sure of."

Lacking that personal voice—or feeling that he lacked it—Gould got great satisfaction in his later years by adapting the ideas of others and creating those marvelous transcriptions of Strauss and Wagner. But as for original work, he finally decided on a completely different course, rejecting all the overworked conventional forms of musical composition and starting to experiment with something quite new, a quite different kind of music.

"The Idea of North"

"What I have in mind, believe it or not," Gould wrote to a friend in San Francisco early in 1965, less than a year after his retirement, "is a trip to the Arctic. I have an enormous compulsion to look upon the Polar seas and I find that this is growing apace each year, so that I really must get it out of my system somehow."

Now that he was free to come and go as he pleased, he really did head north that June to fulfill his "enormous compulsion." To his admirer in Leningrad, Kitty Gvozdeva, he provided a few details: "I went to Hudson's Bay to a point just a few miles above the most northerly growth of forest in that area, which is for the moment the most northern point to which you can take a train in Canada. . . . This train, although it has one car with sleeping accommodations, is not really intended for tourists. Everyone seemed to think I was just slightly mad to be on it in the first place—and practically every member of its crew turned out to be fabulously gifted as a raconteur, in the way that people who have experienced great isolation tend to be. And so for approximately 1000 miles and for two nights and a day (each way), I was able to see an aspect of Canada with which very few people concern themselves. And I have come away from it with an enthusiasm for the North which may even get me through another winter of city living which, as you know, I loathe. . . ."

It was true, at least as of that time, that very few Canadians concerned themselves with the North. "We have administered these vast territories of the north in an almost continuing state of absence of mind," Prime Minister Louis St. Laurent said in 1953, when he first created the Department of Northern Affairs. Yet the North has long haunted the Canadian imagination, not just the Arctic territories themselves but the fundamental idea of North. The North is everything beyond the horizon, beyond the comfortable and the familiar, everything frozen and dark, treeless and windswept. It is a little like the American image of the western frontier, but unlike the compliant West, the hostile Arctic still presents an enormous wilderness. It has no San Diego, no Las Vegas, no Disneyland. "The North is always there," as André Siegfried once wrote. "It is the background of the picture without which Canada would not be Canada."

"It includes great, unrelieved stretches of snow and ice . . ." Barry Lopez wrote in *Arctic Dreams*. "But there are, too, surprising and riveting sights: Wilberforce Falls on the Hood River suddenly tumbles 160 feet into a wild canyon in the midst of the Canadian tundra, and its roar can be heard for miles. . . . The badlands of east-central Melville Island, an eroded country of desert oranges, of muted yellows and reds, reminds a traveler of canyons and arroyos in southern Utah. And there are places more exotic, like the Ruggles River, which flows out of Lake Hazen on Ellesmere Island in winter and runs 2,000 feet through the Stygian darkness, wreathed in frost smoke, before it disappears underneath its own ice. . . ."

In an obscure way, the history of the North makes Canada's national origins older and quite different from those of the United States. "The ferment that led explorers to the Canadian frontier did not begin in the fifteenth-century courts of Lisbon and Madrid, or in the counting houses of London and Bristol," as R.A.J. Phillips wrote in *Canada's North*. "It started much earlier, in Scandinavia." Five centuries before Columbus set sail, Eric the Red had led the Vikings to Greenland. They built settlements there, and on the coast of Newfoundland, which they called Markland. They erected stone houses and barns, brought in farm animals, cut down forests. Throughout the Middle Ages, the Viking settlements in northern Canada were known in Europe as a source of two treasured animals: falcons and polar bears. Canada, then, was not an obstacle discovered during the search for a new route to the Indies but rather, as Phillips put it, "the frontier of northern Europe."

Yet even after the gold rush in the Klondike at the end of the nineteenth century, even after the building of roads and airfields during World War II, the North remained largely untouched. When the Canadian government recovered from its "absence of mind" and began a decade of building and development, the entire population of this vast region still amounted to no more than 25,000. In all the Northwest Territories, there were exactly eight doctors. Education was provided by Anglican and Catholic missionaries, administration by the Royal Canadian Mounted Police. Even today, when icebreakers can force their way through the legendary Northwest Passage, now known as Lancaster Sound, and when trash and garbage can be found littering the bare tundra, there remains a mysterious attraction.

"The towns and telephones, the sound of generators, the grinding of sewage trucks, the ugliness of oil tanks: all this human defilement has not robbed the North of its strange power," Phillips wrote. "When men live in the North, their values change. . . . They live a lifetime alone, and die when they emerge. They become citizens of a different kind of country, a country where nature is overwhelmingly stronger than man. . . . Northern travellers seem to have found an extraordinary fulfillment in this unlikeliest of lands and seas. . . . In success or failure, almost all become missionaries for their cause. When they could return, they did. When they could not return, they relived their northern voyagings throughout their days, the way other men have spent their lives experiencing over and over the trauma of wartime."

Gould, with his Scottish origins, felt an almost mystical sense of that Canadian North and of its connections to the rest of the northern world. If you look at the globe from the North Pole rather than the Equator, Canada joins Russia, Scandinavia, Britain, and Germany on the peripheries of that frozen Mare Nostrum. This international idea of North was never fully articulated in Gould's writings, but it is hardly accidental that he not only loved Bach and Beethoven and Wagner but also recorded less universally admired Scandinavian composers like Grieg and Sibelius and even performed the music of the reclusive and eccentric Norwegian atonalist Fartein Valen. He thoroughly disapproved of the French, Debussy and Ravel, and he seems to have known very little of the great Italian opera composers.

Typically enough, Gould never actually went to the Arctic North.

Most of this frozen wilderness can be reached only by airplane, and nothing could now make Gould get into an airplane. The nearest to the Arctic that he ever ventured was that trip aboard the train known as the *Muskeg Express,* which ran and still runs from Winnipeg a thousand miles north to Churchill, on the southwestern shore of Hudson's Bay. The railroad ends there, and so does the highway system. From a southern perspective, Churchill is almost at the end of the world. But although the tree line ends here, this is barely the beginning of the Canadian North. There are about another 100 miles to the 60th parallel, the southern border of the Northwest Territories, another 200 miles beyond that to Repulse Bay, another 600 miles or so to Resolute Bay and Lancaster Sound and the Northwest Passage, and another 400 miles beyond that to the glaciers of Ellesmere Island. And only there lie the "polar seas" that Gould said he felt "an enormous compulsion to look upon." For an inhabitant of Toronto to describe one train trip to Churchill as a voyage to the North is a little like a Bostonian thinking (as any true Bostonian would think) of a visit to Washington as a journey south, or of a trip to Cleveland as the West.

Still, it was not the reality of the North that fascinated Gould, and he admitted as much, *en passant,* in the introduction to his extraordinary radio documentary, "The Idea of North": "I've been intrigued for quite a long time . . . by that incredible tapestry of tundra and taiga country, as they call it. . . . I've read about it, written about it occasionally, and even pulled up my parka once and gone there. But like all but a very few Canadians, I guess, I've had no direct confrontation with the northern third of our country. I've remained of necessity an outsider, and the north has remained for me a convenient place to dream about, spin tall tales about sometimes, and, in the end, avoid."

"He said, 'Let's go for an automobile ride, and I'll show you Toronto,'" Leonard Bernstein recalls. "So, well, what is there to see? It was cold, and it was getting dark, and I had sort of seen it the day before. So we went out, Glenn in his usual three coats and two hats, and I don't know how many pairs of gloves. We got into his car, which was a black sedan. He turned the heat up to maximum, and the radio volume up to maximum, and he got a station that was playing pop tunes, and Petula Clark was singing, and I said, 'Do you really want to hear this?' It was so hot in that car, I can't tell you, and the music was so loud, and there was nothing to see—it was growing dark—but we drove around for maybe half an hour, having a conversation by shouting over this radio full blast, and that was our tour of Toronto.

"One of the things we talked about was his new love affair with the Arctic. This man who was so afraid of cold, and so geared against it—and I mean literally, the gear he traveled with was immense—why would he seek it out, why would he seek out this enemy? Which was the enemy of his fingers, which were always getting cold at a recording session or a rehearsal, so that he had to have hot water, and many, many mittens. And he tried to answer it in—I don't know—without turning off the radio. It's very hard to tell you what was actually said, but what I came away with was a feeling of a kind of cosmic exploration. There was something spiritual about it. Elements of magic, having to do with the magnetic pole.

"I was terribly moved by it, because I'd have thought that the only explanation would be to seek out the thing that hurts you the most and confront it, in a sort of good old-fashioned Freudian way. The only way you can conquer your fear of elevators is to get into one and say, 'This is an elevator, I'm here, and everything's all right.' But it wasn't that. It was something much more magical and mystical."

"It was through me that Glenn encountered the concept of the radio documentary," says John Roberts of the CBC. "It was in sixty-one, I think—I produced a program called *Music by Royal Composers*, and it was just that, you know, all kinds of interesting people, in all varieties of monarchies of Britain, and it was an exploration of that area. Glenn was very fascinated. He asked me how it was put together, and I explained in immense detail, and he was very, very fascinated. He said, 'You know, I'd like to do that.' And then not long afterwards, he said to me, 'Look, I would like to try and put together a documentary on Schoenberg. Would you be interested?' And I said, 'Terribly interested.' And so, his first Schoenberg documentary was the result of that. And of course, having gone through all that, he was absolutely bitten by the bug, and he wanted to continue, and then other departments were interested in him and what he was doing, and so his scope widened...."

Gould himself recalled his involvement with documentary radio beginning much earlier, in 1945 or 1946. Indeed, there was something about the medium itself, something about hearing a disembodied voice trying to make a connection, that had attracted and delighted the lonely schoolboy. Radio brought him the outside world, and yet it did so without violating his strong sense of privacy. "It's always seemed to me," he wrote, "that when that first person heard that second person's voice by virtue of a crystal set, or whatever it was heard on, that they had not only the most unique experience in music—of music in the sense of voice as sound, obviously, but that they had the one true approach to radio. They were able to get at something quite special . . . that original human contact, that incredible, spine-tingling sense of awareness of some other human voice and persona."

Gould remembered his first documentary on Schoenberg with some dismay, however. "I was always dissatisfied with the kind of documentaries that radio seemed to decree," he said. "You know, they very often came out sounding . . . —okay, I'll borrow Mr. McLuhan's term—linear. They came out sounding 'Over to you, now back to our host, and here for the wrap-up is'—in a word, predictable. I wrote the script, for instance, for a program on Schoenberg in sixty-two . . . [and] it seemed that one had to accept a linear mold in order to pursue any kind of career in radio at that time. So I was very dissatisfied with the available techniques, and in 1967, for the first time, I got a chance to try my hand at producing something on my own."

This was to become "The Idea of North." "What I would most like to do," Gould wrote to a friend in the summer of 1967, "is to examine the effects of solitude and isolation upon those who have lived in the Arctic or Sub-Arctic. In some subtle way, the latitudinal factor does seem to have a modifying influence upon character, although I have no editorial axe to grind in the matter...." And to another friend: "My Arctic bluff has finally been called by Mother CBC, no less. They have suggested that I really do go ahead...."

Gould's plan was to interrogate a number of people who had lived and worked in the North. "Something really does happen to people who go into the north," Gould later wrote, "—they become . . . in effect, philosophers." Then, with razors and glue, he would see what he could make of their taped recollections. One of his first choices was Bob Phillips, who had worked in the Department of Northern Affairs and was now assistant secretary of the cabinet, Privy Council Office. He was also a perceptive and sympathetic observer whose new book on the North had undoubtedly attracted Gould's attention.

"I remember so vividly the first contact," says Phillips, a graying, craggy-faced man who now devotes much of his time to renovating old houses. "It was a Sunday evening when we happened to have guests in, and the phone rang, and it was somebody from—he identified himself as from CBC in Toronto, called Gould, and he said he was doing a series of programs on the North, and asked my help. A couple of years had gone by since I'd been professionally associated with the North, so I offered to introduce him to other people, authorities on the North, but he was very insistent. He said, no, it doesn't matter if you're not up-to-date—it isn't about being up-to-date. It's more philosophical.

"So since we had guests waiting, I finally took the line of least resistance and agreed to meet him at the CBC studios in a day or two, and that was that. Or then—I remember the next stage even more vividly because I think it was the greatest *gaffe* in my life. I met this strange character up on the seventh floor of the Château Laurier, and we first went through a *strange* performance, in which there were more microphones than I'd ever seen laid out before, and finally he said, 'Well, may we talk?' And then he asked really quite penetrating, interesting questions about the North, which required very long answers. And while I was answering, I was astonished at his attitude. He was sort of shaking his head, and smiling, and shaking his head some more, affirmatively, and he seemed to be sort of happy, and then at times it was almost as though he were directing an orchestra, with his hands.

"And so it went, fairly intensely, for about an hour. I had no idea it was so long. And he said, 'Well, look, this is just absolutely marvelous, just what I wanted. Now why don't we take a break? You must be tired.' And so coffee was produced. And so, making conversation over the coffee, I asked him, I said, 'Excuse me, Mr. Gould, but are you related to the pianist?' And he then said that he *was* the pianist. Well, it seemed to me the most extraordinary thing. I had no idea. . . ."

By some mysterious system of his own, Gould chose four other "participants" who had spent substantial amounts of time in the North. "We wanted," he said later, "an enthusiast, a cynic, a government budget-watcher, as well as someone who could represent that limitless expectation and limitless capacity for disillusionment which inevitably affects the questing spirit of those who go north seeking their future." For these roles, he picked, in addition to Bob Phillips, Marianne Schroeder, a nurse; Frank Vallee, a professor of sociology in Ottawa; James Lotz, a British anthropologist; and W. V. (Wally) Maclean, an aged surveyor whom Gould had met on the *Muskeg Express,* an autodidact who loved to quote Shakespeare and to hold forth on the symbolic meanings of the North.

It was Maclean, in a way, who had given Gould the idea for "The Idea of North." A railroad steward had introduced them at the breakfast table, and after some talk about the prospects of the North, Maclean startled Gould by asking, "Are you aware, Mr. Gould, that both Thoreau and Kafka practiced my profession? That both were surveyors?" Gould confessed that he was not. Maclean went on to argue that "there's a real connection between surveying and literature." Gould was fascinated. "For me, to encounter this suddenly in the middle of nowhere was amazing," he later told an interviewer. "And we started an eight-hour conversation—we didn't rise from that table after mid-morning tea, after lunch, or afternoon tea, until four o'clock, by which time I had a headache from the weight of ideas. . . . That was the genesis of his participating."

As usual, though, Gould made of his characters what he imagined in himself. "I think he split his own psyche up into different parts to make the show," Jim Lotz recalls. "The nurturer (the nurse), the objective critic (university professor), the pontificator (the civil servant), and the antiestablishment adventurer (is that me, or am I the idealist?). Then he had the old man in the cave as the commentator. You must see what Glenn did in Jungian terms, not Freudian ones. We were not matched off against each other, but rather set up to complement each other. Glenn played me like a piano, and in fact the program should have been called 'The Idea of Glenn Gould.'"

Still, Gould organized "The Idea of North" by getting each of these people to talk about the North, about their own experiences of loneliness and isolation. Thus Nurse Schroeder: "I didn't have to go to somebody in Coral [Harbor] and say I'm lonesome or I'm depressed. I just had to go and visit them, play a game of chess, whatever they wanted to do, and right away there was a sense of sharing this life. One could realize the value of another human being. You're excluding the rest of the world that will never understand, and you've made your own world with these people, and probably what you'll never know, and what nobody else will ever know, is whether you're kidding yourself or not. Have you really made your peace with these other people . . . because the only alternative to peace is a kind of crackup?"

And Lotz: "I was in many respects solitary, but in a strange way the North has made me more sort of gregarious, because the North does show you exactly how much you rely on your fellow man. What the sense of community means in the North is a matter of life and death. . . . It's so big, it's so vast, it's so immense, it cares so little, and this sort of diminishes you. And then you think, 'My God, I am here. I've got here, I live here. . . .'"

Such observations were reasonably interesting, reasonably perceptive, but they were still only raw material, reels of unedited tape, fodder. Once Gould had his interviews all recorded and transcribed in the south, he once again headed northward, on Route 17, a road that he loved, skirting the shores of Lake Superior. "No. 17 defines for much of its passage across Ontario the northernmost limit of agrarian settlement," he wrote some years later. "It is endowed with habitation, when at all, by fishing villages, mining camps, and timber towns that straddle the highway every fifty miles or so. Among these, names such as Michipicoten and Batchawana advertise the continuing segregation of the Canadian Indian; Rossport and Jackfish proclaim the no-nonsense mapmaking of the early white settlers; and Marathon and Terrace Bay . . . betray the postwar influx of American capital (Terrace is the Brasilia of Kimberly-Clark's Kleenex-Kotex operation in Ontario)."

While driving north, Gould heard on his car radio so many CBC renditions of Petula Clark singing "Who Am I?" that he decided to write an inquiry entitled "The Search for Petula Clark." But on this trip, the singer's question of "Who am I?" led Gould to a little coastal town named Wawa, where he enjoyed tramping along the lakefront piers built of giant timbers. "It's an extraordinary place . . ." he later said, "to sort out some thoughts and try to get some writing done."

"What did he do?" says Lorne Tulk, the skilled editor-engineer who worked with Gould on "The Idea of North." "He rented a motel room, and he sat in the motel room and wrote."

Q: What's up there, in Wawa?

A: Nothing.

Q: He just went up there for a visit?

A: No, he went to Wawa and wrote "North." He had all of his interviews transcribed, and he took all the transcripts with him, locked himself in a motel room in Wawa for two or three weeks, and came back with a program.

If the interviewing had been only a beginning, however, the writing was still only a beginning. In creating what he called "a documentary which thinks of itself as a drama," Gould had made a point of interviewing his five dramatis personae separately; they never met. He had originally planned these five separate interviews as five separate segments, perhaps even to be broadcast on five separate evenings. "And that remained true until something like six weeks prior to broadcast time," Gould later wrote, "which is pretty frightening when you come to think of it. *Five* weeks prior to broadcast time, I suddenly decided that that wasn't at all what I wanted to do—that, obviously, it had to be an integrated unit of some kind in which the texture, the tapestry of the words themselves would differentiate the characters and create dreamlike conjunctions within the documentary. These, of course, would have to be achieved through some rather prodigious editing, and I spent something like two to three weeks occupied with fine editing, still all the while being unsure as to the eventual form that the piece was going to take."

Since Gould had asked his chamber-music players roughly the same questions, he could organize his material into a half-dozen scenes, in which all the characters addressed themselves to the same general point. But when he had finished all this, he found that his hour-long show ran to nearly an hour and a half. "So I thought, 'Well, obviously, one scene has got to go.' We had a scene on the Eskimo—couldn't lose that; we had a scene on isolation and its effects—that had to stay, obviously; we had our closing soliloquy, we had our opening trio and other indispensables—and I couldn't part with any of them. . . . I thought to myself, 'Look, we really could hear some of these people speaking simultaneously—there is no particular reason why not.'"

After telling this story, in "Radio as Music," Gould admitted that "perhaps I exaggerate ever so slightly," but that was essentially how he invented what he later took to calling "contrapuntal radio." Almost nothing, of course, is ever "invented" just like that. Frank Capra, for one, was experimenting with simultaneous dialogue in films as far back as the early 1930's, and all such experimenters were quite aware that even the most banal statements somehow sound, when juxtaposed against other banal statements, less banal. Gould was nonetheless the first professional musician to edit the tapes of spoken words as though they were the notes in a contrapuntal composition.

"The Idea of North" begins with Nurse Schroeder saying, somewhat wistfully: "I was fascinated by the country as such. I flew north from Churchill to Coral Harbor . . . at the end of September. [Note how casually she names as her starting place the northernmost point that Gould ever reached.] Snow had begun to fall, and the country was partially covered by it. Some of the lakes were frozen around the edges, but towards the center of the lakes you could still see the clear, clear water. . . ."

After about a minute of this, Professor Vallee's rather gruff voice begins speaking (Gould, for some reason, never specifically identified any speakers, or any music being played, in any of his radio documentaries): "I don't go—let me say this again—I don't go for this northmanship bit at all. . . ." And so the duet continues:

Schroeder: We seemed to be going into nowhere, and the further north we went . . .

Vallee (simultaneously): I don't knock those people who do claim that they want to go farther and farther north, but . . .

These two people who have never met continue speaking simultaneously for a minute or so, and then, soon after Vallee says, "And the other fellow says, 'Well, I did one of thirty days,'" Bob Phillips's mellow voice starts saying, "And then for another eleven years, I served the North in various capacities. . . ."

This may all seem rather commonplace, but Gould edited these taped observations with a meticulous sense of both meaning and sound. Nurse Schroeder's voice begins almost pianissimo, then very gradually gets louder, and each new voice in this spoken fugato comes in on a specific tangent. Gould described this as "a kind of trio sonata texture." Speaking of Vallee's entrance in the midst of Nurse Schroeder's monologue, he said, "By this time we have become aware of a gentleman who has started to speak and who upon the word 'further' says 'farther'—'farther and farther north' is the context. At that moment, his voice takes precedence over hers in terms of dynamic emphasis. Shortly after, he uses the words 'thirty days,' and by this point we have become aware of a third voice which immediately after 'thirty days' says 'eleven years'—and another crossover point has been effected. The scene is built so that it has a kind of—I don't know if you have ever looked at the tone rows of Anton Webern as distinguished from those of Arnold Schoenberg, but it has a kind of Webern-like continuity-in-crossover in that motives which are similar but not identical are used for the exchange of instrumental ideas. . . ."

It is a little difficult for an ordinary listener to accept Gould's assessment of "The Idea of North" as a musical composition. Granted that it is perfectly possible to treat the speaking voice as a musical instrument, granted that Gould edited his interview tapes just as skillfully and as imaginatively as he edited the tapes of his own performances on the piano, it nonetheless remains true that when Nurse Schroeder observes that "we seemed to be going into nowhere," these are neither abstract sounds being organized according to Gould's aesthetic plan nor are they Gould's words expressing Gould's ideas. Instead of composing a piece of verbal music, in other words, Gould was simply playing the role of editor, and succumbing, as editors often do, to the idea that what he had edited had become his own creation. A professional music critic like William Littler of the Toronto *Star* can be more understanding. "It rather depends on how deeply you want to argue what composition consists of," he says. "If it means the ordering of materials, with a sense of structure, to produce an overall statement—yes, compositional principles were involved in 'The Idea of North.' He's working with words, so he's composing with words. Obviously, if you take it much further and try to analyze it in terms of sonata form, you can't do it. But the general principles of composition are there." Besides, in an era when John Cage composes an *Imaginary Landscape* that includes twelve radios simultaneously playing at random, in an era when Steve Reich takes a taped confession of an accused murderer and then reproduces one or two phrases in a googol of repetitions, how is one to define music, except that it is whatever a gifted musician says it is?

Gould himself indisputably believed that his radio documentaries were musical compositions. "Taking . . . an interview like this one into the studio after the fact," he said not long afterward, "chopping it up and splicing here and there and pulling on this phrase and accentuating that one, throwing some reverb in there and adding a compressor here and a filter there . . . it's unrealistic to think of that as anything but a composition. . . . And . . . it is the way of the future. . . . I think our whole notion of what music really is has forever merged with all the sounds around us, you know, everything our environment makes available." And when he learned in 1972 that a young student named Robert Skelton was planning to write a detailed analysis of his string quartet, he promptly sent him tapes of "The Idea of North" and its sequel, "The Latecomers." "There are . . . certain connecting links," Gould wrote, "which should, I think, be noted: perhaps, most obviously, a concentration on aspects of counterpoint . . . and perhaps, less obviously, a tendency in each case to celebrate, if not precisely a fin de siecle situation, then at least a philosophy which deliberately sought an isolated vantage-point in relation to its time and milieu. . . . There is a true fraternal link, both in subject matter and technique, between the vocal polyphony of 'The Idea of North' . . . and the chromatically constructed counterpoint of the quartet."

When all the theorizing has been done, a radio show depends on one man (or woman) who knows what he (or she) wants, and one who can carry out those wishes. In this case, Lorne Tulk saw his job as the translation into sound of anything that Gould could imagine. "My only function is to play the console, the way you play a piano," says Tulk, a short, stocky man, curly-haired, full of energy. "The difference is that instead of black and white keys, I have turntables and tape recorders. . . . You just say, 'I want something that sounds like—'"

Q: Like what? Can I say that I want it to sound like New York City? Or I want it to sound like blue?

A: Sure. Any of those things.

And so they set to work, night after night. Though Jessie Greig vividly remembers the young Gould playing the piano long after everyone else in the family had gone to bed, Tulk thinks that he was the one who introduced Gould to the rich possibilities of the night. "You can get more done in that time," he says, matter-of-factly. "There's less interruptions. The place is quiet. I don't think Glenn had ever thought in terms of working all night, but once he started doing it, he discovered he loved it. The only thing he didn't like, he didn't like to see the sun come up. So he'd try to get finished and get home before the sunrise."

Q: Like a vampire.

A: It's the one thing that for some reason he found depressing, to see the sun come up. I don't know why.

Q: Perhaps it just meant that the night was gone, and now he had to stop everything and go to bed.

A: I don't know. He just used to say that he didn't want to see the sun rise.

As the deadline approaches, as the opening night draws near, all attention must be focused on getting the job done. The *Star*'s Littler paid a visit to the CBC's Studio K on a pre-Christmas night in 1967 and found a scene of controlled chaos. "By 3 A.M., everyone in Studio K was beginning to look a little like last week's cut flowers," he wrote. "[Producer] Janet Somerville, leaning against the control room wall, stared blankly ahead. Lorne Tulk, bending over his knobs and dials, wore an equally expressionless gaze. And the man in charge, shoes off and shirt hanging out of his trousers, held his face in his hands. The man in charge was Glenn Gould. He had been sitting in CBC Studio K's control room since 6 P.M., drinking coffee, taking tranquilizers, and editing tapes. . . ."

The show was supposed to be broadcast in a couple of days, but it was still far from finished. "You vant qvality, baby? It takes time," Gould offered in yet another of his ethnic impersonations. His listeners smiled weakly. Gould turned serious: "I started Thanksgiving Day, and except for my recording trips to New York, we've been working on this every night since then—last night until 2:30 A.M., the night before 3 A.M. I only regret we didn't start a week earlier to take the pressure off."

Gould then went back to work. Littler watched him and his crew labor over their four Ampex tape machines. "It was quite an oper-ation to observe," he wrote. "Gould would sit up on the control panel, his script resting on a music stand, and cue Tulk with a vocab-ulary of gestures not unlike those of an orchestral conductor. They would talk together about crescendos and diminuendos, Gould would refer to a particular sequence as ternary or a particular voice as lyrical, and in general he seemed to be playing the role of com-poser-conductor. . . . Every now and then, when frustration threat-ened to erupt, he would break into an extravagant German-accented monologue or recall an anecdote associated with his research. His concentration was relentless. Each break would last only a minute or two, until the laughter died down. But he seemed to sense just when that break had to come. His coworkers never questioned him. They were there to help, to tell him what could be done, to activate his ideas. The ideas were almost invariably his."

Gould sustained these late-night sessions by his own enthusiasm, but there were limits. "Toward 5 A.M. . . . " Littler reported, "Gould was still patient with his colleagues and they were still willing to go on as long as he wanted. But reactions were slowing and Gould's lack of sleep had already reduced his eyes to near-slits. 'It's begin-ning to catch up with me,' he smiled. 'I usually get by on seven or eight hours and can make out on four or five for a stretch. But I've stretched the stretch to the limit. Shall we call it a night?'"

Janet Somerville remembers those late-night editing sessions from a somewhat different perspective. "Lorne and Glenn loved each other, and so between them there was utter peace," she says. "It wasn't sick, it wasn't homosexual, it wasn't any of the things we put in a twentieth-century context. It was like a knight and a page, you know, on a great adventure. Lorne should have lived in the Mid-dle Ages. I mean, he has that kind of loyal devotion, which was *the* human virtue of that relationship. And Lorne is just so rich in it. And Glenn found it all totally normal. I mean, he felt that of *course* people would feel that way about him."

A small white parrot suddenly flutters out of a corner of Miss Somerville's living room and swoops past her visitor. "Since it will go on doing that as long as you're here, I might as well put it away," she says, opening the door to the bird's cage and letting it take ref-uge. She remembers now that she had other work to do besides the

Gould show. She was the producer on a nightly program called *Ideas*, of which "The Idea of North" was just one installment, and she was particularly engrossed at that point in taping Martin Luther King's Toronto lectures on nonviolence. But even after working all day, she felt an obligation to spend her nights in the nocturnal world of Glenn Gould. "I was a tired, very hardworking producer who was concerned with five hours a week of other programming at the same time," she says, "but still fascinated by the aesthetic elegance and technical precision of what Glenn was doing. And I enjoyed those all-night sessions, just watching the two of them.

"They would turn out the studio lights and just go by the lights from the console, which was— They were both sort of lit from beneath, and they both have lovely faces, with, you know, strong bone structures. And I would sit there, very tired, having been working all day, and being about to work all the next day, watching the light on their bones and their skin, and watching their fascination. . . ."

Gould never played the piano for her, and now that he is dead, she can only watch him perform on television from time to time. "He looks beautiful," she says. "I mean, in a way, I sometimes feel a little embarrassed, as I sometimes did in watching him edit 'The Idea of North.' Because his physical reaction to beautiful sound, to making beautiful sound—or, in the case of editing, to *hearing* great sound—was so strong that I wanted to look away, sometimes. It was so autoerotic."

Q: Autoerotic?

A: Yes. I felt—you know, I felt sometimes that I was crossing that fine line of voyeurism. Because, I mean, *that's* where Glenn lived, you know, in that *total* response to what he had just created, and in its correspondence to what he had already previously heard in there, inside his head. And that was *so* much more important to him than personal relationships, or money, or, you know, the other things that we mortals get caught up in. That was—that was his *passion* in a very, very full sense.

The show did get done, and it got done just barely in time for Canada's celebration of its own centennial. It is sometimes a little difficult to remember how new the Canadian nation is. Not until well after the battle of Gettysburg, when Americans spent three days slaughtering each other in their struggle over the assertion of a national identity, was the Canadian federation born in 1867. And even then, the provinces of Manitoba and Saskatchewan did not yet exist, nor Alberta, nor British Columbia. So the centennial celebrations of 1967 were an important milestone in the Canadians' still evolving sense of their own identity. The Toronto *Telegram* printed a special magazine section that July 1, Canada Day, and asked various notables like Robertson Davies and Morley Callaghan to explain what it all meant. Gould's views were typically idiosyncratic: "Canada's a place to live comfortably, amicably, and with reasonable anonymity. And I think the latitudinal factor is important to me—the fact we're a northern people, cross-pollinated by influences from the south. But for the moment we're in danger of losing . . . something we Canadians could capitalize on: A synoptic view of the world we live in."

Gould said it all much better in "The Idea of North," which was finally broadcast at the very end of the anniversary year, on December 28. "I found myself listening at two levels simultaneously," Barbara Frum wrote in a clumsy but perceptive review in the Toronto *Star*, "—to the stream of ideas but just as compelling in this production, to the pattern of sounds Gould wove out of his speakers' voices. Using the hypnotic drone of moving train wheels as a bass, Gould wove the voices of the five persons he interviewed into a thick and moody line, fading the voices in and out, under and over each other. . . . There was no attempt to define a 'problem.' No urge to give climatic conditions, population statistics, recent history of the region. . . . Instead Gould used his interviews to create a sound composition about the loneliness, the idealism and the letdowns of those who go North." And the Ottawa *Citizen:* "A poetic and beautiful montage of the North emerged that. . . was more real and honest than the entire ten-foot shelf of standard clichés about Canada's northlands." And the Montreal *Star:* "The Gould broadcast . . . is likely to stand as the forerunner of a new radio art, a wonderfully imaginative striving for a new way to use the only half-explored possibilities of an established form."

Most of Gould's major radio documentaries were inevitably about music, and therein lay both their strengths and their weaknesses.

Strengths because music was Gould's passion, and he had a profound knowledge and experience of it. Weaknesses because music is very hard to capture in the alien language of words. And so Gould's documentaries often turned into music-appreciation seminars, in which various experts sat around and offered comments, until they were all overpowered by the background sounds of the music itself. "Casals: A Portrait for Radio" (1973) was appropriately reverent, and so was "Richard Strauss: The Bourgeois Hero" (1979).

Still, Gould was marvelously inventive. Dissatisfied with his first Schoenberg show in 1962, he eagerly accepted the invitation from John Roberts to celebrate Schoenberg's hundredth birthday in 1974. "It should not be a repeat of our 1962 program, or even a major revision of that very substantial effort," he wrote to Roberts, "though needless to say I would cull from that program such irreplaceable mementoes as Schoenberg's own voice, and almost certainly that of the late Frau Gertrude as well. Basically . . . I would prefer . . . to start from scratch. First of all . . . I would like to make it, overall, a more 'integral' structure—'symphonicizing' it, so to speak, somewhat along the lines of the Stokowski project. . . ."

The standard radio talk show consists of various guests being assembled in a studio and then encouraged to say whatever comes into their heads. Gould's concept of radio was totally different, totally controlled, with himself as the controller. Instead of assembling his experts to chatter at random, Gould interviewed them one by one, recorded them one by one, and then set to work splicing his tapes of these conversations. In contrast to the usual babble, Gould's carefully edited radio documentaries provided the totally implausible (but totally convincing) sound of a half-dozen very interesting people engaged in a very interesting discussion.

And then there was the music that Gould dubbed in, without ever explaining what he was doing. Thus in "Schoenberg: The First Hundred Years," Gould created the remarkable scene of Ernst Krenek recalling how he once went to visit Schoenberg to tell him about his recent discovery of some thirteenth-century motets, and how the atonality of this music provided a background to Schoenberg's own work. And while Krenek's *Mitteleuropäische* voice rolled on, telling how Schoenberg had proved completely uninterested in his visitor's discoveries, Gould dubbed in some of the strange medieval music that the great innovator had refused to hear.

Gould's reference to "the Stokowski project" recalled one of his most remarkable documentaries, "Stokowski: A Portrait for Radio" (1970). In contrast to Schoenberg, who could only be talked about, Stokowski was still there to be questioned. He was eighty-seven years old by now, but nonetheless flourishing, and full of octogenarian opinions. Gould had long admired him. He could remember that he had "hated every minute" of *Fantasia,* which had opened in Toronto when Gould was eight, but Stokowski took pride in unconventional programming, and the new technologies spread his unconventionalities far and wide. "My first encounters with masterpieces I'd read about and wondered about—Schoenberg's *Gurrelieder,* for example, or Mahler's eighth—were via his broadcasts and recordings," Gould later wrote in "Stokowski in Six Scenes," "and after such radio or phonograph exposures I invariably found myself in a state that I can only call exalted.... Stokowski was, for want of a better word, an ecstatic."

They had met, rather absurdly, at the Frankfurt railroad station in 1957. While waiting to board the Amsterdam–Vienna express, the twenty-five-year-old Gould recognized the white-haired conductor pacing to and fro. After trying in vain to think of some elegant means of introducing himself, he finally maneuvered his way into the great man's path, then dropped his ticket and stooped down to retrieve it. "I did manage (or at least I like to think I did) a look of genuine incredulity. 'Why, it's—it's—it's Maestro Stokowski, isn't it?'" Stokowski regarded his interrogator without great interest and said in a "benignly weary" voice, "It is, young man."

An ordinary admirer might have fled at that point, but Gould coolly introduced himself. He was pleasantly surprised to hear the maestro say, "I have read that you were recently in Leningrad." "It was incredible," Gould recalled. "He knew who I was; he knew what I'd been doing." Stokowski even proposed a rendezvous. "'Perhaps, then, later in the evening, I will visit with you. I would be interested to learn your impressions of Leningrad today, and perhaps you might have some interest in my impressions of Leningrad many years ago.' I assured him I would: I would have been interested in his impressions of Mickey Mouse if it had made a visit with him possible."

So they met again when the train was under way, and Stokowski politely inquired where and what Gould had most recently played.

Gould answered "rather proudly" that he had just performed Beethoven's Third Concerto with Herbert von Karajan in Berlin. "The Beethoven third," Stokowski mused. "Is that not the lovely concerto in G major?" Gould was impressed. "It was a superb gambit . . ." he said later. "Lovely or otherwise, the Beethoven third is in the key of C minor, as Stokowski knew all too well; but in one seemingly innocuous, skillfully indirect sentence, he had let me know that he was not in awe of the 'Generalmusikdirektor of Europe [Karajan],' that soloists, as a breed, were to be shunned on principle, and that concertos, as a symphonic subspecies, were quite beneath his notice."

Gould being Gould, he proposed, almost a decade later, after his retirement from the stage, that they record the *Emperor Concerto* together. "With pleasure," said Stokowski, who hadn't accompanied a soloist since working with Rachmaninoff in the 1930's. So it was done, and a splendidly majestic recording it is. There also remains of that 1966 recording session an odd footnote: During a break, someone knocked at the door, and then a woman came in and said to Gould, "Hi. I just wanted to say hello, because I'm a fan, and since we were leaving, I thought I'd just stop by and tell you that." Nobody seemed to know quite what to say, Gould recalled, and so "the lady was finally reduced to adding, 'I'm Barbra Streisand.' And I remember, to my eternal embarrassment, contributing the most maladroit moment of that or any other conversation by saying, 'I know.'" In this odd meeting of mutual fans—for Gould intensely admired Miss Streisand's singing ("With the possible exception of Elisabeth Schwarzkopf," he later wrote, "no vocalist has brought me greater pleasure")—the pianist also became aware that Stokowski "appeared vaguely annoyed about the whole thing—about the interruption of his discourse . . . about the appearance of this talkative young woman whose name he either did not catch or did not know, and that he drummed his fingers on the arm of his chair—more or less in the rhythm of the timpani solo—to indicate his displeasure."

Three years later, John Roberts proposed a radio documentary on Stokowski, and Gould asked the old man whether he would agree to a lengthy interview, for what Gould had in mind now was a kind of monologue in which Stokowski would talk about his view of life while Gould dubbed in background music from Stokowski's recordings. Stokowski agreed, but there was a new difficulty. The New

York educational television station WNET was also planning a documentary on Stokowski, and after some negotiations with CBC, it was agreed that the television cameras would film Gould doing his radio interview. Even though only a bit of this film would be used, Gould and Stokowski were now both prisoners of forces beyond their control. There was a long wait, unsettling, exasperating, while the technicians set up their cameras in Stokowski's elegant Fifth Avenue apartment. Stokowski inquired of Gould what he planned to ask him. Gould artfully took out several pages of notes and read off a few questions. "'Of course,' I smiled, 'I really shouldn't tell you my questions in advance—I should try to surprise you.' (I could afford to smile—I still intended to surprise him.)"

The standard technique is to start with innocuous questions, and then to lead the way gradually into more difficult terrain, and if there is any question that may cause a disaster, save that until the end. Gould loved to overturn standard techniques, though, so now that the TV lights and cameras were all set up, and the irritable old man was impatient to do his turn, Gould started out with a completely incredible question. "Maestro, I have this recurring dream," he began, possibly recalling his triumphant visit to Russia. "In it, I appear to be on some other planet, perhaps in some other solar system, and, at first, it seems as though I am the only Earthman there. And I have a tremendous sense of exhilaration because I seem to believe, in the dream, that I have been given the opportunity—and the authority—to impart my value systems to whatever forms of life there might be on that planet; I have the feeling that I can create a whole planetary value system in my own image. . . ."

Stokowski, who had been staring nervously at the camera while waiting for one of the customary introductory cues ("How did you happen to take up conducting?"), turned in wonderment toward this bizarre interrogator. He began "moving his lips without uttering a word," Gould recalled, "and for some moments I thought that he was not going to answer at all." The extraordinary question that Gould was asking, in his windy and circuitous way, was, What would Stokowski do if he somehow landed on a distant planet where the inhabitants had no knowledge whatever of the arts. What—if anything—would he tell them?

The egomaniac in Stokowski paused for a moment and took a deep breath, and then the old man began an extraordinary peroration: "Think of our solar system, its colossal size," he said. "I have the impression that there are many solar systems, that ours is a very big one, but that there are others which are much larger. . . . I have also the impression that not only is there endless space and the endless mass of the solar systems that are in that space, but there is endless time and endless mental power, that there are great masses of mind, of which ours, in this little Earth that we live on, is only a small part. . . ."

"It was perfect," said Gould, the master manipulator, having gambled that he could surprise this old eagle into expressing the exaltation that nobody had ever before recorded, "it was poetry, it was exactly what I'd come for; if he could keep it up, I had a program."

Keep it up? Stokowski could hardly stop. "Art is like the deep roots of a great oak tree," he said, "and out of these roots grow many branches. . . . If I did have that possibility, I would do my best to give a clear impression to what other form of life there might be on that planet, of what I think is beautiful and orderly, what I think is creative and what I think is destructive. It would be possible, I hope, to let them see what is happening on this Earth—so much destruction, so little that is creative."

Stokowski stopped there, after nearly ten minutes, and eventually Gould took over, first with more questions and finally with razor and glue. He "could not bear to take my leave of Stokowski while he mused upon man's capacity for self-destruction," Gould said, and so he resorted once again to "creative cheating," re-editing the tape to make Stokowski end where he had begun: "Think of our solar system, its colossal size, its possibility." Then, as always, Gould edited himself out of the program, so that Stokowski, instead of answering a provocative question, appeared to be simply prophesying in the manner of some new Ezekiel. And then Gould added music, so that Stokowski's visionary outpourings soared over a background of Schoenberg's *Verklärte Nacht,* Holst's *The Planets,* and Scriabin's *Poem of Ecstasy.*

It was only some months after Gould had sent a tape of this really admirable documentary to Stokowski, and after it had been broadcast to considerable acclaim, that Gould learned that Stokowski, with the serene indifference of old age, had never listened to it.

Before, during, and after the making of the Stokowski program, Gould was deeply involved in extending "The Idea of North" into a number of sequels. The first of these dealt with another remote region, Newfoundland, the land of the Viking settlements, which had joined the Canadian federation only in 1949. Gould called his program "The Latecomers." Newfoundland was considerably more accessible than the Arctic, and more inhabited. Gould actually went there in August of 1968 "in search of characters for a documentary, the subject of which was by no means clear to me."

The subject was, of course, perfectly clear. Once again, Gould was seeking to portray solitude, isolation. Though Newfoundland was less frozen than northern Ontario, it had the additional barrier of the ocean, which Gould used as an underlying *basso continuo* throughout his program. "The reality is in its separateness," he later wrote. "The very fact—the inconvenience—of distance is its great natural blessing. Through that fact, the Newfoundlander has received a few more years of grace—a few more years in which to calculate the odds for individuality in an increasingly coercive cultural milieu."

Gould used thirteen characters this time, and once again none of them ever met. By now, he was seeing in this separateness of his characters all kinds of opportunities. One of the unnamed men he interviewed, for example, compared Newfoundland to Thoreau's Walden and observed that "people who are removed from the center of a society are always able to see it more clearly." One woman, on the other hand, disliked the isolation and felt that she had to escape every once in a while. "I kept saying, 'But why?' and naïve things of that kind," Gould later recalled. "She kept repeating herself, essentially, though with infinite variations . . . and finally turned on me with a fine fury, stopped short of insult, but indicated that my line of questioning was foolish." By splicing these two interviews together, with the interviewer once again removing himself, Gould managed to suggest that the woman who was annoyed at him was actually annoyed at the other man, and that this scene "would appear to be taking place between, I suppose, a man and wife, certainly a lady and gentleman who are engaged in rather intimate conversation. . . . The dialogue represented in that scene never took place as dialogue, and yet I have a strange feeling that had they met, it would have."

Technology gave Gould an even more remarkable opportunity for "creative cheating" in the episode of the fake wave. Gould used the waves on the coast of Newfoundland much as he had used the clacking railroad in "The Idea of North," and since the ocean offers a far greater variety of sounds, Gould taped hours of possibilities, pounding waves, lapping waves, sighing waves, grinding waves. Only when he got back to the editing room in Toronto did he find, as he later confessed, that "there was one scene for which I just couldn't find the right surf sound; I tried everything, every tape of sound we'd recorded in Newfoundland, and nothing quite matched the mood of the voices in that particular scene."

Gould grumbled to someone at the studio about his problem, and so he learned that the CBC had other tapes of other waves beating on other shores. Specifically, he learned that a TV crew had recently returned from making a show about Charles Darwin's voyage aboard the S.S. *Beagle* to the Galápagos Islands off the coast of Ecuador. He couldn't resist listening. "So," he said, "we ended up borrowing a tape from someone who had just returned from the Galápagos, and that worked perfectly."

But what does it actually mean for something to "work perfectly"? One wave in the background may seem a very small point of contention, and yet all the traditions of history, scholarship, and even journalism dictate that every statement must at least try to be true, that the thing should be what it pretends to be. No matter how awkward or implausible it may sound, this is what happened. *"Wie es eigentlich gewesen,"* as Leopold von Ranke said of his history of Rome, "how it really was." So if we are to hear waves beating on the shores of Newfoundland, they are supposed to be waves actually recorded on the shores of Newfoundland. Whether the taped sounds "quite matched the mood of the voices" is quite secondary, tertiary. Indeed, there is no comparison. To "match the mood" of a Newfoundlander's voice with the sound of a wave breaking on the Galápagos Islands is almost a contradiction in terms, an absurdity.

One of the wonders of technology, though, is that it denies the very idea of historical truth. Since everything on tape is a simulation, and since everything can be dubbed, redubbed, overdubbed, what actually happened is of almost no importance. Just as Elisabeth Schwarzkopf could be employed to sing a certain high note that Kirsten Flagstad could no longer reach, and nobody could tell the difference. When this operatic event leaked out as gossip, purists complained that a Flagstad performance should not include a high note secretly sung by Schwarzkopf, but what were the alternatives? No Flagstad performance? A Flagstad performance with mangled high notes? To Gould, such arguments were antiquarian. The goal was not historical accuracy but artistic perfection, and while there might well be very different visions of perfection, Gould was determined to follow his own.

So were the Mennonites, those remarkable descendants of the sixteenth-century Anabaptists, who believed passionately that every injunction of the New Testament must be carried out exactly as written. Gould made these onetime heretics the subject of "Quiet in the Land" (1973), his second sequel to "The Idea of North." It is the most complicated and in some ways the most interesting of these three radio shows because the separateness of the Mennonites is spiritual rather than physical, and chosen rather than compelled.

And Gould's mastery of his medium had by now become overwhelming. The beginning of "Quiet in the Land" is one of the most beautiful things he ever did, first the slow tolling of a church bell, pianissimo, as though from a great distance; then faint chirpings, which sound vaguely like sea gulls but gradually reveal themselves to be the voices of children at play; then, with the church bell still tolling, a sound that resembles surf but is actually the rush of highway traffic; and then the jubilation of a Mennonite congregation singing a hymn.

"Let us bow for prayer," the minister declares. "Lord God, the Holy Ghost, in this accepted hour, as on the day of Pentecost, descend in Thy power. . . ." And as the minister speaks those words, another voice is saying, "I think there is a conflict on the idea of Utopianism versus scattering into the world. . . ." And as the earnest voices continue their explorations of these churchly matters, the music in the background keeps veering between a solo cello playing a reflective Bach saraband and Janis Joplin singing, "Oh, Lord, won't you buy me a Mercedes-Benz?"

Gould was by now possessed by the idea of pushing "contrapuntal radio" to its absolute limits, and beyond. "There's going to be a scene in there which will drive you crazy . . ." he said to a CBC "interviewer" in one of those promotional shows for which he now wrote out both questions and answers. "It's a scene in which nine characters ... talk about the church's relationship to pacifism at what appears to be a church meeting. It's all hooked up from the eight-track, of course. But it's going to make everything I've done up till the present seem like Gregorian chant by comparison."

It is a most impressive scene, about ten minutes long, and almost completely incomprehensible. At one point, for example, while one character says, "The Catholic Church takes a hard teaching like 'You shall not kill,'" a second character simultaneously says, "To me Christianity means unselfishness," and a third says, "When I am threatened as an individual, maybe then we had better reexamine how we have been doing things." Precisely because each of these speakers is saying something that requires concentration and reflection, the simultaneity of their words contradicts their purpose. Gould acknowledged that in such scenes "not every word is going to be audible," but he argued that "by no means every syllable in the final fugue from Verdi's *Falstaff* is either," and "I do believe that most of us are capable of a much more substantial information intake than we give ourselves credit for." The analogy to Verdi is a very debatable one. It does not matter greatly whether we know that the cast of *Falstaff* is singing "Tutto nel mondo è burla" (The whole world is but a joke), for the music is telling us much the same thing, and the music is what we have come to hear. The voices of two or three Christians speaking seriously at cross-purposes is itself almost a *burla*, indeed almost diabolical in its reduction of spiritual statements into spiritual babble.

And Gould's view of himself as the master of these revels did not go unchallenged. Jim Lotz found, on rehearing himself in "The Idea of North," that he could "become a little irritated at the absence of a coherent series of statements." One of Gould's Mennonite subjects, Roy Vogt, a professor of economics at the University of Manitoba in Winnipeg, complained even before the tapes were edited that Gould was manipulating people. "Several times in our conversation," he wrote to Gould, "I was led to believe that my ideas would be used not as the expression of an individual but as a foil for the ideas of others. You can't abstract an individual much more than that, even in a totalitarian society. The musical analogy of counterpoint which you used very often reinforces this impression. Each person becomes a note in a larger symphony, which in social terms is perhaps as good a way as any of describing the underlying assumptions of a totalitarian state. The dictator is a social composer."

Touché. Looking down at his arm and seeing that his accuser had drawn blood, Gould answered with a slashing counterattack. "Counterpoint is not a dry academic exercise . . ." he wrote to Vogt, "but rather a method of composition in which, if all goes well, each individual voice leads a life of its own. Naturally, even in the most complex contrapuntal textures, certain concessions must be demanded of each musical strand as an accommodation to the harmonic and rhythmic pace of the whole. . . . I do not, however, feel that my personal convictions encourage me to distort the interview-material which is made available to me. Quite frankly—and to put it in the most selfish terms—I would do less than justice to my role as a producer if I were to deliberately sacrifice the 'contrapuntal' integrity of one value-system in order to enhance another."

"Quiet in the Land" should have been the end of Gould's exploration of the northlands, but he received a letter from Peking in July of 1978, from John Fraser of the Toronto *Globe and Mail*, suggesting that he do a radio documentary on China. An unusual idea, which Gould inevitably found "fascinating." What made it somewhat absurd, however, was that Gould proposed to add this to his trilogy on solitude—the billion inhabitants of China as an example of solitude!—and the only thing even more absurd was that he contemplated making this documentary on China without leaving Canada. "The prospects for a visit by me to the Orient are nil," he wrote to Fraser. "As you know, I don't fly—haven't for sixteen years—and no assignment, no matter how enticing, will get me aloft again. Furthermore, with each passing year, I become more committed to a sedentary existence and less willing to contemplate any form of travel. . . . Even if a slow boat to China did exist, I would not be on it."

Still, Gould wanted to look into the possibilities. "The big question is: can we find an approach, however oblique, which justifies such a program?" he wrote. "What intrigues me is the possibility of relating a China-essay to the general theme of my so-called 'Solitude Trilogy.' . . . Suppose—and this is strictly off the top of my head—

we would do a program about 'The Last Puritans'—with apologies to George Santayana. Matter of fact, I like the title and I particularly like the relationship it could have to my 'Solitude Trilogy' (Quartet!)—i.e. the political dimension of isolation. What say you?"

Whatever Fraser may have said, nothing ever came of this bizarre project. The "Solitude Trilogy" remained a trilogy.

Since this is the age of television, somebody (possibly Gould himself) decided sometime in 1968 that "The Idea of North" should somehow be converted from "contrapuntal radio" into a television show. Gould was discussing this idea with a friend and producer at Columbia named Paul Myers, and Myers mentioned one of his friends, Judith Pearlman. She was just getting started in television, and she felt passionately about music in general and Gould's music in particular. So they all met and listened to a tape of "The Idea of North."

"That made me pretty nervous," Miss Pearlman recalls. "Because Gould was watching me like a hawk. And at the end, he said, 'Well, what do you think?' And I said, 'I think it's very hard to come to a decision after just hearing it once, and I'd like to listen to it again for the next two weeks.' So that's what I did. I took the tape home and made it my matins and evensong, lauds and complines, for two weeks. As I listened, the patterns of sound became clearer, along with the personalities of the five characters. Then I wrote a treatment, and Glenn read that and liked it."

"At the core of the film is a train journey north to Hudson Bay," the treatment begins. "It is, of course, a real train on a scheduled run—yet also a train of mind and mythology, carrying men still seeking the last frontier as trial or escape. . . ." Miss Pearlman barely realized that she had become a pawn in a complicated power struggle typical of television. The New York public broadcasting executives at WNET wanted to make a deal with the CBC for a series of ten coproduced shows, one of which would almost inevitably feature Glenn Gould, and the fact that Miss Pearlman had written a treatment that Gould had liked gave her a quasi-legal hold on "The Idea of North." It was a hold that was strong enough to survive several shifts and transfers among the executives who were supposed to decide things, and after nearly two years of negotiations and delays, she found herself in Ottawa, bargaining with the Canadian National Railways about what it would cost to rent a railroad car to carry a film crew from Winnipeg to Churchill.

Gould, who was busy making new recordings, elegantly removed himself from all these difficulties. While he sang the praises of technology, he liked to spend hours editing radio tapes with one technician in a studio but not in negotiating the price of a railroad car that would convert a fantasy of sound into a visual reality, or simulation of reality. "So I went over to talk to them, and they wanted five thousand dollars," Miss Pearlman recalls. "Well, my whole budget for such things was only eighteen thousand dollars, so we just kept on negotiating. They said we could have it for four thousand dollars, so I thought, We're making progress. And this went on for *days*. Finally, they said, 'Okay, you can have it for five hundred dollars.'

"So I went back to the CBC studio, and I could hear the producer shouting, the producer they had assigned to take charge of this project, and I knew he was drunk. He shouted that he would do all kinds of lascivious things to me. I was afraid of him, because of the way he talked, and because he was so big. He was about six feet four, and about two hundred fifty pounds. He had made his reputation producing sports events. So I got on the phone to New York, and I said, 'I don't think I can work with this guy.' And then I just held up the phone."

She demonstrates, holding her hand up over her head, holding up the telephone that carried the drunken bellowing of her assigned producer to the ears of supposedly protective coproducers in New York. "And the next Monday," she says, "I was told that he was off the show. Then they just left me on my own." This was not by any means the end of her social problems. She recalls that there was a certain amount of he-man drinking among the technicians, and that drinking repeatedly led to challenges to her authority. "Remember, I was a woman, one of the very few on an executive level at CBC," she says, "and I was from New York, and I was a Jew. I was everything you weren't supposed to be. It was not a good time to be in Canada, at least not for me."

But the work progressed. She hired an actor to play the homespun philosopher, Wally Maclean, and another to play the mute role of a symbolic young man going north for the first time. There had been no such character in the radio drama—he was just somebody Maclean talked about—but TV always needs to *show* everything that radio leaves to the imagination. And occasionally this has a miraculous effect. Miss Pearlman was determined to transfer Gould's whole opening "trio sonata" onto film, so when Nurse Schroeder started talking about the geese flying over Hudson Bay, Miss Pearlman showed us the geese in the air, and when Professor Vallee started grumbling about the North, she showed us the grumbling in a clubby Toronto bar. When Phillips then began talking about the government's role in the North, the camera wandered into Ottawa's Department of Northern Affairs and showed us row on row of filing cabinets. And since Gould wanted his three characters talking simultaneously, Miss Pearlman very skillfully managed to get her three images on the screen simultaneously. Gould's trio sonata thus became a kind of sextet. When he saw it, he loved it. After looking at seven hours of unedited rushes, he pronounced them "absolutely remarkable."

Getting photographic material for such sequences was a lot more complicated than taping five interviews for radio. While Gould had made his one jaunt to Churchill in June, and later done his interviews at his convenience, Miss Pearlman had to take her actors and her TV crew northward on her rented railway car in November. "It was forty-five degrees below zero when we got there," she recalls. "If you took off your glove, your hand began to feel burning. The only hotel was a Quonset hut, but there was a telegram waiting for me:

MAY WE RECOMMEND THE MONTEVIDEO EXCELSIOR—EIGHT PRESIDENTIAL SUITES, 3 BANQUET ROOMS, 2 SALTWATER SWIMMING POOLS, SEASIDE DINER . . . FOR YOUR MID-SEASON VACATION.

CORDIALLY,
G. GOULD, MANAGER

"Churchill was a town of about two thousand souls, and there was just one main street," Miss Pearlman says. "Beyond that, on the edge of town, there was a ring of shacks where the Indians lived, and many of them had no windows. I mean, they were open to the air, at forty-five below zero. I don't know how they survived. A lot of them were drunk all the time. I felt very bad. And another thing was that there were all these abandoned dogs up there. I remember one of them was a Great Dane, and Danes don't have the skin for that kind of weather. They were all scarred and starving and desperate. We were filming there for five days. I felt very bad."

Back in the semitropical metropolis of Toronto, Miss Pearlman found Gould "charming, nourishing, and supportive," but also very busy with his recordings. The language they had in common, while she worked on her film about solitude under his rather distant scrutiny, was not television but music. "It had to do with how lonely I was," she recalls. "I didn't know anyone in Toronto. He knew how I felt, not very happy." This was the occasion on which he played her *Die Frau ohne Schatten,* and the following week there occurred an even more remarkable scene.

Once again, Gould arranged for Miss Pearlman to use a piano in an empty CBC studio, looked in on her after his late-night recording session, and found her on the telephone to New York. Once again, he began to play, this time a Hindemith sonata. Once again, Miss Pearlman emerged from the control room. She happened to mention that she had heard that he had recently taped for the CBC something that nobody could imagine Gould playing, Chopin, the Sonata in B minor.

"Without saying anything, he started playing it," Miss Pearlman recalls. "Then all of a sudden, he got serious about it. It was like a switch being turned on. And he played the whole piece through from beginning to end. And it was the greatest performance I've ever heard in my life. I was more than stunned. At the end, he said, 'What do you think?' I said it was the best performance I'd ever heard. He said, 'Oh, it's not so good as the tape.' But I didn't agree. This was a live performance, and I told him that sometimes, even when he was recording, he should record a straight-through performance. Obviously, it made him acutely uncomfortable to play for a live audience. I remember going to his last performance of the Brahms concerto with Bernstein, and it was obvious that the person playing it was in great pain. But his playing for me now meant that he knew I was feeling awful. It was his gift to me, meaning, 'Hang in there.'"

The reviews in the summer of 1970 were generally favorable. The Toronto *Telegram*'s Kenneth Winters rightly judged that the television version was less daring than the radio original, but he added that it was "the first television production I have ever seen . . . which is a complete, organic and lyrical composition in sounds as well as a composition in pictures." But because television must show what it describes, the cameras showed the snow and ice that the radio had ignored, and this demonstration of what the fabled North actually looks like raised chauvinist hackles. "'The Idea of North' emerges as a foreigner's idea of Canada," the Toronto *Star* complained. "Still and icy landscapes stretch before the camera. Defensively dressed in hooded parkas and boots, inhabitants of shanty towns bustle along bleak streets. And it looks cold. So cold that you wouldn't want to live there. . . ."

Such chamber-of-commerce carping overlooks the most important weakness in "The Idea of North"—and by implication in the whole "solitude trilogy"—which is that Gould never really told us what he thought about solitude. "I've always had some sort of intuition," he once said, "that for every hour that you spend in the company of other human beings you need X number of hours alone." And on another occasion, he declared that the basic theme of this whole trilogy was "that isolation is the indispensable component of human happiness." But how does solitude actually help or harm a man? How does it liberate him or cripple him? How does it enable him to see or prevent him from seeing? Is it a necessity or an accident? These would be difficult questions even if Gould were writing about them in the most straightforward way, but a radio drama spun out of other people's words was obviously the most ambiguous of approaches.

Janet Somerville astutely observed that Gould's passions concerned mainly the sounds that he heard inside his own head, and if this seems bizarre, it is only because we have all been trained in recent years to judge everyone in terms of his relations with other people. Anthony Storr, a lecturer in psychiatry at Oxford, argues that this is a major misconception, and he likes to cite Edward Gibbon's observation that "solitude is the school of genius." "It is widely believed that interpersonal relationships of an intimate kind are the chief, if not the only, source of human happiness," Storr wrote recently in *Solitude, A Return to the Self*. "Yet the lives of creative individuals often seem to run counter to this assumption. For example, many of the world's greatest thinkers have not reared families or formed close personal ties. This is true of Descartes, Newton, Locke, Pascal, Spinoza, Kant, Leibniz, Schopenhauer, Nietzsche, Kierkegaard and Wittgenstein." One could say much the same of Beethoven, Haydn, and Brahms, yet Gould never really tried to formulate or document any such theory, except as a personal preference of his own.

"I think for Gould the question of solitude must have been absolutely central," says Richard Sennett, the N.Y.U. sociology professor who has been working for several years on a book on the subject. "What solitude really does to people's sense of creativity—you can't really create difference without creating the sense of being alone. When you're in a community with other people, when what you express is what could be shared among all of them, that tends to be flat, tends to be ironed out. How does a person get the freedom to reflect, to be self-doubting without being self-indulgent? I suppose the writer who most resembles Gould is Wallace Stevens, with that notion of perfection in retreat. You also hear the silences of that kind of withdrawal in his poetry. Nothing escapes Stevens that isn't deeply, deeply considered. There's a kind of almost supernatural calm in his writing, and yet there's nothing studied about it. You just feel the lines flow one from the other, rather like what you sense in Gould's recording process. . . ."

"Yes, it's very much me, in terms of what it says," Gould told one interviewer about his enigmatic explorations of the North, "—no matter how long Wally Maclean may take to say it—it's about as close to an autobiographical statement as I am likely to make at this stage of my life." As spoken, as broadcast, the aged surveyor's final peroration on the meaning of going north sounds shrewd and sagacious. And perhaps to prevent us from listening too closely, Gould suddenly dubbed in the Arctic strains of Sibelius's Fifth Symphony. But when one reads the actual words that Maclean was declaiming through all that Sibelius—supposedly representing Gould's "autobiographical statement"—they come perilously close to gibberish: "A few years back, certainly in human memory, people thought that this—well, what we call our North—presented a real challenge. Well, what form did they take? Hah! What form? As if everything must somehow have a form. This is hard, this is hard on you. He must notice that you're struggling a bit, eh? But what you're really saying then is something like this: That there was a time when the challenge was understandable. What challenge then? Oh, well, here you have to take it easy. . . ." And so on.

In the way Gould presented "The Idea of North," he made it seem that these were his own ideas, his own creation. And yet he never signed the check. After Gould's brief opening statement, the listener never again hears him express any opinions whatever, never even hears him ask any questions. If anyone wants to take Wally Maclean's peroration as an expression of Gould's own views, all well and good, but Gould never committed himself to that. He remained offstage, the marionette-master, the magician. "Sure, he was a thinker, but very much a by-the-seat-of-the-pants thinker," says Littler of the *Star*. "He thought deeply, but he wasn't as worried by the contradictions in what he was saying as some people with more formal training in logical thought might be. There's an affinity between him and Marshall McLuhan, and I think he admired McLuhan's feeling that everything is provisional, that you make probes. . . ." "What Glenn really thought about solitude, only Glenn knows," Miss Pearlman adds. "He designed his solitude to suit himself, like a pearly shell. He made it a work of art. He distanced himself from other people's emotions—and then he was brilliant."

Yet there were other people who could see through Gould's pearly shell, and read his invisible writings on the walls. More than a decade after making "The Idea of North," when Gould played a tape of it to Margaret Pacsu, who was collaborating with him on his jubilee record album, she began crying. "I suddenly understood what he was trying to do with these voices," she recalls. "It was a quartet of these beautifully balanced—there was a rhythm and a melody to it. Plus the underlying— Now careful, because I'm a good Hungarian-American here, and I will burst into tears in a minute. The sadness of this man was that he was unable to reach out and make a—a—an intimate, warm contact with anyone. That's why I found that devastating. Plus to be sitting there in front of the man and have this happen. He was—surprised, and quite pleased, and quite comforting— Excuse me—" Remembering that moment when she burst into tears while Gould played her "The Idea of North," she bursts into tears all over again.

The TV Star

Music is one of the mysteries that television has never been able to solve. Television exists to show a series of pictures, and music is invisible. The cameras do quite well with opera, since the singers provide something to look at—though long close-ups of a figure like Luciano Pavarotti are a mixed blessing—but when they present a Leonard Bernstein conducting the Vienna Philharmonic, for example, they can only offer those endless shots of violinists sawing and flutists tootling and the white-haired maestro waving, gasping, pointing, sighing, leaping. And when they want to show a pianist, they can only show, from the left side and the right side, from above and below, from front and back and overhead, the pianist belaboring the keyboard. Gould was perfectly aware of this, of course, and when he let patterns of dots drift across the screen while the camera showed his hands playing *The Well-Tempered Clavier*, he told an interviewer, "I had done several TV concerts, and they were static, dull, I wondered if there wasn't a more imaginative way to present good music on TV. . . ."

Gould's first experiments were actually quite conservative. When the CBC first signed him up in 1961 to do four musical specials on its *Festival* series, he originally could think of nothing more imaginative than to create a special stage set for his piano and to talk about what he was going to play. Thus on his second program, when he performed the Shostakovitch Quintet and the Prokofiev Seventh Sonata, he not only gave an informal lecture on Soviet musical life but appeared on what one critic called "a set suggesting the opulence of the court of Peter the Great. . . ." And his commentaries tended

to be, like his record-liner notes, somewhat pretentious and somewhat banal.

The CBC authorities were inclined to let Gould do pretty much
what he wanted, but these early adventures in television were something less than a triumph. After his third program, entitled "Richard
Strauss, A Personal View," the Toronto *Star*'s Roy Shields complained about "having Glenn Gould exercise his ego for an hour on
prime time. . . . It is difficult to understand why Mr. Gould was
allowed to write his own script. . . . His use of language . . . is quite
unintelligible." When the fourth of these shows appeared in the
spring of 1963 and included Gould's "So You Want to Write a
Fugue?," Shields reluctantly conceded that "it was quite good, if you
happened to be a fugue fan," but John Kraglund of the *Globe and
Mail* couldn't resist borrowing part of Gould's libretto to accuse
him of trying to "be clever for the sake of showing off."

Gould was inevitably making the discovery that TV critics could
be even more exasperating than music critics. While most music
critics made some pretense of knowing something about their subject, the TV critics felt it their assignment to make bright remarks
about whatever appeared on their television screens, whether they
knew anything about the subject or not. But the critics were not the
only ones who felt that Gould's first TV shows were exercises in
self-indulgence. "There's nothing wrong with him chatting," said
Eric Till, who had just produced Gould's "Anatomy of Fugue," "but
there are times, and last night was one, when even I couldn't understand what he was talking about. And I had it all explained to me."
Kraglund of the *Globe* said Till then offered a parody, "in familiar
Gould style," about "motivic experimentation, motivic compromise
and so on." And was Gould difficult about making changes? Kraglund inquired. "No, he's most cooperative," the producer said. "But
all we could do was suggest changes. And let's face it, if you had to
say what he says in Gouldese, with all these favorite words of his,
could any changes make it very different?"

Gould was undaunted. In November of that year—just six months
before his retirement from the stage—he turned up in New York
with a tape of his "Anatomy of Fugue," which he persuaded Yehudi
Menuhin to come and watch in a closet-sized room at the CBC
offices. Menuhin made a great show of being impressed by Gould's

savoir-faire. "I find it rather difficult," he said, according to Lillian Ross of *The New Yorker*, "when they put you in front of the camera and say, '*Do* something.'"

Gould smiled. He, of course, had never been put in front of a camera and told to do something. He informed Menuhin that this show had taken two months of conferences, two days of shooting, and thirty thousand dollars. "I don't know if my film is for the mass public," Gould added. "Sometimes I think they don't know what the hell I've said, but they feel elevated."

Throughout this special showing for Menuhin, Gould periodically hopped up from his seat to ask the projectionist to get a sharper focus or to turn up the volume of sound. Miss Ross could not resist comparing images, the confident performer on the screen and the slightly nervous real-life master of ceremonies fidgeting as he watched his own taped performance. Menuhin beamed approval of every piece, following each with a murmur of "Lovely, lovely" or "It comes over beautifully."

"And you spoke throughout so *smoothly*," Menuhin purred. "Was it impromptu?"

"I had it on the TelePrompTer," said Gould, all guilelessness. ("Glenn and Yehudi were always excessively polite to each other," one TV producer observed. "They respected each other greatly, but there was always that sort of top-dog syndrome, always walking around and looking at each other.") And Gould could not stop explaining. "I looked at it often enough to pick up all the cues, but I forced myself to invent phrases as I went along, to keep it sounding natural and not too formal."

"Yes, wonderful," Menuhin said. "Especially if the words are your own."

Gould, according to Miss Ross, "laughed shyly" at the praise for his script-writing. But he also had a plan, and his invitation to Menuhin had clearly been part of it.

"Next year, if you're going to have some time, we might do one together," he said offhandedly. "You ever done the Schoenberg *Fantasia?*"

Gould probably suspected that Menuhin had never played a lot of Schoenberg—and what better way to assert his own initiative?—but Menuhin was quite ready for him.

"Oh!" he said. "What a splended idea! I must look at the music."

Menuhin tried to reinforce his position by inviting Gould to play the Schoenberg as part of one of Menuhin's concerts in England that summer, but Gould brushed the invitation aside. "I'm finished with concerts," he said. "I'm bored with them. It's animal. It's all a circus. It's immoral."

"Yes, I do know what you mean," Menuhin hastened to agree.

They ended with a pledge to meet in front of TV cameras in Toronto. "The Schoenberg, in July," said Gould. "It will be lovely," said Menuhin.

Two years passed before Gould got Menuhin before the cameras for a TV recital of Bach, Beethoven, and the Schoenberg *Phantasy*, a thorny and disagreeable piece that might be said to express all the tormented rage of Schoenberg's last years of obscurity in Hollywood. When Menuhin arrived in Toronto with only one day to rehearse this difficult work, Gould found to his dismay that the violinist still had not done any practicing, indeed "literally did not know [it] at all."

Gould, however, had already written a little script in which he would make Menuhin explain himself.

"You don't really like the Schoenberg, do you?" he asked, a rather remarkable question for two musicians to discuss just before they perform a piece of music.

"Well, Glenn," Menuhin answered (one can generally identify a Gould script by the fact that he thought it highly idiomatic for people to address each other as "Well, Glenn" and "Well, Yehudi," but there are traces of Menuhin's own style in the extreme courtliness of his answers), "I was very anxious to take up your invitation to play it because I admire you, and you know more about Schoenberg . . . than anyone else."

"What disturbs you most?" Gould persisted.

"There is this curious discrepancy between the gesture and the words," Menuhin replied, in a marvelously oblique effort to say that he found the piece senseless. "It's as if you had taken the words of *Hamlet* and then merely strung together a series of syllables that had no meaning as such. . . ."

After all of Gould's anxieties on the eve of taping, however, he found Menuhin's actual performance "one of the great experiences of my life. In some miraculous way, Yehudi had absorbed that extraordinary piece literally overnight and played it with absolutely reckless virtuosity. What was more important, though . . . was that he played it as though for that moment, at least, he loved it." Some critics agreed. Pat Pearce of the Montreal *Star*, for example, called this "an hour of TV grandeur . . . an hour of magnificence. . . . They gave TV a true moment of glory. For this could have been done only by TV." But Dennis Braithwaite of the *Globe and Mail* demonstrated once again that TV could provoke more brutal attacks than anything a music critic could imagine. "The program was really terrible," he wrote. "Worst of all, Glenn Gould was mostly what was wrong with it. . . . Certainly the producer, Eric Till, must be rapped for that nightmarish Victorian set . . . for photographing Gould from the back, thus making him look like something from the Cabinet of Dr. Caligari; for permitting him, while playing tender bits of Bach and Beethoven, to flop his mouth open and shut like a beached bass. . . . All this disarray wouldn't have mattered had their playing been beautiful and moving or if that famous talk had been arresting, or even made some kind of sense. But they fulfilled neither condition."

Many of Gould's thirty or so television shows were simply concerts, some with and some without commentary. The year after the Menuhin recital, for example, he joined the Toronto Symphony in playing the Bach G minor Concerto and the Strauss *Burleske*. In one sense, it was completely contradictory for Gould to be willing to play before the cameras what he refused to play before an audience. This was no longer a matter of not wanting to travel, for he traveled regularly to New York to make records, and a single recital at Carnegie Hall would have sold out within a few hours. Indeed, if he had simply announced that he would give one concert a year in Toronto's Massey Hall, the world would have thronged to fill Massey Hall. Nor was it a matter of his needing privacy or solitude. A pianist taping a concerto in the midst of a hundred orchestral musicians and a platoon of prowling TV technicians can hardly be said to be playing in private. And the camera eye, which brought his image to more people than could ever have watched him in a concert hall, brought that image in intense close-ups, publicizing and exaggerating all

those celebrated gestures, the swaying, the singing, the self-con-
ducting, that the critics so obsessively emphasized.

Gould, as usual, followed a logic of his own about these things.
The fact that he was surrounded by studio listeners could be ignored
because the listeners all had professional reasons to be there; they
were not idle spectators who had paid just to watch. "If they were
there to do a function, he didn't mind that," as Ray Roberts puts it.
"He looked at them and said to himself, 'Oh, well, they're doing a
job, the same as I'm doing a job.'" And though the audiences who
watched him were now enormous, the TV camera provided a kind
of mediation, at least a simulation of protection. If anything went
disastrously wrong—though nothing ever did—it could be repaired.
Gould could hardly help being amused, though, when the currents
of the concert world brought to Toronto in 1970 a pianist just as
eccentric as Gould himself, and just as famous for his eccentricity,
the Italian virtuoso Arturo Benedetti Michelangeli.

"Much against the warnings of a number of more expert people,"
says John Barnes, the retired head of musical programs at CBC-TV,
"I had engaged Michelangeli to do two things, a solo half-hour
thing, a Beethoven sonata, and a concerto with the Toronto Symphony. He wanted to do the *Emperor*. I wasn't that keen on it, but
he wanted to do the *Emperor*, so, you know—if he was going to do
anything, it had to be on his terms, because he was a very difficult
person.

"So he came. And one of the sidelights was that he had bought a
new piano in Hamburg, insisted on flying it over and having it
cleared through customs, but he'd never played it in public before,
and he was dissatisfied with the tuning. So it sat in our main studio
for two days whilst a tuner he'd brought in from Montreal ham-
mered away at it, tried to get it corrected. But Michelangeli got
more and more agitated. With some difficulty, he did the sonata. He
only played it once for us, and we had to tape it live, and that was
it.

"Then he announced that he wasn't going to play any more in the
studio—that we had ruined his piano by the air conditioning, or
something like that, and we were going to have to move to Massey
Hall. By this time, I'd got kind of fed up with him. And coinciden-
tally, we had been doing a series of programs with Glenn, and Glenn

called, on a Tuesday morning, and wanted to speak to Mario Prizek, the producer. And I said 'Glenn, he's tied up to the teeth with Michelangeli, who's proving very difficult.'

"'Oh, yes,' says Glenn. 'I understand he can be tough. Good *luck!*'

"'Well, we'll need that on the show now,' I said. And Glenn said:

"'Well, John, if he doesn't show, I'll do it.' I said:

"'Glenn, I *heard* you. *Don't leave town!*'

"And he laughed. But it all came to a head on Thursday. There was an impasse. We couldn't book Massey Hall, it wasn't available, and we had the Toronto Symphony standing by for Friday morning. So I simply called in the impresario, a chap named Kudriatsev, from Montreal, who has now died. And the manager of Michelangeli. And I said, 'Look, I have to know, *now*, whether your artist is going to perform tomorrow, because otherwise the deal is off.' Kudriatsev was wringing his hands—'Vould you vait till tonight?' I said, 'No, I can't, I have to know now.' Well, they couldn't tell me—so I canceled the contract. Amazement on both their faces.

"'But vot vill you do?' I said:

"'I've got someone else to do it.'

"'But who? *Who?*' And I said:

"'Well, Mr. Gould is going to perform here.'

"There was a long pause by Kudriatsev, and then he *heaved* himself to his feet—he was a great, big, fat, big, big man— He bowed low, and he said, 'I con-*grat*-u-late you!' So I phoned Glenn, and I said, 'Glenn, you're on.'

"'What do you mean, "You're on?"'" I said:

"'You said you'd do the *Emperor Concerto* for us.' He said:

"'You're kidding.' I said:

"'No, I'm not.'

"So Gould was as good as his word. He said, 'My God, just think that the Number One pianist is going to substitute for Number Two.' He canceled a radio show, and sat up most of the night, you know, preparing himself. [Gould had not performed the *Emperor* since recording it with Stokowski four years earlier.]

"The next morning, I went over to the studio with my unit manager, Lad Klimek, who was a Czech, and the orchestra was there, and the conductor, Karel Ancerl, and I said to Mario Prizek, 'You'd better get up and announce that it isn't Michelangeli that's playing this morning, it's going to be Glenn Gould.' So he got up and announced this, and Ancerl was standing there next to my unit manager, and he said something in Czech, and Lad said to me afterward, 'Maybe it's a good thing nobody understood what Ancerl said.' And I said, 'No, what was it?' And he said, 'Ancerl turned to me, and he said, "Michelangeli? *Gould?* Where do you people *get* such kooks?"'"

When the tape of Gould's overnight *Emperor Concerto* was finally broadcast several months later, it was—at safe remove—a triumph. "He was in superb form . . ." Littler wrote in the *Star*. "The camera, all the while, circled the piano, peered into the orchestra, and managed, without getting too fussy about it, to relate its vision to what was happening musically. Glenn Gould, as we all know by now, is television's pianist." Ken Winters of the *Telegram* agreed that Gould was "in stunning form," but he found the recorded sound a "matter for discouragement" and the whole program "discouragingly orthodox television." Talking with Gould afterward, Winters quoted him as saying that "it wasn't quite the kind of televised concert he'd like to do some day. I gathered that he had in mind something more enterprising and more inventive."

Artistic memories are fallible. Mario Prizek tells much the same story about Michelangeli's visit but presents himself rather than Barnes as the principal figure in the negotiations. Well, perhaps he is right. He and Gould worked closely on a number of productions. "The first concert was in 1962," says Prizek, starting to read from a list. He is a rather swarthy man with curling gray hair; he wears a chocolate-colored shirt, chocolate-colored slacks, and a gold necklace. ". . . and then 'Glenn Gould Plays Strauss.' That was with Lois Marshall and an orchestra conducted by Oscar Shumsky . . . And 'Conversations with Glenn Gould.' These were two one-hour shows for WNET in New York. . . ."

Prizek is a professional, and he understands what Gould saw in the possibilities of "creative cheating." There was a spectacular example—far more daring than the Galápagos wave in Newfoundland—during a show on Beethoven. "We were editing a Beethoven sonata," Prizek says, "and at one point the picture on both tapes we had was faulty—it was faulty video—and there was no way we could correct it with the existing materials. And I remembered that a few months before, Glenn had performed a Mozart sonata that had exactly the same beat, and in which he was working the same part of the keyboard. I called up that tape, and we looked at it, and my God, just for those three or four seconds that we needed to cover— It worked beautifully. And so we dropped in the Mozart shot for about three seconds in the middle of the Beethoven, and Glenn was delighted. Not in the fact of trickery but in making right something that wasn't right. When anyone would happen into the editing session while we were still working on other parts of the show, he'd want to show them the Mozart to see if they could notice it. And they couldn't."

Prizek is a gifted painter (he also knows eight languages), and not too long after the *Emperor Concerto,* he had an idea that he wanted to persuade Gould to undertake. "I knew of his interest in contemporary music," Prizek says, "and I wanted to deal, in an interesting, nonacademic way, with the various developments, decade by decade. I compiled a lot of data on the first two decades of this century, what was going on in music and literature and the arts, a sort of calendar of events, and changes in ideas about art. I showed this to Glenn, and he became more and more excited, so we concocted the first episode for John Barnes at CBC."

Barnes was very receptive. "I felt that we wanted to do something with Gould on a more sustained basis," he says. "As with any big artist, you don't just announce what you're going to do, you discuss what they'd like to do and see if you can come to a meeting of minds. So I phoned Glenn and suggested we have a talk, and this was one of the few occasions, by the way, on which *he* invited *me* to lunch. He stopped and picked me up in his car, and we went to lunch at the Westbury Hotel, and he said he was interested in doing some things that involved modern music."

Out of this idea came a series of four extraordinary hour-long shows called *Music in Our Time.* When the first of them, "The Age of Ecstasy (1900–1910)," appeared in 1974, it presented a Gould quite unlike anything ever seen before. For one thing, he was dressed in a neatly buttoned suit. No less unusual, he appeared in a sort of "Age of Ecstasy" living room, with *fin-de-siècle* paintings on the wall, ivory chessmen arrayed on a side table, and a fire burning in the marble fireplace. Most striking of all was that when Gould began playing Scriabin preludes, clouds of colored light began slowly swirling around behind his head, and not just swirling but constantly changing their shapes and their colors.

Gould had good reasons for this extravaganza. He explained to his audience that Scriabin thought musical keys implied equivalents in color, that he believed C major represented red, and D major yellow, and so on, and that he even tried unsuccessfully to invent a color keyboard. If he had succeeded, Gould said from his handsome armchair, the results "might have been something like this." The display of lights was organized by Prizek, who had commissioned Earl Reiback of the Electric Gallery in Toronto to create the chroma-keyed light sculptures. Gould was delighted. "Given the limitations of video-tape," he wrote to Paul Myers in London, "it was, I think, the most effective mating of music and camera we've managed to date and . . . some of the most effective television I've ever seen." Though this program contained other interesting examples of Gould's fascination with musical ecstasy—the Berg Sonata, four Schoenberg songs, and the Debussy Clarinet Rhapsody against a background of Monet water lilies—it was Gould's sensuous version of Scriabin that remains in the memory. "Not everyone will share his enthusiasm for the music of Scriabin," Kraglund wrote in the *Globe and Mail,* "but when he has finished introducing and performing that composer's preludes . . . there is a good chance the viewers will begin to develop an appreciation. That is one of the things about Gould—his ability to command attention in anything for which he has developed a passion."

And for what had Gould not developed a passion? On his second show, "The Flight from Order (1910–1920)," in which Gould's living room had evolved into Jugendstil and boasted a wind-up phonograph with a large trumpet to spread the new sounds, the pianist began with several of Prokofiev's magical *Visions fugitives,* then accompanied his friend Roxolana Roslak in Strauss's *Ophelialieder,* then conducted from the keyboard a dazzling version of *Pierrot Lunaire.* As soon as Patricia Rideout began singing each of Schoenberg's songs, the camera showed hallucinatory images illustrating the text. In "The Washerwoman," for example, the heroine knelt by a stream, scrubbing a piece of cloth, which she then held up and showed to be full of holes. Even when Gould hated a piece, that too was a passion. Thus, after announcing that the music of Stravinsky "sends me up the wall," he walked offstage and left the marvelous *Histoire du soldat* to be conducted by an associate, Boris Brott. He soon returned, though, to sail through his own spectacular transcription of Ravel's *La Valse* (a work of which more will be heard).

Most of the critics remained sympathetic, though some were getting restless. "How many viewers . . . had the slightest idea of what Glenn Gould was talking about . . . ?" Braithwaite complained in the *Star.* "Glenn Gould is a genius. Glenn Gould is a valuable Canadian national resource. But Glenn Gould is a hard man to follow through an analysis of even the familiar classics, let alone one of the twelve-tone labyrinths contrived by Arnold Schoenberg." The CBC didn't seem to mind such outbursts. "Glenn was someone whom we knew and trusted," John Barnes recalls. "He'd worked a great deal with radio. He'd produced things on radio. He'd grown up with us, and we with him, so we treated him very—with a good deal of respect, and let him be part of the team in a way that we probably wouldn't have done with someone else."

The third installment, "New Faces, Old Forms (1920–1930)," required all of the CBC's patience. "Visualize, if you will," Littler wrote in the *Star,* " a potted-palm scene with a vested Boris Brott conducting a chamber ensemble while a deadpan, ice-cream suited Glenn Gould and an eye-bulging Patricia Rideout brogue-accent their way through the Scottish Rhapsody from William Walton's *Façade.* If that isn't the unlikeliest opening for a CBC television music special I don't know what is. And the shenanigans don't end there. Messrs. Brott and Gould wind up in an argument about tempo, Gould and Rideout reappear as arthritic senior citizens, and all this happens within the first few minutes. . . ."

There were other shenanigans that never appeared on camera. During a rehearsal, while Brott was preparing *Façade,* Gould went wandering around and finally sat down on the dais, just behind the conductor, with his fragile hands stretched out on the floor as props. "I was not aware of where Glenn was," Brott recalls, "and I stepped backwards, and I felt my heel just—well, my heel came down on—"

Q: On something squishy?

A: On something squishy. I didn't put my weight on it—thank God!—but Glenn was sitting on the floor, like this, with his hands behind him, and I had landed on one of them. And of course, all the stories that I had heard about various people flashed before my eyes—and the room went dead silent. All the cameramen and gaffers and everybody—the room went absolutely dead quiet. And he blanched. But then he sort of went like this and shook his hand and smiled and said, "It's all right. Don't worry."

And so, after some Bartok, some Schoenberg, some Hindemith and Copland, the program finished with Poulenc's bizarre "choreographic concerto" called *Aubade*. The uninjured Gould played several flashy cadenzas, Brott conducted eighteen instrumentalists, and a half dozen dancers spun and whirled through the roles of Acteon, Diana, and Diana's handmaidens. Poulenc, Gould warned his audience, wrote "some rather lovely things" but also "some of the most shameless claptrap of his time."

The furniture kept changing, so while the Gould of the 1920's sat in a white chair with a curving silver armrest, the Gould of the 1930's lounged in a tan Barcelona chair as he narrated "The Artist as Artisan" and offered Alfredo Casella's *Ricercare on the Name of Bach*, the Hindemith Trumpet Sonata, some Krenek songs, and the Webern Concerto for Nine Instruments. Any pianist might have had difficulties with this repertoire, but Gould's difficulties were of a unique sort. He told a friend that he had to go and practice the Webern, and when the friend expressed surprise at this, since Gould hardly ever practiced, and since he had often played this work during his concert years, Gould confessed. He confessed that he now had the complete score for all nine instruments in his head, "and I have to go and unlearn all the other parts." Yet another unique difficulty was how to translate Webern's abstract score into television. For that, Gould had himself accompanied not only by eight other instruments but by rapidly changing patterns of colored dots, squares, triangles, diamonds, simple shapes that kept expanding and contracting, multiplying and dividing, changing into each other. Gould's TV music had undergone a considerable evolution from the swirling clouds of color that had enveloped Scriabin.

This fourth installment, broadcast in 1977, was as imaginative as ever, but there was something a little perfunctory about it, as though Gould were losing interest, or simply not concentrating, as though his mind were on other things. "It all went along swimmingly for three or four productions, and then Gould had a sort of bad period," John Barnes recalls. "I guess it was maybe when his mother died. And he was ill himself. I don't know what it was, but he claimed to me that he just wasn't feeling well enough to do these things. So he canceled out a couple of times, over a couple of years. We got half of one of them done, but in the end, it just drifted away. It became fairly obvious after a while that he'd kind of lost interest in completing the whole thing."

Even when Gould was not working for the CBC, he had an office there, received mail there, left papers there to be typed, and he was generally treated like what Barnes called "a member of the team." It was because of this that a young director named John McGreevy felt entitled to call on Gould for help with an unusual problem. A newcomer from England, McGreevy had found himself a job in the CBC mailroom, then gotten a chance as a cameraman, then as a director.

"The CBC in the sixties was a place of extraordinary talent and creative vitality," McGreevy recalls, "and of course, coming with that, a lot of wild neurotics populated the corridors. And Glenn was the most exotic of all the neurotics who populated the corridors. I was aware of him long before he was aware of me, because his performances in the studio were always high theatre. And so I became fascinated by this phenomenon.

"Eventually we were aware of each other through the grapevine, but we never really talked until I had a musical problem with a show that I was working on, a one-hour drama called 'Mandelstam's Witness.' This was seventy-five, seventy-six. It was an adaptation of Nadezhda Mandelstam's memoirs, and I got the great Polish actress Ida Kaminska to present a portrait of Mandelstam in her Moscow apartment, describing her life, that fifty years of horror. But it needed something behind it, and the normal musical approaches just weren't going to work. I tried all kinds of things. And so I finally phoned Glenn, right out of the blue, and told him about it. And as it was Christmas Eve when I phoned him, I said, 'Glenn, you know, I would love you to come down and watch this sometime after the holidays.' And he said, 'Well, what are you doing this evening?'"

The idea that Gould had nothing better to do on a Christmas Eve is a little odd, but so is the idea that McGreevy would be similarly unoccupied, and so is the idea that the CBC studios would be wide open for business, but the two of them agreed to meet there. "He came down with stopwatches," McGreevy recalls, "with pencils and papers and so on. And we locked ourselves in a small booth at the CBC. And he was absolutely captivated by the show, and I think we ran it three times that evening. We got out of the booth at four o'clock in the morning—which was a great time for Glenn—and he said, 'I know what you must do. Imagine, in the apartment next door, which we never see, there is a young cellist, a student, and he is rehearsing over and over again a Shostakovitch cello concerto. And then at the very end, he starts to play the slow movement over the closing titles.' And of course it was perfect. When you see the show, you are persuaded that right next door to Mandelstam is a student working away on the cello, and you never need to see him. It was just the most sublime solution to a very, very difficult problem."

McGreevy then became one of the people whom Gould liked to call late at night. "Always at about one o'clock in the morning. 'I hope I'm not disturbing you, John, but I've just finished the first edit of whatever, and it only runs three hours, and I'd like you to hear it.' So one would hang up at four o'clock in the morning. But of course I had a tremendous appetite for all of his gifts and his outpouring of creativity. Being very new to the business myself, I found it grist for the mill for me to be able to listen to somebody in full flight, and in full command of his creative powers, and really pressing the boundaries of what is permissible, in terms of the amount of material you could lay on any individual at any one time. I was fascinated by that whole approach."

McGreevy was just beginning an ambitious project of his own, a series of portraits of the world's great cities, each one to be seen through the eyes of one idiosyncratic observer. Without telling Gould "what the hidden agenda was," McGreevy invited him to look at a show he had just finished. "And up came 'Peter Ustinov's

Leningrad,' with the great man sailing down one of the canals. And Glenn leaped up and said, 'I know exactly why I'm here! You want me to do 'Glenn Gould's Orillia.'* I said, 'Well, not quite Orillia, but almost.' And from there we struck up the arrangement by which he would do this inimitable protrait of Toronto—that was in seventy-eight, I believe, or seventy-nine. And it was a glorious experience."

Q: To what extent was that his own work, and to what extent did you change it around, or redirect it?

A: It was very much a collaboration. His problem was that he really didn't know Toronto today, so I had to—I mean, his Toronto was the Toronto of the forties and fifties—the Toronto that he remembered.

Q: Like so much else in his life, it was all inside his head.

A: Right.

The Toronto of the 1940's, the commercial capital of British Canada, was by most accounts rather stodgy, rather provincial, rather prudish, and rather pleased with itself. It didn't mind the fact that other Canadians often called it "Hogtown," and it didn't mind the fact that other Canadians jeered at the myriad blue laws—no concerts on Sundays, no beer at baseball games—that characterized "Toronto the Good." "In my youth," Gould himself recalled, "it was said that for a really lively weekend, what you had to do was drive to Buffalo."

World War II inevitably began changing Toronto, and the opening of the St. Lawrence Seaway in 1959 changed it still more, turning Hogtown into an international port. "I can still remember, when the Seaway had been completed," Gould said, "how exciting it was to prowl the Toronto waterfront and encounter ships that had brought Volkswagens from Germany or TV sets from Japan and had names like *Wolfgang Russ* or *Munishima Maru*." And as the British influence faded, Toronto's powerful money suddenly asserted itself in the form of exultant skyscrapers. Mies van der Rohe's fifty-four-story Toronto-Dominion Bank became the highest office building in the entire Commonwealth; then I. M. Pei built a slightly higher tower just across Bay Street for the Bank of Com-

---

*The town nearest to the Goulds' cottage on Lake Simcoe.

merce; and then Edward Durrell Stone a still higher one for the Bank of Montreal.

This economic boom attracted whole new populations. One quarter of all postwar immigrants to Canada came to Toronto, until the city's two million inhabitants included more Italians than there are in Florence, more West Indians than in Grenada. The Hungarian revolt of 1956 brought in swarms of refugees from Budapest, and the fall of South Vietnam filled Chinatown with Vietnamese. Despite all the changes and growth, however, Toronto was one of the few major cities in the world where the official passion for bulldozing and skyscraping was stoutly resisted by community opposition in raffish neighborhoods with names like Cabbagetown. The American urbanologist Jane Jacobs not only declared that Toronto was "the most hopeful and healthy city in North America," she went to live there herself. Even now, tourists from south of the border can only marvel at a metropolis where the streets are clean, the storekeepers courteous, the subways safe, and the parks in flower.

Gould could hardly remain unaware of the sudden growth of the cosmopolitan Toronto—he lived there virtually all of his life, and he loved the place—but it is quite possible to ignore such things. Or not ignore, but fail to take in, just as one can fail to notice in the mirror that one has passed from youth into middle age. So while McGreevy's cameras could follow Gould into a number of Toronto institutions that had remained largely unchanged—the zoo, for example, where Gould sang Mahler songs to the mistrustful elephants—the cameras remained somewhat baffled by the Toronto that existed inside Gould's head, the sound of the Sunday-night hymns, for example, that had offered him peace before the return to school on the following morning.

Since TV must show and keep showing, there were only two solutions. One was to illustrate Gould's visions with abstract or symbolic illustrations, as Gould himself had illustrated Scriabin with swirling colors and Webern with dancing dots. The other was to supplement Gould's intangible memories by steering the cameras into the Toronto of today. McGreevy naturally chose the second alternative, took Gould to the megalopolitan Eaton shopping center, and recorded his wonderment—"I don't believe it! It's absurd!" In this rather conventional travelogue of the tourist's Toronto, the

Breakthrough: Gould at his original recording session for the *Goldberg Variations* in 1955.

A left-handed child, unlike all others. Gould at eighteen months (top), and the prodigy with his guardian, Nick.

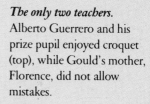

The only two teachers.
Alberto Guerrero and his
prize pupil enjoyed croquet
(top), while Gould's mother,
Florence, did not allow
mistakes.

"He really did wonderful things in the Brahms D-minor concerto, and I adored him for it," says Leonard Bernstein; seen here (top) rehearsing with Gould in the early 1960's, the conductor once made controversial public remarks about his performance of the piece with the pianist. (Bottom) Gould testing pianos at Columbia's Thirtieth Street studio in New York in 1957.

A genius for collaboration. Rehearsing chamber music with Yehudi Menuhin (top) and preparing for a radio interview with Leopold Stokowski.

The sound of a radio was, to Gould "the most unique experience in music." The pianist strikes an Arctic pose on the *Muskeg Express* while making his sound documentary, "The Idea of North" (top), which he spent months editing with engineer Lorne Tulk (bottom, right).

New Directions: A warmly gloved Gould discussing his string quartet with members of the Cleveland Orchestra (top) and working with producer Bruno Monsaingeon to translate his Bach into television.

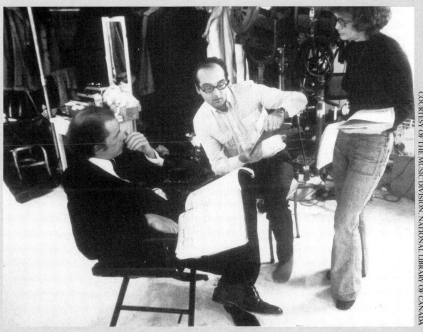

Final Days: Gould was near death when he re-recorded the *Goldberg Variations* in 1981.

cameras even recorded Gould's distaste for the sleazy naughtiness of the city's "strip"—"I always felt that 'Toronto the Good' was a very nice nickname"—and then relentlessly dollied on through the neon-lit vulgarities of Yonge Street. "Glenn Gould's Toronto," in other words, was in many ways not Glenn Gould's Toronto.

But Gould himself was fascinated by the challenge of trying to film his own sense of his own city. He knew that the elaborate technologies of television were far more complex (and more expensive) than anything he had mastered in radio, but he first tried to control the show by writing it. "I told him that these films run about 4,500 words, and so if he did an essay of about 7,000 words, then it gives us a little bit of room to edit," McGreevy recalls. "I went away and shot another couple of episodes of the series and came back to him three months later and he had written about 45,000 words. *And* he said, 'You can't touch a thing.' And I said, 'Well, Glenn, 45,000 words, that's a ten-hour film.' So we spent one very long night hacking our way through it, and he took it all in very great spirit because he knew it had to be done."

Even after all that cutting, there were scenes that Gould couldn't bear to kill, scenes that McGreevy knew he would somehow have to strangle in secrecy. "He had this awful Brando character, Teddy Slutz. And we did shoot a scene where Glenn is driving himself down Yonge Street and suddenly Teddy Slutz comes out of the crowd, hits the car, and they have a huge row with one another. And we double-shot it so that Glenn played all of his stuff [both roles], and quite frankly it was god-awful. So to save him from himself, we left it on the cutting-room floor. I said to him that we had technical problems. I wasn't going to tell him that it was god-awful."

Though Gould could freely indulge himself in such fantasies, the great problem in shooting a nonmusical TV documentary, outside the soundproofed sanctuary of the CBC studios, was that Gould once again had to confront the mindless crowd, the crowd that had once provided his concert audiences and now flowed through the streets. "I mean, one never physically touched Glenn," McGreevy says. "Real, genuine terror about that, and then you multiply that into a crowd, and being trapped in a crowd would be, I imagine, for Glenn, the ultimate horror.... The Eaton Center has thousands of people there all the time, and I think the claustrophobia of that was a problem. If I did things with him, it would draw a crowd, and he'd be very paranoid about everybody looking at him."

McGreevy was shrewdly protective. "I promised him," he recalls, "that I would do everything in such a way that there would be no attention drawn to us. We had to do some very clever and fast foot-work to get him in and out of these places without anybody realizing what we were up to. A lot of that stuff was shot with a concealed camera and Glenn on a radio mike, miles away. We hid behind pot-ted plants and so on, and so people didn't really know. All they saw was another nut talking to himself, and there are many of those."

Gould had other problems as well. McGreevy wanted to shoot the singing-to-the-elephants sequence in the dawn emptiness of the zoo, approximately when Gould went to bed, so they all agreed to meet at the zoo at 5 A.M. "At one o'clock in the morning, my phone rang, and it was Glenn," McGreevy says. "'John, I hope I'm not disturbing you, but I've got a problem, and you may want to start calling the crew because I *may* not be able to make it tomorrow morning. I don't wish to alarm you—' And by that time, of course, I'm sitting up. I said, 'What's the problem?'

"He said, 'Well, I have just contracted all of the symptoms—bar one—of what attacked me in Amsterdam (or was it Copenhagen?), in 1957, in October, when I was on tour, and I was doing the Strauss, I was doing the Schoenberg—I can't remember which opus I was doing—' And going on and on about this. I said, 'Glenn, what is it that you've contracted?' He said, 'Well, subclinical polio.'

"I said, 'I beg your pardon?' He said, 'Well, all the symptoms are there, except for one, and I don't know if it's going to come on, and it may be all right, but I thought I'd better alert you.' I'd never heard of subclinical polio. It sounded—well, he invented a lot of syn-dromes. I wasn't sure if he would actually show, but I arrived on location and set up the equipment, and then Glenn arrived, on time, a little shy, and said, 'I think I'm going to be all right.'"

Q: Could that have been pure stage fright?

A: Yes. Because he was with new people, and he was very, very shy, and he hadn't met my film crew before.

Gould was accustomed to controlling everything, to editing every take of every recording, every tape of his radio interviews, but this was all beyond his grasp. McGreevy was in charge, and McGreevy only let Gould see his editing after the process was all finished. "For Glenn, who had a tremendous desire for control over all the creative elements of his work," McGreevy says, "it was an incredible experience to come in and see the first cutting of this and see a thing that he had spent many hours working on with me, and see that the architecture had completely flown around. . . . Given that he was obsessed by process and structure and architecture within any given piece, this was for him quite fascinating. And so I spent months fending off all kinds of creative brilliance that he applied to me because of what I had done."

When it was all complete, it was, predictably, a big event for Toronto's civic authorities. "I went down to City Hall and persuaded the mayor to let me use the council chamber," McGreevy says. "Have you been in the modern City Hall? Oh, it's quite marvelous—it's *2001*. And to convert the rotunda into a movie theatre and invite several hundred people down to watch 'Glenn Gould's Toronto.'. . ." Gould heard about all this installation of huge screens, and he wanted, within his own rules, to know more. "He said, 'Do you think I could come?'" McGreevy recalls. "'I've never been in City Hall, and I'd just love to see myself thirty feet high.' And so he came and sat through it, an audience of one, and he had the time of his life. But there was no way he could be there with several hundred other people."

GOULD DOESN'T SHOW AT THE PARTY was the headline in the Toronto *Star*. "The big question at City Hall last night was: Would Glenn Gould show up? At least 300 people were on hand in the council chamber for a private screening of Glenn Gould's Toronto. . . . But of course Gould, who is the most reclusive of all performing artists, wasn't there. 'I was hoping this was going to be my chance to meet Glenn Gould but he was smarter than that and decided not to come,' Mayor John Sewell said in welcoming guests. And then Sewell added: 'But someone said it's still daylight out.'"

If such mockery seems unduly patronizing, as though Gould had some kind of moral obligation to stand in the mayor's receiving line and shake the outstretched hands of Toronto's cultural establishment, the newspaper reviews of "Glenn Gould's Toronto" went even further in a new series of personal attacks. The Toronto papers had always been quick to leap to Gould's defense against any outside criticisms, but now that he had made a TV show about their fair city, they found it almost treasonous. "Gould may well be one of the world's greatest interpreters of Bach, yet he has always struck me as a particularly pretentious recluse, cursed with intellectual snobbery," Bob Pennington wrote in the *Sun*. "Failing to show at last week's party in his honor at City Hall seemed just another example of the Garbo syndrome being used as an excuse for poor manners." The *Globe and Mail* was equally disapproving. "He . . . ridicules Toronto's approach to its financial institutions," Don Downey wrote, "and sneers at the city's foundations. . . . There is little, in fact, that escaped Gould's acid tongue."

The *Star* chose to emphasize the fact that Gould was beginning to show his years, that the handsome young virtuoso had grown into a somewhat paunchy and pasty middle age. DRACULA LIVES AS TOUR GUIDE TO TORONTO, the *Star*'s headline proclaimed. "What a marvelous performance it is . . ." wrote TV columnist Ron Base. "Gould announces that he does not arise until after dark. Nosferatu indeed lives! He skulks around Toronto and its shady suburban environs, his hatchet-sharp face shadowed by a floppy cap, his gaunt form swathed in formless overcoat and dark scarf, his wispy hands covered by gloves. Dracula is alive and well and showing us the view from the CN Tower. There is something infinitely cheeky about using a renegade, more concerned with revealing his eccentricities . . . than the city in which he lives. . . . He merely sneers at it all."

Cheeky, yes, infinitely cheeky.

During the mid-1970's, when Gould was beginning to get tired of *Music in Our Time*, when he was deeply disturbed by the death of his mother, and when he began undergoing a number of mysterious medical difficulties, there suddenly came into his life the admiring figure of the French TV producer Bruno Monsaingeon.

Monsaingeon recalls that his own life had been completely overturned by the discovery of Gould's music. "I was in Moscow on a visit in 1965, just to learn the language," he says. "And records were extremely cheap there, so I was buying them by the kilo. I never had heard the name of Gould, but I had a little machine, and I played one of these new records, a live performance of the Bach Inventions that he did in Moscow in fifty-seven. And what happened then is almost indescribable. It was, for me, something of the intensity of a religious revelation. And you know, it completely altered my life. . . . There was something behind the dimensions of the pianist which was of much greater importance than just the genius of the pianist."

Q: What does that mean, exactly? What do you mean when you say it was like a religious experience?

A: My idea was that I heard a voice saying to me, "Come and follow me."

Q: Was that Gould's voice or just a voice?

A: A voice. I hadn't yet met Gould.

Q: But the voice referred to Gould?

A: Yes, yes, it meant that, exactly that.

In the next couple of years, while he still gave violin concerts, Monsaingeon got more and more involved in creating musical programs for French television, first organizing them, then directing them, then realizing that he could produce them on his own. "I was absolutely fascinated by the medium, you know," he says, "and when it appeared that I could have my own projects, the first thing I wanted to do was to try and approach that man of legend whom I'd never met, about whom I knew absolutely nothing, who was Glenn Gould. So I wrote him a long letter, about the way I conceived of television, or music on television, and so on, and could we possibly envision something together, in which you would be *the* subject. . . . I didn't expect an answer, really. It was just like a bottle thrown into the sea. And then six months later, I got a reply from him, an enormous letter, fifteen or twenty pages, saying, 'Well, I'm rather intrigued by your ideas. Why don't you come and see me?'"

If there was one thing that Gould recognized and responded to and appreciated, it was devotion. He needed it. He had received it from his parents, particularly his mother, and from Jessie Greig, and from Lorne Tulk, and from a few other colleagues and comrades, and now he recognized it again in Bruno Monsaingeon. And if Monsaingeon felt overtones of religious inspiration, Gould was not inclined to scorn the idea.

What Monsaingeon had to offer, though, was very practical. He now represented a German corporation named Classart, and Classart wanted to film a series of shows on Gould the hermit, Gould the exile, Gould the lord of the hidden empire. Gould happily agreed, and so Monsaingeon arrived in Toronto in 1974 with a ten-man French film crew. "Starting at two o'clock in the afternoon, we would work until six o'clock in the morning," Monsaingeon recalls. "Every day. And extremely—you know, never tired, simply because the intensity was there. And we also founded a trio at that point, which was—we discovered that my script assistant could read music, and so when there were technical problems, and the technicians were arranging things, we would sing *The Goldberg Variations.* The three of us together. We would give Glenn any part, you know, the soprano as well as the alto or bass, and he was relaxing in his armchair, singing whichever part we gave him to do, and so we sang the complete work. And then one day, Glenn said, 'I've found a title for our trio, for our debut in Town Hall. K for Karen, G for Glenn, and B for Bruno, our trio's going to be called The KGBs.'"

Monsaingeon called his series *Les Chemins de la Musique,* which, by its very insistence on direction, implies a certain disorder. Monsaingeon started like a documentary-maker, with shots of some moving men unloading a piano and carrying it into an empty studio. A narrating voice explains that Gould has not played in public for a number of years, and so we are following him into "La Retraite," as this first installment is called. Gould appears in his usual cap and scarf, takes them off, and starts playing Bach's Partita in E minor.

The documentary approach continues, on a fairly basic level. Why did Gould retire from the concert stage? "I found it an appalling experience, and essentially antimusical. . . . Giving up the concerts was simply a way of giving up an intensely unpleasant experience." These familiar questions and answers serve mainly as accompaniment. Monsaingeon's camera is there primarily to watch Gould play the piano, and so, as it watches, he plays Schoenberg's Suite, Opus 25, and a pavane by Orlando Gibbons, and a bit of his own transcription of Wagner's overture to *Die Meistersinger,* all with a great deal of auxiliary humming and moaning at the keyboard.

Filming with Gould was often less casual than it seemed. "When we had that first session," Monsaingeon recalls, "he hit the microphone at some point—very, very gently—and he collapsed into a chair and said, 'My God, a concussion.' And then he said, 'Well, look, in two hours there should be this effect; in four hours, that; in twelve hours— Now in thirteen hours, if this has not happened, then I'm all right.' And then I—you know, I was terrified. And he said, 'Well, I know, I know, once I let my imagination go, I'm lost.'"

If the first installment seemed diffuse and impressionistic, the second, entitled "L'Alchimiste," was designed to show the master technician pulling all the strands together. Better than any other film, in fact, it did show Gould at work as editor, cutter, mixer, technological creator. The basic subject was a fragment from one of Bach's English Suites, which Gould played in several different ways and then settled down to work on. The dialogue served as illustration:

Gould: Did you manage to get things sharpened up a bit? Is the center mike . . . attenuated now?

Technician: The center mike is a little bit above the other two, to enhance the middle frequencies. . . .

Gould: Are you cued to feed me about ten after the double bar? Okay, if the level isn't right, I'll stop you, but let's see what we can get. . . . Give me about two bars before the splice.

This devotion to the technology of recording reached a still higher point when Gould and his crew moved on from Bach to Scriabin. Camera on Lorne Tulk, moving microphones from place to place. *Gould* (his voice full of enthusiasm): "We're going to try something that may not work at all . . . because we've never done it before. It will involve a whole sequence of different mike perspectives. . . . One very close to the piano, almost like a jazz pickup, the kind of thing where you put the mike right inside the piano instead of in the lower strings, as Oscar Peterson* would do it. . . . Another at the discreet Deutsche Grammophon perspective, you know, a nice view from the balcony. And then, a more distant perspective still, one possibly that will pick up just resonance, just reverb from the back of the walls—and mix all these perspectives. . . . And the music that we're going to do all this for, with, to, is Scriabin. Because I don't think that any other composer has ever needed that

---

*The fact that Gould and one of the most popular jazz pianists both lived in Toronto inspired a number of editors to attempt to sponsor some kind of interview or encounter. Though both pianists were acutely aware of each other, nothing ever came of the idea. After Gould died, Peterson told an interviewer, "I was supposed to do a piano show with him . . . and I am sorry I did not."

help from technology as badly as Scriabin does. . . ." Scriabin, whose music generally sounds beautiful under almost any technological circumstances, sounded very beautiful indeed through Gould's network of microphones.

While Gould was the absolute master of sound, though, one senses that visual technology always remained slightly beyond his reach, a toy to be played with, puzzled over, explored. Monsaingeon's third installment began with a bass singing the opening of "So You Want to Write a Fugue?," and Gould watching on another screen, and then the tenor taking up the fugue theme on a different screen, and Gould watching that on yet another screen. Then Gould started to talk, over the multiplicity of singing voices, and described all of this as "the demolition of a fugue" and also as "a bit of *Waiting for Godot*." This show careened on through Webern and Berg, and then the fourth installment finally returned to the tonic key by showing nothing but Gould again playing Bach's Partita in E minor, Gould's own favorite (with which, remember, the series had begun). Not a word was spoken. Not a word needed to be spoken.

"As the last days approached," Monsaingeon recalls, "everybody was feeling very, very sad because they knew that they would probably never see him again. And unbeknownst to me and to Glenn, the crew had prepared a kind of farewell party. So when the last note or last word or last shot had been completed, a table was pushed forward, and there was plenty of drinks and nuts and all kinds of food and so on, and Glenn was horrified. He said, 'I'm sorry, I can't see all of this, and I have to say good-bye to everybody.' So it was a very abrupt kind of end, and then he wrote to everyone, very wonderful letters. But the feeling of sadness on the part of these people—it was extreme. It was extraordinary to have lived that period of time with that extraordinary man."

The Monsaingeon series had its modest success on European television, but both Gould and Monsaingeon felt that they had barely begun to explore what they and their cameras might create. After all the excursions into Beethoven, Wagner, and Berg, they decided to go back to bedrock and start planning a series on the idea of Gould playing Bach. Because of the nature of television—and because of the nature of Gould, who felt a lifelong yearning to teach, or perhaps to preach, to explain the nature and meaning of his art—Gould could not simply play Bach without writing everything down beforehand. "As is my habit," he wrote in another context in 1977, "the 'dialogue' was entirely scripted by me—I have, in fact, not spoken a spontaneous word via the airwaves for at least a decade. . . . In any case, all of the lines are mine."

Gould's insistence on total control could be disconcerting to his associates. "What about the text on Mozart and Mozart's piano sonatas?" Monsaingeon wrote to him in 1976 about the article that was eventually published under the title "Of Mozart and Related Matters: Glenn Gould in Conversation with Bruno Monsaingeon." "You had said that you would send it to me but it has not arrived. As you may imagine I am very anxious to know what my opinion is and how beautifully 'you' expressed 'my' thoughts." Looking back on these "interviews" now, Monsaingeon sees them as a kind of collaboration. "We spent three years drafting that before we actually started shooting," he says of the TV series, "so that, you know, we spent complete evenings at his studio at the Inn on the Park. And the show was to be very simple, playing and talk and play and talk. Nothing more complicated. What he did at the end was that he made the final draft, you know. And the final draft came from many versions that we had written together."

This final draft consisted mainly of cues. "Glenn, what is it about the fugue that gave it such a central role . . . ?" "Yes, I agree, but don't you think . . . ?" Once Gould picked up his cue, he was almost unstoppable. And sometimes Gould taught more than he realized. Monsaingeon happened to mention, in Gould's script, the beautiful *Chromatic Fantasy,* and Gould proceeded to denounce it in the most extreme terms.

Monsaingeon: You mean that you don't like it?

Gould: Oh, I quite cordially hate it.

Gould went on to call this masterpiece "a monstrosity," to declare that its harmony "wanders all over the lot" (shouldn't fantasies wander?), and even to ridicule its emotional intensity. "If Hitchcock had been working in the eighteenth century," Gould jeered, "Bach would have been working full-time on the Universal lot, writing backgrounds, for sure. I mean, can't you see Peter Lorre or Vincent Price sitting at the manual organ . . . as the clock strikes midnight?" Gould then proceeded to play this splendid piece ("My first and last performance of any part of the *Chromatic Fantasia*") in much the same way that he played the despised sonatas of Mozart, much too fast, with great contempt, and with virtually no sense of the beauties that he was racing through.

Gould's approach to *The Art of the Fugue*, on the other hand, was almost awestruck, and all the more courageous for that. He had often played parts of this monumental work during his concert years, but when he began to record it, in 1962, he took the somewhat evasive step of performing it on an organ, and then, after finishing the first nine of the fifteen fugues, he abandoned the whole project. Now, however, he determined to confront that majestic final fugue that had been interrupted in midmeasure by Bach's death.

"He had never played it before in public," Monsaingeon recalls, "and he said to me, the day before, on the telephone, 'It's the most difficult thing I've ever approached. It's—you've got to keep it going—how do you do that?' He was terribly intimidated. And he said to me, 'I've got several versions—one which would sound like a pavane and another one like a gigue, all very different in tempi and phrasing and articulation and so on. So I'd like to offer you a few, and you tell me which one you choose.'" So they went to the studio, and Gould played and played and played. "And I've never had the same sense of ecstatic abandon as on that particular day," Monsaingeon says. "When he reached the point where Bach introduces the theme of his own name, B-A-C-H, which is an extraordinarily moving passage, Glenn was just in another world, and he started to talk about what he was feeling, and he said, 'There's never been anything more beautiful in all of music.'" That performance too is on the tape, and that performance tells us a great deal about how Gould felt about Bach, about art, about life.

The end of any television series on Gould playing Bach naturally had to present Gould playing *The Goldberg Variations*. The middle-aged man, rather heavy now, and bespectacled, and getting bald, and even relying on makeup—

Q: Did he really use makeup?

A: Oh, always, always.

The middle-aged man had to confront the great triumph of his own youth, at least match it and perhaps somehow surpass it. But between the idea and the reality, nowadays, lies technology, and technology often means breakdown and failure. "I would like to comment in the strongest possible way upon the deplorable state of the physical plant and on the inadequate maintenance of the production hardware in Studio 7," Mario Prizek wrote to the CBC authorities after a taping of Gould's Bach series. There followed, then, a long chronicle of how contemporary technology generally works: On the first day of taping, one of the four cameras broke down, and when the director reorganized everything to work with three cameras, a second camera failed. "Three hours were wasted before the first take could be finished," Prizek said. "On the second day, we had barely started when the Studer began to malfunction. It 'gave up the ghost' before we could get our first 'take.' A maintenance crew was called. They had to disassemble the Studer completely before they could get it into operational condition. . . ." On the third day: "All our 'takes' after the supper-break were aborted by a loud hum and buzz on all tracks. . . ." And so on. "The nature of the delays caused by technical failures would be unacceptable even for an in-house production," Prizek declared, "but for a show which is done as a co-production (in this case with a West German production house) they were both shameful and shaming."

So when Gould began thinking about how to rerecord *The Goldberg Variations,* he began thinking about going back to New York, back to the obsolescent Columbia studio on East Thirtieth Street, back to that onetime church where he had first recorded those marvelous variations so many years ago.

The Romantic Records

In the midst of his early recordings of Bach and Schoenberg and more Bach, Gould surprised many of his admirers by producing late in 1960 a collection of Brahms intermezzi. He might have impressed them by performing these beautifully windblown autumnal trifles in an austerely classical manner, but he indulged himself instead in the most lavish and luscious romanticism. And he was proud of it.

"I have received the test pressing of my latest recording—the first one made since the shoulder trouble—and I really think it is perhaps the best piano playing I have done . . ." he wrote to a friend in Berlin. "I think that you will be quite surprised not only with the repertoire but also with the style of playing which is, if I might say so, rather aristocratic. Come to think of it, I don't really think you will be surprised either. You know what an incurable romantic I am anyway."

To an interviewer, Bernard Asbell, Gould called this "the sexiest interpretation of Brahms intermezzi you have ever heard."

"How do you mean, 'sexiest'?" Asbell asked.

"I have captured, I think, an atmosphere of improvisation which I don't believe has ever been represented in Brahms recordings before," Gould said. "There is a quality as though—this isn't an original comment, but something one of my friends said—as though I were really playing for myself, but left the door open. I think a lot of people are going to hate it, but—"

"But you love it?"

"Yes, I love it. This is one of the things I am most proud of."

Gould's predictions of public rejection were obviously hyperbolic. Raymond Ericson of the New York *Times* found the new record a revelation "that the young Canadian pianist is at heart a highly romantic individual. . . . The Brahms performances are never less than absorbing, for here is an interesting mind at work. Most of them are convincing as interpretations and beautiful to hear." "The reviews of the Brahms, which are now beginning to arrive in force, are almost unanimously glorious . . ." Gould wrote happily to Homburger. "The only exception is the unpredictable Mr. Kolodin, who is violently opposed and says that my view of Brahms' last years is clearly that of a stodgy mooning old codger. . . . The Chicago Sun, which arrived this morning, said 'Gould has the kind of exceptional musicianship that can make him a specialist in any type of music he wishes to cultivate.'"

The Romantic era was, of course, the golden age of piano music, but in belatedly announcing his own romanticism, Gould felt a characteristically wayward impulse to denounce the great piano composers of the period. He repeatedly criticized Chopin, Schumann, and Liszt, and generally ignored Schubert. Just as waywardly, he made an exception of Mendelssohn and announced a recording of his organ sonatas. "I adore Mendelssohn," Gould declared, adding a pugnacious and wholly wrongheaded comparison. "He is a much greater composer than Schumann, for instance."

While Gould scolded the early nineteenth-century masters for their relative indifference to counterpoint, he offered exaggerated praise to the composers who flowered during the decaying years of the Romantic movement. "Actually, I am very much a romantic," he said in one typical outburst. "There are a great many composers of the 19th century whom I would play with the greatest pleasure had they provided any substantial literature for the piano. I think Tchaikowsky was a great composer, one it is now fashionable to dislike on all sorts of grounds such as sentimentality. But I think he was one of the really great symphonic composers, after Beethoven, and I love his music, but not his piano music."*

This particular interviewer, Dennis Braithwaite of the Toronto *Star,* told Gould that Sibelius had once been asked what melody he

---

*There is no evidence that Gould even considered playing Tchaikowsky's popular Concerto in B-flat minor, not to mention the two lesser ones or his voluminous solo pieces.

would take to a lifetime exile on a desert island. "One thing I would take with me," said Gould, "is Strauss' last opera, Capriccio, which I think is one of the most fantastically beautiful works ever written. I have been completely possessed by this work ever since I heard it in Berlin a couple of years ago. . . ." The interviewer casually informed Gould that Sibelius's choice had been the famous Handel "Largo," and then asked him, "What do you say to that?" Gould: "I'm speechless."

Gould was possessed not only by *Capriccio* but by all of Strauss. He once recalled that he had first heard *Ein Heldenleben* when he was seventeen, and he suggested that every adolescent musician probably heard this tone poem as "the work most likely to incorporate all of the doubts and stresses," and that every adolescent musician must grow out of that phase, and that he, Gould, never had. "I believe, quite simply, that Strauss was the greatest musical figure who has lived in this century," he wrote. But one of the elements in Strauss that most appealed to Gould was that he didn't really live in this century, that he turned his back on both the fads and the revolutions and wrote exactly as he pleased. This was the man about whom Gould tried unsuccessfully to write an opera, the man whose richly romantic orchestral scores Gould carried in his head and played on the piano in the small hours of the morning. But Strauss thought in terms of the Wagnerian orchestra, played the piano poorly, and took only a meager interest in it. He wrote little for the instrument, and what he did write was inconsequential.

Gould happened to be in the office of Schuyler Chapin, then the head of Columbia Masterworks, when Chapin got a telephone call from Eugene Ormandy about Strauss's musical setting to Alfred Lord Tennyson's *Enoch Arden*. "It seems difficult to imagine what could have attracted him to Tennyson's drawing-room epic," Gould later wrote of Strauss's extravaganza, but he suggested that "the melodrama setting was a vogue much admired in those days." *Enoch Arden*—has anyone read it since the darkest days of high school English?—tells in the most sonorous Victorian rhetoric the tale of an English sailor who is lost at sea in the far Pacific. He returns home many years later to find his wife happily married to someone else, then decides that she must never know of his survival, and so dies unrecognized and alone. For some reason, Strauss wrote a piano accompaniment—"most uncomfortably sentimental music," as Gould put it—and then took it on tour through Germany, playing the trills and tremolos while a friend declaimed Tennyson's dramatic verses.

"Ormandy wanted to record it," Chapin recalls. "He'd just had Claude Rains as a guest doing an orchestral version in Philadelphia, and they wanted to record it, and no *way* was I interested in that. But Glenn was in my office, and he heard the conversation, and he said, '*Enoch Arden*—it's really a lot of fun. I'd love to do it.' So this was the moment. Claude Rains had just finished it. Why not? I said, 'I can't pay you.' He said, 'I understand, just union scale.' So then I got hold of Rains, and he was a great admirer of Gould's, so all this was tickety-boo. Until we came to Mrs. Claude Rains."

"Mrs. Rains was quick to imagine slights to her husband and right away she picked up the idea that the atmosphere was not right," Chapin wrote in his memoirs, *Musical Chairs*. To keep the two collaborators separate, each was surrounded by a series of screens. "They could look over at one another but pursue their individual parts without distraction . . ." Chapin recalled. "They set to work with mutual suspicion. Gould would romp through the florid piano part while Rains rolled out the language with suppressed chokes and sobs that were so much a part of nineteenth-century declamation. Mrs. Rains was constantly furious and the conversations between the two artists were peppered with her comments. . . . But they did finish it and at the end stiffly acknowledged that they had both done some service to Tennyson and Strauss."

"I thought it was a very amusing thing to do," Chapin says now, "and we got it done at a cost of $1,500, which wasn't much even for those days. It sold about, I don't know, two thousand copies, something like that, but now it has become a collector's item. On Glenn's fiftieth birthday, we were talking on the phone about various things. We talked about *Enoch Arden,* and he said that his 'record spotter' in Toronto had told him it was now going for $150 a copy."

In confronting the world of romantic piano music, Gould confronted a scene completely dominated by two older masters, Arthur Rubinstein and Vladimir Horowitz. They were the most successful instrumentalists of their time, the most extravagantly admired, the most highly paid. They also had their passionate antagonisms. "Horowitz and I were close friends," Rubinstein wrote in his memoirs. "We called each other by our first names with the familiar 'thou,' and he would come some mornings to my place to consult me on his repertoire of effective encores; but I began to feel a subtle difference between us. His friendship for me was that of a king for his subject, which means he *befriended* me and, in a way, used me. In short, he did not consider me his equal. . . . Deep within myself, I felt I was the better musician."

Gould hated such competitive instincts, hated them in himself as well as in others. His friends almost invariably recall his generosity toward other pianists, his reluctance ever to criticize anyone. When he first met Rubinstein, he repeatedly addressed him as "Maestro," and when he later interviewed the famous virtuoso for *Look* in 1971, he offered effusive praises for Rubinstein's new recording of Brahms's F minor Quintet: "I'm drunk on it. I've now heard it five times in the last few weeks. . . . It's the greatest chamber-music performance with piano that I've heard in my life." But when Rubinstein finally wrote his autobiography in the late 1970's, the puritanical Gould could not resist creating a parody that struck directly at Rubinstein's greatest vulnerability, his vulgar boasting about his own celebrity, his popularity, and his romantic conquests. "I had scarcely begun the first supper show of my gala season at the Maude Harbor Festival," Gould began his "Memories of Maude Harbor," "when, as was my habit, I glanced toward the boxes. And there, seated on one marked 'Live Bait—Do Not Refrigerate,' was a vision of such loveliness that it instantly erased from my mind the memory of all four amorous adventures which had befallen me between lunch and five o'clock tea. . . ."

That is still fairly good-natured mockery, but toward Horowitz, Gould felt something more malevolent, something rather like envy, not only envy of Horowitz's transcendent gifts but envy of the admiration that they inspired. Gould probably felt a benign indifference to Rubinstein's cheery love of showmanship and applause, whereas he may have seen darker parallels in Horowitz's tortured retirement from the concert stage. What seems to have plagued him, though, was the widespread view that Horowitz possessed a matchless command of keyboard sonorities, that what he did could not be analyzed or understood, only marveled at.

"I told him once," says Robert Silverman, who published the Rubinstein parody and more than a dozen of Gould's other articles in his *Piano Quarterly*, "about listening to Horowitz play the Tchaikowsky concerto with Toscanini, with my family in the living room and my ear pressed up against the ten-dollar radio, and I'd gone out of my mind at the performance. I can't remember what he said then, but when I mentioned it another time, he *reacted*. He said, 'You *told* me that two years ago.' And then I heard that tone in his voice, and this is the way he sounded—if I can imitate him—'And I have a better technique than Horowitz.' And I laughed. He was so petulant, the way he said it. It was like a little boy saying, you know, 'Doesn't anybody realize that *I* have such a great technique?'"

Joseph Roddy, a graying but ebullient figure who wrote the first major profile of Gould in *The New Yorker* back in 1960, is walking along West Forty-third Street after a pleasant lunch of scampi and white wine when he suddenly remembers a similar scene. He can't recall exactly where it took place, somewhere in New York, when Gould was in town for one reason or another, and he sat down at a piano and whirled through a thunderously Horowitzian chain of double octaves. "And he said, 'I can do *that*,'" Roddy recalls. "'Anybody can do *that*.'" Silverman, sitting on the front porch of the large-beamed house that he built for himself in distant Vermont, laughs at the story. "Yes, right," he says. "As a matter of fact, he said it to me. He said, 'Horowitz's octaves stink.' Or—he'd never use a word like that—I have to be careful because I use my own language in there, but he said, 'Horowitz can't play octaves—he *fakes* them.' I remember him using the word fake."

"He told me," says Roddy, "that he had once done a great service for Horowitz. He had finished a little phrase for one of the Horowitz recording sessions." That seems hardly possible, but Roddy recalls that Gould had rented some space in the RCA Victor studio in New York, "just for some technical stuff that had to be done," and he went there late at night and found one of the engineers in despair. "He was splicing together some Horowitz tapes," Roddy says, "and he had reached the despondency point, because it couldn't be done, because each piece of tape had something wrong with it.

But Gould was as experienced as anyone could be with this whole splicing of tapes, so he sat in and got his brains around what the problem was, and then he said, 'Well, if you do this and this, and get that off there and this off here, then that's it, and you've got it, except that you'll be missing this bar, which I will get for you.' So there exists—" Roddy bursts out laughing, suggesting that somewhere in the legendary recordings of Vladimir Horowitz there is one measure of pure Gould. But *caveat emptor:* Funny stories tend to exfoliate in the retelling. Roddy acknowledges that the authorities at RCA don't "ever recall anything like this ever happening." Bob Silverman says Gould told him the same story about helping to edit a Horowitz tape but without any mention of adding a bit of his own playing. "I don't believe that part," says Silverman. "That part's not true."

Gould never felt any desire to challenge Rubinstein by recording, say, Chopin's Polonaise in A flat or a sheaf of the most beautiul mazurkas, but Horowitz represented a deeper challenge. Just a year after Gould had abandoned the concert stage in the spring of 1964, Horowitz emerged from more than a decade of retirement to appear once again at Carnegie Hall. The clamor surrounding that highly publicized return violated everything that Gould most deeply believed in. "I knew he was getting tired of playing only for a microphone in a studio," Wanda Horowitz was quoted as saying. "He talked of the difference when you play for people in a hall." And then there was all that newspaper publicity about the lines forming outside Carnegie Hall through the night, and Mrs. Horowitz providing the pilgrims with hot coffee, the whole circus atmosphere that Gould feared and loathed.

Gould's response—and it may not even have been a conscious response—was to issue his own recordings of two works that Horowitz virtually owned. One was Prokofiev's Seventh Sonata, one of the three "war sonatas" composed during the dark days of 1942 and given its American premiere by Horowitz. His spectacular recording had been sent to Prokofiev, who sent back a copy of the score inscribed with thanks "to the miraculous pianist from the composer." The second piece was Scriabin's no less miraculous Sonata No. 3 in F-sharp minor. Again, Horowitz seemed to be the unchallengeable champion. The liner notes told the familiar story of how his uncle Alexander, one of Scriabin's pupils at the Moscow Conservatory, had taken the eleven-year-old Vladimir to play for the master, and how Scriabin had told the prodigy's parents not to neglect his literary education. "Your son will always be a good pianist, but that is not enough," Scriabin had said, according to the Horowitz family scripture. "He must be a cultured man also."

Gould recorded the Prokofiev in 1967, the Scriabin in 1968, and both performances were issued in 1969. Since comparisons are said to be odious—"I happen to believe that competition . . . is the root of all evil," said Gould—let us not try to judge whether Gould's recordings are better than those of Horowitz. Both versions are marvelous. If Horowitz is more dramatic and more richly sonorous, the nervous energy and crystalline clarity of Gould's performances make them quite the equals of the older recordings. And though Gould made no mention of any competition, the challenge scarcely went unnoticed. "Choosing no small targets, Gould now has taken on the legend of Vladimir Horowitz by recording two works identified in the public mind with the Russian pianist . . ." Donal Henahan wrote in the New York *Times*. And Henahan was greatly impressed. About the popular finale to the Prokofiev, he wrote: "Who has ever heard this battered, bloodied movement played as a rather giddy, infectious dance? Gould makes it into one, without sacrificing an ounce of its power or motor excitement."

Gould had still further plans for Horowitz, much stranger plans. He wanted to create a parody of that famous Carnegie Hall recital, which Columbia had issued in a very successful two-record album solemnly entitled *An Historic Return*. Gould first suggested his parody in June of 1966 as one of his rather private northern jokes. He made no specific reference to Horowitz, only to the popular practice of recording virtuosos on tour, live, mistakes and all. "I would be presented in recital at White Horse, Yukon Territories; Yellow Knife, Northwest Territories, or some other such romantic spot," Gould wrote. He had originally thought of actually giving such a concert, but, as usual, he now wanted simply to tape it in a Toronto studio because this would be "an opportunity to spoof in a delicious way the whole absurd contradiction of the recorded public recital (Sviatoslav [Richter] at Sofia etc.). . . . It would, of course, be recorded to the best of our ability with perhaps just a few conspicuous clinkers left in to give it credence. . . . Then we would overdub the splutters, sneezes, and sighs of the noisiest damn audience since Neville Chamberlain was shouted down in the House."

Columbia was monumentally uninterested. But Gould would not give up. Writing about future projects in 1972 to Thomas Frost, a producer at Columbia, Gould openly referred to his idea as a burlesque of Columbia's own Horowitz record. "I'd still like to opt for a parody of the Horowitz 'Return' album—set in Moosonee, Ontario, perhaps and, even though several of your colleagues glanced nervously over their shoulders when mention was first made of this five years or so ago—I still like the idea and think it might solve our repertoire problems in a delightfully offbeat way." The repertoire problem was that Gould had intermittently taped a number of short pieces—three Scarlatti sonatas, two Scriabin *poèmes*— that didn't conveniently fit into any marketable package and therefore lay unreleased.

Columbia remained monumentally uninterested. Gould would not give up. Late in 1973, he wrote an eight-page letter to Frost to argue once again for this bizarre project. He enclosed a complete pseudo-Horowitz program, ranging from Scarlatti and Carl Philipp Emanuel Bach to Sibelius and a contemporary Canadian, Barbara Pentland. He even offered suggestions about the printed program notes, which he thought should largely ignore his recital. "I have always felt that one delightfully zany touch should be its almost total absorption with matters anthropological, sociological, and geographical," he wrote. "Through contacts at the Department of Northern Affairs, I have managed to make friends with several people in each of the above-mentioned fields who could, I'm sure, be persuaded to contribute unimpeachably scholarly, but utterly irrelevant, essays on such subjects as, for example, 'the future of permafrost.'"

Despite the manic elements in Gould's obsession with such details, there was a completely serious idea at the core of this project, a new variation on his often-proclaimed idea of how music should be made and how it should not be made. "The joy of the record," he wrote, "would be to invest studio performances with an ambiance which would suggest every conceivable disadvantage of the live concert occasion—a predominantly tubercular audience, a recital hall seemingly in danger of imminent invasion by a pack of timber wolves—indeed the collage possibilities are infinite. . . ." Gould knew, though, that the odds against him were long. He ended with a plea: "Do please let me have some feedback. Eight years and seven months is a long time to wait."

Columbia remained monumentally uninterested.

In July of 1975, Gould's mother, who had begun teaching him at the keyboard forty years earlier, teaching him and singing to him and making him sing to her, suffered a massive stroke. It hadn't yet happened when Bert Gould telephoned her to tell her that he would be home from work within half an hour.

"When I drove into the yard," Gould recalls, "I went to the side door, and she met me at the door and unlocked the door from the inside. And I saw her start to fall. She didn't hit the floor, but she would have if I hadn't caught her. And she never regained consciousness. I sat there in the hospital with her, most of the time, for five days anyway. I guess you really know."

Q: Did she have more strokes, a sequence of strokes?

A: No, just the one, just the one.

Mrs. Gould was 83 then, and she had been failing for some years. Indeed, the struggle to keep up two houses had already become too much for her, and so Bert Gould, earlier in 1975, had sold the lakeside cottage where Glenn had spent his boyhood summers.

"She was *very* attached to it," Jessie Greig recalls, "but I know that she knew that she couldn't do it any longer, keep up two places, packing and going every weekend. I think it played a tremendous part in her death, though. So did Glenn. We talked about it. I said, 'Well, why don't you buy the place?' And he said, 'I'm thinking about it.' I said, 'You should keep it because, you know—' And he said, 'Well, I'm thinking about it, but I don't think I—want—property—there—right—now.'"

To most of his friends, Gould said little or nothing about his mother's death. Even Ray Roberts, who by now worked as his paid factotum and spoke with him several times every day, can recall no signs of the effects of that death. "He went through her funeral and her death with dignity," Roberts told a CBC interviewer. "And one of the things I learnt very early on was not to poke into the personal feelings too— He didn't like that." But Jessie Greig saw more and knew more: "He was really devastated by her death. . . . He missed her terribly, he really did. She was the one to whom he spoke most about his musical accomplishments, and she was the one he shared his reviews with. It was a very traumatic experience for him. And he became more introspective. . . ."

Four years later, Bert Gould decided to marry a family friend, Vera Dobson. He invited his son to act as best man. Gould was quite disturbed by this prospect. His papers contain several drafts of his attempts to answer, and even scraps of real or imagined family dialogue on the subject. Finally, he wrote out his answer in longhand: "Dear Father—I've had an opportunity to give some thought to the matter of your wedding and specifically to the invitation to serve as your best man. I'm sure that, under the circumstances, you would prefer to arrange a private service—one in which any such conventional ceremonial gesture would be inappropriate; in any case, while I appreciate your kindness in extending the invitation, I regret that I must decline. Needless to say, I wish you every happiness, and I would ask you to pass on my good wishes to Mrs. Dobson."

What John Barnes called "a sort of bad period" struck Gould rather suddenly during the summer of 1976. He was at work on the fourth installment of *Music of Our Time* when he suddenly discovered that he couldn't play the piano properly. "During 2nd TV taping (first week in June) lack of coordination was imm. apparent," he scribbled on the legal pads that were to become a year-long journal of diagnosis and desperation. "Opening theme of Casella was unbalanced—notes appeared to stick and scale-like passages were uneven and uncontrolled. . . . An unpleasant experience, and seemingly immune to solution by ad hoc pressures, finger (thumb indent) etc. During next 2 wks., which separated 2nd taping and commentary, problems increased. It was no longer poss. to play even Bach chorale securely—Parts were unbalanced, progression from note to note insecure. . . ."

It is impossible to determine exactly what was the matter with Gould, but his journal records all kinds of problems in his hands and arms, exhausting tensions, tingling in his fingertips, and loss of what had always been Gould's specialty: control. The journal also records apparently related problems, pains in the neck and back, serious eye trouble, an inner-ear disturbance known as labyrinthitis, and disturbances that Gould guardedly mentioned by saying, "It is quite poss., even likely, however, that it had a psychological base."

Gould confided in virtually no one about his difficulties. He did tell Jessie Greig that his legs kept going to sleep, that "he'd go to get up and there'd be absolutely no feeling in his legs." He told her that he thought the tingling "was a form of arthritis, or else poor circulation." She says that she repeatedly urged him to see a doctor. "And he said, 'They don't listen to me. I tell them about it, but they don't listen to me.'" He treated himself with a wax bath, and he got Ray Roberts to apply a thermal device to his stiff arm and shoulder almost every day. "It was a sort of microwave thing, and we'd put pads on," Roberts recalls, "and I used to assist him in doing that. I didn't think it was the healthiest thing in the world, but I have to tell you that I aided and abetted him because he asked me to." Although Gould consulted several doctors about lesser ailments, however, there is no evidence that he ever went to see one of them about this crippling disability. Only the journal tells, in endless and sometimes incomprehensible detail, about his nightly struggles to overcome whatever it was that afflicted him.

The journal discloses Gould's remarkable dependence on visual "images" of himself playing any given passage, as though the ability to see himself playing it were the only prerequisite for actually playing it. And now he seemed to be losing that magical ability. "Nothing prevented the gradual deterioration of image," he wrote in one typical passage, "and, finally, I returned to whole-body system, employing h-k-b rise, high wrist monitor, and constant adjustment re back." This is written mostly in a kind of private code (h-k-b, for example, means hand-knuckle-bridge). Indeed, the whole journal is mostly in code, for Gould was writing this entirely for himself. We can only guess at the possibilities. "Still point," for example, seems to be Gould's shorthand for a passage from Eliot's *Burnt Norton:* "At the still point of the turning world. Neither flesh nor fleshless;/ Neither from nor towards; at the still point, there the dance is,/ But neither arrest nor movement. . . ." "Process—The motto 'still point of the turning world' defines it . . ." Gould wrote. "It related to the revelation that fingers, ideally, should not be required to move— only, so to speak, to 'be there'—and that all other adjustments should be accommodated by body-adjustments."

This is a rather mystical view of the pianist's art, but Gould believed in it strongly. He liked to quote Arnold Schoenberg's story of the centipede "who was asked in which order it moved its hundred legs, and afterwards he could move no legs at all." Yet although Gould seemed to imagine the playing of the piano as a kind of vision, he devoted infinite attention to all the mechanical workings of both the piano and the pianist. And so his journal of this plague year is an exhaustive chronicle of physical details.

"During mid-summer, much effort was directed to the hand knuckles," he wrote in one early entry, "and, initially, it appeared that some progress was made when these were subject to indent pressure. This seemed to foster, on occasion, crescent-like sensation which was sometime solution. . . . In late summer . . . experiments which elevated wrist were tried. These were inaugurated to alleviate unnatural burden in indented fingers, thumbs and knuckles; the experiment resulted only in a complete loss of control. . . ."

That is the heartbreaking thing about this journal, the constant struggle toward a solution, the theorizing and rationalizing about each new experiment, the repeated glimpses of success, the repeated failures. All through that fall and winter, Gould worked on his problem, every night, and by the following April he was reporting a new experiment of relying only on his fingers. "There was initially no neck tension, no vision restriction, no limitation on hovering above keyboard. Beginning on the 2nd or 3rd day, however, there were wrist tightness problems, and, gradually, the separation into bumpy grouping and a general lack of fluidity." And then a breakthrough: "Suddenly, last night, I determined that *the* common denominator in *all* these problems (famous last words?) was the lack of *constancy* in shoulder elevation. For one brief moment, and only in r-h- [right hand] I *had* it; that gleaming lustrous sound was back and I realized, more than ever, that *that* was the sound of control. . . ."

For a time, the recovery seemed like a miracle. Thus, on April 26: "For most of the past 10 days, I was almost afraid to jinx what seemed like the perfect solution by setting down a desc. in these pages. It (the apparent solution) began the day after prev. entry. It involved tipping the head towards right shoulder and moving it as a unit in consequence. . . ." And then, on June 1: "I did try finger-thumb indent in coord with genl top-of-hand pressure—2 or 3 good days ensued. I did try holding wrist tightly from beneath so as to use *it* as a fulcrum-like constant. One day wonder. I did try relating body movt. to *stable* elbows so as to ensure height limitations and legislate front-back polarity.... We may, I think, conclude that nothing has worked."

June 16: "Let us hope there will be no more entries. I do believe the solution has been found. I will have to research these diaries to discover how many times I may have come close to it during the past year. ... Without further procrastination, the solution is in the h-k-b response. It involves letting the h-k-b *rise* (exactly the opposite of the indent theories to which so many pages have been devoted) but *rise* as a result of finger indent motivation. The rise ... treats the hand (from h-k-b to wrist) as a platform from which fingers reach out and explore the keys below. ... Obv., there is a need for further observation and testimony, but I think that the secret of May '67 [there are several mysterious references to some apparently similar breakdown and recovery in 1967] has been rediscovered—I hope and pray that it may not be lost ever again. I do believe it will be poss. to resume work almost imm."

June 23: "I am not sure that everything mentioned in the foregoing entry is beside the point, but it is, unfortunately, far from the last word. Last nite, in a session of close to 3 hrs., every conceivable variant was employed—none with success— For the last several days, right wrist had been unbearably sore after any 10 or 15 min. practice period. It was not partic noticeable *during* performance . . . but imm. upon cessation of activity, the pain was intense."

That very same week, Gould's journal reported that "during taping re 'Music of Man,' no clear 'image' re this system was available; I resorted to wrist control (h-k-b relaxed and relieved). . . .." This casual reference to taping a TV show, in the midst of long descriptions of incapacity, seems to imply that Gould's difficulties were largely imaginary, but he apparently relied once again on a bit of "creative cheating," using a considerably earlier bit of tape for his performance of Scriabin's "Désir."

The Music of Man was the CBC's grandiose, eight-part TV series on the history of music from the earliest Neanderthal pipings to the latest Beatles strummings, all as conceived, organized, and narrated by Yehudi Menuhin. Since Gould and Menuhin were friends, or at least mutual admirers, and since this was a Canadian project, the history of music could not be considered complete without Gould holding forth on the subject. The original script by Curtis Davis says rather vaguely, "We join the YM/Gould conversation. (The talk will include Glenn Gould's reasons for choosing the media as his forum ...)." Gould, however, had to write his own script, which begins with his private notation that this is "a spontaneous, extemporaneous, off-the-cuff, top-of-our-heads conversation between Yehud (Ad lib) Menuhin and Glenn (Wing it) Gould— Commisioned by, and dedicated to Curtis *Damned Audio Verité Is Sinful*." After the camera watches Gould and Menuhin both listening to a playback of a Bach gigue, the "spontaneous, extemporaneous, off-the-cuff" script calls for Gould to say, "Now, Yehudi, you've got to admit that you would not get to hear a sound like *that* in a concert."

Menuhin balked, though, at having Gould tell him what to say on his own television series. "Yes, I'm not sure I'd want to, actually, Glenn," he says in Gould's script, but what he actually said before the cameras was, "I would still recognize your playing. Whatever you've added electronically. . . ." And so on. The memories of the witnesses differ as to whether this was a divergence of musical judgments, or literary judgments, or simply a conflict over turf: Who should write the words that both would agree to speak? There are always intermediaries who can work out compromises, and so when Menuhin said that "machinery" seemed to him "almost an intrusion" on the intimacy of the violinist's art, Gould was allowed to say, "It matters not to me whether I am 'successful' in creating a performance through one take, or whether I do it with 262 tape splices." Menuhin then observed that Gould's radical views on recording were actually becoming commonplace in pop music, almost cripplingly so. "Take the Beatles, who started out playing in public spontaneously; by the time they became accustomed to crutches, which enable them to record tracks separately and put them all together, to add notes and take them away, they could no longer play in public because the public expected something else." Gould: "In a sense, that is also what happened to me."

With both Gould and Menuhin jousting for control over their dialogue, the exchanges sometimes became quite highly charged.

Menuhin: That still doesn't invalidate the concert hall, the experience of which is essential, and remains the standard against which everything else is judged.

Gould: Nonsense, Yehudi. It was the standard until something else came along to replace it, which is exactly what the recording did; and the recording, surely, is now the standard against which the concert must be judged.

Menuhin: If no one is ever going to climb a mountain again, and we have to be satisfied with films about it, where are we?

Gould: We are without people who can climb mountains, which I think is a profoundly good thing. It will save any number of deaths per year.

Though Gould got through that show by playing an old tape of one of his favorite Scriabin pieces, he still had to return home to his piano in the penthouse on St. Clair Avenue, and to his treasury of preludes and fugues and toccatas and fugues and suites and variations and still more fugues, and to find that he could no longer control them as he once had. "Last night witnessed, among other things, a return to shoulder systems ... back-rod, back-rod with collapsed chest, back-rod-head-immobile, with or without collapsed chest, r-shoulder elevation with head tipped to right, etc. In short, everything was tried and nothing worked. . . . It's back to the drawing board."

June 25: "2 days—2 systems—Day before yesterday, I concentrated on wrist control. . . . Wrist pain was largely alleviated. . . . Nevertheless, it, too, appeared a one-day wonder. . . . Nothing prevented the gradual (!) deterioration of image. . . ."

July 1: "It seemed as though everything had returned to normal. . . . New rep.—f—tocc. fugue [Gould means Bach's Toccata in F-sharp minor, which he was planning to record soon], for ex., was studied and everything made sense. I was about to call A.K. [Andrew Kazdin of Columbia] and set up July sessions. Yesterday evening, however, I sensed that all was not well; there was no spec. 'image' threat, just a genl feeling of unease. Being reluctant to admit any extra-psychic principle at work, I went to apt. at 11:30 p.m. The results were horrendous. G [major] Tocc. fugue, which had become a showpiece, was bumpy, inacc., uncertain, unrythmical and ditto everything else that was played. The weird thing was that, so far as I could see, no system-changes were employed. Further tests will follow. . . ."

July 6: "The results desc. in last para have not been repeated. . . .

I am not unmindful of the fact that past 2 wks have, by and large, and excl (very real) problem with wrist, been the most sustained period since problems began. . . ."

July 9: "Wrists were sore and stiff almost from outset. . . ."

July 11: "Last nite (40 min sess) began with arm-drag (shoulder-connect) system. Relaxation ensured—wrist flexibility relieved r-wrist tension *completely*, but usual penalties (overweighted staccato, etc.) followed. . . ."

July 12: "As usual! 2 hr. sess—provided unstable results. Rep. [repertoire] was varied—Bach as usual & Ruggles—Krenek—and, at no point, were results disastrous—merely unimpressive and, in Ruggles-Kreneck, inacc. . . . It *was* poss to switch, from moment to moment, to arm-drag systems; these, thru practice, ensured reasonable stability with Bach rep. but similar results were erratic and unfocussed in Krenek etc. . . ."

And here this long chronicle of suffering simply breaks off. Since Gould went on playing and recording to the end of his life, about five years later, we can only surmise that he somehow found a solution to his problem, or that, as sometimes happens, it simply went away. But exactly what was the problem? Dr. Emil Pascarelli suspects a collapsed spine, quite possibly a result of Gould's fall off that boat rail outside the Goulds' summer cottage on Lake Simcoe. Dr. Pascarelli is an easygoing man with a gray moustache, the medical director of the Kathryn and Gilbert Miller Health Care Institute for Performing Artists at St. Luke's/Roosevelt Hospital on West Fifty-ninth Street in Manhattan. He has read Gould's journal, but he has not been told the name of the patient.

Q: What is a collapsed spine?

A: Well, the vertebrae can erode and cause nerve compression. Maybe I should get a book.

Dr. Pascarelli rummages around in his cluttered office and then returns with a large book on the spine, richly illustrated with skeletal figures, skeletal nerves and tendons. He opens it up and pushes it forward. "The spine is made up of the vertebral body and the tail, and then in between are the disks, okay?" Dr. Pascarelli says. "Now, usually by collapsed spine is meant that a disk erodes, and it collapses. This is a spongy, cartilaginous substance, very rubbery, that acts as a shock absorber between the vertebral bodies. Now in front here is the medullary nervous system. It runs down there, so that if you have a bulge in here, it can compress the spinal column and cause nerve compression, which is—which can be very serious."

Q: He had some kind of spinal injury in his childhood. Could that—?

A: There might have been an exacerbation of the childhood injury, with nerve-root compression, that caused this problem. I don't know.

Q: Is it very painful?

A: It can be painful, but usually it's not. It's usually accompanied by a numbness and a tingling, a discomfort.

Gould's exact symptoms. There are operations to deal with such problems, but back injuries can remain as mysterious in their workings as in their origins. And there is no indication that Gould, although he went to many doctors about many afflictions, real and imaginary, ever consulted anyone about his spine. Yet the illustrations in Dr. Pascarelli's textbook are quite clear: Each cervical nerve affects a specific area of the wrist and hand. "This would be C-5, C-6, C-7," Dr. Pascarelli says as he points to each tentacle in the book. "In other words, these would be—C-7 would be up here in the neck, and these nerves innervate the arm and eventually get down to the muscles in the hand. . . ."

Dr. Pascarelli disapproves of anyone trying, as this nameless pianist did, to treat himself. "One gets the feeling," he says, "that this was a rather weird guy, who had his own notions about—I mean, he did not have too much of a working knowledge of his own body, of physiology and functional anatomy, and he was probably creating new problems. . . . He was trying to change the configuration of his hands, and these kinds of repositioning create more tensions on the tendons. . . . He was experimenting on himself in a pseudo-scientific way, and he didn't have any basic knowledge about what he was doing."

Q: Do you get any sense that any of this is imaginary?

A: I wouldn't say it was imaginary. I would say it's a man struggling with a problem. . . . He's very fearful, and he's attempting to solve it on his own. . . . There's a psychologic overlay here, a very heavy psychologic overlay. . . . Was he going through personal problems at this time? Divorce? Or a wife die, or lover die, or whatever? I mean, these are things you have to think about.

Dr. Fred Hochberg, an eminent neurologist who teaches at the

Harvard Medical School and heads a group of specialists in musicians' ailments at Massachusetts General Hospital, has similar suspicions. He and his colleagues studied Gould's journals (without knowing his name) for several months. After considering the possibility of epilepsy, Hochberg and his associates concluded only "that the individual was unusually preoccupied with medical function and difficulties and that there probably were some features of a paranoid nature." Beyond that, said Dr. Hochberg, no doctor was willing to go.

In sickness and in health, sometimes only after considerable delay, Gould kept on making record after record. He finished *The Well-Tempered Clavier* in 1971, the French and English suites during the early 1970's, and the complete sonatas of Mozart in 1974, but along with these standard classics, he also began producing a strange and hypnotically beautiful series of Romantic works. No Chopin or Schumann, of course. Instead, Gould came forth in 1973 with a gorgeous performance of the Sonata in E minor by his distant relative, Edvard Grieg, and on the back of that he provided a stunning version of Georges Bizet's *Variations chromatiques*. This almost unknown work, he announced, "is one of the very few masterpieces for solo piano to emerge from the third quarter of the 19th century; its almost total neglect is a phenomenon for which I can offer no reasonable explanation."

If Gould could find few masterpieces for solo piano in the third quarter of the nineteenth century (how could he have overlooked, for example, Brahms's Handel Variations?), he could relish the orchestral masterpieces of the period. And so he produced in 1973 his astonishing transcriptions of Wagner's *Meistersinger* prelude, the Rhine journey from *Götterdämmerung*, and the *Siegfried Idyll*. "It was a real labor of love," Gould said later. "I simply wanted to have something of Wagner's I could play."

To achieve that labor of love, Gould discovered that he had to rewrite a lot of Wagner's music, and so he coolly did so, subsequently explaining it all by a theory of his own. According to this theory such old-time transcribers as Franz Liszt had followed their originals too closely. "The Liszt transcriptions . . . tend to be relentlessly faithful . . ." he told Jonathan Cott, just as though he had never heard of such free-form Liszt creations as the *Reminiscences de Lucia di Lammermoor* or *Rigoletto: Paraphrase de Concert.* "If the orchestral texture is thick, Liszt will reproduce the thickness on the piano, and of course a thickness on the piano doesn't sound good, let's face it." And in a long drum roll, "Liszt usually falls back on a tremolando, which is so turn-of-the-century I can't stand it." Instead of such literal copying, Gould said, he "took a solemn oath" that he "would try to re-create the pieces as though somebody like Scriabin, who really knew something about the piano, as Wagner did not, had had a hand in it."

In his revisions of the *Siegfried Idyll,* Gould avoided most of Wagner's doublings of the bass and cello, on the ground that the piano would give this too percussive a sound, and he decided instead "to have the contrabass always enter on the offbeat." That, he said, was just "the prototype for several other little inventions along the way." Since Wagner's long-held chords would die away on the piano, for instance, "what I did was to invent whole other voices that aren't anywhere in the score, except that they are convincingly Wagnerian." At one point, he went even further. "What I did . . . was to invent a dialogue between two offstage horns, one in the tenor and one in the alto, that try to mimic each other, and they go on like this between themselves, and it's gorgeous. . . . Forgive me for saying so, but it's gorgeous!"

Ultimately, Gould's "creative cheating" reached a point where he was not only rewriting Wagner's music for the piano but writing music that the piano could not play. When he had performed the *Meistersinger* prelude for friends, he had always reached a point near the end when the multiplicity of voices becomes so great that "then you say, 'Okay, which themes are we leaving out tonight'?" The recording studio now made all forms of cheating possible, of course. "In order to accommodate the extraordinarily dense polyphony in the 'Meistersinger vorspiel,'" he wrote to a friend, "[I] wrote the last three minutes or thereabouts as though for a piano primo-piano secundo duet . . . and simply over-tracked the material when recording. Consequently, the transcription, strictly speaking, would not be reproducible—except, of course, by two pianists playing in concert—and is effectively realisable only via recording."

Such legerdemain raised a few eyebrows when Gould's Wagner

record appeared, as did his incredibly slow tempo in the *Siegfried Idyll*. ("I've always felt that the piece has an indigenous languor," Gould wrote, "which the 'ruhig bewegt', or whatever, in the score does not adequately delineate.") But the most remarkable thing about Gould's meltingly lyrical performance of Wagner was that it existed at all. Could anything be less likely from the hard-edged master of *The Goldberg Variations?* Could any other pianist even conceive of such a project?

Only an explorer of the Arctic would then have undertaken the task of recording three sonatinas by Sibelius, together with three lyric pieces called *Kyllikki*. And only Gould would have recorded them in a manner wholly divorced from concert performance. As he had done with Scriabin on television, he placed one microphone right inside the piano, another at a respectable distance, and still another in the equivalent of a balcony seat. In praising the results, Joseph McLellan of the Washington *Post* quoted Kazdin's explanation: "Kazdin calls it 'acoustic orchestration' and explains that the performance was recorded 'in a simultaneous variety of perspectives' and then edited to give each passage its ideal acoustic context, like a movie camera shifting from long shots to closeups.... It works particularly well with Gould's performance, which also examines the music 'in a simultaneous variety of perspectives.'"

This late Romantic and "post-Romantic" music was what preoccupied Gould during his last years. When he occasionally played the piano for a friend late at night, he was most likely to play one of his transcriptions of Strauss or Wagner. And when he considered further transcriptions, this was the kind of music that he worked on. Joe Roddy recalls him "playing recordings of Bruckner, or, for maybe the ten thousandth time in his life, the *Metamorphosen* of Strauss, which he decided at that point was the ultimate—was the piece that mattered to him more than any other. The trouble was that Strauss wrote it for twenty-three stringed instruments, and Glenn found that, try as he would, he couldn't really do that on the piano. He just couldn't make it work, and that's why he played it all the time, because it was his food."

Gould did finally record Strauss's youthful Sonata in B minor, Opus 5, along with five *Klavierstücken*, Opus 3, but this was his last recording, taped just a month before his death late in 1982. This and his performance of the Brahms ballades and rhapsodies appeared only after he was gone.

At dawn of May 20, 1980, after six or seven hours spent in editing tapes, Gould left his studio to drive home. "The body of a tiny, presumably new-born squirrel was on the roof of Lance (It had apparently dropped on it from above)," he wrote on a pad later that day, using his private name for one of his cars. "It was an immensely touching sight and, although I was momentarily startled and even frightened by it when I moved the car just before dawn, it was, I think, that sight and the reflections that stemmed from it which was finally resp. [responsible] for the launching of this journal."

The connection is elusive, for Gould kept this new journal for less than two months; it is mostly a chronicle of chores and vexations. It had been twenty-five years since that first recording of *The Goldberg Variations,* and Gould and Columbia had somehow agreed to clean out the cupboard by combining all the unissued miscellany into something to be called *The Glenn Gould Silver Jubilee Album.* So now he was editing those three Scarlatti sonatas that he had taped back in 1968, and a C.P.E. Bach sonata from that same period, and the two Scriabin *poèmes* he had done on TV in 1974, and his 1968 performance of the first movement of Liszt's transcription of Beethoven's Sixth Symphony, and even his 1966 accompaniment to Elisabeth Schwarzkopf's performance of Strauss's "Ophelialieder." This rather strange collection would also include a reissuing of "So You Want to Write a Fugue?"

The only thing it lacked was the repeatedly suppressed parody of Horowitz's "historic return." Seven years after the last rejection of this project, fifteen years after the historic return itself, Gould once again began doggedly pressing CBS for a chance to carry out his strange idea. Horowitz had by now returned to RCA Victor, which made the plan a little bit less implausible, but the general manager of CBS Records remained as monumentally uninterested as ever. Gould and CBS were now discussing the possibility of including some kind of interview or discussion in the jubilee album, but, as Gould noted in his 1980 journal, "Joe Dash has decreed that I must *not* spoof the Horowitz return on the talk disk. . . ."

Gould went to New York that June, partly to talk with CBS,

partly to look for a new piano, and somehow he kept the Horowitz parody alive. Now there was going to be a panel discussion, in which Gould would be the only sane participant, politely parrying the lunacies of his alter egos, Karlheinz Klopweisser, composer of the *Panzersymphonie* that had premiered at El Alamein in 1942; Theodore Slutz, the fine arts editor of New York's *Village Grass Is Greener*; and Sir Nigel Twitt-Thornwaite, conductor laureate of the BBC Light Orchestra (Orkneys) and author of *Beethoven's English Years: The Untold Story*. "It is very difficult," as Gould noted in his journal about his talks at CBS, "to maintain an acceptable level of sobriety at app. moments. I then embellished the idea with one further step—add a compère (real, live-type host) who can control and/ or act as a buffer for me vis a vis the panel. I decided to invite Margaret Pacsu; she's delighted with the idea and will bring along at least one of her own characters, Márta Hortávanyi, to sit in with the panel. . . ."

"I joined the CBC in seventy-two and was in television and moved over to radio and have been in radio ever since," says Miss Pacsu, an extremely attractive brunette who originally came from Princeton, New Jersey. "And one of those days, somewhere around 1976, I was working afternoons, and he came in, what was early for him, and he just bumbled into the music department. It was a hot summer day, and he was in his overcoat and his gloves, all shredded and whatever. He looked like a hobo, to use an Old World word, and we instantly—it was as if I'd known him all my life. Nobody introduced us, he didn't introduce himself, but we started doing these voices, almost instantaneously. He could do Russian, and he did everybody else, but the one he couldn't do was the Hungarian voice, which is my parents' accent, because the darn accent's on the first syllable, and he just couldn't quite get that.

"So I teased him about his ear and his accent, just banter, just jolly conversation, but I knew that he listened to our broadcasts. We had a contest on my program, and we played a brand-new recording— it was some very, very early Schoenberg—and we asked everybody to guess what it was. Well, we had one phone call, from one listener, and it was Glenn. But unfortunately, our free giveaway records were some of his, so we couldn't give them to him. But he loved to do that. I mean, he loved to sort of part the curtains and just emerge and step full-blown into somebody's life.

"Then when he started doing some of his comedy things for radio, he asked me to be his straight man, which I suppose should be a straight person now. Anyway, he was all of the voices, and he wrote all of the sketch and wrote my answers. And before we recorded this, he went into the bathroom and washed his hands, and they were *scarlet* red, and I just said, 'But Glenn, you know, this isn't a concert, this is taped radio. We can redo anything, any mistake.' And he said, 'Well, I suppose that is mildly neurotic, isn't it?' And I said nothing, one of the few times in my life when I said absolutely nothing. . . .

"He called me up—I guess it was the summer of eighty—it was the twenty-fifth of June, two days before my birthday—and he read me the script which he had written. I think he had written it in a matter of hours, or a couple of days, and there were barely any corrections between what he wrote, and what he read me on the phone, and what we finally did. So he must have been thinking about it for a long time.

"We did the record at night, at the Inn on the Park, and I remember he always ordered only *fresh* orange juice for his supper, or whatever meal that was to be at that time, which was about ten o'clock at night, and which he really enjoyed. You could just see that he was really enjoying that one meal, mixed with his—whatever they were, either uppers or slower-downers. I think he was slowing himself down most of the time.

"The pace was really horrendous, and he was very hard to work with, not from my point of view but the technical point of view, because he knew everything, he could hear everything that he wanted. You know, every edit, every single sentence. There weren't four or five versions, there were twenty-five and thirty-five and forty-five. But it was a very satisfactory experience. We were both silly. I mean, we did all kinds of funny things while we were doing this. We were doing animal noises, we did every accent we knew. He sang me a country-and-western song that he had written when he was fifteen. At the same time, he was practicing the next pieces he was going to record, the Haydn sonatas. And this is what happened to me. This whole thing represents three days in my life, from four in the afternoon until two in the morning, in which I did nothing else but that. It was totally focused. I don't remember anything else that happened."

Gould was similarly focused, and when he returned to his journal in mid-August, he was "amazed" to note that he had made no entries since early July. "The reason that I have not written relates . . . directly to the chief product of the intervening wks . . . the talk disc—if one can poss. refer to so magnif. (pardon my modesty) a creation by such a title. . . . Though we hit all manner of snags initially as well as some others subseq., it was apparent early on that we would survive and that the product would be superb. . . . Hilarious and serious by turns, it is, as M.P. [Margaret Pacsu] said at the office meeting (i.e. dub session yesterday) the perfect summing up of 25 yrs."

There are many clever moments in the talk-show section of *A Glenn Gould Fantasy*, but most of the record dealt with questions that Gould had lectured on many times before, his preference for recordings rather than live performances, his belief in the musical possibilities of radio documentaries, and so on. It obviously amused Gould vastly to put his own ideas mainly into the Teutonic accents of Karlheinz Klopweisser, and the attacks of his critics into the Blimpian tones of Sir Nigel Twitt-Thornwaite (the album even includes photographs of Gould schizophrenically playing all these roles, in long white locks as Klopweisser and in walrus moustache as Sir Nigel). Miss Pacsu joined in as not only the mistress of ceremonies but also the Hungarian critic Márta Hortaványi, author of *Fascistic Implications of the 6/4 Chord in Richard Strauss*.

Only when Miss Hortaványi finally asked Gould whether "it is not possible, like other artists who withdraw for a time from the public, that you make then a hysteric return," only then did Gould embark on his long-suppressed Horowitz parody, a piece of wildly surrealistic abandon unlike anything else he ever attempted. For this man who yearned for total control, it was an excursion into the nightmare of total loss of control. The hysteric return had to be set in the Arctic, of course, with Gould performing on the drilling platform of Geyser Petroleum's Exploratory Rig XB 67, while the Aklavic Philharmonic accompanied him via closed-circuit TV from the nuclear submarine *Inextinguishable*, two miles away.

The tape begins with Gould performing the last few bars of Weber's *Konzertstück*, of all things, and then an oleaginous CBC newcaster named Byron Rossiter offers one of those high-toned descriptions of how the audience has been "treated to a veritable feast for eye and ear; they watched as the midnight sun performed its annual mid-summer flirtation with the Beaufort Sea—dipping seductively toward the eager whitecaps on the horizon. . . ." A wave of applause then demonstrates that Gould has returned for an encore, and as he begins to play his spectacular transcription of Ravel's *La Valse*, the CBC commentator goes on describing the scene, telling us not only that Gould is playing on his knees because his famous folding chair was washed overboard but also that the directors of Geyser Petroleum are abandoning Oil Rig XB 67 "even as our soloist, totally absorbed in his performance, continues unaware of their departure." Rossiter then calls in an American correspondent, Cassie Mackerel, for an interview with the president of Geyser Petroleum, while, according to Gould's script, we hear "sounds of high-powered diesel engine with appropriate wave and wind effects; 'La Valse' is still heard, very distantly, in the background."

Miss Mackerel's interview discloses that Geyser has just discovered a major oil field, and all the corporate executives are rushing to call their stockbrokers before the news spreads, but the CBC announcer now takes us back to Gould spraying Ravel in all directions. "It does seem that Mr. Gould is aware that he no longer has an audience; he's increasing the tempo dramatically and—yes, yes, he's made a major cut in the work. . . . However, I've just been notified that, since Mr. Gould no longer has an audience on the rig, and since his recital therefore can no longer be classified as a public event under the provisions of the Public Events Statutes of the Broadcasting Act, our transmission must be terminated forthwith. So on behalf of our host, Geyser Petroleum. . . ." (*"Music up for final seconds to end of* 'La Valse,'" the script concludes, "*after which GG is heard walking off stage to the accompanying applause and barks of a solitary seal.*")

GG: Thank you, thank you, thank you very much.

Gouldian humor is occasionally quite funny, in an Arctic sort of way, and one can only wonder what Horowitz might have made of it. (Horowitz's manager, Peter Gelb, says that he cannot be interviewed.) Intensely aware of each other, these two great virtuosos apparently never met, but John Roberts recalls that Gould's death finally brought them together. "When Glenn died, one of the first telegrams which came was from Horowitz," he says. "They also sent flowers."

Q: But Gould never thought much of Horowitz.

A: Well, yes and no, yes and no. Horowitz pursued a repertoire which Glenn was not very much interested in, but Glenn was full of contradictions. . . .

XII

The Movies

One September day in 1971, without any explanation, a package arrived in Gould's mail. He opened it up and found that someone had sent him a copy of Kurt Vonnegut's *Slaughterhouse-Five*. And so he began reading: "All this happened, more or less. The war parts, anyway, are pretty much true. One guy I knew really *was* shot in Dresden for taking a teapot that wasn't his. Another guy I knew really *did* threaten to have his personal enemies killed by hired gunmen after the war. . . ."

Only a day or two later did Gould receive an explanatory letter from George Roy Hill, the director, whose string of successful movies had recently included *Butch Cassidy and the Sundance Kid*. He was now editing his recently shot film of *Slaughterhouse-Five*, Hill wrote, and "I am starting to think about who is going to do the music for it." Since the major event in the novel was the Allied bombing of Dresden during the last days of World War II, Hill wanted the music to reflect the Baroque style of the ruined city. "I have been thinking of Bach and possibly improvisations on Bach themes throughout the film," he wrote. "Since my knowledge of Bach is closely associated with all your Bach recordings, I thought of you and hope to ask your advice . . . and whether you would be interested in participating in some capacity in this project. . . ."

By this time, Gould had read the novel—indeed, he read it three times—and he didn't much like it. *Slaughterhouse-Five* might have been—should have been—Vonnegut's best and most important novel, for the disaster at Dresden was central to both his own experiences and his view of the world. As a war prisoner, Vonnegut him-

self had survived the most concentrated destruction of the entire
war because he had been confined in an underground slaughter-
house. As a German-American, he was all too well qualified to see
the ironies in the carnage. Perhaps because of that, Vonnegut
avoided any real confrontation with his experience, first by not writing about it for many years, or rather by writing and then throwing
away what he had written.

"I thought it would be easy for me to write about the destruction
of Dresden," he finally declared at the start of *Slaughterhouse-Five,*
"since all I would have to do would be to report what I had seen. . . .
But not many words about Dresden came from my mind then. . . . I
must have written five thousand pages by now, and thrown them all
away. . . . There is nothing intelligent to say about a massacre."
Vonnegut finally solved his problem only by framing his half-sup-
pressed recollections within the familiar amiabilities of his science-
fiction fantasies, of magical flights to the planet Tralfamadore. If
Billy Pilgrim's space travels were fantasy, then so was the bombing
of Dresden, or if the space travel was symbolic, then so too was
Dresden. Either way, we all escape the realities of the firestorm that
killed more than 135,000 people in a single night.

Gould seems to have had more general objections to Vonnegut's
work, though he encountered some difficulties in formulating his
criticisms. "Vonnegut, of course, is to the current crop of college
frosh as J. D. Salinger was to the youth of my day—a dispenser of
those too-easily accessible home truths that one somehow never
does get at home," Gould wrote in a CBC commentary after the film
was released. "And precisely because he quite ruthlessly exploits
certain aspects of the generation gap . . . I suspect that much of his
work will date quickly and reveal the supposed profundities of an
opus like *Slaughterhouse-Five* as the inevitable clichés of an overgen-
eralized, underparticularized view of humanity."

But to create a musical score for the movie—how could Gould
not be tempted? From the earliest beginnings in the age of silent
films, celebrated musicians had been lured into collaboration with
the camera. Prokofiev had provided the music for Sergei Eisen-
stein's *Alexander Nevsky* and *Ivan the Terrible,* and other film makers
hired Shostakovich, Poulenc, Honegger. Aaron Copland wrote the
score for *Of Mice and Men* and Darius Milhaud for *The Private*

Affairs of Bel-Ami. Even Stravinsky and Schoenberg underwent interviews in Hollywood. Part of the temptation was simply money, of course, but part was also the challenge of mastering a new medium, of exploring the possibilities of film, just as Monteverdi and the earliest opera composers had once explored the possibilities of the stage. Gould, who had spoken of his love affair with the microphone, who exulted in his exploits on radio and television, could hardly resist the invitation from George Roy Hill. "I'd be most intrigued to learn about the cinematic notions you intend to apply . . ." he wrote back. "Certainly a baroque ambience for the Dresden sequences sounds both appealing and appropriately ironic. . . ."

Gould later claimed that he imagined great possibilities for *Slaughterhouse-Five*. "I conceived of vast montages," he told William Littler of the Toronto *Star*, "while Hill, who doesn't like much music, thought in terms of set pieces. He kept telling me, 'Keep it simple, keep it simple!'" Hill, savoring a cup of coffee in a sunny office overlooking Rockefeller Plaza, offers no objection to Gould's account, but his own account is quite different. "What happened was—" he says, "I wanted to use Bach throughout, and I wanted to use Glenn Gould throughout. So what I did was, when I scored it, when I cut it, when I edited it, I put in Glenn Gould's records, so that when he—he had already scored it. He just didn't know it. But you can't take records and just use them, and so—I was really kind of afraid, because I didn't have his permission, so I wanted to be on his good side."

Hill diplomatically suggested that he would be happy to make a pilgrimage to Toronto, and Gould graciously agreed to receive him. "So I went up there, and he met me," Hill says. "He had taken a room in a motel that was near the airport, and we just sat there and talked, in this motel room, and I told him what I had done. I told him that I would be perfectly open to suggestions, as long as they were by Bach."

Q: Was he surprised that you'd gone so far ahead without him?

A: He didn't seem to be. In fact, he seemed to take it all in good part, and we sat there and talked for about five hours.

Q: About the movie?

A: About everything. He just started—he was a great raconteur, and he just kept going and going and going. I was fascinated, because I love his music. I think he was one of the giants of the age. So I was listening to this, seated at the foot of Gamaliel.

Despite his admiration and awe, Hill knew exactly what he wanted, and he skillfully maneuvered Gould into both approving what had already been chosen and agreeing to patch over a few gaps. The most difficult of these gaps, which was not really very difficult, was a marching scene in which a selection from Bach's Concerto in D major had to be grafted onto the Fourth Brandenburg Concerto.

"As you can imagine," Gould later told an interviewer, "there is no convenient way of getting from F sharp minor to G major in 18 seconds—not to mention going from 3/8 time to 2/2." Gould proposed that the first section simply fade into the second, but Hill vetoed that. He had permitted no dissolves in his hard-edged filming, and he wanted none on the sound track. He asked Gould to try again, so Gould tried bridging the gap by virtuosity. "I wrote a wildly imaginative canon with themes from the Brandenburg and the other concerto," he said. "George thought that was too sophisticated. We got together in a tiny studio at Film House in downtown Toronto. I felt like Ira Gershwin. I improvised a few versions and George said, 'That's it.'" But that wasn't it. The scene was cut from eighteen seconds to fourteen, and these are big changes in movie music. Gould attempted to make a recording of the agreed-on scene in the Eaton Auditorium in Toronto, and then the phone rang, and Hill reported that yet another four seconds had to be trimmed from the scene.

Gould finally came to New York for the final recording, in which he sat at the harpsichord and conducted a group of musicians from the New York Philharmonic. Gould was by now using the click-track, that movie-musical marvel that a conductor can slip over his ears to synchronize his music with what the film projector shows. "After 35 takes, they told me the click-track was wrong!" Gould marveled. "Now you can't rent the New York Philharmonic for nothing. That cost the studio about $1,000 in overtime pay." The studio, it is probably safe to say, hardly noticed. Bach's music, Gould's version of Bach's music, was a relatively minor part of *Slaughterhouse-Five*.

Hill still retained total control. "The music is all in and it's gorgeous—it exceeds everything I had hoped for," he wrote to Gould in March of 1972. Only then did he confess that he had overruled his hero's wishes on how the music was to be presented. Gould, who had consistently played Bach's harpsichord music on the piano, who had repeatedly declared that it didn't matter what instruments were used in such performances, now felt that the main themes of *Slaughterhouse-Five* should be played on a harpsichord. He recorded both piano and harpsichord versions, but after he was safely back in Toronto, Hill decided on the piano. "I can only say that I took these decisions knowing how strongly you felt, and was willing to make almost any compromise in the world dramatically in order to please you," Hill wrote to him. "However, I am not using the harpsichord in the first arrival of the star. I mixed it and loved it. Then I played the whole picture with it and . . . it failed to do one thing dramatically—the sound of the harpsichord is so different, particularly with the ornamentations, that it simply did not connect. . . ."

Having asserted his view, Hill was quite willing to let Gould take all the credit for the score, and Gould, having been pushed around a bit, was just as willing to take the credit. Indeed, the listings at the start of *Slaughterhouse-Five* ignore Bach and simply announce: "Music: Glenn Gould." According to Littler of the *Star,* the music for *Slaughterhouse-Five* represented "one of the briefest, aptest and most widely praised film scores of the season. As the New Yorker's Penelope Gilliatt writes, 'Bach's music is splendiferously used.'" Littler's own description of the Gould-Hill (Bach) creation was warmly admiring: "His entire score lasts less than a quarter hour and . . . consists entirely of bits of Bach. But what inspired bits! And how crucially placed! The first bit we encounter is the Largo from Bach's F minor Concerto, BWV 1056, which accompanies Billy's wandering, shell-shocked, through the snow-covered Ardennes forest during the war. Not only does this theme offer a marvelous sense of timelessness, its very shape and rhythm seem to pace the figure meandering through the snow. . . . [Music] in this film . . . simultaneously gives added meaning to the setting and an ironic counterpoint to the screen actions."

After such praises, what could Gould say, except that he really didn't like the movie because he really hadn't liked Vonnegut's novel? He liked Hill's direction, he liked all the technical aspects of the film, he felt that everyone had been remarkably faithful to Vonnegut's work, but he didn't think much of that work. "*Slaughterhouse-Five* . . . is a film about the banalities of Middle America which have impeded the moral and cultural evolution of that country," he concluded. "But it's a film produced for, and by, an elitist America, which, instead of turning sympathetically to its past in the hope of achieving some synthesis that might represent its true heritage, diminishes its present and jeopardizes its future by a total lack of faith in the incomparable virtue of charity. It's a film that was challenging and stimulating to work on, superbly crafted within the limits of its genre. . . . But it's not a work of art that one can love."

Vonnegut has become reasonably stoical about such things over the years. "Yes, I know what he said about my novel," he writes in answer to an inquiry. "I do not reply to critics unless they have misrepresented a book some way. His opinion does not offend me. It is yet another idiosyncratic little work of art by a passionate genius. The tone of it is that I have not built on the past, which is what most musicians do. One message of my book, however, is that much of what we have inherited, not music, though, will kill us if we don't stop treating it so respectfully."

Moviemakers periodically thought of Gould's Bach whenever they wanted a sound of coolness and detachment. Thus Warner Brothers used excerpts from *The Goldberg Variations* in the sound track for *The Terminal Man* (1974). Yet it was not until early in 1982, Gould's last year, that a producer actually asked him to provide some music for a film. This was Richard Nielsen, who had been a coproducer of "Glenn Gould's Toronto," and who now was engaged in filming Timothy Findley's *The Wars*. There are curious similarities between Findley's novel and *Slaughterhouse-Five*. Both are portraits of young men very unwillingly at war; both focus on images of fire; both treat war itself as brutal, meaningless, and absurd. *The Wars* was particularly Gouldian in that its hero's act of heroism was a doomed effort to save a troop of horses from German shelling.

Nielsen sent a rough cut of the film to Gould to see if he would like it. Gould liked it very much, Nielsen recalls, but he had one objection. "He said, 'There's a dead horse in one scene, and there is also a scene where a rabbit looks as if it's about to be killed.' He said, 'I know the horse is dead, but if it was killed for the film, I couldn't work on it. That is, if you actually killed that animal—' I said, 'Oh, no.' The horse had long been dead. I think he probably expired from natural causes. I think we got him from an abattoir, where they kill old horses for horsemeat. So we stuck him in a freezer until we needed him. And so Glenn said, 'Well, fine, then we'll do it.'"

Timothy Findley, a very amiable man who lives in an Ontario farmhouse with thirty-three cats, one of whom he claims to have taught to play soccer, remembers his anxiety at meeting Gould even though he had heard that Gould admired both his novel and his film script. "We were supposed to see it together and then talk about the music," Findley recalls. "And I felt: I can't live up to what he thinks of my work. So I was scared of him, and I was scared of the moment. I was sitting in the dimly lit screening room, looking around out of the corner of my eye, and I saw this person come through. And I could hear galoshes. You could hear the galoshes before anything."

Q: Slop-slop-slop?

A: And I thought, It's all true.

Q: This was in midsummer?

A: I can't remember what time of year it was, but he didn't need to dress that way—that was crazy. And so he came in, and my first impression was, He's sick—he's really ill. He looked ill, because the color of his skin was so alarming. And his hair looked dead. It really had that awful look of someone who's been ill in a very major way, so that their hair dies. And it looked like that—it looked like dead hair. . . .

"He was bigger than I thought he would be," Findley goes on, "and he sort of plunked himself down there on my left, and didn't say anything, and I thought, Oh, God! Now I'm going to have to do it all. I'm going to have to lean across and say, 'How do you do? I'm Timothy Findley.' And the joke in all this is that everybody said you never touch his hands, you never try to shake hands with him, but the first thing he did to me was to offer to shake hands. He offered me his hand in a very definite way, none of this tentative, 'don't-touch-me' stuff. Which was lovely, I thought."

It is no longer clear whether anyone really expected Gould to write a musical score for *The Wars*. He was by now less celebrated as a composer than as a kind of virtuoso of technology and pastiche. Gould's own idea was to create a score that would be, like the movie itself, a World War I period piece. That meant Brahms and people like that, and Victorian hymns, "Abide with Me." "I remember him pointing at the screen," Findley recalls, "and saying, 'All the music in the film will come out of that piano bench.' Meaning that everything would be accessible to the people in the film. Nothing would be imposed on them as characters. In other words, there would be no music coming from outside their lives. And I kind of liked that idea."

What Gould did then was to invite Nielsen and his director, Robin Phillips, to his studio for what Nielsen remembers as "really one of the most fascinating nights of my life." Gould had arranged recordings of his own performances to fit each important scene in the movie. "So Glenn did this absolute *tour-de-force* thing that night," Nielsen says, "of taking us through everything he had ever recorded, putting it up on his own electronic equipment, timing it before your eyes with the picture, playing it and modulating it. He literally took us through a whole range of suggestions, from things he had recorded. I remember we had some argument about the Strauss, the Richard Strauss thing in the opening [the third of the *Fünf Klavierstücken*, Opus 3], and he was so delighted with that because he said no one will ever know what this is. 'No one will believe this is Richard Strauss, because he wrote it when he was fourteen.'

"Anyway, we finally finished, and it was agreed that in certain passages, Glenn would compose certain things. Which he did. Sort of cello and bass sequences toward the end. And also the voices that we decided to use for the hymns, Glenn ended up directing those. But anyway, we staggered out of there at seven o'clock in the morning. Robin said, 'He's immensely impressive, but I need to think about him.' And he phoned me at about noon, and he said, 'I'm convinced we've made a mistake.' And I said, 'Well, I have just the opposite reaction.' I said, 'I'm still resonating.'"

Like Dmitri Tiomkin, who startled an Academy Awards audience by crediting his own Oscar to the help of such friends as Beethoven and Wagner, Gould decided to rely mainly on Brahms and Strauss.

Thus one of Brahms's late piano intermezzi (Opus 117, No. 1) became "Rowena's theme," and another one (Opus 118, No. 6) became the "Hospital ashes sequence." This was not plagiarism, for Gould (like Bach) made no secret of his borrowings, but one can hardly help wondering why, when he was finally given such an opportunity to compose whatever he wanted, he limited himself to making a series of arrangements. Even when he undertook to compose a fragment for a soldier to play on a harmonica in one of the nearby trenches, Gould fell back on one of the Brahms intermezzi as his starting point. "The first excerpt is a short set of variations on the theme of Brahms," he wrote to a friend, "the second an arrangment of 'Abide with Me' (both of which themes play a significant leitmotivic role in the score) and together, needless to say, they constitute my first professional exposure to the harmonica. In fact, my ignorance of the instrument was such that I had to ask what the lowest note of the average government-issue harmonica might be—middle C, it turns out, but it's not covered in your average text on orchestration."

Gould put a good deal of work into the performance of this music, not only his piano pieces but the hymns that had helped inspire Canadians to send their youth into the carnage. There is a particularly notable scene in which the hero's despairing mother sits drinking from a flask on the stone stairs of the church while the choir inside sings of patriotic dedication. This was the music, remember, in which Gould heard echoes of his own youth, of those Sunday-night prayers for "the peace that earth cannot give," before the Monday-morning return to school and the "terrifying situations out *there*." "Ever since I was a child," he said in one of his talks with Bruno Monsaingeon, "the music to which I've responded most deeply, the music which has moved me most, is not found in fugues or canons or whatever—it's found in chorales, hymns." Now, in March of 1982, just a few months before that same music sounded at Gould's memorial service, a reporter for the *Star* found the famous recluse out at the distant church of St. Martin-in-the-Fields, overseeing the Canadian Children's Opera Chorus and the choir of St. Simon the Apostle in recording the hymns he had chosen. "Gould specifically worked with three boys . . ." the reporter wrote, "on a piece of music he re-arranged for their voices." "It was a bizarre scene," Dick Nielsen adds, "because Glenn was conducting these boys but he was crouched down in a pew where you couldn't see him. All you could see was a hand reaching out—looked like a totally disembodied hand. Utterly mesmerizing to watch."

Performance, by now, was only the beginning of a Gould creation. After the music had been played and recorded, he started the infinitely detailed process of manipulating the tapes. Of that Strauss *Klavierstück* that he had used in the opening scene of the film, he wrote to the engineer: "Both segments of the Strauss should be dubbed again and/or run straight from the master during the mix. . . . If you do choose to go with the master for the mix, it will involve the all-important pitch alteration (Studer 500 to 504) which occurs at the end of bar 18, immediately before a cut to bar 47; otherwise expressed, it occurs 1 minute, 51 seconds into the opening segment. The other general comment about the Strauss is that, in the Soundmix Theatre, at least, it seemed decidedly bass-oriented. I recall that, during the dubbing session at my studio, I urged Kevin [Doyle, a sound engineer] to effect a steeper bass cut in order to compensate for the dynamic characteristics of the dubber itself. . . ." And so on. That one specimen of engineering instructions continues for seven single-spaced pages.

The Wars was a rather good movie, well acted by various members of Phillips's Stratford repertory company, and ultimately quite moving. Gould liked it a lot. "I think it's a remarkably fine picture," he wrote to a friend, "—very understated, rather slow-moving, interesting particularly for what it leaves unsaid and unshown." That is the kind of praise that implies commercial troubles, however, and those troubles duly arrived. *The Wars* did reasonably well in Toronto and other Canadian cities, but the reviews were mixed, as the phrase goes, and despite Nielsen's best efforts in Los Angeles, he could not find anyone to distribute the picture in the United States at all. In such circumstances, everyone tends to blame everyone else, including Gould. "Robin Phillips said at one point, 'I think the music's too good for the movie,' Nielsen recalls. "And I absolutely love what Glenn did, but I understand. Robin, I think, retains a view that a much more popular music score would have helped the film more."

Gould probably could never have provided that. ("How angry

Glenn was with Robin Phillips!" Jessie Greig recalls. "Glenn would just launch into this tirade on the phone about their working problems. And he would be so angry. . . .") But the most important thing about Gould's role in *The Wars* is that he never really wrote any score at all. Long ago, in his youth, he had talked often about his yearning to become a composer. As a famous virtuoso, he had renounced the concert stage in order to devote his time to composition. He had experimented with various kinds of nonmusical compositions in sound, but *The Wars* represented a kind of last chance, and it was a last chance declined. Sam Carter, Gould's final producer at CBS, later saw just a glimpse of the possibilities when he asked Gould, during a break in a recording session, to improvise on "Abide with Me." "And he did, for twenty minutes," Carter recalls. "And it was beautiful."

The Wars was only a movie, of course, and some authority or other has declared that the basic function of good movie music is to be ignored, not noticed, not heard. That is probably true for believers in the supremacy of visual images, though a rival theory would suggest that the function of a movie composer is to create and exploit one grand idea, the zither theme in *The Third Man*, for example, or the Lara theme in *Doctor Zhivago*. Gould was not really very much interested in such questions. It probably never occurred to him that Nielsen would be the last man to ask him to be what he had once said he wanted to be. Perhaps he had given up such ambitions. In any case, he had quite different plans for his future.

XIII

The Conductor

In one of the lined pads where Gould kept jotting down random thoughts, blood-pressure readings, first drafts of essays, stock-market statistics, letters, shopping lists, and anything else that crossed his restless mind, he now began writing lists of "dream pgms." The first one consisted of Wagner's *Siegfried Idyll*, Schoenberg's First Chamber Symphony, and Strauss's *Metamorphosen*. The second listed Schubert's Fifth Symphony, Strauss's Oboe Concerto, and Schoenberg's *Verklärte Nacht*. Not until the third program did Gould revert to Bach, the Third Brandenburg Concerto, and not until then did he include the first piano work, Bach's Concerto in D minor.

Gould's dream programs no longer featured the piano because he was dreaming of a whole new career for himself as a conductor. In this, he was hardly unique. Liszt had loved conducting; so had Mozart, Schumann, Rachmaninoff, not to mention Bernstein, Ashkenazy, Barenboim. Still, it seems a little strange for someone who had devoted so much of his life to the piano to switch entirely to conducting, to give up the actual performance of music for the sake of directing others in performance.

The main attraction seems to have been the enormously enlarged body of music that would be available to him. This was one of the indirect consequences of Gould's insistence on playing the piano only in the recording studio. It was true, as he had long argued, that the pressures of the concert stage constrained a pianist to perform the same few works over and over again, and thus imposed on him a narrow conservatism. An enthusiastic concert performer like Rubinstein could play some cherished favorite like the A-flat Polonaise again and again without ever tiring of it. For Gould, on the other hand, once he had performed a work, taped it, edited it, spliced it, and put it, as he liked to say, "in the can," that was generally the end. He not only never performed it again but never even looked at it for years on end. And so, once *The Well-Tempered Clavier*, once the partitas and toccatas and the English Suites and French Suites were done, all of Mozart and all of Schoenberg, the prospects seemed to be shrinking.

There were, to be sure, large areas still unfinished. Gould's traversal of the Beethoven sonatas never got much beyond the *Appassionata*, his complete Scriabin sonatas included only the Third and Fifth of the ten, and his beautiful account of the last six Haydn sonatas barely began his idea of recording all sixty. Beyond that, there were those many Romantic masterpieces that Gould professed to despise, the Schubert sonatas, the Chopin études, Schumann's *Carnaval* and *Etudes symphoniques*. Nonetheless, as Gould looked toward his future as a pianist, and as he began recording the oddities of Sibelius and early Strauss, he was apparently beginning to feel a bit hemmed in, restricted, even bored. "I've done it," he said of his entire piano career to Littler of the *Star* in 1981. "It was never something I wanted to spend my entire life doing. To devote the middle thirty years of your life to doing that [playing the piano] is a lot of time—especially the last 20 years, without concerts and other silly diversions. I have pretty well exhausted the music that interests me. . . ."

Gould meant piano music, and he now concentrated much of his emotional energy on the orchestral literature of the late nineteenth century. He kept transcribing Strauss and Wagner on the piano, but why not go back to the original scores, and the sounds that the creators had originally imagined? "I know he was experimenting," says Ronald Wilford, his manager in these later years, "to see whether he wanted to be a conductor, and he was a very great Romantic, and he was having fun. He had done piano transcriptions, and I think what interested him now was doing these pieces in the original orchestration. So whether he was interested in being a conductor or whether he was interested in the original music, I know he was very interested in *his* experimenting to discover whether he could bring it off. . . ."

In a sense, Gould had been conducting all his life. Anyone who ever saw him perform in public saw the extraordinary spectacle of a pianist waving one hand to demonstrate a rhythm while he played the opening statement of a Bach fugue with the other. And when he appeared with an orchestra, he was apt to conduct both himself and the orchestra, regardless of what the official conductor of record might be doing. When he actually mounted the podium, however, there were strange disturbances. He had looked forward "very eagerly," he wrote to a CBC executive in the spring of 1957, to conducting a concert at the Vancouver festival that fall, and on being asked to suggest some programs, he answered that "several ideas have occurred to me—among which would be a Bach or Mozart concerto (from the keyboard)—an all-Bach program—or a more general repertoire, possibly a Mozart or Schubert symphony plus an overture." When that concert was all over, though, his main recollection was of physical torment, "due to a rather involved muscular reaction." There was something about the arm and back muscles that he used in conducting that conflicted with the muscles he used in playing the piano.

"I became quite alarmed," he wrote to Vladimir Golschmann, a fellow conductor at the St. Louis Symphony, "about the danger of conducting at any time close to piano performances. . . . My retirement after a successful career of one concert which was at once my debut and my farewell appearance will, I am sure, be an irreparable loss in the music world. The one logical alternative is to retire from the piano world and devote myself to conducting, which I am seriously considering. . . ."

He was not seriously considering any such thing, of course, and yet the challenge kept luring him back to the podium. There still survives a 1957 TV tape of Gould conducting one movement of Mahler's Second Symphony, with Maureen Forrester as the soloist. Gould conducts without a baton, and he conducts left-handed, with deep, flowing gestures of his arms. One can imagine the back muscles protesting. Once again, Gould announced his retirement. "I had many plans for myself as a conductor," he told an interviewer, "but having done it twice this year, I've given them up. The concerts, in Toronto and Vancouver, were quite successful and I had a wonderful time. But after they were over, I couldn't go near a piano for two weeks. So I cancelled all my other conducting engagements. Don't ask me why; I don't even like to think about it." The reporter added a little elaboration: "A member of Mr. Gould's management organization later explained ... that the gestures involved in conducting—the strong upbeats, downbeats and cue-throwing—had given Mr. Gould such cramps in his arms that he could scarcely move them, much less play a full recital."

Yet the lure kept reappearing. The Stratford Festival was where Gould liked to relax every summer in the 1950's and early 1960's, liked to concoct imaginative programs, engage in chamber music. Here, in one typical festival, he played parts of Strauss's *Capriccio* on the piano, joined Leonard Rose in a Brahms cello sonata, and even sang bits of *Elektra* while accompanying a soprano ("Seeing Glenn Gould through his current Richard Strauss phase," John Beckwith wrote sardonically in the *Star*, "is for the Canadian public somewhat like seeing a difficult child through mumps . . ."). And he again took up conducting, leading two Bach concerti from the keyboard and then the Cantata No. 54, "Thou shalt oppose sin."

And now in his last year, he began making notes on all the possibilities. "Scores to learn," one page in the legal pads begins, and then this remarkable list:

"Beethoven Egmont
"Fidelio
"Coriolanus
"Leonore #3
"Or King Stephen
"Symphony 2, 8
"Grosse Fuge
"Mendelssohn Hebrides . . .
"Ruy Blas
"Symphony 3, 4
"Brahms Symphony 3
"Vln Conc
"Tragic Overture
"Alto Rhapsody
"Song of Destiny?
"Strauss Metamorphosen . . ."

And so on. The list is two pages long, ending with Bach's B minor Mass and all the orchestral suites and Brandenburg Concerti, plus

Krenek's *Symphonic Elegy,* on the death of Anton Webern. Then Gould began writing down the amounts of time to be devoted to studying each of these composers, two hours for Beethoven, one hour and forty minutes for Mendelssohn, thirty minutes for Gluck and Handel. . . .

In all these plans to become a conductor, Gould resolutely ignored many of the most fundamental aspects of that role, those deriving from its intensely public nature. Not only does a conductor create music by extracting it from a hundred more or less willing colleagues but he must serve as the embodiment of his orchestra. He makes speeches, he raises funds, he exchanges ceremonial toasts with dowagers, he is, in every sense of the term, a public figure. Gould, on the other hand, planned to become a conductor in secret. With his own money, about five thousand dollars for an afternoon, he hired an orchestra so that he could rehearse, while his taping machines recorded every fragment. He did not even try this experiment in Toronto but drove thirty miles down the shore of Lake Ontario, in the spring of 1982, to the city of Hamilton.

"He said that he wanted to try," says Boris Brott, the conductor of the Hamilton Philharmonic Orchestra, who had once achieved the unwelcome distinction of having stepped on Gould's hand. "He wasn't sure whether he was going to be successful, or whether he could be successful, in communicating with large groups of people. I think he was a very shy individual, all in all, and yet so much of a showman, as it were. I hate to use the word showman, because it's not the right word. He was very anxious. . . ."

Q: Was there an element of secretiveness in it?

A: Oh, my God, yes! Was there ever! I mean, we literally had to close the hall, and we had security guards. . . .

Apart from having enough money to hire an orchestra—which is how Serge Koussevitzky (with a rich wife) became a conductor, and Sir Thomas Beecham too—how does one actually become a conductor? Is there not a craft and a technique to be learned, for a conductor as much as for a pianist? Brott, who won a post as assistant conductor of the Toronto Symphony at eighteen, is skeptical. "Conducting is such a hit-or-miss affair," he says. "There are so few conductors, if you go through history, who ever really studied conducting. You can learn in a conservatory the basis of conducting—

you know, sort of, what's piano, what's forte, what's four in a bar, what's three in a bar—but that's where it stops. I mean, interpretation, communication, physical communication, all of those things are never taught.

"Glenn had a very gesticulative, naturally gesticulative technique," Brott goes on. "Not a technique per se but an expression. I think, you know, one of the things that's most difficult for young conductors to learn, or for any conductors to learn, is to be uninhibited gesticulatively. That's part of—that's at least fifty percent of the battle. And he had that naturally. It was not a schooled conducting style. It was making music with your hands. At the same time, I didn't find his conducting all that natural or relaxed, to be honest. I felt there was a lot of tension. And one of the things I suppose we all have to learn as conductors is to relax while communicating tension."

Q: But he did get through to the orchestra, what he really wanted from them?

A: Oh, yes. . . . They loved working with him. They adored him. They found him fascinating. As did I.

Brott remembers that Gould wanted to rehearse a Schoenberg piece for piano and wind ensemble, and they talked about how it should go, and Gould was having some kind of difficulty in grasping the complex score. "Finally," Brott recalls, "he said, 'You know, this is ridiculous, but I can't seem to learn this. The only way I'm going to do this is if I play everything.' And so he just sat there at the piano and reduced everything, played his part and everybody else's part at the same time. And without having practiced. He had just decided—you know—it was mind-boggling. The thing that always amazed me about him, both as a pianist and as a musician generally, was that he had an ability to hear contrapuntally, so that all of the polyphonic lines, every line, was so clear in his mind— what was important, what wasn't important, and how it was to come out."

Whether such expensive experiments could ever have led to a career as a conductor remains open to question. Such a question naturally leads to Gould's manager, Ron Wilford of Columbia Artists Management Inc., a silver-haired man in a pin-striped gray suit, who is ready and able to parry any question about anything.

Q: It does seem very odd, when Gould was so reluctant to appear in public, that he should undertake a conducting career, which is a public sort of thing.

A: (Long pause) I don't know what your question is.

Q: How seriously did Gould plan to become a conductor, and what were the possibilities that he would have been successful as a conductor?

A: It depends on how you define the word conductor.

Q: Leading an orchestra.

A: As a music director?

Q: No, standing in front of the orchestra.

A: In a studio?

Q: Well, anywhere. In a studio or—

A: He did that.

Q: Do you think it would have been possible for him to have a career of just recording in a studio?

A: Recording? Yes.

Q: And live on the proceeds of the records?

A: What do you mean by "live on the proceeds of the records"?

Q: I mean, earn a satisfactory income from them.

A: (Long pause) Why not?

Q: Because it had never been done before that I know of.

A: What's never been done?

Q: Having a career as a conductor who doesn't appear in public.

A: (Long pause) The other part of Glenn Gould had never been done either. . . . Every career is unique to itself.

Gould's rehearsals with the Hamilton orchestra lasted no more than a few sessions, and then Gould began working with a free-lance group derived largely from the Toronto Symphony. The only orchestra recording he actually completed, shortly before his death, was a very slow and very beautiful (and still unreleased) performance of *The Siegfried Idyll*. When it was over, the microphones remained open, and Gould's voice can still be heard saying, spontaneously and emotionally, "Gorgeous! Magnificent! Heartbreaking!"

Apart from making orchestral recordings of his own, Gould got interested in the idea of recording a piano concerto without ever seeing the conductor or the orchestra. Specifically, Beethoven and

Herbert von Karajan. This is not an unknown technology. Opera recordings sometimes include dubbed-in arias by singers who have conflicting commitments to perform in the Outer Antipodes. Still, Gould's interest in recording a concerto without ever seeing the orchestra illustrated either his interest in extending the boundaries of technology or his interest in making his life increasingly hermetic, or perhaps simply his interest in experimenting for the sake of experimenting.

The idea was born in 1976, when Karajan was conducting in New York, and Gould wrote out an elaborate scenario for their collaboration on the Bach D minor Concerto and the Beethoven Second, a collaboration that clearly established Gould as the director and Karajan as his deputy:

"Step 1. HvK and GG would first discuss, via phone if poss., all relevant interpretive aspects—temp, dyn. relationships etc.

"2. GG would then proceed to pre-record piano part, editing a two-track submaster which could be approp. leadered, either for tracking or a mix, for stop-tape cues (during tuttis), or . . . in relation to brief orch-solo exchanges (these, if they do not work, could of course be tracked subseq.).

"3. HvK would then record orch. part, using piano pre-tape (and audio feed ear-phone). The procedure would def. necc. stop-tape points so that piano track could be recued etc.

"4. Some segments would clearly benefit by being done the other way around—i.e. orch. material recorded first. . . .

"Thesis and Resolution: That HvK and GG could have a meeting of minds without a meeting.

"Antithesis and Retribution: The result could sound goddamn awful."

These alternative possibilities remained unresolved because of Gould's physical difficulties at the keyboard during the late 1970's. "The project, of course, was canceled due to the problems with my health at that time," he wrote. But when another possibility came up again two years later, when Karajan wanted to bring the Berlin Philharmonic to a taping session with Gould in Toronto, Gould raised objections about the pace of production. "In recent years," he wrote to the prospective producer in Munich, "I have made no recordings with orchestra—the last one, in fact, was in 1969—because of the necessity to adopt a product-per-hour ratio which I find simply unacceptable. I do realize, of course, that the economics of orchestral recording and taping make impractical the sort of leisurely schedule which I insist upon for solo material—a maximum of 10–12 recorded minutes per studio day. However, although in the past, I have worked at a much more accelerated pace in deference to the exigencies of orchestral recording, I am no longer willing to attempt that sort of feat. As I recall, during our ill-fated attempt to tape with the Berlin Philharmonic in the fall of 1976, two concertos—the Bach D minor and the Beethoven B flat major—were tentatively scheduled and two days set aside. This already seemed a breakneck pace to me but within the realm of the possible, nonetheless. In your recent letter, however, you proposed Beethoven No. 1 and 2 plus Bach's D minor and D major 'in a couple of days,' and I frankly cannot imagine committing music to tape at such a pace. . . . I am not willing to tape an average of more than 10 minutes of music per day."

So nothing ever came of the Karajan project, though the exact reasons remain somewhat mysterious. Gould's manager, Wilford, remains reticent.

Q: Do you know why all that came to nothing?

A: (Long pause) Yes. (Longer pause) But nothing which I can tell you.

If Karajan was too difficult, then maybe somebody else could be found. Gould had met Neville Marriner back in the 1950's, when Marriner was a violinist in Josef Krips's London Symphony Orchestra and Gould had performed a cycle of the Beethoven concerti. Despite all of Gould's fascination with novelties and experiments, there remained one part of his mind that always remembered familiar paths and old acquaintances. Marriner, the onetime violinist, had become very successful as the conductor of the London chamber orchestra of St. Martin-in-the-Fields, and Gould kept track of such things. Marriner was serving as guest conductor of the Cleveland Orchestra early in 1982 when Gould telephoned him.

"He said he had his fiftieth birthday coming up, and he was planning to give up playing the piano when he was fifty," Marriner recalls, on a telephone line from Los Angeles, where he is rehearsing Rossini's *La Cenerentola*. "But before he did that, he said, he'd like to make some records with me, and could we talk about it? So I flew up to Toronto one evening, got there about six o'clock, and we settled down to talk. He showed me some of his videos, played me a few records, and then we discussed the possibility of recording the Beethoven concertos. All five.

"It was very difficult," Marriner continues. "I mean, he said that he made one minute's music every hour, and I explained that we couldn't possibly keep an orchestra around for sixty hours, you know, just to make one record. And he agreed. And at about four o'clock in the morning, when I left, we had tentatively decided that he would record the solo parts and then send me the tapes, and I would then put the orchestra around them. And then shortly after that, of course, he died."

While Gould kept mulling over these possibilities, there remained in his mind an idea more radical than anything he had ever attempted. Now that the technology of recording on different tape tracks was perfectly familiar to him, now that he was thinking about recording concerti with different orchestras in different cities at different times, why couldn't he play the roles of both conductor and soloist himself? Not conducting from the keyboard, a part-time, hand-waving sort of effort, but conducting from the podium on one tape track and then performing at the piano on another? What better way could there be to control everything?

Gould had the Hamilton orchestra at his paid command, so all he needed was some young pianist to fill in for himself, some willing impersonator who could play the piano part while Gould conducted the orchestra, and who could then be erased, overdubbed, eliminated, when Gould decided to play the piano part himself. And what better work could be chosen for the experiment than the Beethoven Second Concerto, that bright and beautiful work that Gould had long ago unearthed and made his own? This was what Gould had chosen a quarter of a century ago for his brilliant New York orchestral debut with Bernstein and also for his first brilliant orchestral recording. All he needed now was a dummy, a ghost pianist, an alter ego.

Gould telephoned Martin Canin, a gifted musician whom he had once known on the young-pianists circuit in the 1950's and who now taught at Juilliard. Did Canin know anybody who had completely mastered the Beethoven Second and would like to come to Toronto to play it, knowing that his performance would eventually be erased? Yes, Canin had a pupil named Jon Klibonoff, who knew the work well and would perform the work well and would submit well to being erased.

Gould telephoned Klibonoff, who was then twenty-two, an eager beginner vastly impressed by a call from the master. "It was April Fool's Day, and I couldn't believe it," Klibonoff recalls. Gould wanted to talk. He did one of his Teddy Slutz routines. "In a little while, I'll be able to tell where you come from by your accent," Klibonoff recalls Gould saying. And then, after ten or fifteen minutes, Gould suddenly said, "I'll bet you come from about forty-five minutes west of the Lincoln Tunnel." "And I do," says Klibonoff. "Now that's fantastic, to have that kind of an ear."

So they talked on the telephone from Toronto to New York, talked and sang and rehearsed the whole concerto on the telephone. "Gould just started in and sang the entire orchestral tutti," Klibonoff recalls, "and then I came in, and we sang the whole movement on the telephone. If anybody had heard us, he'd have thought we were crazy."

For what he calls "a handsome honorarium," Klibonoff flew to Toronto. He went to the rehearsal hall in Hamilton, found it empty, climbed up onstage, tried out the piano for a while, and then sat down in the empty auditorium and began reading a book. In due time, a door opened, and the maestro appeared. "He was in a long coat and a hat," Klibonoff recalls, "and I figured, 'That must be him.'" Klibonoff stepped forward, and the coated figure said, "You must be Jon." Gould asked Klibonoff how he liked the piano onstage. Klibonoff, not knowing that the piano had once belonged to Gould, said he had found it rather dry. "I think it will do fine for this Beethoven, or for Bach," he said, "but I don't think you could get a very good Romantic tone from it."

"You couldn't get a good Romantic tone?" Gould echoed. He pushed away the standard-size piano stool and knelt down in front of the piano. "Then he started playing—*very* Romantic," Klibonoff recalls. "He asked me what it was, and I didn't know. I said, 'It doesn't sound like something written for the piano, it sounds like something for orchestra, probably Strauss.' And he said, 'Right. *Elektra.*'"

So they began rehearsing the Beethoven for the taping machines, take after take. Gould had many novel ideas about Beethoven's work. The pace, Klibonoff recalls, was "more stately" than that of the recording Gould had once made with Bernstein, more stately and more articulated, and Gould ignored Beethoven's markings whenever he chose. Klibonoff goes to his piano to demonstrate. "This is what Beethoven wrote," he says, playing the opening march theme and then the smoothly gentle response from the violins. "And this is the way Gould played it." He repeats the sequence, and the slur has disappeared from the violin response. It has become precise and almost staccato, like something from one of the Bach partitas.

The second movement, which Beethoven had marked *adagio*, Gould wanted extremely adagio. The orchestra had some difficulty with this tempo, Klibonoff recalls, difficulty in keeping the melodic line from breaking down. Gould also had some trouble in keeping control of the musicians with the gestures of his hands. In the technique of conducting, Klibonoff recalls, pausing to select the properly diplomatic phrase, Gould still "had a way to go." And Klibonoff himself had trouble with the extremely slow tempo that Gould demanded. Gould's solution, of course, was to go to the keyboard and play the piece himself. "And *he* didn't have any difficulty in giving it a line at that tempo," Klibonoff says. "He could do anything."

Orchestral musicians have labor unions, and labor unions have rules, and the rules would not allow Gould and Klibonoff to continue rehearsing Beethoven's Second on into the night. They had played only a few bars of the concluding rondo when Gould called a halt. He sent the orchestra home, and then he and Klibonoff went down into the basement to listen to the tapes. Were there any disagreements about the interpretation? "No, I knew from the beginning that there weren't going to be any disagreements," Klibonoff says with a wry smile. "I knew I was there 'at your service.'"

Gould seemed pleased. He said to Klibonoff that they should get together again and work on Beethoven's Third Concerto. Klibonoff would have been delighted, but this was in the spring of Gould's last year, and there were other things on his mind, and Klibonoff never heard from him again.

XIV

The Private Life

"Apart from all his work, wasn't there anybody Gould really cared about—passionately?"

"I was afraid you might ask me something like that," says John Roberts, the CBC executive. There is a pause. He offers a faint smile.

"Well, what's the answer?"

"That is the answer," says Roberts.

Gould was an extremely private man. While he fully understood all the techniques for manipulating the media, and while he exploited all those techniques in publicizing his work, he stoutly resisted all intrusions into his private life. Once, during his concert years, when an interviewer hopefully inquired whether Gould was engaged, or even had a steady girl friend, Gould gave a succinct answer: "I am not engaged." Gould's friends continue to guard that sense of privacy, and personal questions are almost invariably met by some variant of the statement that the pianist's private life is nobody's business. Not relevant to his art.

Still, we now live in the age of celebrity, when nothing is conceded to be nobody's business, when all the public heroes pay the price for their fifteen minutes of Warholian fame (and their riches) by permitting the cameras to photograph their mistresses, and even their illegitimate children, all happily at play. For someone to have neither wife nor children, nor acknowledged girl friends, invites dark suspicions that something perverse is being kept secret from the inquiring media. Perhaps inevitably, there has been a certain amount of speculation about Gould's real feelings.

"Glenn came out sort of swishy, and I said, 'Oh, one of those,'" Harvey Olnick says of Gould's first appearance at the University of Toronto. "I always thought he was gay," says Richard Sennett, the sociologist, who knew Gould during his concert years. "Because he seemed so completely indifferent to those vast numbers of fawning women, you know, in the green room." Many women, however, did not find Gould at all indifferent. "Glenn was an eighteenth-century man," says Judith Pearlman, the TV producer, "particularly in his extreme politesse and gallantry toward women. He got along much better with women than with men and was reluctant to be harsh to them in any way."

It is always possible that Gould felt latent homosexual inclinations—many people do, after all—and that he simply suppressed them. Some of the evidence in his private papers is a little ambiguous, and what is one to make of a man naming his two automobiles Lance and Longfellow? When *People* magazine inevitably came to write about Gould, late in his life, Joseph Roddy's story included a slightly enigmatic remark that his "monastic ... solitude is occasionally broken by friends of both sexes, for varying lengths of time." Gould, who had rather naïvely hoped that this article would primarily publicize his new recording of *The Goldberg Variations*, was bitterly dismayed when Roddy first read the story to him over the telephone. "Damn right he hated that," says Ray Roberts. "It was a very clear inference that he was a homosexual. Glenn hit the *ceiling* at that."

Roddy insists that he intended no such thing. But he could sense Gould's dismay about the whole article when he read it to him on the phone. ("I felt sort of terrible about it," he recalls with a laugh. "I felt like a shit, is what I felt.") But on the question of Gould's sexuality, Roddy suddenly mimics Gould's practice of writing out questions for interviewers to ask him. "Why don't you say to me— here's your question—'Why did you *do* that?' And I'll tell you. What I felt, and I felt it with some conviction at that time, was that the homosexual community had swept up Glenn Gould, and I regarded that as wrong. I didn't think he was their property at all."

Q: What you wrote certainly could be construed as suggesting that he was a homosexual—but you didn't intend that?

A: No, I intended just the opposite.

Ray Roberts is even more emphatic. "Just for the record," he says vehemently, "Glenn was *not* a homosexual, absolutely not." Quite apart from the question of homosexuality, Gould undoubtedly found all inquiries about his most private concerns acutely distasteful. "I think Glenn had a tremendous fear of sex, colossal," says one Toronto executive who knew Gould quite well in his later years. "He feared his own sexuality, and he was not naïve or stupid or unsophisticated, so if he feared it, he feared something. There were some huge devils he was fighting. But don't misunderstand me, I think that Glenn would have *expired* before he would actually have done anything wrong." Gould often praised the straitlaced Calvinist morality that had been traditional in Ontario, often criticized Mozart and the whole Mediterranean culture for what he called "hedonism," often referred to himself as a reincarnation of George Santayana's "last Puritan." It seems rather unlikely that anyone who put such nervous emphasis on his own Puritanism might also have been leading a secret life of, shall we say, hedonism.

Still, there seems to have been something strange about Gould's sexuality, or lack of it, or about its direction, or lack of direction. A number of women who were very fond of him, admired him, sensed and felt puzzled by this strangeness, from the beginning and all through his life. Elizabeth Fox, a cheery blonde who now works as a producer of children's shows at the CBC, went out with Gould fairly often when he was twenty and twenty-one, and their dates consisted mainly of listening to music and talking about literature (Gould was in the process of discovering Thomas Mann). "The really personal impression that sticks in my mind is that I didn't know what he was, sexually," she recalls. "I always felt he didn't even shave. He had really smooth skin, and he *looked* sort of androgynous, though I didn't even know what the word was at the time." Repression takes many odd forms. Dr. Joseph Stephens, the Johns Hopkins psychiatrist, recalls that every time he visited Toronto, Gould regularly summoned a Dutch masseur. "And I would sit there with him while he was being massaged," Stephens says. "And I thought, What is this all about? Because my theory, which is absolute theory, is that everybody must be starved for human physical contact, and since he had no other physical contact that I knew of, he had physical contact with this masseur, and these sessions would go on and on." And Nicholas Kilburn, the bassoonist who knew Gould in those same years, recalls that they once were talking about sex, and Gould said, "My ecstasy is my music."

If women seemed threatening, they sometimes really were threatening. All celebrities attract a certain number of demented admirers, but there was something about Gould's remoteness that seemed particularly magnetic. "There was a woman from Boston who must have been around seventy years old," according to Bert Gould, "and she'd drive up to the cottage every summer in a station wagon loaded with her dogs and cats and everything else. She'd park her car over on the road about fifty yards from our door, and every time a boat came to our dock, she'd race down to see if Glenn was on it. It just got so sickening. I remember one day, she parked right in our driveway and started walking across the lawn. I was out sprinkling with the hose, and I just kept going in bigger circles until she walked back to her car. Oh, we'd get so sick of it."

"On a couple of occasions, we had a couple of crazies trying to get at him," says Ray Roberts. "He called me in the middle of the night one night. Some woman was pounding and scratching at his door. And then there was that crazy woman from Texas who kept writing him letters. She wrote him every day. She said she was going to come up and start shooting people on the corner of Bloor and Yonge unless he agreed to marry her."

Other women saw Gould's remoteness in a very different way. "I think Glenn was one of those people who take vows," says Margaret Pacsu, the CBC broadcaster who collaborated on Gould's jubilee record. "I mean, there *are* people who take vows. Buddhists do this, and there are Catholic priests who become devout and secluded people. I think Glenn made a kind of intellectual decision to concentrate entirely on his art." And Gould had once written: "Art on its loftiest mission is scarcely human at all."

Janet Somerville, the producer of "The Idea of North," saw the same dedication but she regards it as less ascetic. "When you watch him playing the piano on television," she says, "that sort of thing is pretty clearly woven into what he's doing. I mean, sexuality can be very *deeply* engaged in a lot of things other than sexual intercourse, and it certainly is engaged in making music. For Glenn and for lots of other people. For all of us, to some extent. I mean, this is not unusual, it's very human. But yes, Glenn had it to an unusual degree. . . ."

Gould did, in fact, have a long romance with the wife of a rather prominent musician, but she is reluctant to talk about any of the details. It began, in a way, when she and her husband were driving to dinner in Los Angeles, and the car radio suddenly began playing a new recording by an obscure young pianist performing *The Goldberg Variations*. The husband pulled up at the side of the road and sat listening, spellbound. The wife recalls that they were very late in arriving at the dinner party. She met Gould at a concert not long afterward, and an elaborate courtship began. She did not like the way he played Bach; he could hardly resist trying to reeducate her. He was always on tour in those days, and so the courtship took elaborate turns. Roddy's article in *People* offered one carefully disguised example. Gould liked to introduce himself on the telephone as one of his many alter egos, Herbert von Hochmeister, the sage of the Arctic, Sir Nigel Twitt-Thornwaite, the dean of British conductors, and so on. When he called his friend and identified himself as one of his comic creations, he often found his call taken by the woman's Chinese maid. It was apparently only when the irritating *People* story appeared that Gould learned that the simpering Chinese maid had actually been the cuckolded husband, who didn't greatly enjoy his own role and therefore inflicted this peculiar revenge on the great impersonator.

In the mid-1960's, shortly after Gould retired from the concert stage, his friend decided to move to Toronto with her two children. She rented a place near his apartment on St. Clair Avenue, and she lived there for four years. "She was a very, very lovely—a nice lady, and I liked her a lot," says Lorne Tulk, the engineer who worked on many of Gould's radio shows during this period. "In some respects, she was something like him. She was—how do I say the words?—'zingy'—would be the wrong word, because it has a bad connotation—"

Q: Lively?

A: Lively. Her mind was going all the time, and his mind was going all the time, so the two of them got on very well.

Gould wanted very much to marry her, she recalls, but she finally decided against it. She decided that he was too—what?—too unstable, too strange, too difficult. And so she returned, with the children, to her patient husband. Gould telephoned her every night for two years, she says, until she finally persuaded him to stop. They never saw each other again.

Despite Gould's self-promoted image as a "recluse," however, he naturally encountered other young women in the course of his work. Toronto is as full of attractive females as any other city, after all, and Glenn Gould's reputation in Toronto was very large indeed. "He was not what you would call a smart dresser," says one of these admirers, a professional singer, as she fingers the yellow beads around her neck, "or cared much about what he looked like, or anything like that, but I found him one of the most glamorous people I'd ever known. Glamorous in the sense that—it was the glamour of his intellect, the glamour of his talent, and even the glamour of his personality. He was a superstar, and he had a superstar personality."

Q: I don't quite know how to ask this, but I feel I have to ask it. Did you have a love affair with him?

A: Oh—uh—I don't think that's—I'm not about to tell you that.

Q: The reason that it's a problem is that one sometimes gets the sense of a man completely cut off from emotional relationships with other people. There have been rumors that he was a homosexual, or that he never had any sex at all.

A: I would prefer not to discuss his sexual life. . . . I have a very strong memory of Glenn, but whether or not he was a homosexual or a heterosexual or asexual or any kind of sexual, that is not the kind of thing that figures very prominently in my recollections. So I'm—you know—I mean, I think he was a very romantic figure. Yes, definitely.

And then there was always Cousin Jessie, who had once waxed his face for dirtying her kitchen floor, who loved him dearly all his life, and who demanded nothing of him. When asked why Gould never got married, the equally unmarried Jessie laughs and says, "Well, I think I would have pitied the woman he was married to. Because he was really married to his music." Jessie could never have married him; she was his cousin, and five years older, but Jessie had something else, her warmth and sympathy and affection.

"You know, I really believe that I was closer to him than any other living person," she says. "He wasn't demonstrative at all, but I remember. . . . I went to Cannington with him when his aunt on his father's side died. He phoned and asked me if I'd go. . . . He was very upset . . . and he reached over and ran his hand down my arm, and he said, 'Jessie, I'll always be good to you.' And I knew he would be. . . . The depth of the love he felt for me is really something, because of the—you know—it was just something special. I've been really fortunate. . . ."

Gould loved games, all kinds of games. He loved to invent new ones. He loved to turn everything he encountered into some kind of a game, which was a little strange for someone who professed to hate all forms of competition. His father still recalls the three-year-old child's fondness for his first piano book, by J. W. Ditson, "because it's more or less a game the whole way through." Gould went on playing musical games all his life. Ray Roberts recalls that he would turn on the radio during the long drives to recording sessions in New York, and he, Roberts, would have to name every piece being played. Like most games, knowledge games are power games—I know something that you don't know. All this was a little unfair to Roberts, since he had no special background in music, but Roberts did his best to learn different styles. "I was a musical nudnick for starters," he says, "but after a while I got a feel for certain periods of time. I got to be pretty good."

A more expert friend, the young New York pianist Monica Gaylord, turned the tables on Gould. She made a tape of twenty selections from her record collection and invited Gould to identify them. She was a little surprised—Gould was probably even more surprised—to find that he knew only three of them. The man who could play Strauss's *Elektra* from memory did not recognize such familiar trifles as Chopin's Nocturne in E minor or Schubert's Impromptu in G flat major.*

But Gould had other ways of playing this game with experts too. "He knew he was a genius, and he loved to exhibit his genius," says Dr. Stephens. "He played that game of 'Play such-and-such in the

---

*This was not the only time Gould revealed strange gaps in his seemingly encyclopedic knowledge of music. Shortly before recording a Beethoven sonata, Opus 31, No. 1, he acknowledged to a colleague that he had "never played it." After listening to a telecast of Wagner's *Tannhäuser* from the Metropolitan Opera, he observed that he had "never even known what it was about."

style of so-and-so,' and he was just incredible at improvising. I have never met anybody who could even vaguely begin to do anything like that. I would say, 'Play me a Beethoven sonata which was not written by Beethoven.' I would say, 'Play a fugue,' and he would just make up all this contrapuntal music, just like that. I said, 'Play me a Chopin nocturne,' and he just made up a Chopin nocturne that was absolutely gorgeous."

Then there was the color game, a supposedly scientific test devised by a Swiss German psychologist named Max Lüscher, in which participants pick their favorite colors and then elaborate psychological analysis ensues. "It is NOT a parlor game, and most emphatically it is not a weapon to be used in a general contest of 'one-upmanship,'" say the publishers of *The Lüscher Color Test,* who report that Dr. Lüscher has been employed as a "color consultant" by firms ranging from Parke-Davis to Volkswagen. Gould similarly used the test on prospective recording engineers, but also, of course, on his friends. Gould's favorite colors were those Arctic shades of gray and black, and he loathed the "aggressive" red. Monica Gaylord likes to wear bright red. Gould was baffled.

Some of Gould's games were quite esoteric. "He would say, 'I'll be Mozart, and you be Beethoven,' and then we would have a philosophical discussion," recalls Nicholas Goldschmidt, the conductor. Most of his games, however, were variations on Twenty Questions or I've Got a Secret. Again, power: I know something that you don't know; try to guess what it is. Gould didn't seem to care, though, whether he played the keeper of the secret or the one trying to discover it. Lorne Tulk recalls that during their midnight dinners while they worked on "The Idea of North," they repeatedly played a game that Gould called Identifications. "I tell you that I am thinking of someone," Tulk says, "and the only clue I give you is that it's either somebody you know or somebody you know of. It's not Twenty Questions because you can take as many questions as you want, but there is a hitch. The hitch is that you can't ask me a direct question. Your questions must be indirect."

Q: Like what? I mean, if I'm thinking of General de Gaulle, can you ask, "Is he an American?"

A: No, that would be a direct question. An indirect question would be: "If you were a dog, what kind of a dog would you be?"

Q: Well, if you were thinking of De Gaulle, what would the answer be?

A: I have a hard time thinking of De Gaulle in terms of a dog.

Q: A bloodhound?

A: I might say, you know, "An oversized French poodle." That's quite a clue, if you see what I'm saying.

Q: Complicated. Was it permissible to give up?

A: Well, that would be—the ultimate humiliation. I don't think Glenn ever gave up. I never knew him to give up.

Gould's games took many forms. He once decided to challenge Columbia Records' nearly incomprehensible royalty statements, and so he wrote a letter of seventeen single-spaced pages debating all the intricacies of payments due from Japan and Australia. He regarded the stock market as a wonderful game, and he played it very shrewdly. ("He used to eat frequently at the Royal York Hotel because the headwaiter there was a stock market buff," says Mario Prizek, "and they spent most of the meal time exchanging stock market tips.") During the troubled economic times in the two years before his death, according to Gould's stockbroker, the pianist was the only one of the broker's clients who made a profit on his trading. His estate, when he died, totaled about $750,000, and much of that came from playing the market.

If all of life is a game, of course, the great question is what the rules are. Gould believed in God, but despite his sternly Presbyterian upbringing, he believed in neither Christianity nor its churches. He believed in extrasensory perception. And in ghosts. He was profoundly superstitious. About the flight times of his friends' airplanes (which he refused to use) or the colors of their cars. "He was terrible about writing checks," says Ray Roberts, who took care of Gould's finances. "He would write a check, and he'd even give it to me sometimes, and then he'd say, 'No, no, it doesn't feel right. Give it back to me.' Sometimes, it would take him six or seven times writing a check before he decided that it was all right."

He adamantly refused to fly anywhere, and yet he drove his cars with wild abandon, repeatedly getting involved in speeding, wrong turns, even occasional collisions. "He learned to drive sitting on my knee," Bert Gould once recalled proudly. "Driving back and forth to the cottage. I'd be controlling the car but he'd be up on my knee, steering it." A little older, Gould absentmindedly steered his father's car into the lake. Older yet, he terrified friends by the heedless way he drove, and yet he refused to let anyone else drive. "I remember when he had that enormous Lincoln Continental which he ultimately smashed up," Harvey Olnick says, "which he liked because he said, 'It gives me more protection.' He went like a madman, and he would cross his legs, and talk and wave, and I would say, 'My God, Glenn, I'd rather take a bus, if you don't mind.'" Dr. Stephens recalls that the first time he ever met Gould, backstage after a concert in Baltimore, Gould proposed that they drive in Stephens's car to Stephens's house. "It was snowing," the psychiatrist says, "and I started to drive through the snow, and he said, 'You don't know anything about how to drive a car in the snow, and I think that *I* should drive.' So we stopped, and he began driving, quite recklessly, I thought. He skidded on the ice at an intersection, and I thought we were going to be killed."

The police record steadily grew. In the mid-1970's, for instance, it read: "25-07-73, speeding 72 mph in 55 mph zone; 25-10-73, speeding 40 mph in 30 mph zone; 29-11-73, speeding 40 mph in 30 mph zone; 05-04-74, prohibited turn; 09-01-75, speeding 44 mph in 30 mph zone; 31-01-75, disobeyed red traffic light. . . ." And so on. None of these were very serious offenses, but the multiplicity of charges is striking. And there were other accidents that never got onto his record. "He tended to bang cars up," Ray Roberts says, recalling an occasion when Gould bumped into somebody and "didn't want to stay around, so I had to get in touch with him and say, 'Get your car fixed, and we'll pay for it.'" Then Cousin Jessie remembers the time Gould hit a truck. "There was a snowstorm, and I'm not sure whether Glenn slipped sideways or the truck slipped sideways or they both slipped sideways," she says. "The truck took to the ditch, and there was nowhere for Glenn to go except into the river."

"He was operating on a different plane, on a different level," Roberts tries to explain, "He had so many things going on up here that he wasn't, you know, that he was sort of accident-prone, bashing things with his car. He drove fast, and sometimes he wouldn't pay attention, he'd have the radio on, and often he'd be conducting." Morris Gross, the attorney, remembers a time when he had to defend Gould for one such episode of "erratic driving." "He was a congenitally absentminded driver, putting it charitably," Gross says. "In this case, there was a police car that followed him for some time, and the policeman couldn't figure out what this crazy driver ahead of him—i.e., Gould—was doing. And when he asked Gould for an explanation, he said, 'Well, I had the radio on, and I was conducting Mahler.' And that was why his arms were waving crazily, both arms, and that's how he got into trouble. My recollection is that the judge hearing the case was very, very sympathetic and let Gould off."

Roberts repeatedly tried to persuade Gould that he would be far safer on an airliner than on the New York Thruway, but his arguments had little effect. Gould, who always wanted to be in control, thought that as long has he had one hand on the wheel of his speeding car, he really was in control. Perhaps to reinforce that idea, he installed a telephone near the wheel. "Yes, he thought he was in control," Harvey Olnick says. "And he loved to risk it. To be in control and yet to be on the edge of out of control. He played the piano that way too. He was always in control, but it seemed reckless at points, didn't it?"

Many of Gould's personal relationships had similar patterns of control and risk, games of discovery and revelation, played according to mysterious rules that Gould invented. As an international celebrity, he was constantly pursued by people who wanted something from him, at the very least his time, but also his ideas, his praise, his emotional energy, his affection. He often had to say no, which he found difficult, and so he found people to say no for him. But when some new acquaintance interested or attracted him, he could suddenly become overwhelmingly friendly. He generally tried to keep his friends separated from each other, but his enthusiasm was a quality that many of them later remarked on. Enthusiasm and encouragement and humor and charm. Gould would ask of a new friend all his time and attention; he would draw him into the Gouldian world of brilliant conversation, and complex games, and late-night music. He talked passionately about God, art, computers, politics (he regarded himself as a Socialist, though he played the stock market and never voted). And then, almost inevitably, there would come a break, and Gould would turn away, turn to other things and other people, and the abandoned friend would never be able to find out what he had done wrong, what mysterious rule he had mysteriously broken. One man who knew Gould well recalls, for example, that a celebrated musician was reported by some third party to have told a joke involving "some kind of cruelty to animals," and so Gould silently broke off all relations with the unsuspecting ex-friend because "this was no longer a person that he wanted to associate with."*

On rare occasions, Gould might try to explain, or explain his lack of explanations. In the National Library in Ottawa, there is a remarkable specimen of Gould telling some unidentified woman who had once thought herself important to him that she was not important after all. "I gather you tried to call me yesterday, so this letter—though difficult—is necessary," Gould begins. "You are as well aware as anyone by what intuition I am sometimes governed, upon what 'unreason' my decisions are sometimes based. And this intuition in the business of human relations is a force which I serve quite without question, and when it seems to demand isolation from one person or from everyone—that too is observed. However illogical and unpredictable and infuriating this may be to others, I have found in this obedience . . . a source of immense strength. And I can only ask you to be charitable and forgive me, and *believe* me when I tell you that you are in no way responsible for this . . . [and] that I hold you in as much affection as ever."

"He would burn—now, I don't want this taken out of context—but he would sort of burn people up," says Roberts. "I mean, he'd literally go at it night and day, night and day, night and day, until the person would be dropping from exhaustion, and he'd still be raring to go, you know? He once said to me that people ultimately disappoint you. One of the things I recognized very early on was that you didn't make demands on him. He liked my relationship because he could turn me on and off at will. I tried to make things as good for him as I could, but probably I would have been burned out sometime. You just couldn't keep up with his ongoingness. And what he

---

*Though Gould had no elaborate philosophy on the subject, he did write to a friend in 1973 that he had "become virtually a vegetarian in the past decade." This was simple enough for a man who described himself as "almost totally indifferent to the process of eating and quite frankly, can just barely manage to open cans." Mario Prizek reports that Gould had virtually no sense of taste.

wanted all the time was control. His whole life was tied up with control."

Control—the word keeps reappearing in almost everyone's recollections of Gould. He had always wanted to control all the circumstances of his life, and over the years it became a passion, an obsession. It was the need to be in control, really, that drove him from the concert stage to the recording studio. And in the recording studio, he had to control all the engineering, where the mikes were placed and how they were used, to make the recording companies come to his native city, to his own studio, where his own equipment would be the only equipment, with everything under his control.

It was the obsessive need for control that made him refuse virtually all interviews unless he could first know all the questions in advance and then eventually write all the questions himself. It was the need for control that made him conduct most of these interviews by means of the telephone and the tape recorder. Gould thought that he was a master of faked improvisation ("Well, Glenn, don't you think . . . ?"), but it is startling to hear some of the tapes that were occasionally made of genuine conversations, and to hear how much more genial and friendly he could become when the interviewing stopped. Similarly, his letters, even to strangers, are much warmer and sunnier than any of his published prose.

Still, the telephone not only preserved his sense of privacy but gave him great opportunities for variety in his social life. Toronto might be a little provincial but the telephone made it possible to have long and frequent conversations with friends in Montreal, New York, London. Gould's rules were, as usual, quite rigid. You did not call him; he called you. If you called him, you got an answering service (though he often eavesdropped on another phone). He might or might not call back, when he chose (always late at night), and for as long as he chose. Often for hours on end, Gould would read some new manuscript that he had just written, or some new version of some manuscript, or he would sing at great length some new musical discovery. Occasionally, at two or three in the morning, one of his listeners would drift off to sleep, and then wake to the sound of Gould sharply asking, "Hello? Hello? Are you there?"

And would it be possible to control people even after one's own death? Well, why not? Margaret Pacsu, in the midst of answering a question about Gould's fondness for Barbra Streisand, suddenly offers a theory: "How much of this was calculated, for *you* to be sitting here asking these questions and falling into this? I mean, you know, did he set this all up?"

Q: Are you talking about us?

A: I'm talking about you, the chosen biographer, who now has to sift through all this material. Did this man—look at that face on the jubilee album. Didn't he just set this all up so that you'd be sitting here asking—

Q: It *is* a rather malicious-looking face.

A: Well, but it's naughty too. Could you imagine that you'd be asking questions about Barbra Streisand? Or that he had carefully set this up so that historians and biographers in future years would be asking *these* very questions? You can go around in circles with that.

The weirdness and intensity of Gould's eccentricities suggest all too easily that these supposed eccentricities were actually symptoms of something more serious. One friend who knew him very well describes him quite bluntly as "a paranoid psychotic," using that term not as some loosely hyperbolic description but as an attempt at clinical diagnosis. Asked to provide specific evidence, this friend snaps back: "You know what a paranoid psychotic is, don't you? They're afraid that somebody is trying to poison their food. They're afraid to go out because somebody might try to kill them."

Q: And you're saying that Gould behaved that way?

A: Yes.

Corroborating evidence seems scarce. Geoffrey Payzant, in his book on the "music and mind" of Gould, which Gould read and okayed, carefully noted that the pianist had "never undergone psychoanalysis," carefully noted that he "has not discussed the psychological significance of his doodling with his friendly neighborhood psychoanalyst," carefully noted that Gould "cheerfully talks about his physical disorders, his hypochondria and his dependence upon tranquilizers and sedatives." And he carefully added: "Perhaps he will let us know about it in the same uninhibited way if ever he should have psychiatric treatment."

"Troubles with Glenn?" says David Oppenheim, the Columbia executive who first signed him up to record *The Goldberg Variations*. "Yeah, there were always troubles with Glenn, but you knew from the beginning that you were dealing with some special breed that had to be handled in a certain way. And this wasn't ever a person who was at peace, even troubled peace. . . . He made demands on the studio environment, on the piano, on the chair, on the temperature, on the— It was always trouble, in that sense. But it was not the kind of trouble that *people* make but just the kind of trouble that a different kind of creature gives us. We have troubles of that kind with our dogs and cats. They are what they are. And he was very much that way. . . . Glenn was queer, and I don't mean that in the sexual sense of the word but the traditional sense, just *queer.*"

"What *is* the connection between insanity and imagination?" John McGreevy asks. "We have to be mad to imagine things that have never been imagined before, and then to insist on the realization of those imaginings. So in that sense Glenn was one of the maddest hatters around, because he did dare to go out onto the furthest rim of what was previously accepted as tolerable behavior, and to live that life. Now the tension of persisting and insisting on that— I'm not talking about his art now, I'm talking about the life that he found for himself—must have induced in him extreme states of anxiety and panic and loneliness and terror from time to time. It must have been unbearable at times—I think he was exhausted by the effort of being Glenn Gould—but I never had a sense that he would have it any other way. Whether he ever went over the edge, I wouldn't say, but he was a fully creative person to the end."

"I certainly never thought of him as crazy," says Leonard Bernstein, but then there are qualifications. "I thought he was eccentric and compulsive, obsessive, contradictory, deliberately contradictory, just to mix people up. That had something to do with his identity. He had some kind of identity problem, and maybe the people he tried to mix up were, number one, himself. I don't like that sort of dime-store psychiatry based on hearsay, but I feel that he had a big problem about who he was, which may have affected every department of his life. Relationships, self-presentation on the stage, sexual life—is he going to be a kid or a grown-up man, is he always going to be this adventurous, surprising little fellow, or is he going to be a serious man? Is he ever going to live with anybody? Get married?

"But you see, I don't have enough evidence. I wouldn't *dare* use the word 'psychotic' about somebody that I had not seen for so long, and based only on tales of peculiarities and sudden shifts of intentions. You could make a convincing case for it. *You* could; I can't, I wouldn't. . . . Why don't you work on the— Take as a totem, as an example, the cold, this tremendous relationship he had with cold, and follow that through. That somebody who would be that fearful of the cold, and at such odds with it, at war with it all the time, should then have gone to seek it out and find magical—and *maybe* even *curative*—powers in the kind of coldness, the extremes of cold that you and I never even experienced— Okay. I loved him very much. And I'm sorry that our relationship stopped, when it did, but it was certainly not of my doing."

To the mystery of Gould's own personality, we must add the mystery of drugs, medications, particularly Valium, which Gould took in large quantities for most of his life. We now know that Valium can be addictive, which we didn't know when it first appeared as a popular psychological panacea in the 1960's, and we now know that there are a number of indeterminate side effects that we also didn't know about then, immeasurable disturbances, irrationalities—what do you call these things? Gould was always tense, intense, and Valium came to seem a necessity. One friend frankly called him "addicted," but these terms are ambiguous.

"He said he wasn't addicted, but he certainly was," says Jessie Greig.

Q: Addicted?

A: Well, I don't know. I thought he was. To me, anybody that takes it is addicted. . . . But he couldn't sleep. You know, his mind seemed to be always restless, probing, and he couldn't sleep without it, I guess. . . .

All these conflicts are at least partly a matter of interpretation. If a friend is discarded for some imagined slight, is that really paranoia or just the artistic personality? If someone insists on eating exactly the same food every day, washes his hands over and over, and follows the injunctions of astrology, numerology, and a theory of colors, is that compulsive neurosis or just whimsicality? At what level does the fear of flying pass from the rational to the irrational? At what level does hypochondria become itself a form of illness, particularly when it leads to self-diagnosis and self-medication? And to what extent do these various peculiarities have a synergistic effect, in which one or two eccentricities might be simply eccentric but the whole array of peculiarities implies a personality almost out of control, held together only by an iron sense of discipline?

If we accept Freud's hypothesis that sanity or normality can be defined as the ability to work and to love, we can look at the aging Gould and suspect that he had become psychologically impaired in both. Psychologically incapable of performing music in public and psychologically incapable of loving anyone as an equal. "If Glenn had managed, in his personal life, to just be a little bit less of a genius, a little bit more normal, I think he'd probably still be with us," says Malcolm Frager, the pianist. "I mean, if he'd settled down, gotten married and had children, and had something to think about besides himself, he probably would have— It could only have helped his playing, could have lent it greater warmth, greater humanity. And I think to have a happy family life is *much* more of a challenge than to have a career."

Many of Gould's friends and admirers feel that conventional psychological judgments simply do not apply to him. Timothy Findley, for example, still recalls his first meeting with the pianist at the screening of *The Wars* as a glimpse of one of "the god-people."

Q: What are god-people?

A: Well, the god-people are the truly, absolutely gifted, almost beyond human dimension or human comprehension. And they are— we might not all know who all of them are, but I think pretty nearly everybody would acknowledge the same ones, the Mozarts and the Shakespeares. There are probably, you know, ten of them in the whole history of the human race. But the substrata, just under them, and so far up that they're beyond all of us, are the people like Beethoven, and I would put Gould almost in that category. It's a quality of mind. When he talked about music, he was incapable of talking about it as a man. He was incapable of talking about it in any terms but his own. And you had to rise to that or you were lost. And as with all of those god-people—not unlike God himself, if you have that kind of belief—if they say things, your striving to understand them delivers what they're saying to you. Do you understand that?

Even in less exalted terms, though, Gould seems to have behaved just as most people would like to behave: He lived exactly as he pleased. He got up when he liked, ate what he liked, worked at what he wanted to work at, whenever he felt like it and however long he felt like it, answered to no bosses, saw or talked with whomever he wanted to talk with, achieved great performances of great music, hugely enjoyed himself, and earned a very good living for doing so. How could anyone ask for more?

Tim Page, the young New York music critic who first visited Gould late in his life, was shocked by the pianist's deteriorating physical appearance ("haggard, weathered, decayed"), but he saw the rich paradoxes in Gould's behavior. "I don't want to be like the people who say there was never anything strange about him," Page reflects. "There was a *lot* that was strange about him, I mean, a weird guy. There must have been a great deal of fear there—you know, fear in airplanes, in enclosed places, in concerts, and they all sort of boiled down to the same fear, which is, I think, a fear of death.

"He was certainly neurotic, and definitely drugged in his later years, but the weird thing is that he was so much *saner* than most people, in a lot of ways. I mean, he was so much more thoughtful and funny and friendly and kind, on his own terms, on his own carefully controlled terms, than most people. He was really jolly, and a really damned good companion."

XV

The Goldberg Variations (II)

Nobody knows exactly what inspired Gould to rerecord his first great triumph, *The Goldberg Variations*. Perhaps it was the spur of devising programs for Monsaingeon's video series. Perhaps it was simply the spur of technology in general, not only Monsaingeon's cameras but Columbia's new digital recording equipment. Perhaps, as he himself said, he had been rethinking the whole work, rethinking the relationship of the parts to the whole. Perhaps he was, like the novelist in Henry James's *The Middle Years*, "a passionate corrector, a fingerer of style." Given an opportunity to revise all his own works for the twenty-three-volume New York edition, James extensively fingered, retouched, and rewrote, adding to the fresh narratives of his youth the complexities of his older vision. In actual fact, Gould almost never recorded anything more than once—two sonatas by Mozart and Haydn were the only examples he cited when the question was raised—but *The Goldberg Variations* represented a kind of challenge. His most popular record, still selling well after a quarter of a century, the variations threatened to define and thus confine him. If he could not surpass the recording he had made at twenty-three, then he had learned and gained very little in all the years since then.

Gould had apparently not even played that famous recording for a long time. According to his own almost unbelievable account, he did not listen to it until three or four days before he went to New York in April of 1981 to redo it. "I just wanted to remind myself of what it was like," he said in a taped interview with Tim Page, "and, to be honest . . . it had, at that point, been so many years since

I'd heard it, that I really was curious about what I'd find." It had
been, Gould said, "a rather spooky experience." He had felt "great
pleasure in many respects." He had found the performance touched
with "a real sense of humor," and he recognized in the actual playing
"the fingerprints of the party responsible." There was one very
important difference, however. "I could *not* recognize, or identify
with, the *spirit* of the person who made that recording. It really
seemed like some other person, some other spirit had been
involved."

Gould now became very critical of this wonderful recording. Of
his beautiful performance of the fifteenth variation, for example, he
said contemptuously that it "sounds suspiciously like a Chopin nocturne, doesn't it?" When Page dutifully said, "It's not that bad,"
Gould retorted, "Would you believe a Bizet nocturne?" And when
Page said, "I think, on its own terms, it's lovely," Gould insisted on
attacking himself: "There's quite a bit of piano-playing going on
there—and I mean that as the most derogatory comment possible."
The reason that this "interview" comes to us in such precise detail,
complete with underlinings for emphasis, is that Gould wrote it all
himself, the questions as well as the answers. "It was about ninety
percent Glenn, maybe ninety-five," says Page, "with some additions
by me as we were working it out. But he did not want anything
spontaneous."

Page had an odd relationship with Gould. He had been a young
music critic on a short-lived New York paper called *The Soho Weekly
News* when he got a call from a Columbia publicist, Susan Koscis,
who was trying to drum up some stories to help sell Gould's jubilee
album. Everything was to be very tightly controlled. Anyone who
would like to inverview Gould should write a letter saying what he
would like to talk about, and then Gould would decide whom he
wanted as an interlocutor, by telephone only. Page asked for an
interview "entirely on your terms," and he felt honored to be chosen. "I was just, you know, a new kid in town," he says. He felt
even more honored when his allotted hour on the telephone
stretched out to about four hours. He was correspondingly horrified
when his newspaper published his much-cut interview under a headline that identified Gould as "Recluse, Philosopher, TV Visionary
and Crank." Page telephoned Toronto to apologize for his employ-

ers, Gould answered that he understood the wicked ways of the press, and so, without ever meeting, they became friends. Gould added Page to that diverse collection of people he lived with on the telephone, calling as often as once or twice a week, always at times of his own choosing, always late at night.

Page shared Gould's infatuation with the odd possibilities of technology. "He called my telephone-answering machine once," Page recalls, "and I had a—I was going through that phase with answering machines where you try to think of cute messages, and I got John McCormack's old recording of 'I hear you calling me,' and I thought it'd be a funny thing to put at the start of a tape. So when Glenn called me, he went—you know, you heard this sharp intake of breath and then 'Good heavens!' And he hung up, but I knew it was him. And then a day later, he called up, and there was John McCormack singing, 'I hear you calling me,' and then the beep, and then Glenn started singing, 'I had expected—' And *foolishly* I interrupted him, because I'd heard his voice, and I thought, My God, it's Glenn, and I'd better pick it up. And he said, 'Oh, you're there. I was just going to leave you a song I'd written.' And I said, 'Oh, well, please, I want to get this on tape.' And he said, 'No, no, no.' And he sang it to me, but I didn't tape it."

To launch the new *Goldberg Variations,* Gould wanted to make sure that all the critics understood what he was doing, so he wrote a self-interview that could be taped and sent out with the recording itself. To play the part of the questioner, he needed a docile collaborator, and so Miss Koscis once again called Page. "It was a typical CBS sleazy maneuver," Page recalls. "I don't mean Susan is sleazy, I mean the company is sleazy. They were willing to pay me seventy-five dollars to go up there and do the interview (they eventually paid a good deal more). They were not willing to pay expenses. They were not willing to pay for my hotel. Glenn called me and said, 'Let's talk about what we want to say. Do you have any questions you'd like to ask me?' I gave him a couple, and we talked about it briefly. He then sat down and wrote out the whole script. Then we both amended it. I finally agreed to go up there even though I had no money, *no* money, because the *Soho News* had folded, but then I thought, Somebody will want this interview with Glenn Gould. I nearly didn't go, but I had just finally qualified for an American Express card, so I put the whole thing on American Express."

Gould's draft of Page's interview is headed, just like his draft of the Menuhin interview, with the ironic notation that this is "a spontaneous, off-the-cuff, top-of-our-heads conversation between Tim (Wing It) Page and Glenn (Ad Lib) Gould." What Gould wanted Page to ask him to explain to the music critics was his new conception of *The Goldberg Variations.* He wanted to explain that the original version that they had loved all these years was simply a collection of unconnected piano pieces, and that he now had a theory that imposed a new relationship on all the variations.

This required, at the beginning, that the saraband theme be played extremely slowly, specifically taking three minutes rather than the one minute and forty-seven seconds of the early version. "I think that the great majority of the music that moves me very deeply is music that I want to hear played—or want to play myself, as the case may be—in a very ruminative, very deliberate way . . ." Gould said. "As I've grown older, I find . . . the great majority of my own early performances too fast for comfort. . . . With really complex contrapuntal textures, one does require a certain deliberation and I think that, to come full circle, it's the . . . lack of that deliberation that bothers me in the first version of the Goldberg."

Even more important, though, was Gould's new view that the tempo of each variation should be closely connected to the tempi of all the others. This was not exactly a new idea. Those few pianists who attempted *The Goldberg Variations* in earlier years had generally followed much the same prescription until Gould himself overturned all the traditions with the bold impetuosity of his 1955 recording. But now that he had made his own way back to the pre-Gould tradition, he saw it as a rare discovery. "I've come to feel, over the years, that a musical work, however long, ought to have basically one—I was going to say tempo but that's the wrong word—one pulse-rate, one constant rhythmic reference point," he said in this spontaneous, off-the-cuff, top-of-our-heads conversation with Page. "Now, obviously, there couldn't be anything more deadly dull than to exploit one beat that went on and on and on, indefinitely. . . . But you can take a basic pulse, and divide it or multiply it—not necessarily on a scale of 2-4-8-16-32, but often with far less obvious divisions—and make the result of those divisions or multiplications act as a *subsidiary* pulse for a particular movement. . . ."

Then he offered examples, starting with Variation 16, the "French Overture." "As you know," Gould's script said, "the French Overture is divided into two sections—the dotted rhythm sequence which gave it its name—which came from French opera tradition—and a little fughetta for the second half. The first section is written with four quarter notes to the bar (sings it) while the fughetta, on the other hand, is in 3/8 time—in other words, each bar in the fughetta contains one and a half quarter notes—a dotted quarter, as musicians like to call it (sings). . . ." And so on, until Page is made to say, "Well, Glenn, I don't think I can keep much more of this in my head at the moment." So they play three variations, and then Page, who already knows the recording perfectly well, now simulates a moment of recognition: "You know something, I felt it; I don't know if I would have actually been able to spot what you did just listening to it—but there *was* a link between those variations— I could feel it in my bones."

Though there are obviously elements of make-believe in all this, Page does not think he said anything that he does not really believe.

Q: He wrote that script for himself to tell you how much better the new version is than the old one, and you agreeing. Is that actually your view?

A: Yes.

Q: I must say that I like the old version much better.

A: Uh-huh, it's a controversial thing, I think. Ivo Pogorelich is with you, and I think a number of other people are too, but yeah, I have to say I really do like the second version better. It doesn't have the same buoyancy and devil-may-care quality, but it's so serene and so reflective.

Having decided that the CBC's recording facilities were technically inadequate, Gould returned to the old Columbia studio on East Thirtieth Street in Manhattan, which CBS, for economic imperatives of its own, was about to shut down. *The Goldberg Variations* was one of the last few recordings made there. But Gould had another reason for this trip to New York. After all his years with Steinway, he wanted to look for a new piano, and though he wanted to try more Steinways, and particularly German-made Steinways, he also wanted to try Bechsteins and other brands. His search eventually brought him to a new Yamaha in the window of the Ostrovsky

Piano Company, just behind Carnegie Hall. He tried playing that new Yamaha and some of the other instruments on display, a spectacle so unusual that the store sought to provide camouflage. "In order to insure his privacy," according to Robert Silverman, who had arranged the tryout, "Mrs. Ostrovsky had sheets hung over the front picture windows. I wonder what people walking along that busy street must have thought as Glenn played—with just some plate glass acting as a sound barrier."

Gould wasn't captivated by any of the pianos on display in the Ostrovsky window, but as he was about to leave, he spotted a much-used Yamaha standing in a back corridor, and he decided to try that. Nobody wanted him to use such an aged instrument, but he insisted. It was like a rediscovery of the battered Chickering in the lakeside cottage of his youth, like the moment in which the prince finds that the glass slipper fits Cinderella's foot. It was "just the instrument he'd been searching for," Silverman said. "He called to report that the long search was at last over." Gould bought the aged Yamaha on the spot and ordered it shipped to East Thirtieth Street for his recording of *The Goldberg Variations*. "We feel a great joy and fulfillment," Debbi Ostrovsky wrote to Gould, "in having nurtured an instrument which ultimately will find its home with you."

"So we went to Thirtieth Street with *tons* of equipment," says Sam Carter, a courtly, graying Southerner who acted as producer on Gould's last records. "We were just entering into the digital period, and so we had two modes of this Sony—we had the first one that they'd come up with, and then we had a 1610, which was a refinement on that, and then we were trying out the Mitsubishi system, and all these systems were still unproved, so every artist insisted that we must still have plenty of analog material, so we'd take along some multitrack tape to be very sure that we were really covered. And at the same time, Mr. Monsaingeon's video truck was sitting out in the street, and we were piping this signal to them."

The basic plan was that Gould would perform *The Goldberg Variations* for both Monsaingeon's cameras and Carter's recorders simultaneously. One variation at a time. Monsaingeon was not a film zealot who wanted his camera to keep nervously moving around to new perspectives; he liked to maintain one documentary point of view for several minutes at a time. And Gould liked that. If some aspect of his own performance before the cameras dissatisfied him, he played the whole variation over again. Only for the recording machines did he later insist on retake after retake. "Some of the variations he'd want to do again and again, until he got just what he wanted," Carter recalls. "A lot of people thought that he just stuck things together, and Glenn talked so much about technology, and he *loved* fooling around with tape, and he *loved* editing, and so some people got the impression that that must be the way he made his records, but that was far from the truth, you know. He had as many one-takers as anybody, and damn near any take he made would have stood on its own."

"The first thing that I became aware of really quickly," says Karen McLaughlin, who worked as Monsaingeon's assistant director, "was that Gould wasn't a kook, you know. He was a very straightforward, lovely guy, who I think had some really serious medical difficulties, which he didn't talk about. I think a lot of what people thought were his little eccentricities and crazinesses were, you know, genuine problems. I think he did have some kind of circulatory trouble because his hands were always cold, and they really *were*, you know. It wasn't a joke. Something in his central nervous system just didn't function as it normally would. He started out saying that he tried to eat moderately and be pretty careful about his diet, but by the—oh, the third day, I'd say, he was eating pizza with the rest of us. We were eating at two in the morning because we always worked at night."

The whole process of rerecording *The Goldberg Variations* was a kind of collective festivity. Even the most unschooled members of the crew felt a certain awe at Gould's performances but also a certain sense of communion. "One day as we were leaving the studio to have a bite to eat," Monsaingeon recalls, "one technician said to me, 'Do you know that piece that goes *Pam*-papa, pa-pa-pa-pa-pa-*pam*-pa-pa?' I said, 'Well, sure, it's Chopin's *Polonaise militaire*,' and he said, 'Do you think he might play that for us?' I said, 'Well, you know, I don't think that he's got any kind of love for Chopin, but why don't you ask him?' When we came back to the studio, that cameraman or cableman or whoever it was said to Glenn, 'Do you know this piece?' And he hummed it. And Glenn said, 'No.' The technician said, 'Well, too bad, I would have liked you to play it for us.' Glenn didn't say a thing, but when the shot was ready, and I said, 'Well, let's do the first take,' or the eighteenth take or whatever, Glenn, instead of playing the variation, made an improvisation on that Chopin theme. And played for about twenty minutes. It was absolutely unbelievable."

Q: In the manner of Bach?

A: No, no, no, it was very Brahmsian, Wagnerian, that kind of harmonic vocabulary. The Chopin theme was there, but he twisted it to all kinds of degrees and made it into a very chromatic piece. And when he finished, you know, he just roared in laughter, and everybody was—it was an incredible piece of display, of pianistic and musical display. And Glenn said to me, "Bruno, I hope you taped that." And, of course, I didn't, so it's gone forever.

Sam Carter recalls that *The Goldberg Variations* was recorded in six very separate sessions. Specifically, they were done from 4 P.M. to midnight on April 22, 23, 24, and May 12, 13, 14, 1981. "We would get a kind of basic thing from our sessions, but then he'd like to take the two-track tape home to Toronto with him and rethink the whole thing," Carter says. "And then we'd discuss it on the phone, and he'd try to put things together himself, and then he'd call me and say, 'Now try this, and see if you can do that, and see if there's any problem about the digital edit.' It wouldn't always work out exactly, because digital editing is a little bit different.

"Actually, I don't know how much you know about recording," Carter goes on, "but when we first started with the digital, it was a circus. Sony only had one digital editing machine making the rounds of Europe and the United States. They had another one in Tokyo. They'd give the machine to us for three days, say, and our engineers had only very brief sessions on how to use it. So we'd get the machine for a weekend, and each of the producers had maybe two or three records to try and edit during that time. So we'd sort of line up, and you'd come in at seven in the morning, or whatever time, you'd try to go through the night, even, as much as you could, because you'd only have a few hours to try desperately to do the records that you were responsible for. And then you'd get in and start, and the machine would break down, or it would not behave properly—it was a *circus*."

Gould seems to have observed a kind of double standard about the video and audio versions of *The Goldberg Variations*. Because he could be seen playing the music in the filmed version, he was slightly less demanding about the quality of the sound; because the recording depended entirely on sound, he wanted that perfect. "They were both meant to be the same," Monsaingeon recalls, "but what happened in fact was that there are a few notes in the record which are different from the film. But just a few notes. For example, one is the final note of the twenty-fifth, the slow variation in G minor. On the film, you can see him, with his right hand, doing this—well, actually, what he's doing, he's conducting a cello. Because he felt that last note was always slightly too loud, and he wanted to keep the cello down. So he redid that last note for the recording. He thought it was quite good enough for the film, because, you know, the picture compensates, but he felt that this particular note should be redone for the record."

The whole process of filming, taping, recording, lasted two months, with Gould traveling to and fro between Toronto and New York. Then he and Monsaingeon, who had collaborated on a detailed shooting script before any taping started, spent that June making the final edit of the video version. It was a kind of milestone, and they both knew it. "When we finally finished the editing," Monsaingeon says, "I remember being on the huge parking lot outside Glenn's studio, the two of us alone, early morning light, extraordinarily exhausted. And Glenn looked *very* tired. I remember looking into his eyes from very close, and seeing those wonderful eyes, very much inside the orbits, looking extremely intense and affectionate. And I felt that I didn't know where I was in the world. You know, I was escaping from some womb, some extraordinary hole in the earth, and landing again in the sunlight."

Now that *The Goldberg Variations* was finished, the beating of drums had to begin, and Gould, for all his reputation as a recluse, was quite an expert at beating drums. (Indeed, his reputation as a recluse was part of the publicity game.) So, for the edification of the prospective reviewers, he began writing that interview with himself, and then summoned Tim Page to Toronto in August of 1982 to play the part of the interviewer. "I was basically an actor," says Page, "an actor who brought something of himself, but an actor.

"So I went up there," Page goes on, "and we spent the first day watching films, watching *The Wars*, watching various tapes, watching him walk around the room, absolutely ecstatic, listening to Barbra Streisand and singing Carl Orff, I mean going around with just this *blissful* look on his face." Page subsequently wrote an account of this visit that provided a rather bleak portrait of the aging virtuoso. "He looked older than his forty-nine years," Page reported. "Gone was the slim, mercurial, oddly beautiful young man whose keyboard acrobatics had dazzled audiences in the late '50s and early '60s. In his place was a stooped, paunchy, rumpled, balding man. . . . Gould's tiny hotel studio was cell-like—the windows blocked, the curtains drawn. His desk was covered with bills, unanswered letters, and penciled first drafts. . . . The bathroom was littered with empty Valium bottles." Yet in the midst of all this, there were touches of something else. "'These are the happiest days of my life,' Gould said suddenly. . . ."

"And then the next night we went to the studio," Page continues, "and we started taping about one-thirty in the morning. We finished about three-thirty. It was a rock studio in downtown Toronto, and, you know, we went through it fairly quickly. I mean, I can tell that there are signs of fatigue in my voice, but it's still a pretty damn good interview, and ninety-five percent of the credit for that goes to Glenn. So what happened then was, I left the room for a minute to get a soda, and then I heard piano music. You know, all night, I'd been thinking, 'Gee, there *is* a piano in that corridor, and maybe he'll go over and play.' And then he sat down, and he started playing through his own transcription of Strauss's *Elektra*. Which is magnificent. And I'm just sitting there and thinking, My God, I'm hearing Glenn Gould play! Wake up! Because, you know, it's four in the morning. Then he played some of the overture of Strauss's *Capriccio,* and then he played Variation Nineteen of *The Goldberg Variations* . . . and then the night was over.

"And one of the things that struck me about all this," Page says, "was that you really had a sense that, for all his solitude, he desperately wanted to be liked. And wanted to be loved. And wanted people really to enjoy him. He was—when I finally said, 'Look, it's six o'clock in the morning, I've got to go to sleep,' it was, like, 'Okay, but I've got these wonderful things, which, you know, I could show you.' He was like a kid, a very sort of self-oriented kid, but he really wanted just to continue."

In contrast to the youthful enthusiasm of Tim Page, the publicity dragnet also brought to Toronto the worldly professionalism of Joe Roddy, on assignment for *People.* "I went up there with Alfred Eisenstadt," Roddy recalls, "and Gould liked the idea of dealing with Eisenstadt. He felt that they had sent the inventor of the camera to take his picture, so he felt very good about that. I think the pictures were for the most part failures, but the visit was excellent, and then I came back without Eisenstadt. We had dinner about ten o'clock that night. In comes the hotel cart with a splendid meal for me. A boiled egg for him. And I sit there like Falstaff, eating, and this conversation goes on, this fantastic discussion of the difference between the two recordings of *The Goldberg Variations,* and the justification for what he had done. He was pointing out what a shabby piece of music *The Goldberg Variations* were, in the early version. One or two of them were of a little interest, but for the most part it was a grab-bag bunch of subgrade Bach. I loved the subject, and so I let him go on and on, and I thought, How false of me. I thought, There isn't going to be one syllable of this in the story."

The surviving tape of that interview contains Gould's astonishing attack not only on his original performance of *The Goldberg Variations* but on the work itself. He accuses Roddy of mistakenly supposing "that I think it's a great work, and I don't. I think it's a very oversold work." He says there are some works that have haunted him for years—notably Strauss's *Metamorphosen*—but *The Goldberg Variations* is not one of them. "There are in the Goldbergs, I think, some of the very best moments in Bach, which is saying an awful lot, but I think there are also some of the silliest. Things such as the canon at the fifth really do move me in an extraordinary way, in as intense a way as anything in *The Art of the Fugue* does, and *The Art of the Fugue* is my favorite Bach work. However, there are also things such as Variations 28 and 29, which are as capricious and silly and dull and as balcony-pleasing as anything he wrote. . . . As a piece, as a concept, I don't really think it quite works." Since Roddy assumed that the readers of *People* magazine would not be interested in such things, the secret of Gould's real opinion of *The Goldberg Variations* went with him to the grave.

By the time this recording neared the market, Tim Page had become a critic at the New York *Times,* and so he was able to use that powerful position to publicize it even before it was officially released. Writing only about the 1955 version in June of 1982, he proclaimed it "a performance of intelligence, originality and fire. I continue to find fresh delights on every rehearing." The *Times* review of the new version was by Edward Rothstein, who took the opportunity to produce a retrospective survey of Gould's career. "The early performance is rambunctious, exuberant, relishing its power and freedom," he wrote. "This record is less viscerally intoxicating, but more affecting, more *serious,* more seductive in its depth. . . . The contemplative meditation of the Aria, the splendid varieties of attack in the 15th variation, the detached and crystalline character of the epic 25th, the almost frightening clarity in the virtuosic parts—all create a 'Goldberg' that gives both a sense of ecstasy and of quiet repose."

Susan Koscis, the Columbia publicist, read the Rothstein story over the telephone to Gould. "I was always a little nervous when I had to read him an article," she recalls, "because if he didn't like it, I would feel terribly responsible, and I never wanted to displease him. Anyway, at the end of this reading, there was silence, and I thought, Oh-oh, he doesn't like it. But then, after a little while, he said that Ed had completely understood him, had grasped the importance of what was important to Glenn, and he said that no journalist had ever written an article with such understanding, and how wonderful it was to finally be understood." When the article itself reached Toronto a day or so later, Gould began reading it aloud over the telephone. He read every word to Jessie Greig, and they both exulted in it. A week later, he had the devastating stroke.

Most of the obituaries noted the ironies of *The Goldberg Variations* being Gould's first and last recordings. Eric McLean of the *Montreal Gazette* noted some deeper oddities. "The album had already been printed, so there could be no question of revamping the cover or the program notes to take his death into account," McLean wrote. "However, you will find in the packaging strange presentiments of what was about to happen. On the back of the album, there is the picture of Gould's piano, and what is obviously Gould's chair . . . but no Gould. Although the program notes make no mention of his death, they are enclosed in a black frame of the sort associated with obituaries. The performance? The 30 variations are played with the same intelligence and clarity that informed the original version. In fact the new interpretation approaches perfection more closely than the first. . . ."

Everything that Rothstein and others heard in this recording is even more explicitly present in Monsaingeon's video version. Gould looks terrible—fat, puffy, pasty, partly unshaven. His dark blue Viyella shirt, with the cuffs unbuttoned, looks simply sleazy. And all the celebrated "mannerisms" are on display; he sways and sings and sighs and makes gestures of conducting himself and more gestures that seem to signify his going into a trance. Yet as one watches, one gradually abandons all these prejudiced observations and becomes a participant in Gould's extraordinary performance. Not only is he playing beautifully, and passionately, but he looks serenely and profoundly happy in his transcendental ability to do what he is doing. Never before has he so clearly achieved his youthful goal of ecstasy. And yet there is also something else. More than a decade earlier, in one of his interviews with himself, Gould had sardonically questioned himself about attempting "to define your quest for martyrdom autobiographically, as I'm sure you will try to do eventually."

"For me," says John McGreevy, the TV director, "it speaks volumes about where he was headed. He's going to another place. This is his farewell. Absolutely. I can hardly bear to listen to it, even today, particularly the closing aria, knowing that he was saying farewell. The prolonged, drawn-out, agonizing poignancy of it. There's a man who was determined to impose, aesthetically and emotionally, his sensibility on his listeners. And he was saying, 'Good-bye.' And this was such an exquisite way of doing it."

Q: I like the first version much better. It had all that courage and enthusiasm.

A: Yes, and life. It's life, whereas the second version is death. He's going away, to another place.

Timothy Findley, the novelist who worked with Gould on *The Wars,* feels much the same way. "I couldn't stop crying when I watched him doing the last moments of *The Goldberg Variations,*" he says.

Q: But he's terribly happy there—

A: Of course. He's gone into another dimension. Yes. He's found sainthood.

Q: Even though he's all alone.

A: Yes, of course. As all saints are. But how ghastly!

XVI

The End

Perhaps the most extraordinary thing about Glenn Gould's last year of life was the diversity of projects to which various people thought he had committed himself. It was like the six blind men and the elephant. Sam Carter of Columbia Records, for example, thought Gould was so bewitched by digital records that he wanted to make new versions of Bach's Two- and Three-Part Inventions, and perhaps the *Italian Concerto.* Jessie Greig recalls him talking at length about writing a historical novel set in Scotland. Neville Marriner believes that he and Gould were going to record all the Beethoven concerti; Jaime Laredo hoped to record more violin sonatas. Bruno Monsaingeon, on the other hand, is one of several people who remember Gould saying, as he approached his fiftieth birthday, that he was going to stop playing the piano, and devote himself to writing, and conducting, and other things. "Just before he died," says Monsaingeon, "we had an appointment to start working on the script of the film that we wanted to do about the *Siegfried Idyll,* with Glenn conducting. And then we wanted to do a film on the B minor Mass of Bach." John McGreevy, the TV director, hoped to make a sequel to "The Idea of North." "We had wanted to do a film on the North," he says, "and, alas, we never got around to it. His radio documentary was fabulous, but I would have done something quite different. I really would have taken him right up to the Arctic, and—

Q: Would he have gone?

A: Yes, he would.

Q: But he'd have to go there by plane, and he wouldn't get into a plane.

A: I know, but we would find some way to get him up there—if it meant taking off by dogsled. He was very, very romantic about the North.

Q: How far north would you have gone?

A: Oh, I'd have taken him right to the roof of the world.

Gould had other plans for the future that were even stranger fantasies. After persuading Ray Roberts to buy a border collie for his children from the Humane Society, Gould began talking about an Arctic animal shelter. "The grand plan—tongue in cheek—was to go to Manitoulin Island, up north, and open the Glenn Gould Puppy Farm," Roberts recalls. "And guess who was going to be the manager? The idea was that we'd keep all the stray dogs from everywhere, and never put a dog out of its misery or anything like that." To Jessie Greig, Gould proposed yet another design for the future. "He said, 'When we get old and senile, I'll buy a house, and you can have the bottom floor, and I'll have the top floor,'" she remembers. "And I said, 'That won't do, because you make too much noise.' And he said, 'Well, then we'll change about.' And I said, 'Still, you'll play the piano all night.' So he was looking forward to being eighty, and at the time, now when I think about it, maybe he really wasn't, maybe that was a cover-up."

Miss Greig remembers that Gould looked much worse in that last summer of 1982. "When I saw him in June, I was absolutely downright floored," she says. "He had gone downhill so much, and just in a few months. His hair had thinned, he was stooped, and his whole face was drawn, you know. I couldn't believe how he'd aged. He'd been so boyish-looking, and he became like an old man. All during that summer, I kept saying to the family, 'I think Glenn's driven.' It's almost as if he was driven to finish those things that he was doing—the Bach and those other ones that he was getting ready to put out. Because he was—he just hardly had time to talk, he was so driven to complete them. And once he did say to me—he gave a big sigh and said, 'I'm *so* tired, Jessie.'"

The lined pads, on which Gould talked to himself, contain endless lists of medical symptoms, tests, medications. One typical specimen says:

"Palpitations

"Heat in arm

"Indigestive-style pains in chest

"Wake-up pulse rate—dream episodes. . . .

"High pulse diminishing with activity

"Freezing sensations—shivers—top of nose. . . .

"Ankle-foot phenomenon

"Recent month's lower abdomen problem—liquid consumption triggers pockets of 'ulcer-like' pains through to back—congestive sensation re bending over. . . ."

Part of this general sense of disintegration was purely the hypochondriac's imagination. At one point, for example, Gould wrote on his pad that he had just discovered some suspicious bluish spots on his stomach, and he wondered what that might portend. Before reporting this to his doctor, he wrote, he would go to the bathroom and check whether the spots might be merely a smear from the ballpoint pen with which he was writing this note. Then he wrote that he did go to the bathroom, and that the spots were indeed just some ink, and that he had washed them away.

Just as paranoiacs do have real enemies, though, hypochondriacs do have real illnesses. Gould did have dangerously high blood pressure, and he did have a whole array of other medical problems: a hyaline hernia, circulation trouble, tingling nerves in his arms and legs, an inner-ear problem called labyrinthitis which affected his sense of balance, eye trouble, hemorrhoids, intestinal gas pains, chronic sore throat, wheezing and shortness of breath, prostatitis, chest pains, and so on and so on. These were both painful and embarrassing. "Heat applied—pain excruciating when lying down in any pos.—and stiff . . . at rest of times," one entry on these pads reads. "3 hrs. sleep tonight . . . spasm effect on waking (r. side, in part., at the moment, is intense) is distressing in the extreme—medication—how many Fiorinal can one take (not that they seem to be doing any good) . . . ?"

He kept compulsively recording how many hours he slept, often three hours on a sofa and three hours in bed, with the radio going, and then he recorded his own pulse rate, sometimes every half hour, and then, when he intermittently woke up, the temperatures in Winnipeg or Calgary. Thus:

"3 A.M. Temp. −7

"HI Vancouver 7

"LO Timmins −30

"Sleep 4½ (interr. hammering) & 2½ est. intermittent. . . ."

And he recorded even the embarrassments. "Interim wakeup almost invariably assoc. with bladder pressure. . . . On two occ. (succ. nights) in June, this resulted in urination while asleep—unprecedented since childhood."

Gould was by now going to no less than four Toronto doctors, but he was also telephoning Cousin Jessie with questions to ask her nephew, who was another doctor. "He'd say, 'Ask Dave this and ask Dave that,'" she says, "about this sensation he was having in his hands and feet and arms and legs." He also acquired weird ideas from various magazine articles. He thought, according to John Roberts, that it was "important to live as close as possible to the summit of a hill because one was less likely to develop cancer." And the doctors kept prescribing drugs. Aldomet for the high blood pressure, Nembutal for sleep, tetracycline and chloromycetin for his constant colds and infections. And Serpasil and Largostil and Stelazine and Resteclin and Librax and Clonidine and Fiorinal and Inderal and Inocid and Aristocort cream and Neocortef and Zyloprim and Butazolidin and Bactra and Septra and phenylbutazone and methyldopa and allopurinol and hydrochlorothiazide. And always, in addition to everything else, lots and lots of Valium.

What are we to make of all this? Mainly, perhaps, that Gould had very little idea of the side effects that might be caused by all these drugs, and that his various doctors may have remained almost equally innocent. In addition, of course, he led a naturally unhealthy life, late hours and bad food. "He did zero exercise," as Ray Roberts puts it, "and he ate scrambled eggs every damn day." For an outside view, we can solicit once again the judgments of Dr. Pascarelli in New York, who is moderately impressed as he reads through Gould's listings of his own symptoms. "'Chest, periodic tightness.' He might have developed angina, coronary insufficiency, so the chest pain might have been a harbinger of cardiac problems. 'Bladder activated wakeup.' He probably had prostatic problems, prostate blockage. 'Some finger pains equivalent to first uric acid findings.' He's alluding to the possibility that he's got some gouty arthritis. 'Stomach pains' could be anything from tension to a serious gastrointestinal problem. He goes and he has heart tests and cholesterol tests, tests for uric acid. 'Hyaline hernia.' That may have been the chest pains. There's a flat valve between the stomach and the esophagus, which allows acid contents of the stomach to regurgitate into the esophagus, and can give heartburn and pain. Particularly a problem at night, when you're lying flat, and the stomach contents can regurgitate into the esophagus. He's using Placido, which is a tranquilizer, to sleep, and he's waking up in the middle of the night, probably from his prostate."

Dr. Pascarelli continues flipping through pages and pages of self-diagnosis. "Okay, here we're talking about epicondylitis, an inflammation of the epicondyles, here in the elbow, which is sometimes called tennis elbow, so he apparently was given steroids, cortisone, muscle relaxant. And he still has urinary tract problems. And he's getting up in the middle of the night. He's on Aldomet. That's for blood pressure. And he refers to myalgia, which is muscle aches. And he says he also has twitches, spasms, and stiffness.

"And he has a bad cold, a virus, which may have caused him to get this arthralgia, pain in the joints. He's striving to keep his blood pressure under control. So then he gets notice of weight increase. . . . Now it seems that he's developed conjunctivitis, which he was treated for, and a middle-ear infection, and then he developed a tingling sensation in the left foot. . . . Black markings on his tongue, which is probably from the antibiotics. He's having trouble with his gastrointestinal tract, his hands and his legs. . . . I don't know what to tell you. I don't think you can really pull this together. I think that you have to just describe it as what it is. I get the feeling that this is a very frightened man, who, for a variety of reasons, is trying to seek a solution to perceived problems by doing a whole series of contrived experiments on himself."

Gould's fiftieth birthday fell on a Saturday, September 25, 1982. He heard vague reports that people were planning festivities in his honor, and he strongly opposed any such idea. "He phoned me a week before his birthday," Jessie Greig recalls. "He knew that his dad was planning a birthday party, and he didn't want *any* birthday party. He said that he knew that some of the people at CBS were

planning a birthday party, and he said, 'I really don't want any birthday party. And if they invite you, don't go.' And I said, 'Well, okay.'
He didn't even want you to send him a birthday card, you know. It
really was funny. He never wanted you to mention his birthday."

Q: Was that a dislike of growing older?

A: I don't know. I don't know. I think he hated any celebration
or anything that set him apart, you know. He really disliked
celebrations.*

And he really was quite sick, with a bad cold or a flu. He was
dosing himself with Vitamin C compounds, but they didn't help, and
people did keep calling, from all over, to wish him happy birthday.
Geoffrey Payzant recalls that Gould "thanked me for writing my
book because it meant that he wouldn't have to spend a lot of time
answering questions from the media on turning fifty." Edward
Rothstein called and arranged to talk again at greater length later that
week. "I looked forward, with eagerness, to a developing friendship," Rothstein says. John McGreevy called, and Rothstein's article
had to be read to him. And Bob Silverman recalls that he and Gould
discussed the Rothstein article "sentence by sentence, literally."
Schuyler Chapin called, and said, as one always does, that he
"couldn't believe Glenn was fifty." Gould sang parts of the new version of *The Goldberg Variations,* which Chapin had not yet heard.
They talked for nearly an hour about the old days at Columbia, and
Gould recalled having told somebody that "the really exciting days
were when Schuyler Chapin was there."

"And then he said, 'Tell me about your children,'" Chapin recalls.
"He was particularly interested in our youngest, Miles. And I'd forgotten a little incident when Miles was five. . . ." Chapin had been
at home, sick, and Gould had come to visit, wearing "his raggedy
overcoat and his gloves," and they had talked, and then Gould had
spotted a collection of Strauss songs near the piano, and he wanted
to play them. "Well, our piano stool was an ordinary Steinway piano
stool," Chapin says. "No, no, no, of course that wouldn't do. We

*Another invitation that Gould scorned came from Jack Behrens, dean of the faculty of
music at the University of Western Ontario, who had the marvelous idea of asking Gould to
come on the day after his birthday and perform John Cage's *4′ 33″,* that celebrated oddity in
which a pianist sits motionless before a piano throughout three silent movements of 33 seconds, 2 minutes 40 seconds, and 1 minute 20 seconds. The world's most famous nonper-
former was not amused.

had to look around the apartment to find an adequate stool, and we did. It was the wastebasket in the library, so I emptied the wastebasket, put it down, and there he sat. He must have spent nearly an hour, playing and singing, with that awful voice, but absolutely on pitch. Then he said, 'I'm hungry,' so I scrambled some eggs. And suddenly I looked over, and Glenn had ceased talking and was sort of looking this way. Standing in the doorway was my little boy, Miles, absolutely mesmerized by this strange apparition in the kitchen. I introduced them, and Miles walked in, and kept looking at Glenn, and hopped into a chair, and had a glass of milk and a cookie while we were having scrambled eggs. And Glenn started to talk to him, while this kid started to talk right back to him, and they had a very interesting—you know, I mean, it's just an incident in one's life that is pleasurable and nice at the time, without one's thinking very much about it. But now Glenn went through the whole thing on the phone, chapter and verse—wastebasket, Strauss—"

Q: You mean ten years later?

A: More than ten years later. Twenty years later, I would say.

Gould's relations with his father were somewhat less tender, but Bert Gould thought he should do something to observe his son's fiftieth birthday. Gould played turtle, hard-shelled, withdrawn. "He phoned us that he was—he had a bad cold and wasn't feeling too good," Bert Gould recalls. Vera Gould nonetheless made him some cookies, and bought him a sweater, and then they both took the short drive over to the Inn on the Park to present their birthday presents. Gould remained wary. "He wasn't laid up or anything like that," Bert Gould recalls. "He came up to the car—outside—with us—and so on."

Gould had rather reluctantly made a will, two years earlier, leaving everything to the Salvation Army and the Toronto Humane Society, those guardians of the destitute and the helpless. Steve Posen pushed him into making the will ("He was angry at me for having suggested it to him from time to time"), but the attorney balked at Gould's peremptory instructions. "I said to him, 'Glenn, I'm sorry, but I need to be able to discuss with you what your assets and liabilities are, who are the people who could be dependent upon you, discuss with you what it is that you're doing.' He said something like, 'You have your instructions, sir.' He also said, 'When we are in our eighties, we will sit down together and make out the perfect will.' He said, 'This isn't for anything that we need. This isn't going to happen.'"

But Gould was superstitious, and the will haunted him. "I remember when Glenn told me on the phone that he had been asked to make up a will," Ron Wilford recalls. "He said, 'I've just come from signing my will, and it bothers me. I hope it isn't prophetic. It gives me a very bad feeling.'"

Two days after his birthday, on Monday, September 27, Gould woke up at about 2 P.M. and realized that there was something very wrong. That is the way strokes often come, not in some dramatic collapse but simply a sudden realization that something is very wrong. "He went to the bathroom," Roberts says, trying to reconstruct the critical moment, "and that's when he realized—he was sitting there—he was sleeping and woke up and realized that he'd had a stroke. He called me at my office."

Q: How did he realize it?

A: Well, he had a numbness down one side. So he called me at the office, and I tore right over to the Inn on the Park. And he actually got up and unlocked the door and let me in. We started calling doctors and everything else—trying to get—what to do— because he wanted the doctors to come over there. He didn't want to go down to the hospital. And the more calling around I did, trying to get hold of these various people, the more I became convinced that there was no way—we had to go down to the hospital. But the last thing he wanted was an ambulance pulling up, and that whole bit, so what I did was contact the management of the hotel, who very discreetly brought him up a chair, a wheelchair, and we took him down and put him into the Lincoln. *I* put him in the car. I don't know how in hell I ever did that, but I got him into the car and drove him down to the hospital.

Q: Was he conscious during all this?

A: Oh, yes.

Q: Was he talking?

A: Yes, oh, yes.

Q: But he knew it was serious?

A: Oh, yes. Well, he didn't think it was *that* serious, okay? He certainly didn't think it was life-threatening. Not at that point. So I got him down to the hospital, and got him admitted, and started making calls, you know, his father and that sort of thing. We took him upstairs, and they examined him, and put him in a room—not intensive care, I don't think—and he seemed quite normal. I mean, he was, you know, he slurred his speech—one side was—but he was fine.

Roberts stayed at the hospital, alone, until about midnight, then went home, then returned early the next morning to deal with things. He had called Jessie Greig the night before—she was in the midst of the laborious process of moving into a new apartment— and told her about the stroke. "Then they phoned me again at about six in the morning—I was so tired from moving—and said that Glenn had been asking for me all night long," Miss Greig recalls. "I went to the hospital, and they allowed me three minutes. I went over to his bed. I said, 'It's Jessie.' And he said, 'I know.' He said, 'I sent for you.' He had one hand behind his head, and I could see there was a swelling in his head, you know, and his eyes would close, but then they'd open again. And so I put my hand down, and he gripped it real tight, and he held my hand, and he said, 'I'm ter-ribly ill.' And I said, 'I know you're terribly ill, but we Greigs are fighters, you know.' And he said, 'Yes, but it's too late now. It's just too late.'

"I only stayed—I was so tired I could hardly stand up—and they only allowed me three minutes. And I came out really upset. I think he knew from my face that I was upset. I didn't cry. I didn't do anything to show him I was upset. But we knew each other well enough for him to know I was upset."

Bert Gould came to the hospital with his wife, but she remained outside. Gould seemed to be asleep. "I sat there beside the bed and held his hand some," Bert Gould recalls, "but he wasn't conscious at all. Except in this way: I was talking to him, trying to make him hear or understand, and all of a sudden, one arm came up and started conducting." The old man, remembering, waves his own arm up in the air, to and fro. "Which he always did, you know, even driving the car or the boat or anything—he'd conduct. But you can't say that he was conscious. I presume that somehow he knew it was me. I don't know."

Gould did come awake again, after his father had gone, and he began struggling to resume his ordinary activities. "At one point there, he was still carrying on business things," Roberts recalls. "He wanted me to go and get in touch with his lawyers and get power of attorney so I could carry on those—we had to get all his income tax paid. There were going to be some fairly heavy fines if you didn't get it paid by the end of the company year. So he wanted to get this money issue cleared up, and he wanted to know what the stock market was doing, and, you know. But he was also dozing a lot, sleeping a tremendous amount. And he's having, you know, he's numb on one side. And he just deteriorated. Late Tuesday evening, we got him a TV set so he could watch, and he kept talking about wanting to tape some guy that was on some channel. Things started to get less and less coherent."

"At ten o'clock that Tuesday night," Jessie Greig says, "he had Ray phone me. Ray apparently was there the whole time. And Glenn wanted to play a guessing game. He wanted me to guess who else was at the hospital. There was a Catholic priest that he wasn't very fond of, and he was mixed up, because that priest wouldn't be at that hospital. He'd be at St. Mike's; he wouldn't be at Toronto General. Anyway, we played Twenty Questions through Ray. He sent Ray to the phone, and I was to guess who was there, and Ray went back and forth with the answers. And I came off the phone, and I was so happy. I said to my sister Betty, 'Glenn is going to be all right.' And Betty said, 'I hate to tell you, Jessie, but, you know, they quite often do that, and have a lucid time before they—' And then the next morning, they phoned and said that he had slipped into another deep coma."

Q: Did he have another stroke?

A: Yes.

Q: That second night?

A: Yes.

"It works this way," says Ray Roberts. "What happens is, when you have a stroke, one side of the brain swells up. And eventually what will happen, as it did in Glenn's case, it causes pressure on the other side, cuts the circulation on the other side, and the other side has a stroke. What happened was that that swelling was so extreme— He had a lot of headaches and things, you know, and his headaches were getting stronger, and by Tuesday night, he was getting to the point where you couldn't make any sense—"

Q: He was trying to talk?

A: Very much. He was crying out things like, "Ray, where are you?" But what he said didn't make any sense. He was very clear—you could understand him well enough—but, you know, like when somebody has a fever, they start making silly requests and things like that. That's what we were getting.

Q: And you stayed there that night?

A: I stayed up until about tennish.

Q: And on Wednesday what happened?

A: By Wednesday, he was into a—

Q: Coma?

A: He was basically completely incoherent, and everything else that's evident in a coma.

"It's funny how life—you know, it's funny in life what happens," says Jessie Greig. "A friend of mine who's a teacher here visited a friend at a cottage in Finland, and this girl there had nursed Glenn in the hospital. And she said, 'I never saw a man so at peace with himself.' She said the only thing he wasn't at peace with was that he wanted Jessie, and the nurses thought I must be a girl friend or something. But he said that when they talked to him, they had never seen a man so at peace with himself. So, you know, he must have come to accept it really quickly, in those two days."

Gould's stroke was kept secret from the press all during these first days. "We did ask the hospital authorities to keep it quiet, not announce it to the public," Bert Gould says. "We didn't want the press to get it because we knew there'd be no peace at all after that, so they held it up for several days until they came to us and said they felt they'd really have to announce it or they'd be in trouble. So they went and had it announced. I figured at the time that within an hour after the press had published it here we'd have telephone calls from Europe—friends there, and so on."

GOULD SUFFERS STROKE said the front page of the *Globe and Mail* on October 2. "Pianist Glenn Gould is in the intensive care ward of Toronto General Hospital after suffering 'a severe stroke' on Monday, his family revealed yesterday. A terse announcement issued by the hospital on the Gould family's behalf said it was 'still too early to determine if there will be any residual problems.'" And the phones began ringing, and kept ringing.

"I got a call to come in to Joe Dash's office [the president of Columbia Masterworks]," Susan Koscis recalls. "They said it was very important, some other people were there waiting for me, and I thought, That's it, they're going to tell me I'm fired. I was absolutely sure. I prepared myself. I walked in, sat down, and I saw all these somber faces, and I thought, Oh, for sure, I'm being fired. And then they told me that Glenn had had a stroke. And it didn't register, because I was so prepared to be fired. I said, 'What did you say?' And they said, 'Glenn had a stroke, and he's going to die, it is only a matter of time, so would you please prepare the press release, update the bio, get the photos ready?' You know, all that kind of thing. Oh, it was unbelievable."

When the hospital announced that it was "still too early to determine if there will be any residual problems," Gould was lying in a coma in the intensive care unit, kept alive by the hospital's life-support systems, and it was becoming increasingly clear that he was not going to recover, ever. Should the machinery go on indefinitely, pumping Gould's blood, breathing his air, when there was no hope that he could recover, or even regain consciousness? No, it was decided to end the torment, and at 11:30 A.M. on Monday, October 4, Gould was allowed to die.

It was Ray Roberts who reported that the life-support systems had been deliberately shut off, and he wanted that kept confidential. "Why do you need to include that anyway?" he asked.

Q: Because I want to tell the complete story, and that's part of it.
A: Yes, that's part of it.

Roberts did not then know that this part of the story had already been published in the Anglican magazine *Canadian Churchman*, in its obituary in November of 1982. "The massive stroke he suffered . . . left him almost totally paralyzed," it said. "He sank into a coma, was put on life-support systems, but within a few days his family made the agonizing decision to withdraw those systems."

Q: So what is the confidentiality here?
A: I guess there isn't any. Sure as hell I didn't tell them. Damn!

"I worked all weekend long, updating the bio and all this kind of thing," Susan Koscis recalls, "and I remember thinking, How strange I haven't heard from him. But I thought, Well, okay, he's working on a project, and he'll call me when he's finished. Then after working on the bio all weekend, I was at my desk typing it, and Joe Dash came in and said, 'Well, he's dead. Get the press release ready.' Just like that."

Many people heard about Gould's death not from newspapers or television but from calls from friends. Tim Page remembers that he turned on his answering machine and heard two messages, one from the New York *Times* announcing that he had just been formally hired, the second from a friend at CBS Records telling him of Gould's stroke. "So it was like these two pieces of news which were just bizarre," Page says. "I spent that weekend in just this state of frenzy and fury. Because I cared a lot for Glenn. I mean, it hit me very, very hard. I went out with Susan Koscis, and we just said, you know, 'What are we going to *do*?' This man who we barely ever saw—it was not like some kind of hero worship—it was real, genuine fondness, even love.

"I covered a couple of concerts that weekend, and then I came into the office just as the news came through that he had died. I'll never forget how eerie it felt to go to the *Times*, pick up the first copy of an edition with my writing in it as a regular critic, and to see that the front page has Glenn's obit."

So they took Gould's body out to the graveyard, Mount Pleasant Cemetery, and they buried him there, near his mother. Mount Pleasant is an enormous place, stretching east from Yonge Street to Bayview Avenue, not far from the Inn on the Park, not far from the apartment on St. Clair, not far from Bert and Vera Gould's house in Don Mills, not far from most of the places where Gould lived most of his life. The authorities at the cemetery take pride in the distinguished figures buried there, who range from William Lyon Mackenzie King, the onetime prime minister, to Zlitcho Demitro, identified as "world king of the gypsies," to Alexander Muir, who wrote "The Maple Leaf Forever." The rows and rows of less exalted graves reflect the cosmopolitanism of contemporary Toronto. Near Gould's grave are those of Veronica Molnar, Stephen Ching, Olga Vool, Heinz Rothermel, Stuart MacNaughton, John Haluza.

The Gould family plot contains one simple granite gravestone, with rosebuds carved along the edges. It says:

GOULD
Florence E.
July 26, 1975
Beloved wife of
Russell H. Gould

Their dearly loved son
Glenn H. Gould
Oct. 4, 1982

Seven or eight feet in front of that gravestone, and just a bit to the right, there is a granite plaque in the ground, about one foot by two. The plaque itself is dark gray granite. Mortised into it, in lighter gray, is the outline of a piano top. Inside that figure are the words:

Glenn Gould
1932–1982

Just below that date is a musical stave, in the treble clef, and upon it the opening notes of *The Goldberg Variations*.

Here lies Glenn Gould, his bones—*Requiescat in pace*—but he is not really here. Or rather, he is and is not. It is like and not like the National Library in Ottawa, which has collected and preserved his letters, his note pads, his scores, his books, his cuff links, his tapes, his piano. He is there and not there.

It is easy enough to say that he is in every house that has a record player and a recording of *The Goldberg Variations* or the partitas or the Beethoven Second Concerto or the Schoenberg Suite, and there are many of those. There was in Gould's recordings, in that detachment that could swerve into passion, in that coolness, that serenity, that ecstasy—there was a strange power unlike anything in the work of any other pianist. It was a power that made many people feel that their lives had somehow been changed, deepened, enriched. One woman, for example, told Bert Gould that she had recovered from a nervous breakdown by spending hours with Gould's Bach. A heart surgeon in London made it a practice to operate only after he and his patient had both listened to Gould recordings.

All during his last years, people kept writing to Gould to try to tell him what his music had meant to them. They always failed, and Gould, trying to answer them, also failed. "I most certainly agree with you about the therapeutic effects of music and musical performance," he wrote to one inquiring admirer two years before his death. "I have always believed that if this relationshp does not exist, it *should* exist. At the same time, vis-a-vis my own work, I prefer not to attempt to ascertain from precisely what sources any therapeutic value might be forthcoming. . . ." Therapeutic is perhaps too technical a term. Lillian Ross of *The New Yorker* expressed a more general feeling when she said, "I always feel grateful when listening to Gould play on records or over the radio these days."

In all those houses, on all those records and tapes, Gould is and is not there.

And then there are the *Voyagers*. In August of 1977, while Gould was still alive, the United States government sent off into the unknown two spacecraft destined for Jupiter, Saturn, and beyond. In the hope that somebody somewhere might eventually intercept these spacecraft, they were loaded with a variety of messages that were supposed to report the existence of thinking beings on a planet known as earth. Official committees met to decide on what should be said. Originally, the messages were supposed to include a golden plaque showing what a human male and female looked like, but congressional opposition to such "smut" persuaded the authorities to abandon that idea. Official committees continued their studies. What resulted was a twelve-inch copper recording, together with a record-playing machine and pictorial instructions on how the machine could be made to play.

The record included a declaration of good cheer from President Jimmy Carter ("This is a present from a small, distant world . . ."), and another from U.N. Secretary General Kurt Waldheim, who was not then suspected of being a Nazi war criminal, but perhaps that is all too richly part of the earth's message. Then came a series of greetings in a series of languages, starting with Sumerian, the oldest one known, and ending with a child saying in English, "Hello from the children of planet earth." Then came something called "sounds of earth," which included whales breathing, volcanoes rumbling, dogs barking, trains whistling, trucks roaring, people laughing, kissing. And then, finally, the intergalactic language of music: pygmy girls in Zaire singing an initiation song, Louis Armstrong crooning "Melancholy Blues," a Japanese flute "depicting the cranes in their nest," the Queen of the Night aria from *The Magic Flute*, a woman's wedding song from Peru, and Glenn Gould playing the prelude and fugue in C major from the first book of Bach's *Well-Tempered Clavier*.

The two *Voyager* spacecraft, designed to last more than a billion years, sailed past Jupiter and Saturn on schedule, passed Pluto and departed from the solar system late in 1987. Remember now how Gould had once told Stokowski that he had "this recurring dream," that he had gone to "some other planet, perhaps in some other solar system," and that he had been "given the opportunity—and the authority—to impart my value systems to whatever forms of life there might be. . . ."

According to Michael R. Helton, of the Jet Propulsion Laboratory in California, who ran a computer analysis of where the two *Voyager* spacecraft were going, *Voyager I* would head toward the constellation Ophiuchus and *Voyager II* toward Capricornus. "In about 40,000 years," according to a report in *Science News*, "both craft should pass within 1 to 2 light years of a fourth-magnitude star (AC +79 3888)—not exactly grabbing distance. Voyager II should pass a similar distance to another star (AC −24 2833-183) 110,000 years later, and about 375,000 years after that, Voyager I will pass perhaps 1.5 light years from DM +21 652 in Taurus."

If some space patrol in Taurus ever gathers in one of these *Voyager* vehicles some 500,000 years from now, and if the authorities there ever crack open their catch, and if they manage to decipher the pictorial instructions and figure out how to play the copper record that contains the first prelude and fugue from Bach's *Well-Tempered Clavier*, God knows what they will make of Glenn Gould, who is and is not there, or of us.

A Note on Sources

It is not easy to determine how the traditional kind of scholarly documentation could be provided for this book. Most of it is based on great quantities of material that were privately obtained and not systematically organized. There are three basic areas to be considered.

I. The Gould papers at the National Library of Canada in Ottawa. About a year after Gould's death, in November 1983, the library acquired for an undisclosed sum the complete collection of Gould's writings, tapes, letters, and other papers, as well as many of his personal possessions (as described in Chapter I). Ruth Pincoe, the Toronto researcher assigned to sort out these papers, has written a striking description of the confusion she found in Gould's apartment: "Most of the papers, especially those dating back more than five years or so, were stored in one room, in boxes, in filing cabinets, and piled on shelves. Some were in file folders (quite probably arranged by someone else); many more were stuffed in large envelopes with vague titles indicating their contents. Some of the correspondence was separated out; much more of it bore every evidence of being completely accidental."

Ms. Pincoe apparently tried to follow whatever Gouldian organizational patterns she could discern, rather than trying to create one of her own. When I looked through all these papers in the fall of 1986, they were collected in rows of large cardboard boxes, all filled with folders. Some of these boxes were of relatively little interest (e.g., three filled with material on various Grammy nominations). The significant ones were: Outgoing correspondence, four boxes; incoming correspondence, six boxes; manuscript pads (restricted), three boxes; manuscript fragments (restricted), two boxes; scripts, sixteen boxes; drafts of articles and scripts, nineteen boxes; music manuscripts, five boxes. Perhaps of interest, though not to me, were seven boxes of financial papers and four boxes of canceled checks. Not "significant" but a great convenience were ten boxes of newspaper clippings, two boxes of magazine articles, and two boxes of photos.

When I studied all these papers, the boxes were simply standing on shelves, and I could look at anything I wanted to see. Though some other researchers have also been granted access to most or all of these papers, the collection was not opened to public use until the spring of 1988. As noted above, certain papers were and still are "restricted," which basically means that the library and the Glenn Gould Estate retain the right to control who sees them and what use may be made of them, if any. I do not really know why any such restrictions should exist. The restricted papers do confirm the reasonably obvious fact that Gould had many real medical problems, but if anyone comes here looking for anything scandalous, he will find precious few signs of it.

The letters, which I have generally identified as such in the course of this book, are numerous but only moderately interesting—much routine business correspondence, a surprising number of detailed answers to fan mail. There are occasionally letters of substance to faraway friends like John Roberts or Paul Myers, but nothing either confessional or revelatory. Ms. Pincoe has written that "it is strongly suspected he did his own weeding during his life," and Ray Roberts confirms that Gould destroyed a certain amount of correspondence that he did not want preserved.

The restricted pads and fragments are more complicated. They include many pages of preliminary drafts of various articles but also school papers and endless listings of Gould's blood pressure, hours of sleep, and repetitions of his own signature. Gould almost never dated any of these entries, and a disquisition on Schoenberg that begins in the midst of a list of stock market holdings may suddenly break off ten pages later in the midst of a list of medications, only to reappear just as suddenly in the midst of another pad containing shopping lists. Clearly, Ms. Pincoe's original ordering of all these documents could only be provisional, and one periodically hears talk that more comprehensive cataloguing is planned or under way, even that someone is transcribing all the scrawls on Gould's pads. One also hears that everything will be or is being computerized, which may or may not be an improvement. In any case, there seems no purpose in my trying to specify here which box contains which quotation. The general reader can reasonably trust my reliability, and any scholar who wants to undertake similar research will simply have to do the digging for himself.

II. The interviews. I conducted more than eighty interviews for this book, a number of them two or three hours in length. They were all done on tape (except twice when the tape recorder broke) and the tapes were then transcribed, but since all this material remains in my attic, there again seems little point in offering detailed documentation. It should be clear enough that when anyone starts talking at length, and in the present tense or in Q and A, this material comes from my interviews.

My heavy use of Q and A is a little unorthodox, but I like it partly because it conveys a sense of process, of a search for Gould actually taking place, and partly because the information being conveyed often derives from the questions as well as from the answers, or else from the interplay between the two. I think there is considerable value in reporting these things pretty much as they occur rather than simply mixing them into a smoothly homogenized account. And one does not have to look at many transcripts before one realizes that most people do not speak in complete sentences or with any great regard for the rules of syntax. In quoting what people said exactly as they said it, I have no intention of belittling or mocking any irregularities of speech, only of recording everything accurately.

I should add that in a very few instances, I have quoted from interviews conducted by other people and kindly loaned to me. Specifically, Tim Page conducted long interviews with Bert Gould and Jessie Greig, which the Glenn Gould Estate made available to me; Joe Roddy sent me the tape of the *People* interview in which Gould denounced *The Goldberg Variations*; and Vincent Tovell gave me a transcript of the excellent TV show "Glenn Gould: A Portrait" that he and Eric Till produced for the CBC.

III. Printed materials. There are four basic Gould books. First on any list, of course, is *The Glenn Gould Reader*, skillfully compiled and edited by Tim Page (1984). This substantial volume contains just about all of Gould's most significant writings, including notably "The Prospects of Recording," "Radio as Music," "Music and Technology," "Stokowski in Six Scenes," the self-interviews, the parody of Rubinstein, the essay on Toronto, the conversation with Bruno Monsaingeon on Mozart, the record-liner commentaries, and several major articles on Strauss and Schoenberg. This is the basic Gouldian canon.

(Monsaingeon has assembled and translated into French a somewhat larger but essentially similar collection of Gould's writings and interviews, published in Paris in three volumes: *Le Dernier Puritain* [1983], *Contrepoint à la Ligne* [1985], and *Non, Je Ne Suis Pas du Tout un Excentrique* [1986].)

The pioneering *Glenn Gould, Music and Mind,* by Geoffrey Payzant (1978), contains a certain amount of biographical material but is essentially an analysis of Gould's aesthetic philosophy, and Payzant is quite adept in pulling together the ideas in Gould's scattered writings. Since he was working on this during Gould's lifetime, he did not have any access to private or unpublished papers, but conversely he did have the advantage of getting Gould's views about his manuscript.

Glenn Gould Variations, By Himself and His Friends, edited by John McGreevy (1983), contains a number of valuable memoirs, notably Leonard Bernstein's "The Truth about a Legend," Robert Silverman's "Memories," and John Lee Roberts's "Reminiscences." It also reprints several important earlier accounts, particularly Joseph Roddy's *New Yorker* profile, "Apollonian," Richard Kostelanetz's "Glenn Gould: Bach in the Electronic Age," and Robert Fulford's "Growing Up Gould."

Conversations with Glenn Gould, by Jonathan Cott (1984), reflects the kind of situation that Gould liked best: an intelligent and admiring interviewer, an open telephone line, an endless amount of time, and a verbatim tape transcript (subject to editorial retouching). Cott covers a great deal of territory, often, as in his account of the Wagner transcriptions or the George Szell episode, more thoroughly than anyone else.

More modest Q & A interviews with Gould appear in *Reflections from the Keyboard, The World of the Concert Pianist,* by David Dubal

(1984), and *Great Pianists Speak for Themselves,* by Elyse Mach (1980). Several recent books also contain interesting chapters on Gould, notably *The Recording Angel, Explorations in Phonography,* by Evan Eisenberg (1987); *The House of Music, Art in an Era of Institutions,* by Samuel Lipman (1984); and *The Solitary Outlaw,* by B. W. Powe (1987).

I should perhaps mention here one mysterious Gould book that I deliberately did not quote, a novel of sorts entitled *Der Untergeher* (1986), by Thomas Bernhard. The narrator is much involved with a fictitious character named Glenn Gould, "the most important piano virtuoso of the century," whom he supposedly met when they were both pupils of Vladimir Horowitz at a master class at the Salzburg Festival. Bernhard's Gould also has a Rockefeller Foundation grant, practices Chopin for hours on end, and in general bears no relation to reality. I wrote to Bernhard to ask him to explain why he had created this fantasy, but he never answered.

On the general and more or less recent music scene, I have read with interest *Musical Chairs, A Life in the Arts,* by Schuyler Chapin (1977); *Current Convictions, Views and Reviews,* by Robert Craft (1977), and *Present Perspectives, Critical Writings,* by Robert Craft (1984); *Music Talks, Conversations with Musicians,* by Helen Epstein (1987); *Out of Character, A Memoir,* by Maureen Forrester, with Marci McDonald (1986); *I Really Should Be Practicing, Reflections on the Pleasures and Perils of Playing the Piano in Public,* by Gary Graffman (1981); *Understanding Toscanini, How He Became an American Culture-God and Helped Create a New Audience for Old Music,* by Joseph Horowitz (1987); *Bernstein, A Biography,* by Joan Peyser (1987); and *My Many Years,* by Arthur Rubinstein (1980).

Some major interviews and commentaries on Gould have never been collected, of course. One good one that I have quoted often is "An Interview with Glenn Gould," by Bernard Asbell, an early and lengthy Q & A that appeared in *Horizon* in January of 1962. And since no record of Gouldian interviews should be confined to the printed page, I should mention that among TV and radio interrogations, the best was a series of four conducted for BBC-TV by Humphrey Burton in 1966. It is remarkable for the fact that Burton, unlike many interviewers, often challenged Gould and made him explain and defend his views.

Other notable press accounts of Gould's activities include "Making a Record with Leonard Bernstein," by Jay Harrison, in *The Reporter*, July 11, 1957; "Inner Voices of Glenn Gould," Harold Schonberg's controversial review of the Brahms D minor Concerto in the New York *Times*, April 7, 1962; "The Glenn Gould Contrapuntal Radio Show," by Robert Hurwitz, New York *Times*, January 5, 1975; "Glenn Gould," by Joseph Roddy, *People*, November 30, 1981; "Glenn Gould Revisits a Masterwork," by Edward Rothstein, New York *Times*, September 26, 1982; and "Pilgrim Pianist," by Sanford Schwartz, *The New Republic*, September 1, 1986.

All the main music critics wrote repeatedly about Gould's concerts and recordings, so the files in Ottawa bulge with their observations. Since New York is indisputably the musical capital of the continent, I have quoted mainly from the New York critics, particularly Harold Schonberg, Donal Henahan, Tim Page, and Edward Rothstein of the *Times*, Jay Harrison and Paul Henry Lang of the *Herald-Tribune*, Winthrop Sargeant of *The New Yorker*, B. H. Haggin of *The New Republic*, Irving Kolodin of *The Saturday Review*, and Martin Mayer of *Esquire*. In Canada, Gould naturally received even heavier press coverage. Perhaps the best of it came from William Littler of the Toronto *Star*, though there were also good stories by his predecessors, John Beckwith and Dennis Braithwaite, and Eric McLean of the Montreal *Star*.

On the general subject of Canada, I have done my best to rise from a characteristically American state of abysmal ignorance to one of merely woeful ignorance. Works of use in that rise have included *France and England in North America* by Francis Parkman; *O Canada, An American's Notes on Canadian Culture*, by Edmund Wilson; *The Scotch*, by John Kenneth Galbraith; *Canada's North*, by R.A.J. Phillips; and *Northern Realities*, by Jim Lotz, the latter two being both participants in Gould's "The Idea of North."

Gould's Concerts

Date	Place	Main works performed (titles abbreviated when repeated)
1945		
Feb. 16	Toronto (Conservatory)	Bach Fantasia and Fugue in C minor (organ)
		Dupuis Organ Concerto in G (1 mvt.)
1944–46	Toronto	Several joint concerts of Kiwanis Festival winners
June 22	Toronto	Chopin Impromptu in F sharp, Etude Op. 10 #3; Brahms Ballade in G minor; Liszt *Valse oubliée*
Nov. 29	Toronto	Beethoven Concerto #4 (1st mvt.), two-piano version with Alberto Guerrero
Dec. 12	Toronto	Mendelssohn Organ Sonata #6 (2 mvts.); Dupuis Organ Concerto (1 mvt.); Bach Fugue in G minor
1946		
Feb. 3	Toronto	Mendelssohn Organ Sonata #1; Dupuis; Bach fugue
April 10	Toronto	Bach *Well-Tempered Clavier* Prelude & Fugue in B-flat minor, Partita #2 (Rondeaux, Capriccio); Chopin Impromptu, Waltz in E minor

Date	Place	*Main works performed* (titles abbreviated when repeated)
May 8	Toronto (Massey Hall)	Beethoven Concerto #4 (1st mvt.) (Ettore Mazzoleni conducting Toronto Conservatory Symphony Orchestra)
Oct. 28	Toronto	Beethoven Sonata Op. 2 #3 (last mvt.), Chopin Impromptu

1947

Jan. 14, 15	Toronto	Beethoven #4 (Bernard Heinze, Toronto Symphony)
April 10	Toronto	Haydn Sonata in E flat; Bach Preludes and Fugues in B-flat minor, C-sharp minor; Beethoven Sonata Op. 10 #3, Chopin Impromptu; Mendelssohn Andante and Rondo Capricioso
May 1	Toronto	Recital, program unknown
June 8	Toronto	Organ recital: Dupuis Concerto; Mozart *Romanze;* four Bach chorale preludes
Oct. 20	Toronto (Eaton Auditorium)	Five Scarlatti sonatas; Beethoven *Tempest Sonata;* Couperin *Passacaille* (arr. Guerrero); Chopin Waltz in A flat (Op. 42), Impromptu; Liszt *Au Bord d'une source;* Mendelssohn Rondo (official debut solo recital)
Nov. 16	Toronto	Same as Oct. 20 recital
Dec. 3	Hamilton	Beethoven Concerto #1 (Sir Ernest MacMillan, Toronto Symphony)

1948

Nov. 4	Toronto	Mozart Fantasia in C minor; Czerny Variations on a Theme of Rodé; Chopin Etude, Op. 10 #7
Nov. 11	Toronto	Dupuis Organ Concerto; MacDowell "To a Wild Rose"

Date	Place	*Main works performed* (titles abbreviated when repeated)
1949		
March 6	Toronto	Two Scarlatti sonatas; Beethoven Sonata, Op. 81a; Mendelssohn *Variations sérieuses*
April 21	Toronto	Program unknown
May 3	Toronto	Two Scarlatti sonatas; two Chopin waltzes; Czerny
Oct. 9	Toronto	Beethoven Variations in F; Prokofiev Sonata #7
1950		
Jan. 19	Toronto	Hindemith Sonata #3
Feb. 12	Toronto	Bach *Italian Concerto*; Beethoven *Eroica Variations*
April 21	Toronto	*Italian Concerto*; Beethoven variations; Prokofiev
May 18	Toronto	Beethoven #4 (Ettore Mazzoleni, Conservatory Symphony)
Sept. 1	Toronto	Bach Toccata in E minor; Czerny Variations on "La Ricordanza"; Chopin Etude in C-sharp minor
Nov. 26	London, Ont.	Bach Toccata; Mozart Fantasia; *Eroica Variations*
1951		
Jan. 4	Toronto	Hindemith Sonata #3; Gould Bassoon Sonata (with Nicholas Kilburn); Gould Five Short Piano Pieces; Morawetz Fantasy in D minor; Krenek Sonata #3
Jan. 23	Toronto	Beethoven #1 (MacMillan, Toronto Symphony)
March 6	Toronto	Weber *Konzertstück* (MacMillan, Toronto Symphony)

Date	Place	*Main works performed* (titles abbreviated when repeated)
May 2	Hamilton	Beethoven #3 (Jan Wolanek, Hamilton Philharmonic)
May 27	St. Catherines, Ont.	Beethoven #3 (Wolanek, St. Catherines Civic Orchestra)
Oct. 28, 29	Vancouver	Beethoven #4 (William Steinberg, Vancouver Symphony)
Nov. 7	Calgary	Bach Partita #5; Beethoven Op. 81a; Variations in F
Dec. 12	Toronto	Beethoven #2 (MacMillan, Toronto Symphony)

1952

Feb. 10	Toronto	Sweelinck Fantasia; Partita #5; Brahms intermezzi; Berg Sonata
Aug. 30	Toronto	Beethoven three bagatelles, Op. 126; Prokofiev Sonata #7
Oct. 4	Toronto	Schoenberg six miscellaneous songs (with Elizabeth Benson Guy), Piano Pieces Op. 11, Piano Suite Op. 25, *Ode to Napoleon Bonaparte* (Victor Feldbrill, chamber group)
Nov. 6	Montreal	Partita #5; Beethoven Sonata Op. 101; Brahms intermezzi; Berg

1953

Feb. 16	Ottawa	Toccata, Partita; Beethoven Sonata Op. 109; Brahms; Berg
July 31	Stratford Festival	Beethoven Trio Op. 70 #1; Brahms Op. 101 (with Albert Pratz, violin, and Isaac Mamott, cello)
Aug. 4	Stratford Festival	Bach three Sinfonias, Partita #5; Op. 109; Berg Sonata
Oct. 3	Toronto	Webern Variations Op. 27; Berg; Schoenberg *Hanging Gardens* (with Roma Butler)

Date	Place	Main works performed (titles abbreviated when repeated)
Oct. 19	Peterborough	Gibbons Pavane; Partita #5; Beethoven Sonata Op. 110; Berg
Nov. 19	Toronto	Partita #5; Op. 110; Schoenberg Pieces Op. 11; Berg
Nov. 23	St. John, N.B.	Bach four Sinfonias, Partita #5; Op. 110; Berg

1954

Jan. 24	Montreal	Bach fifteen Sinfonias; Schoenberg Suite Op. 25; Hindemith Sonata #3
April 1	Brantford, Ont.	Bach fifteen Sinfonias; Op. 109; Brahms intermezzi; Berg
Oct. 16	Toronto	All-Bach concert (no details)
Oct. 25	Toronto	Bach fifteen Sinfonias; Beethoven *Eroica Variations*; Morawetz Fantasy
Nov. 4	Montreal	Morawetz; Bach three *WTC* preludes and fugues; *Eroica Variations*
Nov. 15	Winnipeg	Webern Variations; Partita #5; Berg; Op. 109
Dec. 14, 15	Montreal	Beethoven #1 (Désiré Defauw, Montreal Symphony)

1955

Jan. 2	Washington	Gibbons Pavane; Sweelinck Fantasia; Bach five Sinfonias, Partita #5; Webern Variations; Op. 109; Berg (U.S. debut)
Jan. 11	New York	Same as Washington
March 14	Ottawa	Bach *Goldberg Variations*; Hindemith #3; Krenek #3
March 29	Toronto	Bach D minor; Strauss *Burleske* (MacMillan, Toronto Symphony)
July 12	Stratford	Beethoven #2 (Boyd Neel, Hart House Orchestra)
July 29	Stratford	*Goldberg Variations*

Date	Place	Main works performed (titles abbreviated when repeated)
Aug. 8	Montreal	Beethoven #4 (Jean Marie Beaudet, Toronto Symphony)
Nov. 7	Montreal	*Goldberg Variations;* Beethoven Sonata Op. 111; Hindemith #3
Nov. 10	Ottawa	Beethoven #2 (Eugene Kash, Ottawa Philharmonic)
Nov. 15	Sherbrooke	Beethoven #4 (Sylvio Lacharité, Sherbrooke Symphony)
Dec. 4, 5	Victoria	Beethoven #5 (Hans Gruber, Victoria Symphony)
Dec. 11	Edmonton	Beethoven #4 (Lee Hepner, Edmonton Symphony)
Dec. 12	Winnipeg	Beethoven #1 (Walter Kaufman, Winnipeg Symphony)

1956

Date	Place	Main works performed
March 15	Detroit	Beethoven #4 (Paul Paray, Detroit Symphony)
March 18	Windsor	Repetition of Detroit concert
March 21	Hamilton	Bach D minor (MacMillan, Toronto Symphony)
April 16	Toronto	Bach *Art of the Fugue* (#2, 4, 7) Partita #5; Op. 109; Hindemith #3
May 7	New York	Bach *Art of the Fugue* (excerpts)
July 9	Stratford	Krenek #3; Berg. Also conducted Schoenberg *Ode to Napoleon Bonaparte.* Gould String Quartet also performed
Oct. 10	Mount Lebanon, Pa.	Beethoven #3 (William Steinberg, Pittsburgh Symphony)
Oct. 15	Watertown, Conn.	Bach fifteen Sinfonias; Op. 109; Hindemith #3
Oct. 23, 24	Toronto	Beethoven #2 (Walter Susskind, Toronto Symphony)

Date	Place	*Main works performed* (titles abbreviated when repeated)
Oct. 30, 31	Montreal	Bach D minor; Strauss *Burleske* (Milton Katims, Montreal Symphony)
Nov. 2	Delaware, Ohio	Bach fifteen Sinfonias, *Art of the Fugue* (#1, 2, 4, 7); Op. 109
Nov. 16	New York (Metropolitan Museum)	Bach fifteen Sinfonias; Krenek #3; Hindemith #3
Nov. 19	Dallas	Beethoven #5 (Walter Hendel, Dallas Symphony)
Nov. 26	Niagara Falls, Ont.	Not known
Nov. 28	Hamilton	Bach *Italian Concerto;* Op. 110; Mendelssohn *Variations sérieuses*
Dec. 5	Spokane	Op. 110; Mendelssohn Variations; two Brahms intermezzi
Dec. 9	Vancouver	Beethoven #3 (Irwin Hoffman, Vancouver Symphony)
Dec. 11	Vancouver	Beethoven #5 (1st mvt.); Bach *Goldberg Variations* (excerpts) (Hoffman, etc.)
Dec. 13	Winnipeg	Bach D minor (Walter Kaufman, Winnipeg Symphony)
Dec. 29, 30	St. Louis	Beethoven #4 (Vladimir Golschmann, St. Louis Symphony)

1957

Jan. 26, 27	New York	Beethoven #2 (Leonard Bernstein, N.Y. Philharmonic)
Feb. 4	Burlington, Vt.	Op. 109; Hindemith #3
Feb. 11	Quebec	Bach fifteen Sinfonias; Op. 109; Berg
Feb. 14	Brockville, Ont.	Partita #6; Op. 109; Hindemith #3
Feb. 28, March 1, 2	San Francisco	Bach F minor; *Burleske* (Enrique Jordá, San Francisco Symphony)

Date	Place	Main works performed (titles abbreviated when repeated)
March 8	Pasadena	Partita #6; Op. 109; Berg
March 17, 18	Victoria	Beethoven #4 (Hans Gruber, Victoria Symphony)
March 28, 30	Cleveland	Beethoven #2 (George Szell, Cleveland Orchestra)
May 7	Moscow	Partita #6; Op. 109; Berg
May 8	Moscow	Beethoven #4, Bach D minor (Moscow Philharmonic, conductor ??)
May 11	Moscow	Goldberg Variations; two Brahms intermezzi; Hindemith #3
May 12	Moscow	Berg; Schoenberg excerpts; Webern Variations; Krenek #3; Bach Art of the Fugue (excerpts)
May 14	Leningrad	Partita #6; Op. 109; Berg
May 16	Leningrad	Berg Sonata (rest unknown)
May 18	Leningrad	Bach D minor; Beethoven #2 (Vladislav Slovak, Leningrad Philharmonic)
May 19	Leningrad	Informal student concert; program unknown
May 24, 25, 26	Berlin	Beethoven #3 (Von Karajan, Berlin Philharmonic)
June 7	Vienna	Bach fifteen Sinfonias; Op. 109; Webern Variations
Aug. 20	Montreal	Brahms Quintet in F minor (with Montreal Quartet)
Aug. 27	Hollywood	Not known
Sept. 11	Toronto	Bach F minor; Beethoven #4 (Nicholas Goldschmidt, CBC Symphony)
Oct. 29, 30, 31	Washington	Beethoven #2 (Howard Mitchell, National Symphony)
Nov. 3	Syracuse, N.Y.	Partita #5; Mozart Fantasy in C minor and Sonata K. 330; two Brahams intermezzi; Hindemith #3

Date	Place	*Main works performed* (titles abbreviated when repeated)
Nov. 7	Rochester, N.Y.	Beethoven #2 (Gerard Samuel, Rochester Philharmonic)
Nov. 11	Toronto	*Goldberg Variations;* Haydn Sonata in E flat; K. 330
Nov. 16	Pittsburgh	*Goldberg Variations;* Haydn sonata; Schoenberg Piano Suite Op. 25
Nov. 20	Cincinnati	*Goldberg Variations;* Schoenberg Suite; Haydn sonata
Dec. 7	New York	Schoenberg Suite; K. 330; *Goldberg Variations*
Dec. 13	Miami	Partita #5; K. 330; two Brahms intermezzi; Berg

1958

Date	Place	Main works performed
Jan. 23	Philadelphia	Haydn sonata; K. 330; *Goldberg Variations*
Jan. 28	New Orleans	Beethoven #2 (Alfred Wallenstein, New Orleans Philharmonic)
Feb. 7	Buffalo	Beethoven #3 (Josef Krips, Buffalo Philharmonic)
Feb. 12	Kingston	*Goldberg Variations;* Beethoven Sonata Op. 10 #2; K. 330
Feb. 17	Winnipeg	Same as Kingston
Feb. 20	Saskatoon	Partita #5; Haydn sonata; Op. 110; Berg
Feb. 24, 25	Vancouver	Bach D minor; *Burleske* (Milton Katims, Seattle Symphony)
Feb. 26	Tacoma	Same as Vancouver
March 7	San Francisco	Bach F minor; Strauss *Burleske* (Enrique Jordá, San Francisco Symphony)
March 13, 14, 16	New York	Bach D minor; Schoenberg Concerto (Dimitri Mitropoulos, New York Philharmonic)

Date	Place	Main works performed (titles abbreviated when repeated)
March 21	Boston	*Goldberg Variations;* K. 330; Berg
March 23	Montreal	Same as Boston
March 28	Lexington, Ky.	*Goldberg Variations;* Op. 111
April 3	Ottawa	Bach fifteen Sinfonias, Partita #6; Beethoven Op. 111
May 4	Ann Arbor	Beethoven #4 (Eugene Ormandy, Philadelphia Orchestra)
May 27	Toronto	Bach Partitas #1 and 6
July 23	Vancouver	Haydn sonata; Op. 110; *Goldberg Variations*
July 27	Vancouver	Beethoven #2 (Irwin Hoffman, Vancouver Festival Orchestra)
July 30	Vancouver	Bach D minor, Brandenburg Concerto #5 (John Avison, CBC Chamber Orchestra)
Aug. 10	Salzburg	Bach D minor (Dimitri Mitropoulos, Concertgebouw Orchestra)
Aug. 25	Brussels	Bach D minor (Boyd Neel, Hart House Orchestra)
Sept. ?	Stockholm	Program not known
Sept. 21, 22	Berlin	Bach D minor (Von Karajan, Berlin Philharmonic)
Oct. 9	Wiesbaden	Beethoven #3 (Wolfgang Sawallisch, orchestra uncertain)
Nov. 15	Florence	Schoenberg Suite; K. 330; *Goldberg Variations*
Nov. 30	Tel Aviv	Beethoven #2 (Jean Martinon, Israel Philharmonic)
Dec. 4	Jerusalem	Same as Tel Aviv
Dec. ?	Tel Aviv	Three recitals; programs unknown
Dec. ?	Haifa	Three recitals; programs unknown

Date	Place	Main works performed (titles abbreviated when repeated)
Dec. 14, 16	Tel Aviv	Schoenberg Suite; K. 330; *Goldberg Variations*
Dec. 26, 27	Detroit	Bach F minor; Mozart C minor (Paul Paray, Detroit Symphony)

1959

Date	Place	Main works performed
Jan. 2	Minneapolis	Beethoven #4 (Antal Dorati, Minneapolis Symphony)
Jan. 5, 6	Houston	Beethoven #5 (André Kostelanetz, Houston Symphony)
Jan. 9	Pasadena	Schoenberg Suite; K. 330; *Goldberg Variations*
Jan. 14, 15, 16	San Francisco	Beethoven #3 (Enrique Jordá, San Francisco Symphony)
Jan. 24, 25	St. Louis	Beethoven #5 (Harry Farbman, St. Louis Symphony)
Jan. 31	Edmonton	Not known
Feb. 2	Calgary	Not known
Feb. 13	New York	Partita #6; Schoenberg Piano Pieces Op. 19; Op. 110; Berg
Feb. 18	Salt Lake City	Beethoven #3 (Maurice Abravenel, Utah Symphony)
Feb. 19	Ogden, Utah	Not known
Feb. 24	Buffalo	Op. 110; *Goldberg Variations*
March 1	Washington	Schoenberg Suite; K. 330; *Goldberg Variations*
March 3	Oberlin	Not known
March 8	Boston	Partita #6; Op. 110; two Brahms intermezzi; Hindemith #3
March 10	Quebec	Partita #6; Op. 110; Schoenberg Six Pieces; Hindemith #3
April 2, 3, 4	New York	Mozart C minor (Bernstein, New York Philharmonic)

Date	Place	*Main works performed* (titles abbreviated when repeated)
April 5	New York	Beethoven #3 (Bernstein, New York Philharmonic)
April 7, 8	Montreal	Beethoven #5 (Igor Markevich, Montreal Symphony)
April 14, 15	Toronto	Beethoven #3 (Walter Susskind, Toronto Symphony)
April 18	Birmingham, Ala.	Not known
April 20	Knoxville, Tenn.	Not known
April 22	Columbia, S.C.	Not known
May 16	Berlin	Schoenberg Suite; K. 330; *Goldberg Variations*
May 20	London	Beethoven #4 (Josef Krips, London Symphony)
May 22	London	Beethoven #1 (Krips, London Symphony)
May 30	London	Beethoven #2 (Krips, London Symphony)
June 1	London	Beethoven #3 (Krips, London Symphony)
Aug. 25	Salzburg	Schoenberg Suite; K. 330; *Goldberg Variations*
Aug. 31	Lucerne	Bach D minor (Von Karajan, Philharmonia Orchestra)
Oct. 8	Winnipeg	Brahms Concerto #1 in D minor (Victor Feldbrill, Winnipeg Symphony Orchestra)
Oct. 12	Ann Arbor	Sweelinck; Schoenberg Suite; K. 330; *Goldberg Variations*
Oct. 14	London, Ont.	Beethoven #2 (Martin Boundy, London Symphony)

Date	*Place*	*Main works performed* (titles abbreviated when repeated)
Oct. 25	Berkeley	Berg; Schoenberg Pieces; Hindemith #3; Krenek #3; Morawetz
Oct. 27	Denver	Bach D minor; *Burleske* (Saul Caston, Denver Symphony)
Nov. 1	San Francisco	Sweelinck; Schoenberg Suite; K. 330; *Goldberg Variations*
Nov. 5, 6	Atlanta	Beethoven #4 (Henry Sopkin, Atlanta Symphony)
Nov. 9	Rock Hill, S.C.	Partita #1; Berg; K. 330; Schoenberg Pieces; Op. 110
Nov. 20, 21	Cincinnati	Beethoven #4 (Max Rudolf, Cincinnati Symphony)
Nov. 23	Bloomington, Ind.	Partita #1; K. 330; Op. 110; Berg
Nov. 26	Cleveland	Schoenberg Concerto; Brandenburg #5 (Louis Lane, Cleveland Orchestra)
Dec. 10	Syracuse	Partita #1; Haydn sonata; Schoenberg Pieces; Op. 110; Berg
Dec. 17	Oklahoma City	Beethoven #4 (Guy Fraser Harrison, Oklahoma City Symphony)

1960

Date	Place	Main works
March 2	Baltimore	Beethoven #4 (Peter Herman Adler, Baltimore Symphony)
March 18	Toledo	Beethoven #4 (Joseph Hawthorne, Toledo Orchestra)
March 27, 28	Victoria	Beethoven #3 (Hans Gruber, Victoria Symphony)
April 5	Washington	Beethoven #1 (Howard Mitchell, National Symphony)
April 9	Rochester	Partita #1; *Eroica Variations*; Berg
April 19	Montreal	Beethoven #5 (Igor Markevich, Montreal Symphony)

Date	Place	Main works performed (titles abbreviated when repeated)
April 24	South Bend, Ind.	Brahms D minor (Edwyn H. Hames, South Bend Symphony)
July 24	Stratford	Bach D minor, Brandenburg #5 (Oscar Shumsky, National Festival Orchestra)
July 27	Vancouver	Beethoven #4; Mozart C minor (Louis Lane, Vancouver Festival Chamber Orchestra)
July 29	Vancouver	Beethoven *Tempest Sonata, Eroica Variations*; Berg
Aug. 2	Vancouver	Schoenberg songs, *Book of Hanging Gardens*, Suite, *Ode to Napoleon Bonaparte*
Aug. 7	Stratford	All Beethoven; details not known
Oct. 4	New Haven	Mozart C minor (Frank Brieff, New Haven Symphony)
Oct. 12	Detroit	*Burleske* (Paray, Detroit Symphony)
Oct. 13	Detroit	Beethoven #2; Brandenburg #5 (Paray, Detroit Symphony)
Nov. 6	Buffalo	Beethoven #5 (Krips, Buffalo Philharmonic)
Nov. 15	Cincinnati	*Tempest Sonata, Eroica Variations*; Brahms three intermezzi; Berg
Nov. 29	Akron	Same as Cincinnati
Dec. 1	Minneapolis	Not known
Dec. 6, 7	Toronto	Schoenberg Concerto; Mozart C minor (Susskind, Toronto Symphony)

1961

Jan. 31	Denver	Beethoven #3 (Saul Caston, Denver Symphony)
Feb. 5	St. Louis	Beethoven #2, #4 (Edouard van Remoortel, St. Louis Symphony)
Feb. 8	St. Louis	Beethoven #1, #5 (van Remoortel, St. Louis Symphony)

Date	Place	*Main works performed* (titles abbreviated when repeated)
Feb. 11	St. Louis	Beethoven #3, Triple Concerto (van Remoortel, St. Louis Symphony, and Harry Farbman, violin; Leslie Parnas, cello)
Feb. 20	Houston	Bach D minor (Sir Malcolm Sargent, Houston Symphony)
Feb. 23, 24	Tulsa	Beethoven #4 (Franco Autori, Tulsa Philharmonic)
March 4	Minneapolis	*Tempest Sonata, Eroica Variations*; Brahms intermezzi; Berg
March 12	Boston	Partita #3; Haydn sonata; *Tempest Sonata*; Berg
March 17, 18, 19	New York	Beethoven #4 (Bernstein, New York Philharmonic)
March 22	Miami	Partita #3; *Tempest Sonata, Eroica Variations*; Haydn sonata
March 25	Atlanta	Byrd three pieces; Partita #3; K. 330; Op. 109; Berg
April 9	Montreal	Krenek #3; Partita #3; Haydn sonata; Op. 110
April 25	Los Angeles	*Goldberg Variations*; Webern Variations; Op. 110; Berg
May 2	Cleveland	Partita #3; K. 330; Op. 109; Berg
July 16	Stratford	Brahms Cello Sonata #1, Violin Sonata #1, Trio #3 (Oscar Shumsky, violin, Leonard Rose, cello)
July 23	Stratford	Strauss songs, Violin Sonata, Op. 18, *Capriccio* (arr. Gould) (Ellen Faull, Victor Braun, Oscar Shumsky)
Aug. 4	Vancouver	Beethoven Sonata Op. 31 #3
Aug. 9	Vancouver	Bach Cantata #54 and unspecified concerto (Gould as pianist and conductor)

Date	Place	*Main works performed* (titles abbreviated when repeated)
Aug. 13	Stratford	Bach Concerto in D minor, Sonata #3 for gamba and harpsichord (Leonard Rose, cello, National Festival Orchestra)
Aug. 17	Vancouver	Brahms D minor (with Zubin Mehta, Vancouver Symphony)
Oct. 8	White Plains, N.Y.	Beethoven #5 (Simon Asen, Symphony of the Air)
Oct. 12, 14	Madison, Wis.	Not known
Oct. 22	Boston	Brandenburg #5; *Burkeske* (Paray, Detroit Symphony)
Oct. 26, 28	Cincinnati	Beethoven #5 (Max Rudolf, Cincinnati Symphony)
Nov. 3, 4	Madison, Wis.	Partita #3; K. 330; Op. 109; Berg
Nov. 17	Minneapolis	Beethoven #5 (Stanislaw Skrowaczewski, Minneapolis Symphony)

1962

Date	Place	Main works performed
Jan. 2	Baltimore	Brandenburg #5; *Burleske* (Peter Herman Adler, Baltimore Symphony)
Feb. 6	Oakland	Beethoven #4 (Gerhard Samuel, Oakland Symphony)
Feb. 11	Berkeley	*Tempest Sonata*, Op. 110, *Eroica Variations*
Feb. 27	Winnipeg	Partita #3; *Tempest Sonata;* Prokofiev Sonata #7
March 5, 6	Portland, Ore.	Brahms D minor (Gregory Millar, Portland Symphony)
March 22, 24	Cleveland	Bach D minor; *Burleske* (Louis Lane, Cleveland Orchestra)
March 25	Cleveland	Bach D minor; Beethoven #3 (Louis Lane, Cleveland Orchestra)
April 6, 8	New York	Brahms D minor (Bernstein, New York Philharmonic)

Date	Place	*Main works performed* (titles abbreviated when repeated)
April 12	Toledo	Beethoven #3 (Joseph Hawthorne, Toledo Symphony)
April 14	Columbus, Ohio	Bach D minor; Beethoven #2 (Evan Whallon, Columbus Symphony)
April 22	Chicago	Byrd three pieces; Schoenberg Suite; Partita #3; Op. 109; Berg
April 26	Lexington, Ky.	Byrd three pieces; Partita #3; Haydn sonata; Op. 109; Berg
July 8	Stratford	Bach *Musical Offering, Art of the Fugue* (1–8) (Shumsky, Rose, members of National Festival Orchestra)
July 29	Stratford	Hindemith *Das Marienleben*, Sonata #3 (Lois Marshall)
Aug. 5	Stratford	Mendelssohn Trio in D minor, songs (Shumsky, Rose, Leopold Simoneau)
Aug. 10	Stratford	Not known
Oct. 9, 10	Baltimore	Brahms D minor (Adler, Baltimore Symphony)
Oct. 23	Atlanta	Beethoven #5 (Sopkin, Atlanta Symphony)
Nov. 8	Detroit	Beethoven #3 (Paray, Detroit Symphony)
Nov. 20	Cincinnati	*Art of the Fugue* (four fugues), Partita #4; Op. 109; Hindemith #3
Nov. 23	Kansas City	Byrd three pieces; Haydn sonata; Op. 109; Berg
Nov. 27	Louisville, Ky.	*Art of the Fugue* (four), Partita #4; Brahms three intermezzi; Hindemith #3

1963

Date	Place	Main works performed
Feb. 13, 14, 15	San Francisco	Bach D minor; Schoenberg (Jordá, San Francisco Symphony)
March 5	Denver	Brahms D minor (Caston, Denver Symphony)

Date	Place	Main works performed (titles abbreviated when repeated)
April 16	Rochester	*Art of the Fugue* (four), Partita #4; Op. 109; Hindemith #3
July 7	Stratford	Bach Violin Sonata #1, Concerto #6 (Shumsky, violin; Mario Bernardi, conductor; National Festival Orchestra)
July 28	Stratford	Glinka *Trio Pathétique;* Prokofiev Violin Sonata, Op. 94 (Shumsky; Sol Schoenbach, bassoon)
Oct. 26	Detroit	*Art of the Fugue* (four); Op. 109; Hindemith #3

1964

| March 29 | Chicago | *Art of the Fugue* (four); Partita #4; Krenek #3; Op. 110 |
| April 10 | Los Angeles | *Art of the Fugue* (four); Partita #4; Op. 110; Hindemith #3 |

Discography
by Nancy Canning

NOTE:

1. This catalogue is organized chronologically by recording date. Where possible, cuts from the same album have been grouped together to avoid redundancy in release information.
2. All recordings were released by CBS Masterworks on 33⅓ rpm discs unless otherwise specified.
3. With the exception of the non-CBS recordings, all release dates refer to first releases in North America. Only the first release of each piece is listed, with the exceptions of the non-CBS and CBS collections, e.g., *The Glenn Gould Legacy* series.

Abbreviations

  * Recorded in New York City, usually at CBS's 30th Street Studio
 ** Recorded in Toronto at Eaton Auditorium, unless otherwise specified
  § Unreleased: in CBS archives
   Produced by:
 ¹ Samuel H. Carter
 ² Thomas Frost
 ³ Glenn Gould
 ⁴ Andrew Kazdin
 ⁵ John McClure
 ⁶ Paul Myers
 ⁷ Joseph Scianni
 ⁸ Howard Scott
 ⁹ Richard Killough

CBS Catalogue Numbers

  BS Bonus Special
  IM Digital
  ML Mono
  MS Stereo
  Mn Stereo, with multiple (n = number) discs
 MnX Stereo series
   S Soundtrack

RECORDING DATE	COMPOSER	WORKS	CATALOGUE NUMBER	RELEASE DATE	NOTES
1940s**	Mozart	Fantasy No. 1 in F minor (Four Hands), KV 594	TV 34793X	1983	With Alberto Guerrero, piano. Released by Vox as *The Young Glenn Gould: In Memoriam 1932–1982, Vol. 2*
	Mozart	Five Variations in G major (Four Hands), KV 501			
	Mozart	Sonata No. 4 in F major (Four Hands), KV 497			
	Mozart	Sonata No. 5 in C major (Four Hands), KV 521			
1951**	Berg	Sonata, Op. 1	RS3	1953	Released by Hallmark
	Prokofiev	"The Winter Fairy" from *Cinderella*			With Albert Pratz, violin
	Shostakovich	Three Fantastic Dances			With Albert Pratz, violin
	Taneyev	The Birth of the Harp			With Albert Pratz, violin
			TV 34792X	1982	Released by Vox as *The Young Glenn Gould: In Memoriam 1932–1982, Vol. 1*
Oct. 1954	Bach	Partita No. 5 in G major, BWV 829	120	1954	Released by the CBC Transcription Service Program
	Morawetz	Fantasy in D minor			

Date	Composer	Work	Catalog	Year	Notes
June 1955*	Bach	Goldberg Variations, BWV 988	ML 5060[8]	1956	
			S 31333[8]	1972	Var. 18 and 25 included on the sound track for Slaughterhouse-Five
			M4X 38616[8]	1984	The Glenn Gould Legacy, Vol. 1
1956	Gould	String Quartet, Op. 1	142	1956	Montreal String Quartet. Released by the CBC International Service Program
Feb./June 1956*	Beethoven	Sonata No. 30 in E major, Op. 109	ML 5130[8]	1956	
			M3 39036[8]	1985	The Glenn Gould Legacy, Vol. 2
Feb. 1956, July/Aug. 1957*	Bach	Partita No. 5 in G major, BWV 829	ML 5186[8]	1957	
	Bach	Partita No. 6 in E minor, BWV 830	M4X 38616[8]	1984	The Glenn Gould Legacy, Vol. 1
June 1956*	Beethoven	Sonata No. 32 in C minor, Op. 111	ML 5130[8]	1956	
			M3 39036[8]	1985	The Glenn Gould Legacy, Vol. 2

RECORDING DATE	COMPOSER	WORKS	CATALOGUE NUMBER	RELEASE DATE	NOTES
June 1956*	Beethoven	Sonata No. 31 in A-flat major, Op. 110	ML 5130[8]	1956	
			M3 39036[8]	1985	*The Glenn Gould Legacy, Vol. 2*
April 1957*	Beethoven	Concerto No. 2 in B-flat major, Op. 19	ML 5211[8]	1957	With Leonard Bernstein conducting the Columbia Symphony Orchestra
	Bach	Concerto No. 1 in D minor, BWV 1052			With Leonard Bernstein conducting the Columbia Symphony Orchestra
May 1957, Moscow	Bach	Three-Part Inventions, Nos. 2–15, BWV 788–801		§	Not released
May 1957, Moscow Conservatory	Bach	*Art of the Fugue*, BWV 1080	LDX 78799	1986	Nos. 1, 2, and 4. Gould comments between pieces, and speaks about composers of the New Viennese School of twelve-tone composers and of Ernst Krenek. Released by Harmonium Mundi/France as *Concert du Moscou*. Produced by Nicholas Saba
	Bach	*Goldberg Variations*, BWV 988			Variations 3, 9, 10, 18, 24, and 30
	Berg	Sonata, Op. 1			

Date/Location	Composer	Work	Catalog No.	Year	Notes
May 1957, Leningrad	Krenek	Sonata No. 3, Op. 92, No. 4			Excerpt
	Webern	Passacaglia for Orchestra			Excerpt
	Webern	Variations for Piano, Op. 27			
	Bach	Concerto No. 1 in D minor, BWV 1052	M4X 38616	1984	Live performance with Vladislav Slovak conducting the Leningrad Philharmonic Orchestra. *The Glenn Gould Legacy, Vol. 1*
May 1957, Leningrad	Beethoven	Concerto No. 2 in B-flat major, Op. 19	M3 39036	1985	Live performance with Vladislav Slovak conducting the Academic Symphony Orchestra. *The Glenn Gould Legacy, Vol. 2*
May 1957, Berlin	Beethoven	Concerto No. 3 in C minor, Op. 37	013.6323	1988	Live performance with Herbert von Karajan conducting the Berlin Philharmonic. Released by Nuova Era on CD only
July/Aug. 1957*	Bach	*The Well-Tempered Clavier*, Book II: Fugue No. 14 in F-sharp minor, BWV 883	ML 5186[8]	1957	
	Bach	*The Well-Tempered Clavier*, Book II: Fugue No. 9 in E major, BWV 878	M4X 38616[8]	1984	*The Glenn Gould Legacy, Vol. 1*

RECORDING DATE	COMPOSER	WORKS	CATALOGUE NUMBER	RELEASE DATE	NOTES
Aug. 1957	Brahms	Quintet in F minor, Op. 34	140	1957	With the Montreal String Quartet. Released by the CBC Transcription Service Program
Jan. 1958*	Haydn	Sonata No. 59 in E-flat major, XVI/49	ML 5274[8]	1958	
	Mozart	Sonata No. 10 in C major, KV 330			
	Mozart	Fantasia and Fugue in C major, KV 394	M3 39036[8]	1985	*The Glenn Gould Legacy, Vol. 2*
March 1958*	Schoenberg	Piano Concerto, Op. 42	013.6306	1986	Live performance with Dimitri Mitropoulos conducting the New York Philharmonic Orchestra. Released by Nuova Era on CD only
Apr./July 1958*	Beethoven	Concerto No. 1 in C major, Op. 15	ML 5298/MS 6017[8]	1958	With Vladimir Golschmann conducting the Columbia Symphony Orchestra. Cadenza by Gould
			M3 39036[8]	1985	*The Glenn Gould Legacy, Vol. 2*

Date	Composer	Work	Catalogue	Year	Notes
May 1958*	Bach	Concerto No. 5 in F minor, BWV 1056	ML 5298/MS 6017[8]	1958	With Vladimir Golschmann conducting the Columbia Symphony Orchestra
			S31333[8]	1972	Included on the sound track for *Slaughterhouse-Five*
June/July 1958*	Krenek	Sonata No. 3, Op. 92, No. 4	ML 5336[8]	1959	
			M3 42150[8]	1986	*The Glenn Gould Legacy, Vol. 4*
June/July 1958*	Schoenberg	Three Piano Pieces, Op. 11	ML 5336[8]	1959	
			M3 42150[8]	1986	*The Glenn Gould Legacy, Vol. 4*
July 1958*	Berg	Sonata, Op. 1	ML 5336[8]	1959	
			M3 42150[8]	1986	*The Glenn Gould Legacy, Vol. 4*
Aug. 1958, Salzburg	Bach	Concerto No. 1 in D minor, BWV 1052	013.6306	1986	Live performance with Dimitri Mitropoulos conducting the Concertgebouw Orchestra of Amsterdam. Released by Nuova Era on CD only
			D15119	1986	Released by Price Less on CD only

RECORDING DATE	COMPOSER	WORKS	CATALOGUE NUMBER	RELEASE DATE	NOTES
Sept. 1958, Stockholm	Mozart	Concerto No. 24 in C minor, KV 491	CD 323	1986	With Georg Ludwig Jochum conducting the Swedish Radio Symphony Orchestra at the Musical Academy in Stockholm. Released by BIS on CD only as *Glenn Gould in Stockholm 1958*
Oct. 1958, Stockholm	Beethoven	Concerto No. 2 in B-flat major, Op. 19			
Oct. 1958, Stockholm	Beethoven	Sonata No. 31 in A-flat major, Op. 110	CD 324	1986	Released by BIS on CD only as *Glenn Gould in Stockholm 1958*
	Berg	Sonata, Op. 1			
	Haydn	Sonata No. 59 in E-flat major, XVI/49			
May/Sept. 1959[*]	Bach	Partita No. 1 in B-flat major, BWV 825	ML 5472/MS 6141[6]	1960	
May 1959, July/ Sept./Nov. 1960[*]	Brahms	Intermezzi, Op. 76, Nos. 6 and 7, Op. 116, No. 4, Op. 117, Nos. 1–3, Op. 118, Nos. 1, 2, and 6, Op. 119, No. 1	ML 5637/MS 6237[7]	1961	
			M3 42107[7]	1986	*The Glenn Gould Legacy, Vol. 3*

Date	Composer	Work	Catalog	Year	Notes
May 1959*	Beethoven	Concerto No. 3 in C minor, Op. 37	ML 5418/MS 6096[8]	1960	With Leonard Bernstein conducting the Columbia Symphony Orchestra
June 1959*	Bach	Partita No. 2 in C minor, BWV 826	ML 5472/MS 6141[8]	1960	
	Bach	Italian Concerto (in F major), BWV 971			
Aug. 1959, Salzburg	Bach	*Goldberg Variations*, BWV 988	D15119	1986	Live performance. Released by Price Less on CD only
	Mozart	Sonata No. 10 in C major, KV 330			
Aug. 1959, Salzburg	Bach	*Goldberg Variations*, BWV 988	CMG1	1986	Live performance. Released by Frequenz on CD only as *Glenn Gould in Salzburg*
	Mozart	Sonata No. 10 in C major, KV 330			
	Schoenberg	Suite for Piano, Op. 25			
	Sweelinck	Fantasia in D minor for Organ (arr. for Piano)			
Aug. 1959, Salzburg	Bach	Brandenburg Concerto No. 5 in D major, BWV 1050		§	
March 1960, Cleveland, Severance Hall	Gould	String Quartet, Op. 1	ML 5578/MS 6178[8]	1960	Symphonia Quartet

RECORDING DATE	COMPOSER	WORKS	CATALOGUE NUMBER	RELEASE DATE	NOTES
July/Sept. 1960, Jan 1967, Aug. 1971*	Beethoven	Sonata No. 17 in D minor, *Tempest*, Op. 31, No. 2	M 32349[8]	1973	
July/Aug. 1960, Feb. 1967*	Beethoven	*Eroica Variations*, Op. 35	M 30080[4]	1970	
July 1960, May 1967*	Beethoven	Variations in F major, Op. 34			
Jan. 1961, Toronto, Massey Hall**	Mozart	Concerto No. 24 in C minor, KV 491	ML 5739/MS 6339[2/8]	1962	With Walter Susskind conducting the CBC Symphony Orchestra
	Schoenberg	Piano Concerto, Op. 42			With Robert Craft conducting the CBC Symphony Orchestra
March 1961*	Beethoven	Concerto No. 4 in G major, Op. 58	ML 5662/MS 6262[8]	1961	With Leonard Bernstein conducting the New York Philharmonic
Oct. 1961	Strauss	*Enoch Arden*, Op. 38	ML 5741/MS 6341[7]	1962	With Claude Rains, narrator
1962, Stratford, Ontario	Beethoven	Sonata No. 3 for Cello and Piano in A major, Op. 69	234	1986	With Leonard Rose, cello, at the 1962 Stratford Festival. Released by Melodram
	Beethoven	Trio in D major, *Ghost*, Op. 70, No. 1			With Leonard Rose, cello, and Oscar Shumsky, violin

Date	Composer	Work	Number	Year	Notes
Jan./Feb. 1962	Bach	Art of the Fugue, Nos. 1–9, BWV 1080	ML 5738/MS 6338[7]	1962	Fugues I–IX played on organ. Recorded at All Saint's Church in Kingsway, Ontario
June/Sept. 1962*	Bach	The Well-Tempered Clavier, Book I: Nos. 1–8, BWV 846–853	ML 5808/MS 6408[6]	1963	
Sept. 1962*	Brahms	Concerto No. 1 in D minor, Op. 15	234	1986	With Leonard Bernstein conducting the New York Philharmonic. Released by Melodram
				1987	Radiothon Special Edition Historic Recordings, Vol. 7. A joint release between the New York Philharmonic and radio station WQXR
Oct. 1962*	Bach	Partita No. 3 in A minor, BWV 827	ML 5898/MS 6498[6]	1963	
Dec. 1962, March/ Apr. 1963*	Bach	Partita No. 4 in D major, BWV 828			
Apr. 1963*	Bach	Toccata in E minor, BWV 914			
Apr./June 1963, Aug. 1964*	Bach	The Well-Tempered Clavier, Book I: Nos. 9–16, BWV 854–861	ML 5938/MS 6538[6]	1964	
June 1963, Feb./ Aug. 1965*	Bach	The Well-Tempered Clavier, Book I: Nos. 17–24, BWV 862–869	ML 6176/MS 6776[6]	1965	

RECORDING DATE	COMPOSER	WORKS	CATALOGUE NUMBER	RELEASE DATE	NOTES
Dec. 1963, Jan. 1964*	Bach	Two- and Three-Part Inventions, BWV 772–801	ML 6022/MS 6622[6]	1964	
	Bach	Two- and Three-Part Inventions: No. 4 in D minor, BWV 775/790; No. 6 in E major, BWV 777/792; and No. 13 in A minor, BWV 784/799	M4X 38616[6]	1984	*The Glenn Gould Legacy, Vol. 1*
Dec. 1963*	Gould	"So You Want to Write a Fugue?"	M2X 35914[6]	1980	With Vladimir Golschmann conducting the Juilliard String Quartet, Elizabeth Guy-Benson (soprano), Anita Darian (mezzo-soprano), Charles Bressler (tenor), and Donald Gramm (baritone). *The Glenn Gould Silver Jubilee Album*
Jan. 1964*	Schoenberg	Suite for Piano, Op. 25	ML 6217/MS 6817[2]	1966	
			M3 42150[2]	1986	*The Glenn Gould Legacy, Vol. 4*
Jan. 1964, Jan. 1965*	Schoenberg	Six Songs, Op. 3	M 31312[2]	1972	With Donald Gramm, baritone, and Helen Vanni, soprano

Date/Location	Composer	Work	Catalog Number	Year	Notes
June 1964, Jan. 1965*	Schoenberg	Four Songs, Op. 2	ML 6216/MS 6816[2/4]	1966	With Ellen Faull, soprano
June 1964, Manhattan Center*	Beethoven	Sonata No. 6 in F major, Op. 10, No. 2	ML 6086/MS 6686[2]	1965	
June 1964, Sept. 1965*	Schoenberg	Six Little Piano Pieces, Op. 19	ML 6217/MS 6817[2]	1966	
July 1964*	Schoenberg	Phantasy for Violin and Piano, Op. 47	ML 6436/MS 7036[6]	1967	With Israel Baker, violin
Sept. 1964, Manhattan Center*	Beethoven	Sonata No. 5 in C minor, Op. 10, No. 1	ML 6086/MS 6686[2]	1965	
Nov. 1964, Manhattan Center*	Beethoven	Sonata No. 7 in D major, Op. 10, No. 3			
Jan./Nov. 1965*	Schoenberg	Two Songs, Op. 1	ML 6216/MS 6816[2/4]	1966	With Donald Gramm, bass-baritone
Feb. 1965*	Schoenberg	Ode to Napoleon Bonaparte, Op. 41	ML 6437/MS 7037[9]	1967	With the Juilliard String Quartet and John Horton, speaker
March/Aug. 1965, May 1966, Jan./Aug. 1970*	Mozart	Sonata No. 13 in B-flat major, KV 333	M 31073[4]	1972	The Mozart Piano Sonatas, Vol. 3
June 1965*	Schoenberg	Das Buch der hängenden Garten, Op. 15	ML 6216/MS 6816[4]	1966	With Helen Vanni, mezzo-soprano
June/Sept. 1965, May 1966*	Mozart	Sonata No. 12 in F major, KV 332	M 31073[4]	1972	The Mozart Piano Sonatas, Vol. 3

RECORDING DATE	COMPOSER	WORKS	CATALOGUE NUMBER	RELEASE DATE	NOTES
Sept./Nov. 1965*	Schoenberg	Five Piano Pieces, Op. 23	ML 6217/MS 6817⁴	1966	*The Glenn Gould Legacy, Vol. 4*
			M3 42150⁴	1986	
Nov. 1965*	Schoenberg	Piano Pieces, Op. 33a and b	ML 6217/MS 6817⁴	1966	*The Glenn Gould Legacy, Vol. 4*
			M3 42150⁴	1986	
Dec. 1965, Aug. 1970*	Mozart	Sonata No. 11 in A major, KV 331	M 32348⁴	1973	*The Mozart Piano Sonatas, Vol. 4*
Jan. 1966*	Strauss	Three Ophelia Songs, Op. 67	M2X 35914⁶	1980	With Elisabeth Schwarzkopf, soprano. *The Glenn Gould Silver Jubilee Album*
Jan. 1966*	Strauss	Four Songs, Op. 27, No. 4: "Morgen"		§	With Elisabeth Schwarzkopf, soprano
Jan. 1966*	Strauss	Eight Songs, Op. 49, No. 7: "Wer lieben will, muss leiden"		§	With Elisabeth Schwarzkopf, soprano
Jan. 1966*	Strauss	Four Songs, Op. 27, No. 3: "Heimliche Aufforderung"		§	With Elisabeth Schwarzkopf, soprano
Jan. 1966*	Strauss	Five Songs, Op. 48, No. 4: "Winterweihe"		§	With Elisabeth Schwarzkopf, soprano

Date	Composer	Work	Catalog	Year	Notes
Feb. 1966*	Beethoven	Sonata No. 9 in E major, Op. 14, No. 1	ML 6345/MS 6945[4]	1967	
Feb./May 1966*	Beethoven	Sonata No. 10 in G major, Op. 14, No. 2			
March 1966, Manhattan Center*	Beethoven	Concerto No. 5 in E-flat major, *Emperor*, Op. 73	ML 6288/MS 6888[4]	1966	With Leopold Stokowski conducting the American Symphony Orchestra
Apr. 1966, Oct. 1967*	Beethoven	Sonata No. 23 in F minor, *Appassionata*, Op. 57	MS 7413[4]	1970	
Apr. 1966*	Beethoven	Sonata No. 8 in C minor, *Pathétique*, Op. 13	ML 6345/MS 6945[4]	1967	
June 1966*	Morawetz	Fantasy in D minor	32110045/46[4]	1967	*Canadian Music in the 20th Century*
Aug. 1966, Jan./Feb. 1967*	Bach	*The Well-Tempered Clavier*, Book II: Nos. 1–8, BWV 870–877	MS 7099[4]	1968	
Oct. 1966, Feb. 1973*	Hindemith	Sonata No. 1 in A major	M 32350[4]	1973	
Nov. 1966*	Beethoven	Thirty-two Variations in C minor, WoO. 80	M 30080[4]	1970	
Nov. 1966*	Mozart	Fantasia in C minor, KV 475	M 33515[4]	1975	*The Mozart Piano Sonatas, Vol. 5*

RECORDING DATE	COMPOSER	WORKS	CATALOGUE NUMBER	RELEASE DATE	NOTES
Dec. 1966, Jan. 1967*	Hindemith	Sonata No. 3 in B-flat major	M 32350[4]	1973	
			M3 42150[4]	1986	*The Glenn Gould Legacy, Vol. 4*
March 1967*	Beethoven	Sonata No. 18 in E-flat major, Op. 31, No. 3	M 32349[4]	1973	
May 1967*	Bach	Concerto No. 3 in D major, BWV 1054	ML 6401/MS 7001[4]	1967	With Vladimir Golschmann conducting the Columbia Symphony Orchestra
			S 31333[4]	1972	Included on the sound track for *Slaughterhouse-Five*
May 1967*	Bach	Concerto No. 7 in G minor, BWV 1058	ML 6401/MS 7001[4]	1967	With Vladimir Golschmann conducting the Columbia Symphony Orchestra
May 1967*	Beethoven	Sonata No. 14 in C-sharp minor, *Moonlight*, Op. 27, No. 2	MS 7413[4]	1970	
May 1967*	Mozart	Sonata No. 5 in G major, KV 283	MS 7097[4]	1968	*The Mozart Piano Sonatas, Vol. 1*
May/Nov. 1967*	Mozart	Sonata No. 3 in B-flat major, KV 281			

Date	Composer	Work	Catalogue	Year	Album
May 1967*	Byrd	A Voluntary	M 30825[4]	1971	*A Consort of Musicke Bye William Byrde and Orlando Gibbons*
	Byrd	Sixth Pavan and Galliard			
June/July 1967*	Prokofiev	Sonata No. 7 in B-flat major, Op. 83	MS 7173[4]	1969	
			M3 42150[4]	1986	*The Glenn Gould Legacy, Vol. 4*
July 1967*	Byrd	First Pavan and Galliard	M 30825[4]	1971	*A Consort of Musicke Bye William Byrde and Orlando Gibbons*
July 1967*	Anhalt	Fantasia for Piano	32110045/46[4]	1967	*Canadian Music in the 20th Century*
July 1967*	Mozart	Sonata No. 15 in C major, KV 545	MS 7323/MGP 13[4]	1969	
			M 32348[4]	1973	*The Mozart Piano Sonatas, Vol. 4*
July 1967*	Pentland	*Shadows (Ombres)*		§	
July/Nov. 1967*	Mozart	Sonata No. 4 in E-flat major, KV 282	MS 7097[4]	1968	*The Mozart Piano Sonatas, Vol. 1*
Aug. 1967*	Hétu	*Variations pour piano*	32110045/46[4]	1967	*Canadian Music in the 20th Century*

RECORDING DATE	COMPOSER	WORKS	CATALOGUE NUMBER	RELEASE DATE	NOTES
Aug./Oct./Nov. 1967*	Mozart	Sonata No. 2 in F major, KV 280	MS 7097[4]	1968	The Mozart Piano Sonatas, Vol. 1
Nov. 1967*	Mozart	Sonata No. 1 in C major, KV 279			
Nov./Dec. 1967, Jan 1968*	Beethoven/Liszt	Symphony No. 5 in C minor, Op. 67	MS 7095[4]	1968	
Jan. 1968*	Schoenberg	Two Songs, Posth.	M 31312[4]	1972	With Helen Vanni, soprano
	Schoenberg	Two Songs, Op. 14			
Jan. 1968*	Schumann	Quartet in E-flat major for piano and strings, Op. 47	MS 7325[9]	1969	With the Juilliard String Quartet
Jan. 1968, Sept. 1970*	Schoenberg	Three Songs, Op. 48	M 31312[4]	1972	With Helen Vanni, soprano
Jan. 1968*		Glenn Gould: Concert Dropout; Glenn Gould in Conversation with John McClure	BS 15[4]	1968	Bonus record included with MS 7095
			M4X 38616[4]	1984	The Glenn Gould Legacy, Vol. 1
Jan./Feb. 1968*	Scriabin	Sonata No. 3 in F-sharp minor, Op. 23	MS 7173[4]	1969	
			M3 42150[4]	1986	The Glenn Gould Legacy, Vol. 4

Date	Composer	Work		Year	
	Scarlatti	Sonata in D major, L. 465			
Jan. 1968*	C.P.E. Bach	*Würtemburg* Sonatas: No. 1 in A minor, WQ 49	M2X 35914[4]	1980	*The Glenn Gould Silver Jubilee Album*
Jan. 1968, Feb. 1980*/**	Scarlatti	Sonata in D minor, L. 413			
	Scarlatti	Sonata in D major, L. 463			
	Scarlatti	Sonata in G major, L. 486			
Feb. 1968*	Beethoven	Sonata No. 24 in F-sharp major, Op. 78		§	
Feb. 1968*	Schoenberg	Eight Songs, Op. 6	M 31312[4]	1972	With Helen Vanni, soprano
Apr. 1968*	Schoenberg	Two Ballads, Op. 12, No. 1: "Jane Grey"			
July 1968*	Mozart	Sonata No. 9 in D major, KV 311	MS 7274[4]	1969	*The Mozart Piano Sonatas, Vol. 2*
July/Aug. 1968*	Beethoven/Liszt	Symphony No. 6 in F major, *Pastoral*, Op. 68: First Movement	M2X 35914[4]	1980	*The Glenn Gould Silver Jubilee Album.* Fifth movement recorded, but not released
Aug. 1968*	Gibbons	Lord of Salisbury Pavan and Galliard	M 30825[4]	1971	*A Consort Of Musicke Bye William Byrde and Orlando Gibbons*

RECORDING DATE	COMPOSER	WORKS	CATALOGUE NUMBER	RELEASE DATE	NOTES
Aug. 1968*	Gibbons	Allemand, or Italian Ground			
	Gibbons	Fantasy in C major			
Sept./Oct. 1968*	Mozart	Sonata No. 6 in D major, KV 284	MS 7274[4]	1969	*The Mozart Piano Sonatas, Vol. 2*
Sept. 1968*	Mozart	Sonata No. 7 in C major, KV 309			
1969	Gould	The Idea of North	PR8[3]	1971	Released by CBC Learning Systems
Jan./Feb. 1969*	Mozart	Sonata No. 8 in A minor, KV 310	M 31073[4]	1972	*The Mozart Piano Sonatas, Vol. 3*
Feb. 1969*	Bach	Concerto No. 2 in E major, BWV 1053	MS 7294[4]	1969	With Vladimir Golschmann conducting the Columbia Symphony Orchestra
	Bach	Concerto No. 4 in A major, BWV 1055			
Sept./Dec. 1969*	Bach	*The Well-Tempered Clavier*, Book II: Nos. 9–16, BWV 878–885	MS 7409[4]	1970	
Sept. 1969, Jan. 1971**	Bach	*The Well-Tempered Clavier*, Book II: Nos. 17–24, BWV 886–893	M 30537[4]	1971	

Date	Composer	Work	Catalog	Year	Collection
Aug./Sept. 1970, Nov. 1974**	Mozart	Sonata No. 16 in B-flat major, KV 570	M 35515[4]	1975	*The Mozart Piano Sonatas, Vol. 5*
Aug. 1970*	Mozart	Sonata No. 10 in C major, KV 330	M 31073[4]	1972	*The Mozart Piano Sonatas, Vol. 3*
1971	Gould	The Latecomers	PR9[3]	1971	Released by CBC Learning Systems
Jan./Feb. 1971, Nov. 1973**	Bach	Overture in the French Style, BWV 831	M 32853[4]	1974	
Feb./May 1971, Feb. 1973**	Bach	French Suite No. 5 in G major, BWV 816			
March/May 1971**	Bach	French Suite No. 6 in E major, BWV 817	M 32853[4]	1974	
			M4X 38616[4]	1984	*The Glenn Gould Legacy, Vol. 1*
March/May 1971**	Grieg	Sonata in E minor, Op. 7	M 32040[4]	1973	
			M3 42107[4]	1986	*The Glenn Gould Legacy, Vol. 3*
Apr. 1971**	Bach	Variations in the Italian Style, BWV 989	[4]	§	

RECORDING DATE	COMPOSER	WORKS	CATALOGUE NUMBER	RELEASE DATE	NOTES
Apr. 1971**	Byrd	Hughe Ashton's Ground	M 30825[4]	1971	*A Consort of Musicke Bye William Byrde and Orlando Gibbons*
	Byrd	Sellinger's Round			
May 1971**	Bizet	*Variations chromatiques*, Op. 3	M 32040[4]	1973	
May 1971**	Schoenberg	Two Ballads, Op. 12, No. 2: "Der verlorene Haufen"	M 31312[4]	1972	With Cornelius Opthof, baritone
May 1971**	Bach	English Suite No. 2 in A minor, BWV 807	M2 34578[4]	1977	
			M4X 38616[4]	1984	*The Glenn Gould Legacy, Vol. 1*
Aug. 1971, May 1973**	Beethoven	Sonata No. 16 in G major, Op. 31, No. 1	M 32349[4]	1973	
March 1972, Feb. 1973**	Hindemith	Sonata No. 2 in G major	M 32350[4]	1973	
March/May 1972**	Handel	Suites for Harpsichord, Nos. 1–4	M 31512[4]	1972	Played on harpsichord

Date	Composer	Work	Catalogue	Year	Collection
Apr./Nov. 1972, March 1973*/**	Mozart	Sonata in F major with Rondo, KV 533/494	M 32348[4]	1973	*The Mozart Piano Sonatas, Vol. 4*
Nov. 1972**	Mozart	Fantasia in D minor, KV 397			
Nov. 1972**	Bach	French Suite No. 2 in C minor, BWV 813	M 32347[4]	1973	
	Bach	French Suite No. 1 in D minor, BWV 812			
Dec. 1972, Feb. 1973**	Bach	French Suite No. 3 in B minor, BWV 814			
Dec. 1972**	Bizet	*Premier Nocturne* in D major	M 32040[4]	1973	
Dec. 1972**	Scriabin	Two Pieces, Op. 57, "Désir" and "Caresse dansée"	M2X 35914/M 36504[4]	1980	*The Glenn Gould Silver Jubilee Album*
			M3 42150[4]	1986	*The Glenn Gould Legacy, Vol. 4*
Feb./May/June 1973**	Wagner/Gould	*Siegfried Idyll*	M 32351[4]	1973	
Feb./May/June 1973**	Wagner/Gould	"Dawn" and "Siegfried's Rhine Journey" from *Götterdämmerung*	M 32351[4]	1973	
	Wagner/Gould	*Meistersinger* Prelude	M3 42107[4]	1986	*The Glenn Gould Legacy, Vol. 3*

RECORDING DATE	COMPOSER	WORKS	CATALOGUE NUMBER	RELEASE DATE	NOTES
Feb. 1973**	Bach	French Suite No. 4 in E-flat major, BWV 815	M 32347[4]	1973	
March/May 1973**	Bach	English Suite No. 1 in A major, BWV 806	M2 34578[4]	1977	
Nov. 1973, June/Sept. 1974**	Mozart	Sonata No. 14 in C minor, KV 457	M 33515[4]	1975	*The Mozart Piano Sonatas, Vol. 5*
Dec. 1973**	Bach	Sonata for Viola da Gamba and Keyboard: No. 3 in G minor, BWV 1029	M 32934[4]	1974	With Leonard Rose, cello
	Bach	Sonata for Viola da Gamba and Keyboard: No. 2 in D major, BWV 1028			
May 1974**	Bach	Sonata for Viola da Gamba and Keyboard: No. 1 in G major, BWV 1027			
May/June 1974**	Beethoven	Bagatelles, Op. 33 and 126	M 33265[4]	1975	
June 1974**	Bach	English Suite No. 3 in G minor, BWV 808	M2 34578[4]	1977	
Sept. 1974**	Mozart	Sonata No. 17 in D major, KV 576	M 33515[4]	1975	*The Mozart Piano Sonatas, Vol. 5*

Date	Composer	Work	Catalog No.	Year	Notes
Nov. 1974**	Beethoven	Sonata No. 1 in F minor, Op. 2, No. 1	M2 35911$^{3/4}$	1980	
Dec. 1974, May 1976**	Bach	English Suite No. 5 in E minor, BWV 810	M2 34578^4	1977	
	Bach	English Suite No. 4 in F major, BWV 809			
Jan. 1975**	Hindemith	Sonata for Trumpet in B-flat major and Piano	M2 33971/M 33973^4	1976	With Gilbert Johnson, trumpet
Feb. 1975**	Bach	Sonata for Violin and Harpsichord: No. 1 in B minor, BWV 1014	M2 34226^4	1976	With Jaime Laredo, violin
	Bach	Sonata for Violin and Harpsichord: No. 2 in A major, BWV 1015			
July 1975**	Hindemith	Sonata for Horn and Piano	M2 33971/M 33972^4	1976	With Mason Jones, horn
Sept. 1975**	Hindemith	Sonata for Bass Tuba and Piano			With Abe Torchinsky, tuba
Sept. 1975, Feb. 1976**	Hindemith	Sonata for Alto Horn in E-flat and Piano			With Mason Jones, horn
	Hindemith	Sonata for Trombone and Piano			With Henry Charles Smith, trombone
Oct. 1975, May 1976**	Bach	English Suite No. 6 in D minor, BWV 811	M2 34578^4	1977	

RECORDING DATE	COMPOSER	WORKS	CATALOGUE NUMBER	RELEASE DATE	NOTES
Nov. 1975**	Bach	Sonata for Violin and Harpsichord: No. 4 in C minor, BWV 1017	M2 34226[4]	1976	With Jaime Laredo, violin
	Bach	Sonata for Violin and Harpsichord: No. 3 in E major, BWV 1016			
Jan. 1976**	Bach	Sonata for Violin and Harpsichord: No. 5 in F minor, BWV 1018			
	Bach	Sonata for Violin and Harpsichord: No. 6 in G major, BWV 1019			
July 1976**	Beethoven	Sonata No. 2 in A major, Op. 2, No. 2	M2 35911[3/4]	1980	
Aug. 1976, Aug. 1979**	Beethoven	Sonata No. 3 in C major, Op. 2, No. 3			
Oct. 1976**	Bach	Toccata in D minor, BWV 913	M 35144[4]	1979	
Oct./Nov. 1976**	Bach	Toccata in F-sharp minor, BWV 910			
Oct./Nov. 1976**	Bach	Toccata in D major, BWV 912	M 35144[4]	1979	
			M4X 38616[4]	1984	*The Glenn Gould Legacy, Vol. 1*

Date	Composer	Work	Catalog	Year	Notes
Nov. 1976, Jan./March 1977**	Hindemith	*Das Marienleben*, Op. 27	M2 34597[4]	1978	With Roxolana Roslak, soprano
Dec. 1976/March 1977**	Sibelius	*Sonatine*, Op. 67, Nos. 1–3	M 34555[4]	1977	
			M3 42107[4]	1986	*The Glenn Gould Legacy, Vol. 3*
March 1977**	Sibelius	*Kyllikki:* Three Lyric Pieces for Piano, Op. 41	M 34555[4]	1977	
1977	Bach	Fugue in A major on a Theme by Albinoni, BWV 950		§	
Apr./Aug. 1979**	Strauss	Five Piano Pieces, Op. 3	IM 38659[3/4]	1984	Nos. 1 and 3 recorded in April at the St. Lawrence Town Hall
May 1979**	Bach	Toccata in G major, BWV 916	M 35831[4]	1980	
	Bach	Toccata in C minor, BWV 911			
June 1979**	Bach	Toccata in G minor, BWV 915			
June 1979**	Bach	Concerto in B-flat major after Marcello, BWV 974		§	
June/July 1979**	Beethoven	Sonata No. 15 in D major, *Pastoral*, Op. 28	M2 35911[3/4]	1980	

RECORDING DATE	COMPOSER	WORKS	CATALOGUE NUMBER	RELEASE DATE	NOTES
July 1979, Feb. 1980	Beethoven	Sonata No. 11 in B-flat major, Op. 22		§	Second and fourth movements only
Aug. 1979**	Bach	Fugue in B minor on a Theme by Albinoni, BWV 951		§	
Sept. 1979**	Beethoven	Sonata No. 12 in A-flat major, Op. 26	M 3783$^{3/4}$	1983	
Oct. 1979, Jan./ Feb. 1980**	Bach	Preludes and Fughettas, BWV 899, 902, and 902A	M 3589$^{3/4}$	1980	
	Bach	Preludes and Fugues, BWV 895 and 900			
	Bach	Six Little Preludes, BWV 933–938			
	Bach	Three Little Fugues, BWV 952, 953, and 961			
	Bach	Nine Little Preludes, BWV 924–928 and 930			
Oct. 1979**	Bach	Chromatic Fantasy and Fugue in D minor, BWV 903		§	
Apr. 1980	Bach	Fantasia in C minor, BWV 919		§	

Date	Composer	Work	Catalogue No.	Year	Notes
Apr. 1980	Bach	Fantasia in G minor, BWV 917		§	
Apr. 1980	Bach	Prelude and Fugue on BACH, BWV 898		§	
July/Aug. 1980**	Gould	A Glenn Gould Fantasy	M2X 35914[3]	1980	The Glenn Gould Silver Jubilee Album
Oct. 1980*	Haydn	Sonata No. 61 in D Major, XVI/51	I2M 36947/IM 37559[1/3]	1982	
	Haydn	Sonata No. 60 in C major, XVI/50			
Feb. 1981*	Haydn	Sonata No. 59 in E-flat major, XVI/49			
Feb./March 1981	Haydn	Sonata No. 62 in E-flat major, XVI/52			
March 1981*	Haydn	Sonata No. 56 in D major, XVI/42			
March/May 1981*	Haydn	Sonata No. 58 in C major, XVI/48			
Apr./May 1981*	Bach	Goldberg Variations, BWV 988	IM 37779[1/3]	1982	In co-production with Clasart Films
Aug. 1981**	Beethoven	Sonata No. 13 in E-flat major, Op. 27, No. 1	M 37831[3/4]	1983	
Aug. 1981	Bach	Italian Concerto, BWV 971		§	

RECORDING DATE	COMPOSER	WORKS	CATALOGUE NUMBER	RELEASE DATE	NOTES
Feb. 1982, RCA Studio A*	Brahms	Ballades, Op. 10	IM 37800$^{1/3}$	1983	
Apr. 1982	Beethoven	Concerto No. 2 in B-flat major, Op. 19		§	With Gould conducting members of the Hamilton Philharmonic and Jon Klibanoff, piano
June/July 1982, RCA Studio A*	Brahms	Rhapsodies, Op. 79	IM 37800$^{1/3}$	1903	No. 1 only. *The Glenn Gould Legacy, Vol. 3*
			M3 42107$^{1/3}$	1986	
July 1982, Toronto	Wagner	*Siegfried Idyll*		§	With Gould conducting members of the Toronto Symphony Orchestra
Sept 1982, RCA Studio A*	Strauss	Sonata in B minor, Op. 5	IM 38659^{1}	1984	
			M3 42107^{1}	1986	*The Glenn Gould Legacy, Vol. 3*

CBC Radio and TV Shows

by Nancy Canning

NOTE:
1. All entries are live performances unless otherwise noted.
2. Virtually all broadcasts after 1957 include Gould introducing each work, and in many cases commenting extensively upon them.
3. All programs written or produced by Gould are so noted.

SOURCE	AIRDATE	SERIES NAME	COMPOSER	WORKS	NOTES
Radio	1950's		Bach	Fifteen Sinfonias, BWV 787–801	
			Bach	The Well-Tempered Clavier, Book II: Fugue No. 14 in F-sharp minor, BWV 883	
Radio	1950's		Beethoven	Concerto No. 2 in B-flat major, Op. 19	Roland LeDuc conducting the CBC Little Symphony Orchestra
Radio	1950's		Scarlatti	Sonata in F minor, L. 475	
Radio	1950's		Webern	Variations for Piano, Op. 27	
Radio	3-6-51		Weber	Konzertstück	Sir Ernest MacMillan conducting the Toronto Symphony Orchestra in Massey Hall, Toronto. Gould plays a fragment of this recording in The Glenn Gould Silver Jubilee Album
Radio	10-29-51	Vancouver Symphony Orchestra	Beethoven	Concerto No. 4 in G major, Op. 58	William Steinberg conducting the Vancouver Symphony
Radio	9-28-52	Distinguished Artists	Beethoven	Six Bagatelles, Op. 126	
			Beethoven	Variations in F major, Op. 34	

			Beethoven	Sonata in G minor, Op. 49, No. 1	
Radio	10-12-52	Distinguished Artists	Beethoven	Sonata No. 28 in A major, Op. 101	Largo
Radio	10-14-52		Beethoven	Sonata No. 4 in E-flat major, Op. 7	
Radio	10-21-52	CBC Concert Hall	Berg	Sonata, Op. 1	
			Schoenberg	Suite for Piano, Op. 25	
Radio	10-21-52	CBC Concert Hall	Sweelinck	Fantasia in D minor for Organ (arr. for Piano)	
Radio	1953	CBC Recital	Brahms	Sonata for Violin No. 2, Op. 100	With Morry Kernerman, violin
Radio	12-21-53	CBC Symphony Orchestra	Schoenberg	Piano Concerto, Op. 42	Canadian premiere of this work, Jean-Marie Beaudet conducting the CBC Symphony Orchestra
Radio	2-28-54		Bach	*The Well-Tempered Clavier*, Book II: Fugue No. 14 in F-sharp minor, BWV 883; Fugue No. 22 in B-flat minor, BWV 891; Fugue No. 7 in E-flat major, BWV 876	
			Bach	No. 11 in G minor, No. 14 in B-flat major, No. 4 in D minor, No. 7 in E minor, No. 8 in F major	

SOURCE	AIRDATE	SERIES NAME	COMPOSER	WORKS	NOTES
Radio	6-7-54	Distinguished Artists	Bach	Partita No. 5 in G major, BWV 829	
			Bach	No. 13 in A minor, BWV 799	
			Hindemith	*Ludus Tonalis:* Fugue No. 1 in C major	
			Hindemith	Sonata No. 3 in B-flat major	Incomplete
Radio	7-18-54	Summer Festival	Beethoven	Trio in B-flat major, WoO. 39	With Alexander Schneider, violin, and Zara Nelsova, cello
			Beethoven	Trio in D major, *Ghost,* Op. 70, No. 1	
TV	12-16-54	L'Heure du Concert	Beethoven	Concerto No. 1 in C major, Op. 15	First movement only, with Paul Scherman conducting an unidentified orchestra. Plays own cadenza. Only video of Gould in performance before a live audience
Radio	2-21-55	CBC Symphony Orchestra	Beethoven	Concerto No. 3 in C minor, Op. 37	Heinz Unger conducting CBC Symphony Orchestra
Radio	3-29-55	Toronto Symphony Orchestra	Bach	Concerto No. 1 in D minor, BWV 1052	Sir Ernest MacMillan conducting Toronto Symphony Orchestra
Radio	10-19-55	CBC Wednesday Night	Beethoven	Sonata No. 32 in C minor, Op. 111	

Medium	Date	Program	Composer	Work	Notes
Radio	1-17-56	CBC Concert Hall	Bach	Partita No. 6 in E minor, BWV 830	
			Gibbons	Pavan and Galliard for the Lord of Salisbury	
Radio	4-25-56	Glenn Gould Interview			Gould interviewed by Eric McLean
Radio	10-23-56	Toronto Symphony Orchestra	Beethoven	Concerto No. 2 in B-flat major, Op. 19	Incomplete. Walter Susskind conducting Toronto Symphony
Radio	1957	Glenn Gould Interview			Interviewed by Ted Viets in Vienna during 1957 European tour
TV	2-20-57	Chrysler Festival	Bach	Partita No. 5 in G major, BWV 829	Allemand, Sarabande, and Courante movements
			Mahler	Symphony No. 2 in C minor, *Resurrection*	Gould conducting an unidentified orchestra with Maureen Forrester, soprano, in the fourth movement, "*Urlicht*"
Radio	5-26-57		Beethoven	Concerto No. 3 in C minor, Op. 37	Herbert von Karajan conducting the Berlin Philharmonic
Radio	9-11-57	International Geophysical Year Concert	Bach	Concerto No. 5 in F minor, BWV 1056	Nicholas Goldschmidt conducting the CBC Orchestra in Massey Hall, Toronto
TV	10-22-57	L'Heure du Concert	Bach	Concerto No. 1 in D minor, BWV 1052	Thomas Mayer conducting the Ottawa Symphony Orchestra in Montreal

SOURCE	AIRDATE	SERIES NAME	COMPOSER	WORKS	NOTES
Radio	7-15-58	Assignment			Interviewed by Hugh Thomson
TV	1959	On the Record	Bach	*Italian Concerto*, BWV 971	Excerpt. National Film Board production, filmed in CBS Studios, New York
TV	1959	Off the Record	Bach Bach	Partita No. 2 in C minor, BWV 826 *The Well-Tempered Clavier*, Book I: Fugue No. 6 in D minor, BWV 851	Excerpt
Radio	1959		Mozart Schubert	Symphony No. 1 in E-flat major, KV 16 Symphony No. 4	Gould conducting the CBC Vancouver Orchestra
Radio	8-59	Glenn Gould at Salzburg Festival, 1959	Bach	*Goldberg Variations*, BWV 988	
Radio	12-4-59	Project 60/At Home with Glenn Gould			Interviewed at his Lake Simcoe home by CBC producer Vincent Tovell, with brief musical examples transcribed for piano from a Bruckner Quintet, Sibelius's Fifth Symphony, and Gould's own Quartet
Radio	12-30-59	Glenn Gould Interview			American music critic Alan Rich interviews Gould in Berkeley, California

Medium	Date	Program	Composer	Work	Notes
Radio	1960's	Summertime/Vancouver International Festival	Schoenberg	*Das Buch der hängenden Garten*, Op. 15; Eight Songs: Op. 6 "Traumleben"; Four Songs: Op. 2 "Waldsonne"	With Kerstin Meyer, soprano
			Schoenberg	*Ode to Napoleon Bonaparte*, Op. 41	With Donald Brown, narrator, and the Vancouver String Quartet
			Schoenberg	Suite for Piano, Op. 25	
TV	7-26-60	Special/Stratford Festival	Beethoven	Violin Sonata in C minor, Op. 30, No. 2	In rehearsal of third movement with violinist Oscar Shumsky. Opens with Gould playing excerpts from Tchaikowsky's *Romeo and Juliet*
TV	10-11-60	Recital	Beethoven	Sonata No. 17 in D minor, *Tempest*, Op. 31, No. 2	
			Brahms	Intermezzo in E-flat major, Op. 117, No. 1	Excerpt
			Sweelinck	Fantasia in D minor in Organ (arr. for Piano)	
TV	2-6-61	Festival 61/The Subject Is Beethoven	Beethoven	Sonata for Cello and Piano No. 3 in A major, Op. 69	With Leonard Rose, cello
			Beethoven	*Eroica Variations*, Op. 35	
			Mendelssohn	*Variations sérieuses*	Excerpt
TV	1-14-61	Parade	Beethoven	Sonata in E-flat major, Op. 31, No. 3	Gould in comedy routine for children, filmed in Vancouver. Plays brief excerpt

SOURCE	AIRDATE	SERIES NAME	COMPOSER	WORKS	NOTES
Radio	1962	Stratford Music Festival 1962	Beethoven	Sonata for Cello and Piano No. 3 in A major, Op. 69	With Leonard Rose, cello
			Beethoven	Trio in D major, *Ghost*, Op. 70, No. 1	With Leonard Rose, cello, and Oscar Shumsky, violin
TV	1-14-62	Sunday Concert/ Music in the USSR			Includes discussion and excerpts from Balakirev, Glinka, and Tchaichovsky
			Prokofiev	Sonata No. 7 in B-flat major, Op. 83	
			Shostakovich	Piano Quintet, Op. 57	With the Symphonia Quartet
Radio	3-13-62	Ten Minutes with .../National School Telecast			Vincent Tovell interviews Gould on music and instruction
TV	4-8-62	Sunday Concert/ Glenn Gould on Bach	Bach	*Art of the Fugue:* No. 4, BWV 1080	Played on Gould's "harpsipiano" CD-318
			Bach	Brandenburg Concerto No. 5 in D Major, BWV 1050	Gould conducts from piano, with Oscar Shumsky, violin, and Julius Baker, flute
			Bach	St. Anne Fugue in E-flat major, BWV 552	On organ
			Bach	*Wiederstehe doch der Sünde*, BWV 54	With Russell Oberlin, countertenor

Medium	Date	Program	Composer	Work	Notes
Radio	8-8-62	CBC Wednesday Night/Arnold Schoenberg: The Man Who Changed Music			Documentary on Schoenberg's life and works written and narrated by Gould. Includes interviews with Gertrude Schoenberg, Aaron Copland, Goddard Lieberson, Peter Ostwald, Istvan Anhalt, and Winthrop Sargeant. Some material used for 1974 *Music of Schoenberg* series
Radio	9-4-62		Brahms	Concerto No. 1 in D minor, Op. 15	Leonard Bernstein conducting the New York Philharmonic
TV	10-15-62	Festival/Richard Strauss: A Personal View	Strauss	Four Last Songs: No. 3, "Beim Schlafengehen"	With Lois Marshall, soprano. Interprets and talks about his affinity for Strauss's music
			Strauss	Four Songs Op. 27: No. 2, "Cäcilie"	With Lois Marshall
			Strauss	*Le Bourgeois Gentilhomme* Suite, Op. 60	With Oscar Shumsky playing violin and conducting an unidentified orchestra
			Strauss	Three Ophelia Songs, Op. 67	With Lois Marshall, soprano
			Strauss	Violin Sonata in E flat, major Op. 18	First movement, with Oscar Shumsky, violin
Radio	12-5-62	CBC Wednesday Night/Glenn Gould Recital	Bach	Partita No. 4 in D major, BWV 828	15th anniversary of this program series

SOURCE	AIRDATE	SERIES NAME	COMPOSER	WORKS	NOTES
TV	10-15-63	Festival/The Anatomy of Fugue	Bach	*The Well-Tempered Clavier*, Book II: Fugue No. 22 in B-flat minor, BWV 891; Fugue No. 7 in E-flat major, BWV 876	Introduces works and discusses the history and development of fugues and counterpoint. Program includes extensive discussion by Gould, using Elizabeth Benson-Guy and Patricia Rideout's performance of Lassus's "Who Followeth Me?" and Marenzio's "Spring Returns," madrigals, the fugue from Mozart's Adagio and Fugue in C minor performed by the Canadian String Quartet, Do Re Mi, and his own contrapuntal improvisation developed from the American and British national anthems as illustration
			Beethoven	Sonata No. 29 in B-flat major, *Hammerklavier*, Op. 106; Sonata No. 31 in A-flat major, Op. 110	
			Gould	"So You Want to Write a Fugue?"	Gould introduces his work and conducts the Canadian String Quartet and Concert Singers
			Hindemith	Sonata No. 3 in B-flat major	Last movement

TV	6-17-64	Festival/Concert for four Wednesdays	Bach	*Goldberg Variations*, BWV 988	speaks about the *Goldbergs* and then performs Variation No. 30 and the Nine Canonic Variations
			Beethoven	Sonata No. 30 in E major, Op. 109	
			Sweelinck	Fantasia in D minor	
			Webern	Variations for Piano, Op. 27	
Radio	1-10-65	CBC Sunday Night/ Dialogues on the Prospects of Recording			Program written and narrated by Gould. Explores the roles of artists, editors, critics and engineers in the music of modern society. Includes interviews with Schuyler Chapin, John Hammond, Paul Myers, Marshall McLuhan, Diana Menuhin, Robert Offergeld, Leon Fleisher and Ludwig Diehn. Musical illustrations from Foss, Raaijmaker, Martin, Pousseur, and Stravinsky
Radio	1-27-65	Glenn Gould Interview			Interviewed by Patricia Moore of the CBC International Service Bureau on Schoenberg, Stravinsky, and recording. Broadcast in Moscow as five separate programs

SOURCE	AIRDATE	SERIES NAME	COMPOSER	WORKS	NOTES
TV	1966	Conversations with Glenn Gould: Bach			First of a four-part program co-produced by the BBC and PBS/Washington, D.C., of Gould in conversation with Humphrey Burton of the BBC. Opens with *Goldberg Variation* No. 4. They discuss the role of the performer and listener, and the advantages of recording over the concert experience.
TV	1966	Conversations with Glenn Gould: Beethoven			Focuses on tempi, using illustrations from the Third and *Emperor* Concerti, Op. 10, Nos. 1 and 2, and Op. 109
TV	1966	Conversations with Glenn Gould: Richard Strauss			Gould speaks of his love for Strauss's music. Plays excerpts from *Metamorphosen* and the Three Ophelia Songs
TV	1966	Conversations with Glenn Gould: Arnold Schoenberg			Discusses his view of Schoenberg's development, using excerpts from *Ode to Napoleon Bonaparte*, Op. 41, and Suite for Piano, Op. 25, and the Second Chamber Symphony, Op. 38

5-18-66	TV	Festival/Duo: Yehudi Menuhin and Glenn Gould	Bach	Sonata for Violin and Harpsichord: No. 4 in C minor, BWV 1017	Gould and Menuhin discuss each piece before their performance
			Beethoven	Violin Sonata in G major, Op. 96, No. 10	
			Schoenberg	*Phantasy* for Violin and Piano, Op. 47	
11-9-66	TV	Intertel/The Culture Explosion			Gould is one of many interviewed by Alan Trebek on whether a cultural explosion has occurred
11-13-66	Radio	The Art of Glenn Gould/On Records and Recording	Bach	*Art of the Fugue:* No. 3, BWV 1080; *Goldberg Variations*, BWV 988; Partita No. 5 in G major, BWV 829; *The Well-Tempered Clavier*, Book I: Prelude No. 8 in E-flat minor, BWV 853	First of a weekly program series which ran from 11-13-66 to 4-30-67 which aired all of Gould's CBS recordings. The four programs listed below include Gould's comments. On this broadcast Gould explored the question of honesty in recording versus live performance
					Excerpts
					Aria
					Preambulum

SOURCE	AIRDATE	SERIES NAME	COMPOSER	WORKS	NOTES
			Beethoven	Concerto No. 5 in E-flat major, *Emperor*, Op. 73	With Leopold Stokowski conducting the American Symphony Orchestra
			Schoenberg	Five Piano Pieces, Op. 23, No. 2; Three Piano Pieces, Op. 11	Excerpts
			Strauss	*Enoch Arden*, Op. 38	Excerpt, with Claude Rains, narrator
Radio	11-23-66	Ideas/The Psychology of Improvisation			Discusses the nature of improvisation
Radio	11-29-66	CBC Tuesday Night/ Glenn Gould in Recital	Bach	*The Well-Tempered Clavier*, Book II: Fugues No. 1 in C major, BWV 870; No. 2 in C minor, BWV 871; No. 6 in D minor, BWV 875; No. 7 in E-flat major, BWV 876	
			Hindemith	Sonata No. 1 in A major	
			Mozart	Fantasia in C minor, KV 475	

Medium	Date	Program	Composer	Work	Notes
Radio	1967	CBC Tuesday Night/ Glenn Gould in Recital	Beethoven	Sonata No. 29 in B-flat major, *Hammerklavier*, Op. 106	
			Mozart	Fantasia in C minor, KV 396	
Radio	3-12-67	The Art of Glenn Gould	Bach	*The Well-Tempered Clavier*, Book I: No. 1 in C major, BWV 846; No. 2 in C minor, BWV 847; No. 3 in C-sharp major, BWV 848; No. 4 in C-sharp minor, BWV 849	
			Gould	String Quartet, Op. 1	Discusses the structure of his quartet
TV	3-19-67	Music for a Sunday Afternoon	Beethoven	Sonata No. 17 in D minor, *Tempest*, Op. 31, No. 2; Thirty-two Variations in C minor	Excerpts
			Mozart	Sonata No. 13 in B-flat major, KV 333	
Radio	3-19-67	The Art of Glenn Gould	Bach	Two- and Three-Part Inventions, BWV 772–801	
			Gould	"So You Want to Write a Fugue?"	Discusses the theory and structure of his composition

SOURCE	AIRDATE	SERIES NAME	COMPOSER	WORKS	NOTES
TV	3-29-67	Festival/To Every Man His Own Bach			Discusses the obsolescence of the concert hall and the future of recording with Humphrey Burton of the BBC
			Bach	*Goldberg Variations*, BWV 988	Performs Variation No. 4 for the opening and Variation No. 30 for the closing of the program
			Beethoven	Concerto No. 5 in E-flat major, *Emperor*, Op. 73	Excerpt
			Beethoven	Sonata No. 5 in C minor, Op. 10, No. 1; Thirty-two Variations in C minor	
Radio	4-2-67	The Art of Glenn Gould	Gould	Conference at Port Chillkoot	Satirical documentary written by Gould on music critics' conference. Musical illustrations are from Schoenberg's Songs, Op. 2, and Book I of *The Well-Tempered Clavier*
Radio	5-7-67	Master Musician/Yehudi Menuhin			Gould introduces this series airing Menuhin's complete discography. Plays a recording of Menuhin at 14 performing Elgar's Violin Concerto
Radio	5-23-67	CBC Tuesday Night/Glenn Gould in Recital	Beethoven	Bagatelles, Op. 126: No. 1 in G major; No. 2 in G	

				minor; No. 5 in G major; *Eroica Variations*, Op. 35; Sonata No. 18 in E-flat major, Op. 31, No. 3	
Radio	9-19-67	CBC Tuesday Night/Glenn Gould in Recital	Anhalt	Fantasia for Piano	
			Byrd	My Ladye Nevelle's Booke: Sixth Pavan and Galliard; A Voluntary; First Galliard	
			Mozart	Sonata No. 5 in G major, KV 283	
			Prokofiev	Sonata No. 7 in B-flat major, Op. 83	
TV	11-15-67	Centennial Performance	Bach	Concerto No. 7 in G minor, BWV 1058	Vladimir Golschmann conducting the Toronto Symphony Orchestra
			Strauss	*Burleske* for Piano and Orchestra in D minor	
Radio	11-23-67	CBC Centenary Concerts/Glenn Gould in Recital	Bach	*Art of the Fugue:* Nos. 9, 11, 13, BWV 1080; English Suite No. 1 in A major, BWV 806; Toccata in D minor, BWV 913	

SOURCE	AIRDATE	SERIES NAME	COMPOSER	WORKS	NOTES
Radio	12-11-67	The Best of Ideas		The Search for Petula Clark	Discusses the music and image of Petula Clark
Radio	12-28-67	Ideas	Gould	The Idea of North	The first documentary in the *Solitude Trilogy*, written and produced by Gould. Cast: Wally Maclean (narrator), R.A.J. Phillips, James Lotz, Frank Vallee, Marianne Schroeder
TV	1968	World of Music			Host for weekly series which ran from 2-4 to 3-17-68. On the last program, Gould introduces and comments extensively between acts of Mozart's *Abduction from the Seraglio*, KV 384
Radio	2-8-68	CBC Thursday Night/Glenn Gould in Recital	Beethoven	Sonata No. 24 in F-sharp major, Op. 78	Written and introduced by Gould
			C.P.E. Bach	*Würtemburg* Sonata No. 1 in A minor, WQ 49	
			Scarlatti	Sonata in D major, L. 463; Sonata in G major, L. 486	
			Scriabin	Sonata No. 3 in F-sharp minor, Op. 23	
Radio	5-20-68	Ideas		Anti Alea	Written and produced by Gould. Interviews Milton Babbitt, James Lyons, and Paul Myers on the subject of "chance" in music

Medium	Date	Program	Composer	Work	Description
Radio	6-11-68	CBC Tuesday Night/ Glenn Gould in Recital	Beethoven/ Liszt	Symphony No. 6 in F major, *Pastoral*, Op. 68	Outlines the background of Liszt's transcriptions of Beethoven's nine symphonies
Radio	6-11-68	CBC Tuesday Night/ The Stratford Festival			Discusses music festivals with Louis Applebaum
Radio	11-10-68	Sunday Supplement			A news magazine and public affairs program hosted and co-produced by Gould. Subjects include Walter Carlos's *Switched-on Bach*, the closing of the mines on Belle Isle, Newfoundland, and the movie *Charge of the Light Brigade*
Radio	12-3-68	CBC Tuesday Night	Mozart	Sonata No. 6 in D major, KV 284; No. 7 in C major, KV 309; No. 8 in A minor, KV 310	Discusses Mozart with James Kent
Radio	12-26-68	CBC Thursday Music	Gibbons	Fantasy in C major; Pavan and Galliard for the Earl of Salisbury; Italian Ground Bass	Discusses the music of Gibbons and Hindemith's *Gebrauchsmusik* with James Kent
			Haydn	Sonata No. 59 in E-flat major, XVI/49	
			Hindemith	Sonata No. 3 in B flat	

SOURCE	AIRDATE	SERIES NAME	COMPOSER	WORKS	NOTES
Radio	3-13-69	CBC Thursday Music/Glenn Gould in Recital	Bach	Overture in the French Style, BWV 831	Discusses the role of keys in diatonic music, Bach's affinity for B minor, and Berg's "tonal feelings" with James Kent
			Berg	Sonata, Op. 1	
			Brahms	Intermezzo in B minor, Op. 119, No. 1	
TV	5-8-69	Telescope/Variations on Glenn Gould	Beethoven/ Liszt	Symphony No. 6 in F Major, *Pastoral*, Op. 68	Excerpt acts as backdrop
Radio	5-20-69	The Art of Glenn Gould/Take One	Bach	Concerto No. 1 in D minor, BWV 1052	Incomplete rehearsal with Vladimir Golschmann conducting Columbia Symphony Orchestra. Gould and co-host Ken Haslam discuss concert versus live performance
			Bach	Partita No. 5 in G major, BWV 829	
Radio	5-27-69	The Art of Glenn Gould/Take Two	Brahms	Intermezzo in A minor, Op. 76, No. 7	Gould and Hasdam perform a skit on concert-going public
			Prokofiev	Sonata No. 7 in B-flat major	
Radio	6-3-69	The Art of Glenn Gould/Take Three	Gould	The Search for Petula Clark	Rebroadcast
			Strauss	*Enoch Arden*, Op. 38	Claude Rains, narrator; Gould and Haslam discuss Strauss

Radio	6-10-69	The Art of Glenn Gould/Take Four	Schoenberg	Piano Concerto, Op. 42	Robert Craft conducting the CBC Symphony Orchestra. Gould and Haslam play tapes of Arnold and Gertrude Schoenberg
Radio	6-17-69	The Art of Glenn Gould/Take Five	Mozart	Concerto No. 24 in C minor, KV 491	Walter Susskind conducting the CBC Symphony Orchestra in Massey Hall, Toronto. Gould and Haslam discuss Mozart
			Mozart	Sonata No. 15, KV 545; No. 3 in B-flat major, KV 281; No. 5 in G major, KV 283	
Radio	6-24-69	The Art of Glenn Gould/Take Six	Bach	Concerto No. 7 in G minor, BWV 1058	Vladimir Golschmann conducting the Columbia Symphony Orchestra
			Bach	Sinfonia and Invention in B minor, BWV 786; E minor, BWV 778; G minor, BWV 782; G major, BWV 781	
			Bach	*The Well-Tempered Clavier*, Book I: Fugues No. 1 in C major, BWV 846; No. 2 in C minor, BWV 847; No. 3 in C-sharp major, BWV 848	

SOURCE	AIRDATE	SERIES NAME	COMPOSER	WORKS	NOTES
Radio	6-31-69	The Art of Glenn Gould/Take Seven	Anhalt	Fantasia for Piano	Gould and Lamont Tilden, co-hosts. Gould interviews Anhalt about his *Cento* (excerpt played)
			Brahms	Intermezzo in A major, Op. 118, No. 2	
			Scriabin	Sonata No. 3 in F-sharp minor, Op. 23	
Radio	7-8-69	The Art of Glenn Gould/Take Eight	Beethoven	Concerto No. 4 in G major, Op. 58	Gould discusses with co-host Bill Hawes his trouble with the opening of the 4th Concerto
Radio	7-15-69	The Art of Glenn Gould/Take Nine	Beethoven	Concerto No. 5 in E-flat major, *Emperor*, Op. 73	Leopold Stokowski conducting the American Symphony. Gould plays his interview with psychiatrist Joseph Stevens about the psychology of the virtuoso
Radio	7-22-69	The Art of Glenn Gould/Take Ten	Gould	Anti-Alea	Rebroadcast
			Krenek	Sonata No. 3	First and last movements. Gould discusses twelve-tone music
Radio	7-29-69	The Art of Glenn Gould/Take Eleven			Gould discusses with cohost Alan Maitland his desert island discography

Radio	8-5-69	The Art of Glenn Gould/Take Twelve	Beethoven/Liszt	Symphony No. 5 in C minor, Op. 67	Co-hosts Gould and Haslam play a skit on a musicologists' conference evaluating Gould's recording, featuring Gould as Sir Humphrey Pryce-Davies
Radio	8-12-69	The Art of Glenn Gould/Take Thirteen	Schoenberg	*Das Buch der hängenden Gärten*, Op. 15	Gould discusses with Haslam how a rift developed with the Juilliard Quartet over interpretation of the Schumann Quartet
			Schumann	Quartet in E-flat major	
Radio	8-19-69	The Art of Glenn Gould/Take Fourteen	Brahms	Intermezzo in E-flat major, Op. 117, No. 1; Intermezzo in B-flat minor, Op. 117. No. 2	Co-hosted by Gould and Bill Hawes. Gould interviews pianist David Bar-Illan about new approaches to concert programs
			Hétu	*Variations pour piano*	
			Mozart	Sonata No. 9 in D major, KV 311	
Radio	8-26-69	The Art of Glenn Gould/Take Fifteen	Beethoven	Concerto No. 3 in C minor, Op. 37	Co-hosted by Gould and Bill Hawes. Gould interviews Norman McLaren about the soundtracks for his films *Spheres, Pas de Deux, Mosaic,* and *Canon*
Radio	9-2-69	The Art of Glenn Gould/Take Sixteen	Bach	Partita No. 5 in G major, BWV 829; Partita No. 6 in E minor, BWV 830	Gould and cohost Ken Haslam discuss the relationship between harmonic and rhythmic elements in Bach, and Schoenberg's use of the dance form in his Suite
			Schoenberg	Suite for Piano, Op. 25	

SOURCE	AIRDATE	SERIES NAME	COMPOSER	WORKS	NOTES
Radio	9-9-69	The Art of Glenn Gould/Take Seventeen	Beethoven	Sonata No. 32 in C minor, Op. 111; No. 4 in C-sharp minor, *Moonlight*, Op. 27, No. 2; No. 8 in C minor, *Pathétique*, Op. 13	Host Ken Haslam with Gould as Theodore Slutz
Radio	9-16-69	The Art of Glenn Gould/Take Eighteen	Gould	The Idea of North	Gould rebroadcasts and talks about his documentary
Radio	9-23-69	The Art of Glenn Gould/Take Nineteen	Bach	*Art of the Fugue*, BWV 1080	Gould speaks with co-host Ken Haslam about the fugues of Bach, Mozart, Bartok, Verdi, Buxtehude, and Beethoven
			Gould	"So You You Want to Write a Fugue?"	
Radio	9-30-69	The Art of Glenn Gould/Take Twenty	Gould	Conference at Port Chillkoot	Gould and Haslam discuss critics and criticism. Rebroadcast of 4-2-67 program
			Mozart	Sonata in D major, KV 284	Last movement
Radio	10-7-69	The Art of Glenn Gould/Take Twenty-one	Gould	On the Moog	Gould and Haslam talk about Walter Carlos's recordings. Rebroadcast of 11-10-68 program

Medium	Date	Program	Composer	Work	Notes
Radio	11-12-69		Gould	The Latecomers	Broadcast in Ottawa, Vancouver, and Winnipeg only. Gould's contrapuntal documentary on Newfoundland, the second in his *Solitude Triology*
Radio	11-29-69	CBC Tuesday Night/ Glenn Gould in Recital	Brahms	Intermezzo in A major, Op. 118, No. 2	Includes Gould discussion with Haslam on Scriabin in relation to the Impressionists
			Mozart	Sonatas in B-flat major, KV 333; B-flat major, KV 570	
			Pentland	Shadows (Ombres)	
			Scriabin	Sonata, No. 5, Op. 53	
Radio	1970's	EBU Recital	Bach	Variations in the Italian Style, BWV 989	Co-production with the European Broadcast Union and CBC
			Beethoven	Variations in F major, Op. 34	
			Bizet	*Variations chromatiques*, Op. 3	
			Byrd	My Ladye Nevelle's Booke: Hugh Ashton's Ground; Sellinger's Round	
			Webern	Variations for Piano, Op. 27	

SOURCE	AIRDATE	SERIES NAME	COMPOSER	WORKS	NOTES
TV	2-18-70	Special/The Well-Tempered Listener			Conceived and developed by Gould. Talks with Curtis Davis about counterpoint and its demise with the development of the sonata form
			Bach	*The Well-Tempered Clavier*, Book II: Fugue No. 14 in F-sharp minor, BWV 883	Played on harpsichord
			Bach	*The Well-Tempered Clavier*, Book II: Fugue No. 22 in B-flat minor, BWV 891	First 25 bars played alternately on piano and harpsichord
			Bach	*The Well-Tempered Clavier*, Book II: Fugue No. 3 in C-sharp major, BWV 872	Excerpt, combination of harpsichord and piano performances
			Bach	*The Well-Tempered Clavier*, Book II: Fugue No. 9 in E major, BWV 878	Excerpt, combination of piano, harpsichord, and organ performances
Radio	7-23-70	CBC Thursday Night/Glenn Gould in Recital	Chopin	Sonata No. 3 in B minor, Op. 58	Gould in conversation with Haslam on the revival of interest in Romantic composers. Gould plays tape he has prepared on the music of the 1960's, which includes composers Terry Riley, Boulez, Barber, and Babbitt
			Mendelssohn	Songs Without Words, Op. 19, No. 1; Op. 19, No. 2; Op. 30, No. 3; Op. 85, No. 2; Op. 85, No. 5	

Medium	Date	Program	Composer	Work	Notes
TV	8-5-70	Special		The Idea of North	Television version of original radio broadcast, directed by Judith Pearlman
TV	12-9-70	Special/Glenn Gould Plays Beethoven	Beethoven	Bagatelles, Op. 126: No. 3 in E-flat major	
			Beethoven	Concerto No. 5 in E-flat major, *Emperor*, Op. 73	Karel Ancerl conducting the Toronto Symphony
			Beethoven	Variations in F major, Op. 34	
Radio	2-2-71	CBC Tuesday Night/Encore		On Stokowski	Documentary written and produced by Gould in cooperation with the BBC, CBC, and NET/Boston
Radio	9-30-71	Musicscope	Bach	English Suite No. 2 in A minor, BWV 807; French Suites No. 5 in G major, BWV 816; No. 6 in E major, BWV 817	Gould interviews Hans Eichner of the University of Toronto on the influences of French culture on Germany in Bach's time
Radio	7-18-72	CBC Tuesday Night/Glenn Gould in Recital	Grieg	Sonata in E minor, Op. 7	Program on Norwegian composers, written and produced by Gould. Also aired by Norwegian radio NRK
			Valen	Sonata No. 2, Op. 38	
Radio	8-26-72	The Scene			Interviewed about his sound track for the film of Vonnegut's *Slaughterhouse-Five*

SOURCE	AIRDATE	SERIES NAME	COMPOSER	WORKS	NOTES
Radio	10-7-72	The Scene			Debate with Harry Brown on the value of competitive sports and games. Gould impersonates boxer Dominico Pastrono and others
Radio	2-27-73	CBC Tuesday Night/ Glenn Gould in Recital	Bach	French Suites No. 1 in D minor, BWV 812; No. 2 in C minor, BWV 813	
			Scriabin	Two Pieces Op. 57: "Désir" and "Caresse dansée"	
			Wagner/ Gould	*Siegfried Idyll*	Discusses his Wagner transcription with Ken Haslam, playing a few bars "straight," and then showing how he transcribed them
TV	1974	Chemins de la Musique/Glenn Gould: La Retraite	Bach	Partita No. 6 in E minor, BWV 830	First of four shows directed by Bruno Monsaingeon for ORTF
			Byrd	Sixth Galliard	
			Gibbons	Pavane for the Earl of Salisbury	
			Schoenberg	Suite for Piano, Op. 25.	
			Wagner/ Gould	*Meistersinger* Prelude	Excerpts

Medium	Date	Program	Composer	Work	Notes
TV	1974	Chemins de la Musique/Glenn Gould: L'Alchimiste	Bach	English Suite No. 1 in A major, BWV 806	Recording session in Eaton Auditorium of Sarabande, and Bourées I and II with Engineer Lorne Tulk and Producer James Kent. Directed by Bruno Monsaingeon for French national television, ORTF
			Scriabin	Two Pieces Op. 57: "Désir" and "Caresse dansée"	
TV	1974	Chemins de la Musique/Glenn Gould: 1974	Berg	Sonata, Op. 1	Discusses "So You Want to Write a Fugue?"; shows kinescope, and The Idea of North. Directed by Bruno Monsaingeon for ORTF
			Schoenberg	Suite for Piano, Op. 25	Intermezzo
			Webern	Variations for Piano, Op. 27	
TV	1974	Chemins de la Musique/Glenn Gould: Partita No. 6	Bach	Partita No. 6 in E minor, BWV 830	Directed by Monsaingeon for ORTF
Radio	1-15-74	CBC Tuesday Night		Pablo Casals: A Radio Portrait	Written and produced by Gould. Uses the same contrapuntal radio techniques as in his Solitude Trilogy. Includes interviews with Casals' biographer Albert Kahn, several of his Marlboro Music Festival students, and Casals in rehearsal talking about Bach

SOURCE	AIRDATE	SERIES NAME	COMPOSER	WORKS	NOTES
TV	2-20-74	Musicamera/Music in Our Time: No. 1 The Age of Ecstasy, 1900–1910	Berg	Sonata, Op. 1	First of an unfinished series in which Gould discusses modern art and music, decade by decade. Directed by Mario Prizek
			Debussy	Rhapsodie for Clarinet, No. 1	With James Campbell, clarinet
			Schoenberg	Eight Songs, Op. 6: No. 1, "Traumleben"; No. 4, "Verlassen"; No. 7, "Lockung"; No. 8, "Der Wanderer"	With Helen Vanni, soprano
			Scriabin	Albumleaf, Op. 58; Prelude in E major, Op. 33, No. 1; Prelude in C major, Op. 33, No. 2; Prelude in E-flat major, Op. 49, No. 2; Prelude in F major, Op. 45, No. 3; Two Pieces: "Désir" and "Caresse dansée," Op. 57	
Radio	9-11-74	Music of Today/ Schoenberg Series: No. 1			Series commemorating the 100th anniversary of Schoenberg's birth, written and hosted by Gould. Entire series uses recordings and includes no live performance. In this first program, Gould discusses the accessibility of Schoenberg's music

			Schoenberg	Eight Songs Op. 6: No. 4, "Verlassen"	With Helen Vanni, soprano
Radio	9-18-74	Music of Today/Schoenberg Series: No. 2 A Schoenberg Liederabend	Schoenberg	Eight Songs Op. 6: No. 1, "Traumleben"; No. 7, "Lockung"; No. 8, "Der Wanderer"	With Helen Vanni, soprano. Gould discusses early vocal composition
			Schoenberg	Four Songs Op. 2: No. 4, "Waldsonne"	With Ellen Faull, soprano
			Schoenberg	Six Songs Op. 3: No. 4, "Hochzeitslied"	With Helen Vanni, soprano
			Schoenberg	Two Songs Op. 1: No. 1, "Dank"	With Donald Gramm, bass-baritone
Radio	9-25-74	Music of Today/Schoenberg Series: No. 3 Schoenberg the Inventor	Schoenberg	Six Little Piano Pieces, Op. 19	Gould discusses Schoenberg's middle period, his early experiments with vocal composition, and the "ten silent years."
			Schoenberg	Suite for Piano, Op. 25	
Radio	10-2-74	Music of Today/Schoenberg Series: No. 4 The Crusader	Schoenberg	Ode to Napoleon Bonaparte, Op. 41	Gould's recording, with the Juilliard Quartet and John Horton, reciter. Discusses Schoenberg's American period with Eric Leinsdorf.
Radio	10-9-74	Music of Today/Schoenberg Series: No. 5 The Symphonist Part 1	Schoenberg	Pelleas und Melisande, Op. 5	Excerpts. Gould discusses Strauss's and Mahler's influence on Schoenberg's symphonic style and their personal relationships

SOURCE	AIRDATE	SERIES NAME	COMPOSER	WORKS	NOTES
Radio	10-16-74	Music of Today/ Schoenberg Series: No. 6 The Symphonist Part 2	Schoenberg	Piano Concerto, Op. 42	Robert Craft conducting the CBC Symphony Orchestra. Gould discusses Schoenberg's American compositions and the 19th-century traditions
Radio	10-23-74	Music of Today/ Schoenberg Series: No. 7 Operatic Works	Schoenberg	*Moses und Aaron* and *Erwartung*, Op. 17	Excerpts. Show includes clips from 1962 interviews between Gould and Gertrude Schoenberg and others
Radio	10-23-74	Musicamera			Gould introduces the series that is to follow, excerpting clips from each program
Radio	10-30-74	Music of Today/ Schoenberg Series: No. 8 The Transcriptionist			Co-hosts Gould and Haslam discuss Schoenberg's transcriptions, including those of Bach and Brahms
Radio	11-6-74	Music of Today/ Schoenberg Series: No. 9			Includes clips from Gould's 1962 interview with John Cage, discussing his study with Schoenberg
Radio	11-13-74	Music of Today/ Schoenberg Series: No. 10	Schoenberg	*Phantasy* for Violin and Piano, Op. 47	With Israel Baker, violin.

Type	Date	Program	Work	Composer	Notes
Radio	11-19-74		Schoenberg, the First Hundred Years—A Documentary Fantasy for Radio		Written and produced by Gould, using his contrapuntal radio construction. Includes interviews with Krenek, Cage, and Leinsdorf. Music includes excerpts from eleven works by Schoenberg
Radio	1-27-75	CBC Tuesday Night/Music of Schoenberg	Six Little Piano Pieces, Op. 19; Suite for Piano, Op. 25	Schoenberg	
TV	2-5-75	Musicamera/Music in Our Time: No. 2 The Flight From Order, 1910–1920	Visions fugitives, No. 2, Op. 22	Prokofiev	
			La Valse, Op. 45	Ravel/Gould	Gould performs his own transcription
			Pierrot Lunaire, Op. 21	Schoenberg	"Introduction," "Columbine," "The Dandy," "Washerwoman," "Chopin Waltz," "Madonna," and "The Sick Moon." With Patricia Rideout, narrator, and instrumental ensemble
			Three Ophelia Songs, Op. 67	Strauss	With Roxolana Roslak, soprano
TV	8-29-75	Radio As Music			Documentary of Gould discussing the construction of his radio documentaries "The Idea of North" and "Quiet in the Land" with engineers Donald Logan and John Thomson

SOURCE	AIRDATE	SERIES NAME	COMPOSER	WORKS	NOTES
TV	11-26-75	Musicamera/Music in Our Time: No. 3 New Faces, Old Forms, 1920–30	Hindemith	*Das Marienleben*, Op. 27	With Roxolana Roslak, soprano
			Poulenc	*Aubade*	Boris Brott conducting an unidentified orchestra and the Robyn Lee and Jeremy Blanton dancers
			Schoenberg	Suite for Piano, Op. 25	Intermezzo
			Walton	*Façade Suite*	Boris Brott conducting unidentified excerpts. Gould performs in duet with Patricia Rideout, soprano, for the Rhapsody
TV	1976	Musicanada	Bach	Overture in the French Style, BWV 831	Recording session in Eaton Auditorium in Toronto with engineer Lorne Tulk
Radio	1976		Gould	Documentary: Ernst Krenek	Written, produced and performed by Gould. Rejected by the BBC, and never aired
Radio	4-25-77	Ideas	Gould	Quiet in the Land	Last part of the *Solitude Trilogy*, written and produced by Gould. Explores a Mennonite community

Radio	8-22-77	August Arts National			As host, Gould plays recordings of some favorite composers, Mendelssohn and Sibelius
Radio	8-23-77	August Arts National			As host, Gould plays recordings of some favorite composers, Gibbons, Schoenberg, Bruckner
Radio	8-24-77	August Arts National			As host, Gould plays recordings of music he doesn't particularly like, but played by performers he does: Krips conducting Mozart's *Haffner* and *Jupiter* symphonies, and Alexis Weissenberg playing Schumann's *Carnaval*
Radio	8-25-77	August Arts National			As host, Gould plays recordings of late Richard Strauss: *Deutsche Motet*, Oboe Concerto, *Capriccio*, and *Metamorphosen*
Radio	8-26-77	August Arts National			As host, Gould plays recordings of Streisand and Bach
TV	12-14-77	Musicamera/Music in Our Time: No. 4 The Artist As Artisan, 1930–40	Casella	*Due ricercari sul nome BACH*, No. 1	
			Hindemith	Sonata for Trumpet in B-flat major and Piano	First and third movements, with Raymond Crisera, trumpet
			Krenek	*Wanderlied im Herbst*, Op. 71	With Patricia Rideout, soprano

SOURCE	AIRDATE	SERIES NAME	COMPOSER	WORKS	NOTES
			Prokofiev	Sonata No. 7 in B-flat major, Op. 83	First movement
			Webern	Concerto for Nine Instruments	With Boris Brott conducting an unidentified ensemble
Radio	4-2-79	Mostly Music		Le Bourgeois Hero, Part I	Contrapuntal documentary written by Gould, on Richard Strauss. Includes interviews with composers Wolfgang Sawallisch, Stanley Silverman, and Wolfgang Fortner, producer John Culshaw, Strauss biographer Norman Del Mar
Radio	4-9-79	Mostly Music		Le Bourgeois Hero, Part II	
TV	9-27-79	Cities/Glenn Gould's Toronto			Written and narrated by Gould. Directed by John McGreevy.
TV	12-12-79	The Music of Man/ Sound or Unsound	Scriabin	Two Pieces Op. 57, No. 1: "Désir"	As part of Yehudi Menuhin's TV series, Gould discusses recording with Menuhin and illustrates mixing Scriabin's "Désir" CBC-MAET-OECA co-production
Radio	12-81	Booktime	Gould	The Three-Cornered World	Against a musical backdrop, Gould reads selections from the first chapter of Soseki's novel

	Date	Title	Composer	Works	Notes
TV	9-29-83	Glenn Gould Plays Bach/No. 1: Gould Plays Bach	Bach	*Art of the Fugue:* No. 1, BWV 1080	First of four Clasart co-productions, directed by Bruno Monsaingeon, who interviews Gould about Bach
			Bach	Chromatic Fantasy and Fugue in D minor, BWV 903; Partita No. 4 in D major, BWV 828; *Italian Concerto,* BWV 971; Overture in the French Style, BWV 831; Partita No. 6 in E minor, BWV 830; *The Well-Tempered Clavier,* Book II: Fugue No. 3 in C-sharp major, BWV 872	Excerpts in several cases
TV	10-6-83	Glenn Gould Plays Bach/No. 2: Bach and the Fugue	Bach	*Art of the Fugue:* Nos. 2, 4, 15, BWV 1080; Fugue from Fantasia and Fugue on the Name BACH, BWV 898; Sinfonia No. 1 in C major, BWV 787; *The Well-Tempered Clavier,* Book II: No. 19 in A major, BWV 888; Book II: No. 22 in B-flat minor, BWV 891; No. 9 in E major, BWV 878	Clasart co-production, directed by Bruno Monsaingeon. Excerpts in several cases
TV	10-17-83	Glenn Gould Plays Bach/No. 3: The Goldberg Variations	Bach	*Goldberg Variations,* BWV 988	Clasart coproduction, directed by Bruno Monsaingeon. Filmed in CBS Studios, New York, simultaneously with CBS recording of this work

Gould's Published Writings
by Nancy Canning

Note: This chronological bibliography contains published material only, and does not list the radio transcripts, and unpublished items included in Tim Page's anthology, *The Glenn Gould Reader*. Several articles which were either reworked under the same or different titles are noted as such.

Books
Arnold Schoenberg—A Perspective, University of Cincinnati Press, 1964

Periodicals, Program and Liner Notes
"A Consideration of Anton Webern," program notes for the New Musical Associates' second annual presentation at the Royal Conservatory, January 9, 1954
"The Goldberg Variations," liner notes on Gould's CBS recording ML 5060, March 1956
"Beethoven's Last Three Piano Sonatas," liner notes on Gould's CBS recording ML 5130, September 1956
"The Dodecacophonist's Dilemma," *Canadian Music Journal*, Autumn 1956
"Some Beethoven and Bach Concertos," liner notes on Gould's CBS recordings ML 5211, October 1957, and ML 5298, May 1958
"Piano Music of Berg, Schoenberg, and Krenek," liner notes on Gould's CBS recording ML 5336, July 1958
"String Quartet, Op. 1," program notes for a concert of chamber music at the Cleveland Institute of Music, March 25, 1960
    Also as "Gould's String Quartet, Op. 1," liner notes on CBS recording MS 6178, October 1960
"Bodky on Bach," book review of *The Interpretation of Bach's Keyboard Works* by Erwin Bodky in *Saturday Review*, November 26, 1960
"Let's Ban Applause!" *High Fidelity*, February 1962

"An Argument for Strauss," *High Fidelity*, March 1962

"Piano Concertos by Mozart and Schoenberg," liner notes on Gould's CBS recording MS 6339, May 1962

"Richard Strauss's *Enoch Arden*," liner notes on Gould's CBS recording MS 6341, May 1962

"The Schoenberg Heritage," program notes for 1962 Stratford Festival, July 13, 1962

"Hindemith—The Early Years," program notes for 1962 Stratford Festival, July 29, 1962

"Bach and Schoenberg Concertos," program notes for a San Francisco Symphony concert, February 13–15, 1963

"Not Defector," letter to the editor in Toronto *Daily Star*, May 27, 1963

"A Strauss and Schoenberg Concert," program notes for Strauss Festival Concert, July 7, 1963

"Russian Concert," program notes for 1963 Stratford Festival, July 28, 1963

"Bach: The Six Partitas; Glenn Gould Interviewed by David Johnson," liner notes on Gould's CBS recording M2S 693, September 1963

"So You Want to Write a Fugue?," *High Fidelity*, April 1964

"Strauss and the Electronic Future," *Saturday Review*, May 30, 1964
  Also as "An Argument for Music in the Electronic Age," *Varsity Graduate*/University of Toronto, December 1964

"Advice to a Graduation," *Bulletin of the Royal Conservatory of Music of Toronto*, December, 1964

"The CBC, Camera-Wise,"* *Musical America*, March 1965

"Dialogue on the Prospects of Recordings," *Varsity Graduate: Explorations*/University of Toronto, April 1965
  Also as "The Prospects of Recording," *High Fidelity*, April 1966

"Ives' Fourth," *High Fidelity*, July 1965

"Of Time and Time Beaters,"* *High Fidelity*, August 1965

"L'Esprit de jeunesse, et de corps, et d'art,"* *High Fidelity*, December 1965

"We, Who Are About to Be Disqualified, Salute You!" *High Fidelity*, December 1966

"The Piano Music of Arnold Schoenberg," liner notes on Gould's CBS recording M2S 736, April 1966

"Yehudi Menuhin: Musician of the Year," *High Fidelity*, December 1966

"The Search for Petula Clark," *High Fidelity*, November 1967
  Also as "Why Glenn Gould *Loves* Petula Clark," Toronto *Daily Star*, November 18, 1967

"Canadian Music in the Twentieth Century," liner notes on Gould's CBS recording 32110046, November 1967

*Published under the pseudonym Dr. Herbert von Hochmeister

"Arnold Schoenberg's Chamber Symphony No. 2," liner notes on *The Music of Arnold Schoenberg*, Volume 3, M2S 709, 1967

"Beethoven's 5th Symphony on the Piano: Four Imaginary Reviews," liner notes on Gould's CBS recording MS 7095, March 1968

"Recording of the Decade . . . Is Bach Played on, of All Things, a Moog Synthesizer?" *Saturday Night*, December 1968

"Piano Sonatas by Scriabin and Prokofiev," liner notes on Gould's CBS recording MS 7173, January 1969

"'Oh, For Heaven's Sake, Cynthia, There Must Be Something Else On,'" *High Fidelity*, April 1969

"The Well-Tempered Synthesizer," liner notes on Walter Carlos's CBS recording MS 7286, October 1969

"Should We Dig Up the Rare Romantics? . . . No, They're Only a Fad," New York *Times*, November 23, 1969

"Beethoven's 'Pathétique,' 'Moonlight,' and 'Appassionata' Sonatas," liner notes on Gould's CBS recording MS 7413, February 1970

"Beethoven: The Man and His Time," The Guelph Spring Festival program, May 1–16, 1970

    Also as "Admit It, Mr. Gould, You Do Have Doubts About Beethoven," Toronto *Globe and Mail Magazine*, June 6, 1970

    "Gould Quizzed: (a Gouldish Encounter)," *American Guild of Organists and Royal Canadian College of Organists Magazine*, November 1971

    "Glenn Gould Interviews Himself About Beethoven," *Piano Quarterly*, Fall 1972

"His Country's 'Most Experienced Hermit' Chooses a Desert Island Discography," *High Fidelity*, June 1970

"Liszt's Lament? Beethoven's Bagatelle? Or Rosemary's Babies?" review of Rosemary Brown's Philips recording PHS-900256, *High Fidelity*, December 1970

"The Idea of North," liner notes on Gould's recording, CBC Learning Systems PR-8, 1971

"The Latecomers," liner notes on Gould's recording, CBC Learning Systems PR-9, 1971

"Rubinstein: Interview," *Look*, March 9, 1971

"Radio as Music: Glenn Gould in Conversation with John Jessop," *The Canadian Music Book*, Spring/Summer 1971

"William Byrd and Orlando Gibbons," liner notes on Gould's CBS recording M 30825, September 1971

"Gould's Second Choice Is a Heintzman," letter to the editor, Toronto *Telegram*, September 4, 1971

"Art of the Fugue," introduction to *The Well-Tempered Clavier, Book I*, 1972

"Wagner Transcriptions," liner notes on Gould's CBS recording M 32351, 1973

"Piano Music by Grieg & Bizet, with a Confidential Caution to Critics," liner notes on Gould's CBS recording M 32040, February 1973

"Hindemith: Will His Time Come? Again?" liner notes on Gould's CBS recording M 32350, September 1973

   Also as "Hindemith: Kommt seine Zeit (wieder)?" *Hindemith-Jahrbuch*, 1973, trans. Peter Mueller

   "Glenn Gould: Hindemith," *Stereo Guide*, Winter 1974

"Data Bank on the Upward Scuttling Mahler," book review of *Mahler, Volume 1*, by Henry-Louis de la Grange in Toronto *Globe and Mail*, November 10, 1973

   Also in *Piano Quarterly*, Spring 1974

"Glenn Gould Interviews Glenn Gould about Glenn Gould," *High Fidelity*, March 1974

"Conference at Port Chillkoot," *Piano Quarterly*, Summer 1974

"Today, Simply Politics and Prejudices in Musical America Circa 1970 . . . but for Time Capsule Scholars It's Babbit vs. Flat Foot Floogie," book review of *Dictionary of Contemporary Music*, edited by John Vinton, in Toronto *Globe and Mail*, July 20, 1974

   Also as "The Future and 'Flat-Foot Floogie'" in *Piano Quarterly*, Fall 1974

"A Festschrift for 'Ernst Who'???" book review of *Horizons Circled: Reflections on My Music* by Ernst Krenek in *Piano Quarterly*, Winter 1974/75

   Also as "Krenek, the Prolific, Is Probably Best Known to the Public at Large as—Ernst Who?" in Toronto *Globe and Mail*, July 19, 1975

"An Epistle to the Parisians: Music and Technology, Part 1," *Piano Quarterly*, Winter 1974/75

"Korngold and the Crisis of the Piano Sonata," liner notes on Anton Kubalek's recording, produced by Gould, GENESIS GS1055, 1974

"Glenn Gould Talks Back," letter to the editor in Toronto *Star*, February 9, 1975

"The Grass Is Always Greener on the Outtakes: An Experiment in Listening," *High Fidelity*, August 1975

"Streisand as Schwarzkopf," *High Fidelity*, May 1976

"Back to Bach (and Belly to Belly)," book review of *The Definitive Biography of P.D.Q. Bach (1807–1742)?* by Peter Schickele in Toronto *Globe and Mail*, May 29, 1976

   Also as "Fact, Fancy, or Psychohistory: Notes from the PDQ Underground," in *Piano Quarterly*, Summer 1976

"Of Mozart & Related Matters: Glenn Gould in Conversation with Bruno Monsaingeon," *Piano Quarterly*, Fall 1976

   Also as "Mozart: A Personal View . . . A Conversation with Bruno Monsaingeon," liner notes on Gould's CBS recording M 35899, July 1979

"Boulez," book review of *Boulez* by Joan Peyser in *New Republic*, December 25, 1976

"Critics," *The Canadian*, February 2, 1977

"Sibelius and the Post-Romantic Piano Style," *Piano Quarterly*, Fall 1977

"The Piano Music of Sibelius," liner notes on Gould's CBS recording M 34555, November 1977

"Portrait of a Cantankerous Composer," book review of *Schoenberg: His Life, World and Work* by H. H. Stuckenschmidt in Toronto *Globe and Mail*, March 18, 1978

"In Praise of Maestro Stokowski," New York *Times Magazine*, May 14, 1978

> Also as "Stokowski in Six Scenes, Part I," *Piano Quarterly*, Winter 1977–78, "Part II," Spring 1978, and "Part III," Summer 1978
>
> "Stokowski: A Recollection," *Toccata: The Magazine of the Leopold Stokowski Society*, Spring 1982

"Glenn Gould," book review of *Glenn Gould: Music and Mind* by Geoffrey Payzant in Toronto *Globe and Mail*, May 27, 1978

> Also as "A Biography of Glenn Gould," in *Piano Quarterly*, Fall 1978

"A Tale of Two *Marienlebens*," liner notes on Gould's CBS recording M 234597, July 1978

"A Hawk, a Dove, and a Rabbit Called Franz Joseph," *Piano Quarterly*, Fall 1978

"Memories of Maude Harbour, or Variations on a Theme of Rubinstein," *Piano Quarterly*, Summer 1980

"The Glenn Gould Silver Jubilee Album," liner notes on Gould's CBS recording M 35914, 1980

"What the Recording Process Means to Me," *High Fidelity*, January 1983

Index

Gould's lecture on, 112, 165
Gould's performances of, 17, 19, 41, 64,
  75–76, 81, 164, 210, 216–17, 218,
  228, 277
Gould's radio documentaries about, 177,
  178, 190
Gould's recordings of, 119, 128–29, 139,
  234, 256, 273, 328
quoted by Gould, 20, 119, 246
radio discussed by, 119
Schoenberg, Arnold, works of:
Book of the Hanging Gardens, Opus 15,
  129
First Chamber Symphony, 272
Gurrelieder, 191
Ode to Napoleon Bonaparte, Opus 41, 129,
  164
Pelleas und Melisande, 17, 119
Phantasy for Violin and Piano, Opus 47,
  128, 209, 210
Piano Concerto, Opus 42, 75–76, 119
piano pieces, 19, 129
Pierrot Lunaire, Opus 21, 216
songs, 128, 136, 216–17
Suite for Piano, Opus 25, 41, 75, 81,
  128, 228, 328
Verklärte Nacht, 194, 272
"Washerwoman," 216–17
Schoenberg, Gertrude, 190
"Schoenberg: The First Hundred Years,"
  190
Schonberg, Harold, 54, 69–70, 73, 75, 105–
  7
Schroeder, Marianne, 180, 181, 183, 184,
  202
Schubert, Franz, 18, 141, 158, 172, 235,
  272, 273, 274, 290
Schumann, Robert, 43, 101, 129–30, 141,
  235, 252, 272
Schumann, Robert, works of:
Carnaval, 273
Etudes symphoniques, 273
Schütz, Heinrich, 131
Schwarzkopf, Elisabeth, 75, 116, 192, 196–
  97, 255
Schweitzer, Albert, 130
Scott, Howard, 72
Scriabin, Alexander, 116, 168, 253
color theory of, 216
Gould's recordings of, 240, 241, 242,
  273
Gould's television performances of, 12,
  216, 218, 222, 229–30, 247, 249, 254,
  255
Scriabin, Alexander, works of:
"Désir," Opus 57, 247
Horowitz's meeting with, 240–41
Poem of Ecstasy, 194

Sonata No. 3 in F-sharp minor, Opus 23,
  241, 273
Sonata No. 5, Opus 53, 273
"Search for Petula Clark, The" (Gould),
  181
"Season on the Road, A" (Gould), 78
Seltzer, Elmer, 165
Sennett, Richard, 205, 285
Sergeant Pepper's Lonely Hearts Club Band,
  124
Serkin, Rudolf, 34, 43
Sewanee Review, 144
Sewell, John, 225
Shields, Roy, 208
Shostakovitch, Dimitri, 220, 262
Piano Quintet, Opus 57, 207
Shumsky, Oscar, 92, 214
Sibelius, Jean, 235–36, 242
Gould's recordings of, 6, 175, 254
Sibelius, Jean, works of:
Fifth Symphony, 205
Kyllikki, Opus 41, 254
Sonatinas, Opus 67, Nos. 1–3, 254
Siegfried, André, 174
Siegfried Idyll, The (Wagner), 252, 253,
  254, 272, 278, 315
Silverman, Robert, 78n, 112, 239, 240, 307,
  320
Silvester, Fredk. C., 30
Simcoe Lake, Gould's summer cottage on,
  17, 25–26, 27, 32, 40, 54, 83, 84, 109,
  221n, 243, 250, 287, 307
Skelton, Robert, 185
Slaughterhouse-Five (film), 261–66
Slaughterhouse-Five (Vonnegut), 261–62,
  266
Slovak, Vladislav, 63
Smith, Miriam, 33
Soho Weekly News, 303, 304
Soir, Le, 77
Soldier's Tale, A (Stravinsky), 42, 217
Solitude, A Return to the Self (Storr), 204–5
Solitude Trilogy, 12, 199–200, 204
Solti, Sir Georg, 117
Somerville, Janet, 186, 187–88, 204, 287–
  88
sonatas, *see specific composers*
Sonatinas, Opus 67, Nos. 1–3 (Sibelius),
  254
"So You Want to Write a Fugue" (Gould),
  167–68, 208, 230, 255
Speaking of Pianists (Chasins), 72
Spector, Phil, 124
Spohr, Ludwig, 142
Spokane *Daily Chronicle*, 61
Staunton, Howard, 21
Stein, Irvin, 90–91
Steinway, Frederick "Fritz," 89

About the Author

OTTO FRIEDRICH, a senior writer for *Time*, is the author of numerous works of nonfiction including *City of Nets*, *Before the Deluge*, *Going Crazy* and *Decline and Fall*. He has written extensively for numerous magazines including *Smithsonian*, *Harper's*, *The Atlantic* and *Esquire* and is the former managing editor of the old *Saturday Evening Post*. He lives on Long Island.